NATURE WALKS

NORTH

ALAN McPHERSON

and the

Hoosier Chapter / Sierra Club

with

Drawings by:

Angie Neidlinger & Debbie Wilkerson

Photography by: Alan McPherson

Edited by: Alfred Strickholm

Central Avenue Beach, Indiana Dunes National Lakeshore

NATURE WALKS IN NORTHERN INDIANA

" We today are called upon to answer for our

stewardship of this plethora of riches and beauties.

We admit that we handled these natural wonders

in the spirit of recklessness.

Today we are squarely facing the problem

of reparation for we must make reparation

or we must meet disaster. "

Gene Stratton Porter (1868-1924)

from the <u>Weekender</u> of

the Isaac Walton League

This Book is Dedicated to the Founding of the Sierra Club in 1892 and its Founder John Muir, whose efforts began the preservation of unspoiled natural places, and who spent part of his youth in Indianapolis where he began his thousand mile journey to Florida.

Books by Alan McPherson

Nature Walks in Southern Indiana
Hoosier: Illustrated Origins of Indiana's Sobriquet
Indian Names in Indiana
Nature Walks in Southern Florida
Fifty Nature Walks in Southern Illinois
Nature Walks in Orange County, CA
Wild Food Plants of Indiana and Adjacent States
Wild Plants of the Urban West
100 Nature Walks in the Missouri Ozarks

Published by the Hoosier Chapter of the Sierra Club
212 West 10th Street, Suite A-335
Indianapolis, IN 46202 (317) 972-1903

Edited by: Alfred Strickholm / Hoosier Chapter, Sierra Club
Drawings by: Angie Neidlinger & Debbie Wilkerson
Photography by: Alan McPherson

Cover: Indiana Dunes State Park, near Beach House Blowout

ISBN 0-9628469-1-0

Distribution and Marketing: Hoosier Chapter / Sierra Club
212 West 10th Street, Suite A-335
Indianapolis, IN 46202, (317) 972-1903

Manufactured in the United States of America
on Acid Neutral Paper

FOREWORD

"... To explore, enjoy, and preserve the nation's forests, waters, wildlife, and wilderness..."

-Sierra Club

Preparation of this nature walks and hiking guide to northern Indiana began after the publication of *Nature Walks in Southern Indiana* by Alan McPherson. Its origins were however earlier. Often, the Hoosier Chapter of the Sierra Club would meet in the Indiana Dunes at the home of Lee Botts who was a major contributor in the creation of the Indiana Dunes National Lakeshore. Having enjoyed the natural beauty of the Dunes, it was difficult to understand the opposition that existed to preserve this national treasure. Once destroyed, it would be almost impossible to return it to its previous glory. To Lee Botts, and the many others who worked ceaselessly to preserve the Indiana Dunes, we are grateful.

On our way to meetings at the Dunes, we would stop at the Jasper-Pulaski State Fish and Wildlife Area. This wildlife area is a remnant of the great Kankakee marsh which once harbored millions of birds and other wildlife. This once existing treasure is now gone and what little remains is due to the efforts of those before us who worked ceaselessly to preserve something of this heritage for future generations to view. In talks with the author Alan McPherson who lives in northern Indiana, I became aware of other unique areas, which had been preserved by the efforts of those dedicated. With little encouragement, Alan began over several years the enjoyable and sometimes arduous task of exploring, hiking, writing, photographing, and compiling as much as he could of the well known and also less known wonderful places of northern Indiana. This guide could not have been created without his dedication and love of the wild places.

The nature outings described in this guidebook include many preserves which only recently have been rescued from oblivion. Many organizations in addition to the Sierra Club, such as The Nature Conservancy and ACRES, Inc. have been in the forefront of this preservation and deserve all our support. A people and country are often judged by how they treat their places of beauty. We have saved our Yellowstone and Yosemite. It is equally important to save the smaller places which are also worthy. When using this guide, it is hoped that one remembers those who have made the preservation of these places possible, for it is in these places, that there is rejuvenation of the spirit.

Alfred Strickholm
Hoosier Chapter / Sierra Club

CONTENTS: NATURE WALKS IN NORTHERN INDIANA

Nearby Nature Walks

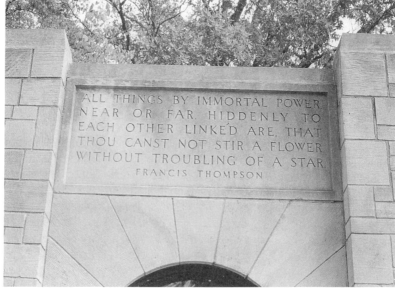

Entry Gate at Indiana Dunes State Park

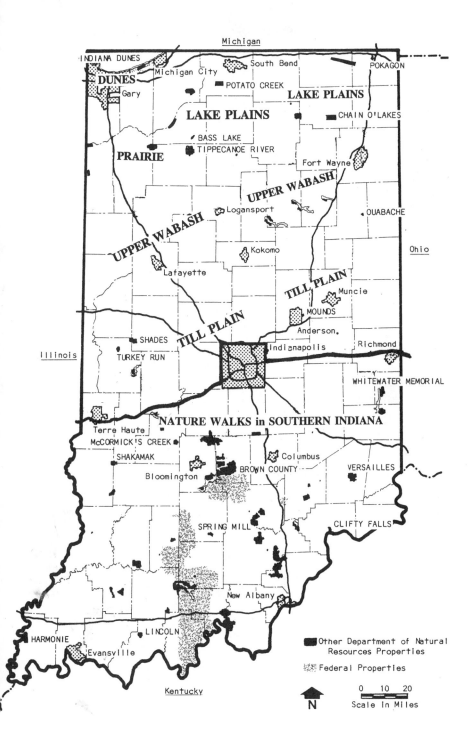

Michigan

INDIANA DUNES
South Bend
POKAGON

DUNES
Michigan City
POTATO CREEK
LAKE PLAINS

Gary
LAKE PLAINS
CHAIN O'LAKES

BASS LAKE
TIPPECANOE RIVER

PRAIRIE
Fort Wayne

UPPER WABASH

UPPER WABASH
Logansport
OUABACHE

Ohio

Kokomo

Lafayette

TILL PLAIN
Muncie

TILL PLAIN
MOUNDS

Anderson.

SHADES
Indianapolis
Richmond

Illinois
TURKEY RUN
WHITEWATER MEMORIAL

NATURE WALKS in SOUTHERN INDIANA

Terre Haute
McCORMICK'S CREEK

SHAKAMAK
Columbus
VERSAILLES

Bloomington
BROWN COUNTY

SPRING MILL
CLIFTY FALLS

New Albany

HARMONIE
LINCOLN

Evansville

Kentucky

■ Other Department of Natural
Resources Properties

░ Federal Properties

N

0   10   20
Scale in Miles

7

NATURE WALKS IN NORTHERN INDIANA: A LISTING

NEARBY NATURE WALKS

PREFACE

Northern Indiana, to the casual observer, is a flat to gently rolling agricultural landscape, dotted with woodlots, wetlands, small towns and industrialized cities. Upon closer inspection, the northern half of Indiana reveals a unique mix of natural areas. Unlike the obvious, omnipresent beauty of southern Indiana's hill country, northern Indiana's enchantment is more subtle and the special areas need to be sought out on foot.

We, the members of the Sierra Club, appreciate the varied public and private lands that are open to visitation. We commend the many individuals, groups, and agencies who established these life-sustaining natural resources which add to the fullness of life. This compilation of nature walks informs the interested public where they are located in northern Indiana.

There are trails for all seasons. Trails that follow the shoreline of the Great Lake Michigan and the adjacent dunes. Trails that move through a tall grass prairie or oak savanna. Trails which encircle a natural shoreline of an undeveloped lake. Trails that parallel Indiana's State river, the Wabash. Trails that lead through wildflower-filled meadows and autumn-tinged deciduous forests. Trails that weave through silent forests in winter that are open to cross country skiing or snowshoeing. There are also "trails" that access natural history sites, botanical and zoological gardens, historical monuments, buildings and grounds.

With Nature Walks in Northern Indiana, the walking enthusiast will be able to locate over 200 trails ranging from easy to rugged. The majority of the nature experiences in this guide may be walked in a day or less. The first five sections includes trails located in the 49 northern Indiana counties north of Interstate Highway 70, "the New National Road". In addition, the neighboring border areas of Ohio, Michigan and Illinois are included. Indianapolis is found in the companion book Nature Walks in Southern Indiana.

All nature walks were experienced, photographed and written by the author between 1988 and 1994. The brief write-ups include a capsule heading at the page top that lists the name of the nature walk, community or nearest community, county or counties located, name or names of United States Geological Survey map(s) (USGS, scale 1:24,000), trail(s) distance, acreage, activities, and fees. The main focus of the write-ups is about outstanding site features or essence of place, parking and trailhead location(s), trail surface, and highway travel directions. More than a trail guide, flora, fauna, folklore, history, geology, and other recreational sites and activities are mentioned to further enhance and enjoy the many splendors.

Development of this easy-to-use guide was encouraged by the Hoosier Chapter of the Sierra Club after the successful publication of <u>Nature Walks in Southern Indiana</u> in 1991. The author thanks Photo Solutions of Bloomington for the care in printing the featured photos. Al Strickholm designed the trail and highway maps that accompany the text, and also did the arduous task of editing. Angie Neidlinger and Debbie Wilkerson drew the fine pen and ink illustrations of native wildlife. A special thank you with deep gratitude to all individuals who generously contributed to the making of this guide.

Alan McPherson

Anna Brand Hammer Reserve
Wildness preserved by ACRES, Inc.

DISCOVERING NORTHERN INDIANA: OVERVIEW

"Trails are the footprints of the ages"

-Jens Jensen, American Landscape Architect, Midwest
in Siftings (1939), Chapter: Art has its Roots in the Soil.

Northern Indiana's natural attractions and invigorating climate makes an outdoor setting that is foot-accessible year around. The benefits of walking, especially in a natural area, are many and is considered safe and virtually injury free. Although wilderness is non-existent, there are numerous nature places that have wildness. Nearly everyone in northern Indiana is within moderate driving distance of a natural parkland or preserve that has paths or areas for walking. Knowing what trails exist, what to expect of the natural experience, and how to arrive at the site are the three essential questions this guidebook addresses.

The nature walks are listed by natural region. The main body of the guide includes five northern Indiana natural regions: Dunes, Prairie, Lake Plains, Upper Wabash River valley, and Till Plain.

The nature walks are numbered and correspond to a regional map at the beginning of each of the five main sections. Expanded listings of nature walks will be found in three additional sections: Ohio Borderlands, Michigan Lakelands, and Chicago and Illinois Prairie.

Municipal, township, county, state and federal government agencies administer public accessible parklands for recreation and other purposes in northern Indiana. So do private organizations such as The Nature Conservancy, a national conservation organization whose objective is the preservation and protection of environmentally significant land, and ACRES, Inc., a regional northeast Indiana non-profit conservation group with similar objectives as The Nature Conservancy.

No special skills are required to be a walker but to further enhance your enjoyment and safety in the outdoors there are tips that are worthy of mention. Plan and study ahead your special needs for either a short walk, a day hike or several overnights. Consider your physical comfort in our humid continental climate. Soft soled footwear such as quality tennis shoes or light-weight hiking shoes are best for the terrain of northern Indiana. The average walking speed is three miles per hour or 20 minutes per mile. Good fitting and roomy clothing are essential. Cotton for summer and wool for winter. Recent development in synthetics are versatile enough to wear in any weather. Layering, dark clothing, natural wool, some cottons,

Hoary Puccoon, Ober Savanna

and high-tech synthetics are best for winter. Be cautious of frostbite, hypothermia and dehydration in winter and heat exhaustion and stroke in summer. Several sporting and outdoor stores have all hiking and backpacking needs in our area.

Suggested day pack essentials or options may include raingear, maps, compass, flashlight, pocket knife, water, butane lighter, first aid kit, whistle, dry food and fresh fruit, toilet paper, bug repellent, and a guidebook to your favorite nature study like birds or geology. A hat, sunglasses and binoculars and the gear should fit nicely in one or two day or fanny packs.

Backpacking for overnights will require additional gear of course, especially in winter. An extra change of clothes and evening wear may include a sweater or light coat, wool socks, and a parka. Sleeping gear such as bag, ground pad and cloth, and tent adds to the pounds.

Cooking gear and food will also add to your load and may require heavier shoes for support. Additional overnight items that may be included are candles, repair kits, toilet articles, towels and garden trowel. Plastic bags may serve as emergency raincoats for backpacks or for hikers. If matches are preferred, you may waterproof the heads with nail polish or purchase specialty matches. Gear should be compact, simple, and light, generally speaking. All in all, you can explore without expensive gear. Before leaving, always tell your family or friends your hiking plans and make sure your vehicle is road-worthy to take you and others to a destination and back. Arrive alive.

Trail quality and their conditions will vary from experience to experience. Few trails are paved and handicapped accessible, most are found in urban areas and state parks. Trail brochures are available at some trailheads such as nature preserves. Fish and Wildlife Areas as a general rule do not have established trails but are open to roaming. When planning a hike consider the length of daytime especially during the short days of late fall and winter. Trail rules may vary but basically all expect fire control, trash, and sanitary containment and respect for private property and people. Hikers should be aware of the potential dangers of hunters during the fall and winter hunting seasons. Accidents do occur.

Off-trail exploration is more secure if a compass and maps are available. Topographic quadrangle maps feature natural detail with symbols. On a map in the scale of 1:24,000, one inch on the map equals 2,000 feet in the real setting. Color is used somewhat real to life: green for woodland, brown lines for contour earth, blue for water and black for human works. Topos and other maps may be purchased from:

Publications Office,   Map Sales Unit
Indiana Geological Survey   Indiana Department of
Geology Building   Natural Resources
Indiana University   402 W. Washington Street
10th Street & Walnut   Room W160
Bloomington, IN 47401   Indianapolis, IN 46204-2742

Maps may also be examined and occasionally checked out at the various universities and colleges. Several backpacking and outdoor stores in the larger cities carry topographic maps. Prices will vary. Expect to pay from $3.00 to $5.00 each.

Insect pests are also part of being outside and northern Indiana has its share of noxious creatures. The female mosquito is by far the major pest of the outdoors. The pesky flying insect is usually common in low swampy areas or poorly drained bottomlands and are particularly noticeable at sunset, evening and sunrise. Fifty-two species occur in Indiana and one, the Culex species does carry disease. There are numerous insect repellents which are effective which include the component DEET, and most hikers have a favorite.

There are nature walks that will be off limits at certain times because of the mosquitoes. Normally the mosquito population subsides after middle August but with wet and hot summers they will thrive until frost.

The female deer fly, like the female mosquito, needs blood for protein to produce young. Deer flies breed in wet areas and are especially noticeable along reservoirs, wet woodland and swamp. A hat, longsleeve shirt and pants helps keep them from biting as do certain insecticides. They are strong fliers and will pursue their victims for miles. Usually they are not seen after mid-July but may persist as late as mid-August.

Chiggers, harvest mites or red bugs are not as prolific in the north half of the state as the south half but certain years they are noticeable particularly from June to September or frost. The nearly invisible larvae of the mite (Arachnid) feeds on humans and other animals by dropping off brushy or herbaceous vegetation and feeds by piercing the skin. They cause a red welt by injecting a fluid that breaks down the skin tissue and a tube is formed in which the chigger lives and feeds. The larvae bites ankles, waist, and arm pits. Little can be done after bitten except apply itch relief ointments or take a salt water bath. Best prevention entails staying away from brushy areas and applying a sulphur-vaseline ointment around the legs and ankles. Kerosene is reputed to be the best prevention. Drugstore insecticides are available as well as health food store insecticides.

Adult eastern North American wood and brown ticks or "dog ticks" are a particular problem mainly in early spring to mid-spring but are found during warm weather in grassy open areas and woodlands. Ticks are crab-shaped and the largest of the mites, closely related to chiggers. They transmit disease such as Rocky Mountain spotted fever which is uncommon to rare in Indiana. They are unlikely to transmit Lyme disease. Ticks feed on the blood by injecting their mouth parts into the skin.

Most of the reported cases of Lyme disease in Indiana are in the northwestern counties. The bear or deer ticks (Ixodes scapularis) are the major carriers of the Lyme disease, spreading south from its concentration in Wisconsin and Minnesota. The best prevention is avoid brushing up against vegetation, checking often, wearing light colored clothing to make it easier to find, tuck and button down clothing, and wear repellent containing DEET or permethrin. If a tick does attach, use alcohol or kerosene to make it "back out". The best way to remove a tick is to grasp it with tweezers as close to the skin as possible and gently, but firmly, pull it straight out. Do not leave the infectious mouthparts behind.

The wood eye gnat can be a pest of the eye, ear, nose and mouth in mid to late summer. Repellents work to a degree. An annoying but harmless spider of late summer and early fall is the spiny back woods spider who builds its webs seemingly everywhere along the trail. Yellow jackets, bees, hornets, and wasps may sting, sometimes repeatedly. Centipedes rarely bite and are non-poisonous. Baking soda moistened is reputed to relieve the bite and sting of insects as is honey applied to the skin.

There are about 35 species of snakes found in Indiana. The common harmless snakes in northern Indiana include the garter, water, brown, hognose, fox, racers, rat, bull, and king snakes. Be advised that non-poisonous snakes will bite if disturbed. Snakes are normally active from April to October and most are basically nocturnal but do venture out in the day. Occasionally hikers will come across a garter or water snake basking in a sunny opening along the trail. Blue racers have been known to "chase" people. The two poisonous snakes found in northern Indiana are the copperhead and the west central massasauga rattlesnake. The water moccasin or cottonmouth is non-existent in northern Indiana and only isolated colonies are found in extreme southern Indiana. The banded watersnake is often falsely confused with the cottonmouth.

Indiana's most common poisonous snake is the northern copperhead and in central Indiana it is found in the western upland of Till Plain, in Parke and Putnam counties. The copperhead inhabits high, rocky, dry upland ridges and it is also found under rocks near streams and wood piles. Its bite is rarely fatal. It is difficult to see on the forest floor since the snake's chestnut brown body and red-bronze copper head blend well with the leaf litter. Like the rattlesnake, the copperhead is a pit viper with retractable hollow fangs and bears young alive in September. Watch out for this "highland moccasin" when stepping over logs since there is no warning of their presence and they will strike from any position.

The eastern massasauga rattlesnake of northern Indiana's wetlands and wet prairie and occasionally woodland is also poisonous. The mild mannered small rattlesnake reaches three feet in length and feeds primarily on rodents. It has a pattern of black spots or blotches down the back. They prefer crayfish holes for shelter. Once found north of Indianapolis, the massasauga is now found near marshes and lakes in the northern two tiers of counties. Massasauga is a corruption of the Algonquian Indian name for the Mississauga River in Ontario, Canada, possibly meaning, "at the mouth". The nature centers at Potato Creek and Pokagon State Parks have displays of captured wild snakes including the massasauga.

Eastern Massasauga Rattlesnake (photo by Harold Smith, Winamac)

Poison ivy should be identified and learned to be avoided. Poison sumac is a white-berried shrub of low ground about lakes and in tamarack bogs in the Lake Plains and is considered the most poisonous to the touch. Woodland stinging nettle can be painful as can be greenbriar and briars from roses, rasp and blackberry canes. It is remotely possible than an encounter with a skunk may result in being sprayed. Even more remote is a bite from a rabid raccoon or other animal. The safety rule for lightning is seek out dense woods, ravines, ditches and groves of immature trees and not shelter underneath large solitary trees, hilltops, high ground, or rock ledge outcrops. The spring months, especially April and May, are tornado season.

The summer months of July and August are hot and humid and walks along water bodies are refreshing. Avoid the sun, especially at mid-day and cover exposed skin with sunscreen. While winter walking, cross country skiing, snowshoeing, or camping, stay as dry as possible. Old timers often said there were two seasons in northern Indiana; summer and winter. Drinkable water and restrooms are available at most of the listed nature walks. Prepare for your visit by having an Indiana state highway map and obtain and learn to use a compass.

Pigeon River Fish & Wildlife Area

After a long hike, treat your feet to a warm soaking, a cool rinse, easy drying, and maybe some foot powder. Put on a fresh pair of socks, if handy. Be flexible and prepared for all your trips in the outdoors. Whether hiking with a friend or alone, always inform others of your route.

Trail routes are always changing. New trails are being added, and old trails are neglected, re-routed, improved, or abandoned. All trails herein have been read and checked for accuracy by administering agencies but errors will exist. Errors and corrections should be brought to the attention of the author through the publishers; The Sierra Club, Hoosier Chapter, 212 West 10th Street, Suite A-335, Indianapolis, Indiana 46202, Phone (317) 972-1903. Be aware the Sierra Club and the author are not responsible for any accidents that may incur while using this guidebook.

DUNES: OVERVIEW

*"Here, beyond the horizon of the yellow dunes,
I entered, for a time, a glorious,
primitive world of the past. "*

Edwin Way Teale
Dune Boy, (1943) page 166

Hiking the Indiana Dunes is by far one of the most rewarding natural experiences in northern Indiana despite the fact it is located in one of the most heavily populated and industrialized regions in the world. The main attraction is Lake Michigan, a 22,400 square mile inland sea, and the miles of golden sand beaches. The extreme southern shore of the planet's sixth largest freshwater lake shapes Indiana's northwest border which is shared by the Calumet Region counties of LaPorte, Porter and Lake. The uniqueness of this special natural area does not end at the shore, but continues inland some distance.

Geologically, the dunes began thousands of years ago at the end of the last glacial ice age. The ice meltwaters of postglacial Lake Chicago receded several times, forming beaches and dunes as far south as US Highway 30 near Dyer, Indiana. These old inactive beaches and dunes have over the ages, undergone natural succession as recognized by Henry C. Cowles, "the Father of North American plant ecology". These same natural forces are still active and all their results are especially noticeable near the present day Lake Michigan shore where wave eroded sands become wind borne, forming "living" dunes such as Mt. Baldy.

Today hikers may enjoy miles of short and long nature walks from easy to rugged through, over and along beaches, foredunes, blowouts, interdunal swales, backdunes, swamps, marsh, bog, fen, ponds, lakes, rivers, savanna, prairie and moraine. The plants and animals that inhabit these natural places are just as special. Species from all directions merge at the dunes and present arresting contrasts. For the past century, natural history scientists have explored the dunes in an attempt to "read" the diverse landscape. Over 1,400 species of plants and animals have been observed and recorded.

The majority of nature walks of the dunes are found within the Indiana Dunes National Lakeshore, whereas the remainder belong to local municipalities and county park and recreation departments, the Indiana Department of Natural Resources, and The Nature Conservancy.

INDIANA DUNES, WESTERN REGION

National Lakeshore

State Park or Nature Preserve

Hiking trail

Bicycle trail

Ranger station

Wheelchair accessible

Interpretive trail

0   1   4 Kilometers
0   1   4 Miles

North

Campground

Snack bar

Lifeguarded swimming area

Picnic area

Cross-country ski trail

WATER SAFETY
Lake Michigan waters can be hazardous. Rip currents occur frequently during periods of high wind and waves. During the winter, shelf ice forms along the lakeshore and is never safe to walk on. Check with local authorities regarding conditions and potential hazards.

LAKE MICHIGAN

West Beach
Bathhouse
First Aid

DUNES

Midwest Steel

INDIANA

MARQUETTE PARK
Boat launch

West Beach Visitor Center

OGDEN DUNES
Dune Succession Loop Trail
West Beach Loop Trail
Ogden Dunes RR station

Chica

Oak   Street

Long Lake Loop Trail

Long Lake

U.S. Steel

River

Miller Woods Trail

Inland Marsh Trail

Grand   Calumet

Paul H. Douglas Center for Environmental Education
Information

Entrance Station

Marquette Trail

County Line   Road

Miller Avenue
Miller RR station

CALUMET PRAIRIE STATE NATURE PRESERVE

Calumet   River

Little

Prairie

Deep   River

PORTAGE

To Hobart Prairie Grove

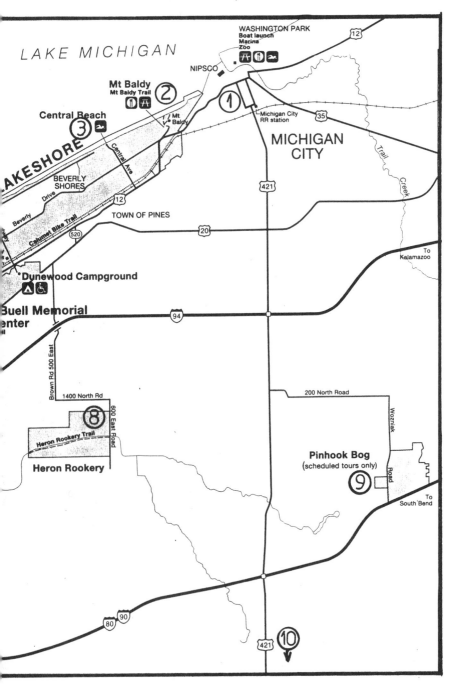

Big Blowout & Tree Grave Yard, Indiana Dunes State Park

Historically, the Indiana Dunes National Lakeshore, an urban American national park which was modelled after the Cape Cod National Seashore, was established in 1966, and dedicated in 1972. The first attempt to preserve the dunes began in 1916 with Stephen Mather, National Park Director, and the Illinois-based Prairie Club. Those early efforts resulted in the establishment of the Indiana Dunes State Park in 1925. As time went on, concerned citizens wanted to preserve more of the dunes from evergrowing populations and industrial development, thus Save The Dunes Council was formed in 1952 by Dorothy Buell. When the council failed to win support from Indiana politicians, they turned to Illinois Senator Paul H. Douglas, who introduced numerous bills starting in 1958 to save the dunes. Despite tremendous opposition and after numerous picturesque dunes were levelled by sand mining, a compromise between pro and anti-park factions was reached during the Kennedy years and signed into law by President Johnson in 1966. Today that struggle continues.

Recently a congressional bill passed adding 1,117 acres more to the National Lakeshore, saving such places as Crescent Dune, east of Mt. Baldy from condominiums, and some prairie lands of Hobart, Calumet and Gaylord Butterfly. The present acreage is over 15,000 acres but ideally, 4,000 acres more should be preserved including the Salt Creek and Little Calumet River corridors.

Mount Baldy, Dunes National Lakeshore

Recreation-wise, the dunal parklands provide swimming, wind surfing, sailing, boating, fishing, picnicking, horseback riding, cross country skiing, camping and more. Year-round camping is at Dunes State Park, and from April through October, at the recently established National Lakeshore Dunewood campground near US 12 and Broadway, two miles east of the Dorothy Buell Memorial Visitor Center (on Kemil Road) and 0.25 mile south of the Beverly Shores railroad station.

Hikers should be aware that mosquitoes and deer flies and other insects can be a problem in warm weather especially inland away from the open beach. Walking the sandy trails can be tiring. Tennis shoes or other light weight shoes are best for the terrain. The cooler air near the lake is refreshing during the summer but additional clothing will be required other times of the year. If walking barefoot on the beach, condition your feet slowly since the grainy sand can damage skin after a distance. The firm wet sand near the shore makes for easier walking. Be cautious in hot weather and wear layers of clothing in cold. The sun can be especially bright reflecting off the water. The "singing sands" can be stinging on a windy day near the foredunes. This unstable world can be inundated by people as well as sand. Nearly 2 million outdoor seekers visit the dunes each year, so plan your visit, if possible, during weekdays and camp. Plan your hikes in the more remote areas and expect the beach and adjacent parking areas to be near capacity during nice weather weekends.

In the future, it is expected the National Lakeshore will expand their trail system and create a more interconnecting network stretching from Mt. Baldy from the east to Miller Woods in the west, a distance of 25 miles. People as diverse as Henry David Thoreau, Henry Cowles and Alice Gray or "Diana of the Dunes" have visited, studied and lived the dunes. It is only recently we have come to realize just how special these "singing sands" are for the spirit. In the words of poet Carl Sandburg, "they constitute a signature of time and eternity".

For maps and further information contact:

Park Superintendent
Indiana Dunes National Lakeshore
1100 North Mineral Springs Road
Porter, Indiana 46304
(219) 926-7561

Indiana Dunes State Park
1600 North 25E (N. Terminus of Indiana 49)
Chesterton, Indiana 46304
(219) 926-1952

Friends of the Indiana Dunes
P.O. Box 166
Beverly Shores, IN 46301
(Information for Friends Group and membership only)

The Friends of the Indiana Dunes is a non-profit organization dedicated to the support of programs and activities of the Indiana Dunes National Lakeshore and the Indiana Dunes State Park.

1. MICHIGAN CITY, IN/NATURE PLACES

ACTIVITIES: nature walks, nature preserves, county park, beach, swimming, lighthouse, marina, museum, historic sites, picnicking, fishing, boat launch ramp, bandshell concerts, amphitheatre, playgrounds, mini golf, tennis courts, zoo, special events, concessions
FEE(s): lakefront parking, museum & zoo entrance, picnic shelter reservation

Michigan City at the mouth of Trail Creek is located on the eastward boundary of the Indiana Dunes National Lakeshore at the southern edge of Lake Michigan. The city's geographic position accounts for much of the special nature places to explore.

The Michigan City public beach at Washington Park. and adjacent sea-going harbor is one special area influenced by Lake Michigan. The scenic lakefront is at the top of the richest ornithological sites in the Middle West especially for rare sightings. The lands edge of the lakeshore gives migratory birds a well-defined flyway route. Birders as well as nature walkers and fishermen enjoy the concrete walk along the breakwater jetty to Indiana's only working lighthouse. The scenic lighthouse juts out north about 200 yards from the W. P. Marina and yacht basin with its maritime atmosphere of slips, piers and boat launch. Views of the dunes shoreline to the west are spectacular.

Where the Northern Indiana Public Service Company (NIPSCO) power plant and cooling tower are situated at the mouth of Trail Creek, was once the tallest of the Indiana dunes. The 200 foot "Hoosier Slide", a former tourist attraction visible from Chicago, was removed by the train loads for commercial purposes such as glassmaking at the turn of the 20th century. There is a fisherman's path along the chain link fence adjacent to the NIPSCO power plant and Trail Creek to the beach. Michigan City's 99 acre Washington beach park and zoo just east and south of the working lighthouse and marina is a legacy left by former Mayor Martin Krueger who was inspired by Chicago's Lincoln Park over a century ago. What could have been a steel mill is now one of the best city parks along lake Michigan.

The wide and level golden sand beach stretches for 2.25 miles to the east towards Long Beach and Duneland Beach communities. There are numerous picnicking sites sheltered in the wooded back dunal ridges. The historic 1911 Washington Park bandstand is still used for weekend summer concerts. Further west is the Old Lighthouse Museum and Indiana's oldest lighthouse which served Great Lakes sailors for over 100 years (1837-1940). The museum features marine artifacts, local history, a marine library, the former living quarters of the lighthouse keeper and a Children's Room. The museum is situated south of the U.S. Coast Guard station on Heisman Harbor Road, west of Franklin Street and Lake Shore Drive. There is a small entrance fee and the museum is open all year from 1 pm - 4 pm Tuesday - Sunday, closed Mondays and holidays.

The Washington Park Zoo, one of the oldest and largest Indiana zoos, is located across from the fee parking area of the beach, along Lake Shore Drive at the intersection with Fedder Drive. Visitors will appreciate the natural woodland setting and the winding stone paved trails set among the many animal exhibits such as the Feline House, Monkey House and Island, Golden Eagle exhibit, Children's Castle, Petting Barn, Observation Tower and more. There is a nominal admission fee and hours seasonally vary from 10:30 am to 3 pm in winter and longer hours in summer until 6 pm weekdays and 8 pm on weekends.

Creek Ridge County Park, Michigan City

The lakefront marina and park/zoo complex are located at the north end of Franklin Street/US 421, 0.5 mile north of US 12 and seven miles north of I-94 in Michigan City. The parking fee is the main expense and the lot may be overfilled on summer weekends.

Further inland several miles along the West Branch of Trail Creek is LaPorte County's Creek Ridge Park. Dedicated in 1992, the 76 acre suburban green space provides about three miles of nature trails including a boardwalk to Trail Creek. There are also loop trails around the perimeter of an old field along Waterford Creek and Trail Creek and in a maturing mixed deciduous woodland elevated above a wetland. All three trails originate at the parking area. The developing regional park also provides picnicking, fishing and playgrounds and in the future a pioneer demonstration farm.

To reach Creek Ridge County Park from I-94, go north on US 421 about one mile to Grienke Road/CR 400N and turn right/ east. Proceed east on Grienke Road/CR 400N about two miles to the park entrance on the left/north side of the road. The day-use park is open dawn to dusk.

Two additional nature walks in the Michigan City area require permission from The Nature Conservancy to visit. Permission to visit 30 acre Barker Woods and 17 acre Stockwell Woods may be obtained by calling the TNC property steward at Barker Woods (219) 872-8012, 444 Barker Road in south Michigan City, 46360.

Superintendent
Washington Park, Lakefront Office
Michigan City, IN 46360
(219) 873-1506

LaPorte County Parks & Recr.
Courthouse Square
LaPorte, Indiana 46350

The Nature Conservancy
1330 West 38th Street
Indianapolis, IN 46208-4103
(317) 923-7547

2. INDIANA DUNES NATIONAL LAKESHORE
Trip 1: Mt. Baldy Trail & Beach
USGS MAP(s): Michigan City West 1:24,000
TRAIL(s) DISTANCE: 0.5 mile round trip
BEACH FRONTAGE: apprx. 2 miles
ACREAGE: 90 acres
ACTIVITIES: nature walks, swimming, seasonal lifeguards, picnicking, shelter, fishing, x-country skiing, hang gliding, seasonal concessions

One of the largest dunes on the south shore of Lake Michigan, Mount Baldy is a 123 foot high "living" sand dune that "moves" inland about 4.5 feet a year, slowly burying the wooded back dunes. Except for a few clumps of struggling marram grass and small groves of partially buried cottonwood trees, the active wind-formed sand dune is devoid of vegetation or "bald" at or near the summit.

The trail begins at the north end of the parking area where sheltered picnicking, concessions and restrooms are available. The sandy well-used path curves around the base of Mt. Baldy's backsides, uphill along wooden stairs and then turns north again at the junction of an old service road towards the beach. There are several user paths but the trail forks; right leading uphill towards sloping Mt. Baldy or left towards the stairs leading to the beach.

The views from the dune crest are worth the climb. On a clear day the Chicago skyline is in view to the northwest. Wooded dune ridges are to the immediate west and to the south they appear to extend for miles. To the east is the Crescent Dune area. Michigan City's NIPSCO power plant and cooling tower, once the site of the taller "Hoosier Slide" dune (200 feet), appears oddly out of place here.

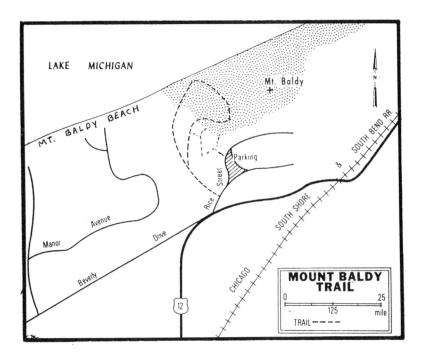

Mount Baldy Trail

Hang gliders here must receive a permit from the Ranger Station at Park Headquarters at 1100 N. Mineral Springs Rd. in Porter, IN. Mount Baldy seems ideal for soaring hawks and other birds, but not for hang gliding due to wrong prevailing winds. On windy days the blowing sands appear as a "wisp of smoke" or as snow drifting in winter. A quick and fun descent back to the parking area is down the steep backsides of Mt. Baldy.

Along the narrow beach, walkers may explore in either direction, but the shore is slightly wider to the west and Central Beach. Blue clay ledges and darker exposed ridge-like patterns in the sand reveal buried forests. One obstacle to walking to Central Beach can be the high waters of Kintzele Ditch but normally it is easy to cross and continue your journey to Central Beach and return. There are also old roads being vacated that weave through the wooded oak-hickory backdunes between the Mt. Baldy parking area and Lake Park Avenue to the west.

Access to the Mt. Baldy parking area is at the intersection of US 12 and Beverly Drive, just west of Michigan City on Rice Street north, at the LaPorte-Porter county line. Mt. Baldy is at the eastern extent of the Indiana Dunes National Lakeshore. The parking lot fills quickly on summer weekends. Visitation hours are from 6 am to 11 pm in summer.

3. INDIANA DUNES NATIONAL LAKESHORE
Trip 2: Central Avenue Beach
USGS MAP(s): Michigan City West 1:24,000
BEACH FRONTAGE: appx. 2 miles
TRAIL(S) DISTANCE: no est. trails
ACTIVITIES: nature walks, nature study, swimming, picnicking

Central Avenue Beach is a natural stretch of sandy strand and scenic dunes positioned east of Lake Front Drive and Beverly Shores, Indiana and west of Mt. Baldy and Michigan City, Indiana. Beach walkers may consider Central Avenue and Mt. Baldy beaches as one unbroken beach, except for Kintzele Ditch, with nearly two miles of frontage.

Walking west, the beach ends at the rip rapped cul de sac of Lake Front Drive. Some user paths follow the dune crest but these undesignated trails can be unsafe in places. The use of undesignated trails is to be discouraged here since they are detrimental to dune stability and may destroy rare plant species.

Walking east towards Mt. Baldy, the sloping dunes comes right to the lake at certain points and the Kintzele Ditch can have high water after a rain but the adventuresome will prevail. At several spots user trails descend from the dune tops to the beach. (The use of "self made trails" here are to be discouraged).

Central Beach is a non-lifeguarded beach, but is a fine place to sunbathe or explore, located 5.3 miles east of the National Lakeshore Visitors Center via US 12 to Central Avenue north. From the Mt. Baldy entrance road or Rice Street off of US 12, drive about one mile due west to the intersection of Beverly Drive and Central Avenue. Turn right/north towards the lake on Central Avenue and continue to the dead end and parking area on the west/left side of the road. Park in the spacious lot, which can be crowded on weekends in summer, go up the steps past the picnic tables along a shaded path to the old paved portion of Central Avenue and the restrooms. Continue north through a dune cut to the open beach. Beach hours are from 8 am to sunset daily. In the summer they are 6 am to 11 pm. Follow the posted directional signs.

4. INDIANA DUNES NATIONAL LAKESHORE

Trip 3: Kemil Beach & Dune Ridge Trail
USGS MAP(s): Dune Acres, Michigan City West 1:24,000
BEACH FRONTAGE: appx. 1 mile
TRAIL DISTANCE: 0.5 mile loop
ACTIVITIES: nature walks, nature study, swimming, lifeguards, picnicking, fishing

Parking for Kemil Beach and Dune Ridge Trail is directly north of the National Lakeshore visitors center at the intersection of US 12 and Kemil Road/State Park Road/CR 300E. Drive about one mile north of Kemil Road to the designated parking area on the right side of the road Additional parking is limited lakeside along Lake Front Drive but available for about six vehicles at the first house from the curved intersection with Kemil Road. There is also parking available at the National Lakeshore Lake View site, just west of Broadway Avenue in Beverly Shores, Indiana where parking for about 30 vehicles is posted. Both of these lakeside parking areas tend to fill quickly in warm weather.

The Dune Ridge Trail loop trailhead is located at the southeast corner of the Kemil Road parking area. An amphitheatre lies south about 60 yards from the trailhead. The 0.5 mile trail explores the oak-hickory forested back dunes and a good portion of the path is up and down, as the trail name implies. The halfway point is at the high dune crest vista where an observation platform has been constructed. Downhill from the observation platform where the trail curves back west/left to the trailhead, is a gate that accesses old unimproved roads in Beverly Shores. If adventuresome, consider exploring the several miles of old roads that traverse maturing forest-covered stable dunes. Many of the houses are slated for removal when their Reservation Use Agreements expire. Retrace your steps back to the Kemil Beach parking area and restrooms.

To reach the beach from Kemil Road parking area requires about a 200 yard walk to the lake along a paved path alongside Kemil Road. To the west, Kemil Beach borders Indiana Dunes State Park. To the east, a walk along a wide strand with beached sailboats and catamarans will lead to the Lake View National Lakeshore site (restrooms, picnicking, interpretive signs, fishing, limited parking) and beyond to where the rip rap rock shoreline begins at Shore Street. The Beverly Shores beach is public but parking is for residents only with displayed permit. The rip rap limestone has replaced the former beach which has washed away, separating Kemil Beach from Central Avenue Beach. Above, along Lake Front Drive are five historic houses that are architectural gems brought to Beverly Shores via barge and truck from the Chicago World's Fair in 1933.

Back Dunes, Indiana Dunes National Lakeshore

These historic homes are the Rostone House, Armco-Ferro House, House of Tomorrow, Florida Tropical House and the Cypress House. Unfortunately, they are not open for display to the public but may be in the future.

Kemil Beach is open 6 am - 11 pm, summer hours are 6 am to 11 pm

5. INDIANA DUNES NATIONAL LAKESHORE
Trip 4: Visitor Center/Calumet Dune Trail
USGS MAP(s): Dune Acres 1:24,000
TRAIL(s) DISTANCE: 0.5 mile loop
ACTIVITIES: nature walk, nature study, interpretive displays, theater, bookstore, programs, information

The Dorothy Buell Memorial Visitor Center, named in honor of the founder of the Save The Dunes Council, is the best place to become acquainted with the natural and social history of the Indiana Dunes. Besides providing trail information and maps, the center features a slide program about the National Lakeshore, has interpretive displays, books and other dune-related materials, a library, activity schedules, telephone and restrooms.

The Calumet Dune Trail begins and ends on the south backside of the visitor center. The paved, handicapped accessible trail is self-guiding and a trail brochure is available that corresponds to the thirteen interpretive stations enroute. Topics covered on this short walk include blowouts, fire scars, increment borers, forest clearing, succession, meadow plants, wetlands, oaks, forest humus, wintergreen and the former beach of prehistoric Lake Chicago. The Calumet Dune Trail also runs adjacent to the north terminus of the Ly-co-ki-we Trail network. Recently, a Visitor Center to Campground trail, the "Dunewood Trace" has been completed.

To reach the visitor center and the Calumet Dune Trail from I-94 exit 26 north onto Indiana 49 and drive to US 12. Turn east on US 12 and drive three miles to Kemil Road and turn right/south. The visitor center parking area is to the immediate right or west side of the road. The Dorothy Buell Memorial Visitor Center is open daily from 8 am to 5 pm except Thanksgiving, Christmas and New Year's Day.

6. CALUMET BIKE TRAIL
USGS MAP(s): Dune Acres, Michigan City West 1:24,000
TRAIL(s) DISTANCE: 9.2 miles one-way
ACTIVITIES: biking, hiking, x-country skiing, accesses recreational sites

Although open to hiking, bicyclists rather than hikers find the Calumet Bike Trail more to their liking since the route follows a gravel service road adjacent to the South Shore railroad and US 12. Maintained by the Indiana Department of Natural Resources, the Calumet Trail (also a National Recreation Trail and Hoosier Bikeway path) parallels the transportation and energy corridor for 9.2 linear miles, from the Beverly Drive and US 12 intersection near Mt. Baldy, west to Mineral Springs Road at the closed Dune Acres railroad station. Enroute the trail connects several recreational sites of the National Lakeshore and Indiana Dunes State Park.

Best time to bike or hike is during autumn when the abundant red maples are in full color as well as the abutting open fields and wetlands. Due to condition of the road only mountain bikes are recommended.

The National Lakeshore visitor center parking area at Kemil Road and US 12 is a good place to park and access the trail. Additional access points include the following east to west sites:

Access Points:

Central Avenue
500 E/Beverly Shores, Indiana
Broadway Avenue
Kemil Road (next to the visitor center)
Tremont Road
Indiana 49 (just south of Indiana Dunes State Park entrance)
Waverly Road
Mineral Springs Road

Recreational Sites: (connecting or close proximity)

Mt. Baldy
Central Beach
National Lakeshore Campground
Visitor Center/Calumet Dune Trail/Ly-co-ki-we Trail
Kemil Beach/Dune Ridge Trail
Indiana Dunes State Park
Cowles Bog
Chelberg Farm/Bailly Homestead/Little Calumet River Trail

7. INDIANA DUNES NATIONAL LAKESHORE
Trip 5: Ly-co-ki-we Trail
USGS MAP(s): Dune Acres 1:24,000
TRAIL(s) DISTANCE: 10 miles
ACTIVITIES: hiking, x-country skiing, bridle trail, picnicking, shelter, visitor center

The longest distance trail in the National Lakeshore is the Ly-co-ki-we Trail. The Miami Indian name, Ly-co-ki-we meaning "sandy ground", appropriately describes the trail surface which can be trying and tiring after a short trek especially if horse traffic is heavy. However the trail is seldom used by horses or hikers.

There are two trailheads with plenty of parking. The visitor center at the intersection of US 12 and Kemil Road has overflow parking if the main lot is crowded across the road from the center and there are restrooms, picnic spots and information. The second trailhead and parking site is

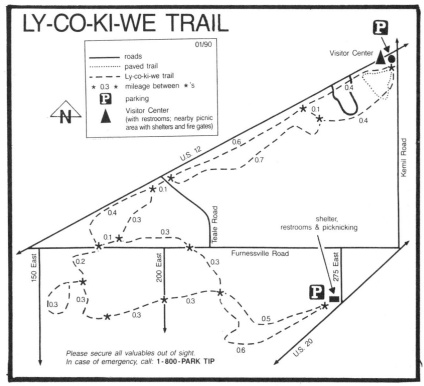

LY-CO-KI-WE TRAIL

01/90

————	roads
··············	paved trail
— — —	Ly-co-ki-we trail
★ 0.3 ★	mileage between ★'s
🅿	parking
▲	Visitor Center (with restrooms; nearby picnic area with shelters and fire gates)

N

Visitor Center

Kemil Road

U.S. 12

0.4
0.1
0.4
0.6
0.7
0.1
0.4
0.3
0.1
0.3
0.1
Teale Road
shelter, restrooms & picknicking
Furnessville Road
150 East
200 East
275 East
0.2
0.3
0.3
0.3
0.3
0.3
0.5
0.6
U.S. 20

🅿

Please secure all valuables out of sight. In case of emergency, call: **1-800-PARK TIP**

located at the intersection of US 20 and CR 275E about two miles south and west of the visitor center. The second trailhead includes a warming hut, picnic shelters and restrooms.

The Ly-co-ki-we Trail traverses black oak wooded gentle ridges, old fields reverting to grassy scrub and marsh wetlands. The area was once covered by Lake Chicago several thousand years ago. There are four color coded interconnecting trails that comprise the ten mile distance: Blue 2.2 miles, Green 3.3. miles, Red 2.8 miles and a combination segment of Red, Green and Yellow 1.1 mile. The color markers are in the process of being changed and removed.

Basically the Blue segment lies between the visitor center and Teale Road, forming a double loop. The Green segment is between Teale Road and the Furnessville Road forming a loop. The Red segment is situated south of the Furnessville Road, between CR 150E and CR 200E/Veden Road. The fourth trail segment is between the Furnessville Road, Veden Road and the second trailhead at US 20 and CR 275E. Exercise caution when crossing Teale, Veden, and the busy Furnessville roads. The flat to gently rolling terrain is perfect for beginning cross country skiers.

8. INDIANA DUNES NATIONAL LAKESHORE
Trip 6: Heron Rookery
USGS MAP(s): Westville 1:24,000
TRAIL(s) DISTANCE: 1.6 mile one-way
ACTIVITIES: nature walk, nature study

Heron Rookery is about five miles south of Lake Michigan as the crow flies. Surrounded by farm fields, the isolated area is a large block of lowland forest along the upper reaches of the Little Calumet River, situated between two moraines. A great blue heron rookery of forty nesting pair is located in the northeastern portion of the densely wooded property, giving rise to the property's place name. Classified as a rare nester, the shy and retiring large majestic bird nests by the dozens in the tallest trees especially sycamores, reusing the same bulky stick nests with added materials for years. The decrease in rookeries is attributed primarily to the destruction of habitats and chemicals in the food chain.

An east and west trailhead accesses the wooded property. The point to point trail follows the south spoil bank of the channeled stream for the entire 1.6 mile distance. The flat level path may be wet in places. There are several deadfalls in the river and occasionally along the path, some caused by beaver. Spring wildflowers and wildlife are plentiful and so are mosquitoes during the warm weather. Nonetheless the hike through the maturing floodplain forest is worth the trek. Retrace your steps.

To reach Heron Rookery in rural Porter County from US 20 west of The Pines, Indiana, turn south on CR 500E and drive under the I-94 overpass to CR 1400N Road. To reach the eastern trailhead turn left/east on CR 1400N and drive to the next road south, 600E. Continue on CR 600E 0.5 mile, just beyond the bridge crossing over the Little Calumet River and the east trailhead parking area. The trail begins at the northwest corner.

To reach the west trailhead, turn west on 1400N Road and drive to the next road south, CR 450E. Turn south on CR 450E and proceed 0.5 mile to the parking lot and trailhead just beyond the bridge over the Little Calumet River. The trailhead is at the northeast corner.

Further downstream on the Little Calumet River is the state-owned Langeluttig Marsh - Little Calumet Wetland Conservation Area, the National Lakeshore's Bailly Homestead and Chellberg Farm, and Little Calumet River Trail.

9. INDIANA DUNES NATIONAL LAKESHORE
Trip 7: Pinhook Bog
USGS MAP(s): Westville, LaPorte West 1:24,000
TRAIL(s) DISTANCE: 0.3 mile boardwalk tours only
ACREAGE: 406 acres
ACTIVITIES: guided nature walks by tour only, nature study

A few miles south and east of Heron Rookery is Pinhook Bog, an entirely different type of wetland. Pinhook Bog was created about 14,000 years ago when a large block of glacial ice broke off from a larger retreating parent glacier. The ice gouged out a "kettle hole" and formed a small lake, the bottom sealed by clayish glacial "till" or outwash. Over the ages, the lake filled in with organic materials and today what remains is a bog; a highly acidic wetland that survives by rainwater and snow. Dead organic plant material continues to accumulate but does not decay, but instead turns into peat since the vinegar-like waters are so acidic that decay cannot take place. In time, bogs will fill in and (as is here) be a quaking bog, and then eventually become stable land.

Due to its fragile nature, Pinhook Bog is only open by appointment and when accompanied by a member of the National Lakeshore interpretive staff. Tours are available by calling (219) 926-7561 ext. 265 and asking for reservations. Groups of 15 individuals is the limit for each tour. Tour times are also listed in the Ranger Guided Activity Schedule.

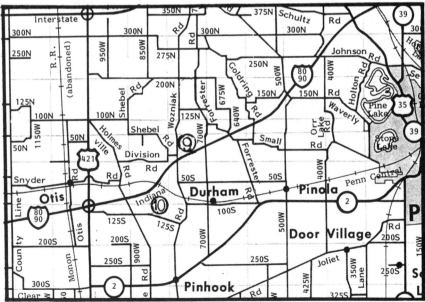

Pinhook Bog (9) & Hildebrand Lake (10)

10. HILDEBRAND LAKE
Pinhook, IN/LaPorte County
USGS MAP(s): LaPorte West, Westville 1:24,000
TRAIL(s) DISTANCE: no est. trails
ACREAGE: 36 acres
ACTIVITIES: hiking, nature study

Located about three miles south and west of Pinhook Bog is Hildebrand Lake, an undisturbed kettle moraine lake that was purchased by The Nature Conservancy and is now in the ownership of the DNR's Division of Nature Preserves. The "kettle" was formed by the melting of a large detached block of ice that was buried in glacial moraine when the ice sheet covering the region receded. As the buried ice melted, the moraine material above and about it filled in, forming a "kettle shaped" basin.

The shoreline of Hildebrand Lake has a buttonbush shrub ring that harbors northern type plants. The south and west shore of the preserve is forested and there are several deep ravines. The north and east shore is private land. There are no trails but the preserve is open to visitation. Parking for two cars is available along the roadside shoulder at the open lakeside overlook. Enter the woods and follow the vehicle-wide path between the lake and the upland knoll for about 0.25 miles to where the path ends.

Hildebrand Lake is easily reached from US 421 just south of the Indiana Toll Road/80-90 junction at CR 125S, the first road south, just north of the Purdue Westville Campus. Turn east/left onto CR 125S and drive 1.8 miles to the preserve's southwest property boundary on the left/north side of CR 125S.

To reach Pinhook Bog, National Lakeshore property from Hildebrand Lake, continue east on CR 125S to the "T" and turn left/north on Wozniak Road and continue to the area just beyond the toll road overpass. Visitation is by tours only.

11. MORAINE NATURE PRESERVE

Valparaiso, IN/Porter County
USGS MAP(s): Chesterton 1:24,000
TRAIL(s) DISTANCE: appx. 3 miles of service road trails
ACREAGE: 570 acres
ACTIVITIES: hiking, nature study

Geographically located on the south edge of the Indiana dunes by a few miles, Moraine Nature Preserve exemplifies the geology of the Valparaiso Moraine with its rolling steep hills, gorges, muck pockets, potholes and a natural kettle pond. Defined, a moraine is an accumulation of earth and stone called till, carried and deposited by a glacier. Created by a lobe of the Wisconsin glacier, the Valparaiso Moraine extended around the southern edge of Lake Michigan forming a U-shaped land mass that acted as a dam barrier separating drainage patterns of Lake Michigan from the Kankakee River valley. Today this glacial carved landscape is primarily covered with young and maturing beech-maple forest. The nature preserve is the result of several land gifts and bargain sales to The Nature Conservancy but is owned and managed by the DNR's Division of Nature Preserves.

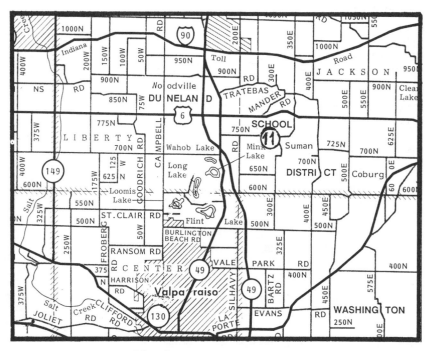

Moraine Nature preserve (11)

43

Permission to visit Moraine Nature Preserve is necessary either from the Indiana DNR Division of Nature Preserves (317) 232-4052 or from the preserve stewards, Mr. and Mrs. John Womer (219) 464-4941.

To reach the nature preserve from Valparaiso and US 30 drive north on Indiana 49 and exit US 6 east. Go east on US 6 about 0.5 mile to the first stop light and old Indiana 49 and turn right/south. Drive one mile on old Indiana 49 to CR 750N and turn left/east. Follow CR 750N 0.5 mile to the preserve's entrance and continue following the gravel road about 0.5 mile to a parking pullout where the road jogs south (the south drive is the property stewards). Along the entrance road you will pass three gated service roads on the north side and one on the south side. An old service road begins north where you park. Most of the service road trails are found in the north portion of the property and interconnect. Trails lead through the woods to the largest wetland on the property at the northwest edge. The service road trail on the south side of the entry road/750N leads to the Carlson Pond area. In some areas off of the old road trails, rose bushes are thick in the understory.

12. INDIANA DUNES STATE PARK
Chesterton, IN/Porter County
USGS MAP(s): Dune Acres 1:24,000
TRAIL(s) DISTANCE: 8 trails total appx. 16.5 miles
BEACH FRONTAGE: 3 miles
ACREAGE: 2,182 acres
ACTIVITIES: hiking, nature study, nature center, naturalist, x-country skiing, nearby bicycle trail, beach swimming, lifeguards, bathhouse, picnicking, shelters, playground, playfields, smelt fishing only, A, B & youth camping, concessions, camp store, cultural arts programs
FEE(s): entrance, shelter reservations, camping

Established in 1925, Indiana Dunes State Park is one of the crown jewels in the Hoosier state park system. The three miles of golden sand beach along the shores of Lake Michigan, the unique geographical mixture of plants and animals, the high quality dune ecosystem, and the largest nature preserve of any state park combine to form the finest natural, scientific and recreational area in Indiana. However with all of these attractions it is also Indiana's most heavily visited state park especially on summer and fall weekends. Therefore it is recommended that plans for visiting during the busy season be made during the less hectic weekdays.

The seven trails encompass several habitats: beach, dunal ridges, blowouts, savanna, marsh, swamp, riparian, prairie and upland forests.

Trail 1 which is described on the map no longer exists due to a break in the water tower which has eroded the trail away. It should no longer be used due to further continuing erosion.

Trail 3 may be seen to the immediate south of the lookout tower. The 0.75 mile non-looping trail begins near the gatehouse entrance and travels west through dunal forest and then north along a gentle pathway among a jack pine grove to conclude at the lookout tower and parking lot.

Trail 2 is a three mile long hike that interconnects Trails 8 and 10 for a longer combined loop. The trailhead begins on the south side of Wilson Road just west of Dunes Creek and shortly thereafter crosses the creek. The trail turns east to cross the youth camp access road and continues another mile following Dunes Creek east to cross a third park road, just north of the Duneside picnic shelter and parking area. The next half of the trail, before joining Trail 10, explores the southeast portion of the 1,530 acre Dunes Nature Preserve.

From the Duneside picnic shelter the trail enters a climax forest and parallels the south edge of the Great Marsh heading east. Spring flowers, ferns and birding is excellent. The final segment of the trail bisects the marsh via a boardwalk and joins Trail 10. A loop may be formed by going west/left on Trail 10 to Trail 8 and south to rejoin Trail 2 and Wilson Shelter. This loop also forms the Trail B cross country ski trail in winter snows.

Trail 4 is a 0.75 mile long journey that heads north from the campground uphill alongside ravines to join Trail 8 on the east slope of 192' Mt. Tom, the highest Indiana dune. The sandy trail jogs east on Trail 8 along the base of Mt. Tom. After descending several flights of steps, Trail 4 then leaves Trail 8 and goes north through a hardwood cove to end at the junction of Trail 7 overlooking the beach. Loop trails may be formed from Trail 7 and 8.

Trail 7 is a 1.1 mile moderate path that begins at the nature center parking area and heads northwest through the wooded dunes to cross Trail 8 south of 184' Mt. Holden. The trail continues on through woods intersecting Trail 4, finally ending at the beach and Trail 10. Take some time to enjoy the modern nature center with its outstanding exhibits, aquarium, observation windows, library, and Jens Jensen fountain. The nature center is open daily 9 am to 5 pm in summer. The rest of the year it is open from 9 am to 4 pm on weekends and from 12 noon to 4 pm on weekdays.

INDIANA DUNES STATE PARK

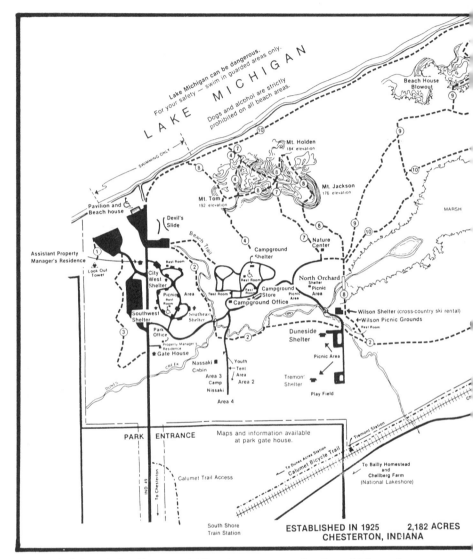

Trail 8 is a 1.5 mile rugged hike that traverses the three highest dunes enroute to the beach, intersecting Trails 9, 10, 7, and 4. Trail 8 begins at the Wilson picnic shelter and heads north crossing Trails 9 and 10 east of the nature center. The trail continues uphill to 176' Mt. Jackson then down the saddle and up to 184' Mt. Holden, then down crossing Trails 7 and 4. The trail continues uphill to 192' Mt. Tom and on to the beach and Trail 10. There are some boardwalk segments and many steps.

INDIANA DUNES STATE PARK

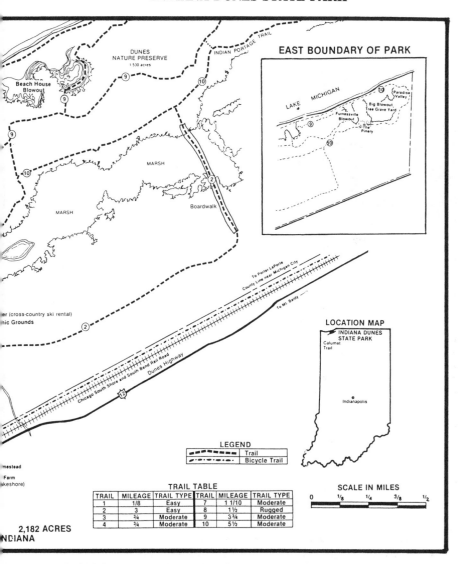

EAST BOUNDARY OF PARK

DUNES
NATURE PRESERVE
1,530 acres

Beach House
Blowout

LAKE   MICHIGAN

Paradise
Valley

Big Blowout
Tree Grave Yard

Furnessville
Blowout

The
Pinery

MARSH

MARSH

Boardwalk

To Porter LaPorte
County Line near Michigan City

To Mt. Baldy

LOCATION MAP

INDIANA DUNES
STATE PARK
Calumet
Trail

er (cross-country ski rental)
nic Grounds

Indianapolis

Chicago South Shore and South Bend Rail Road
Dunes Highway

LEGEND

▬ ▬ ▬ ▬ ▬	Trail
▬·▬·▬·▬·▬·	Bicycle Trail

mestead
Farm
akeshore)

2,182 ACRES
NDIANA

TRAIL TABLE

TRAIL	MILEAGE	TRAIL TYPE	TRAIL	MILEAGE	TRAIL TYPE
1	1/8	Easy	7	1 1/10	Moderate
2	3	Easy	8	1½	Rugged
3	¾	Moderate	9	3¾	Moderate
4	¾	Moderate	10	5½	Moderate

SCALE IN MILES

0	1/8	1/4	3/8	1/2

Trail 9 is a 3.75 mile moderate linear and loop hike through the more remote Dunes Nature Preserve. The foot trail begins at the nature center and runs northeast through a stable dunal forest along the backside of active dunes. The trail ascends the dunal ridges near the Furnessville Blowout and follows the ridgeline looping back to Beach House Blowout. The blowout exposes ancient tree "graveyards"; forests buried by the advancing wind blown dunes then re-exposed by strong winds. This trail affords some of the most spectacular views in the park.

Mount Tom, Indiana Dunes State Park

The 5.5 mile Trail 10 is the best longest distance hike for the nature seeking. Hikers may begin/end at the beach house pavilion or the nature center. Basically the trail follows the beach for 2.75 miles and then turns inland at the east boundary to Paradise Valley leading past The Pinery, natural stands of mature white pines. The trail continues southwest potentially connecting Trail 9 and intersecting Trail 2. It then skirts the north side of the Great Marsh wetland, reconnecting Trail 9 and crossing Trail 8 before ending at the nature center.

In addition, the 9.2 mile Calumet Bike Trail is easily accessed near the park's entrance to the south.

To reach Indiana Dunes State Park from I-94 exit 26 north on Indiana 49 and continue to the park entrance where the highway terminates. The park beach is bordered by Kemil Beach National Lakeshore to the east (Kemil Road north from US 12) and Porter Beach to the west (Waverly Road north from US 12).

13. INDIANA DUNES NATIONAL LAKESHORE

Trip 8: Bailly Homestead/Chellberg Farm/Little Calumet River Trail
USGS MAP(s): Dune Acres 1:24,000
TRAIL(s) DISTANCE: 2 loop trails total appx. 4.7 miles
ACTIVITIES: nature walks, nature study, living historic sites, picnicking, shelters, visitor center, bookstore, activities, programs, special events, festivals, x-country skiing

The Bailly Homestead and Chellberg Farm offers visitors an opportunity to experience what settlement history was like over the past 150 years by providing working living history re-creations. A two mile loop trail and linear spur spans the two historic dwellings, the visitor center and Bailly Cemetery and for those who seek more walking, the 2.7 mile Little Calumet River Trail loops along the riparian corridor and adjacent wetlands and upland forest. Both trails can be wet and mushy at times. The visitor center just southwest of the parking area is the best place to begin.

The Bailly Homestead, located 0.3 mile west of the visitor center, was the domicile of French-Canadian trader Honore Gratien Joseph Bailly de Messein (1774-1835) during the early 1800s. He was involved in trading with the Potawatomi and was accepted as family largely due to his half-Ottawa wife, Marie, who was related to the local Indians. The site was a crossroads of Indian trails and a canoe route. Bailly sold most of his furs to Jacob Astor's American Fur Company.

When the wilderness fur trade declined he turned to a more settled way of life and bought more land, established Baillytown and built a tavern on what is now Bethlehem Steel Corporation. The Bailly Homestead site also includes a coachman's house, kitchen/chapel, main house, brick house and storehouse. North one mile along the loop trail is a linear spur that crosses Oak Hill Road, leading to the Bailly Cemetery where Joseph, his wife Marie, and other family members and early settlers are buried.

Retracing your steps 0.3 mile back to the main loop across Oak Hill Road, continue another 0.3 mile to the Chellberg Farm. Anders and Johanna Kjellberg (later anglicized to Chellberg) were Swedish immigrants who bought 80 acres of the Bailly estate in 1874. Three generations worked the farm, growing grains, milking dairy cows and producing maple syrup.

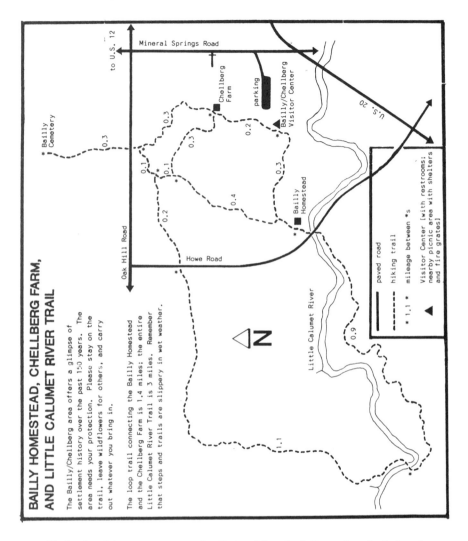

BAILLY HOMESTEAD, CHELLBERG FARM, AND LITTLE CALUMET RIVER TRAIL

The Bailly/Chellberg area offers a glimpse of settlement history over the past 150 years. The area needs your protection. Please stay on the trail, leave wildflowers for others, and carry out whatever you bring in.

The loop trail connecting the Bailly Homestead and the Chellberg Farm is 1.4 miles; the entire Little Calumet River Trail is 3 miles. Remember that steps and trails are slippery in wet weather.

Today's visitors may tour the living historical farm that includes the 1885 farm house, barn, chicken house, corn crib, windmill, granary, tenant house, maple sugar house, gardens and fields. Demonstrations, scheduled programs and activities by volunteers and park employees bring life to the farm throughout the year, simulating the lifestyles of those who lived it. Chellberg Farm and Bailly Homestead are also the site of the annual Maple Sugar Festival in early March and the Duneland Harvest Festival in September.

The Little Calumet River Trail begins near the stream at the Bailly Homestead. The trail crosses the river and Howe Road and follows the floodplain west nearly a mile to recross the water body and head north.

The federally endangered Indiana bat and state endangered black-crowned night heron forage along the stream while steelhead trout, coho and chinook salmon, northern pike and brown trout spawn in its waters. The trail continues through marsh, ravine and upland forest and curves east again to recross Howe Road, a distance of 1.1 miles. An additional 0.2 mile through woods reconnects the Bailly-Chellberg loop. Turn right/south and walk 0.1 mile to a short cut if not preferring to walk the total loop back to Bailly Homestead. The shortcut connecting spur leads to Chellberg Farm, 0.3 mile away. From the farm walk south to the parking area and visitor center. A trail map is available at the center.

To reach the Bailly Homestead, Chellberg Farm and Little Calumet River Trail from I-94 exit 26 north onto Indiana 49 and drive north to US 12 and turn left/west. Proceed west on US 12 about 1.5 miles to Mineral Springs Road and turn left/south. Continue about 0.75 mile (past the National Lakeshore Administration and Maintenance Center) to the visitor parking entry road on the right/west side of the road. Follow the directional signs.

Great lakes Indian Wigwam Hut in Winter, Bailley Homestead

14. IMAGINATION GLEN PARK

Portage, IN/Porter County
USGS MAP(s): Portage 1:24,000
TRAIL(s) DISTANCE: appx. 5 miles of interconnected nature trails
ACREAGE: 256 acres
ACTIVITIES: nature walks, nature study, picnicking, shelters, fishing, canoeing, launch ramp, bicycling, playgrounds, ballfields, archery range, x-country skiing, concessions
FEE(s): summer weekends and holiday parking

Portage is Porter County's largest city and Imagination Glen is the community's largest park. The active recreational area of the 256 acre park occupies the high level ground above Salt Creek while the nature trails wind along the floodplain forest of the glen.

The unmarked but obvious trails begin at the parking lot, heading east and south. The east trail leads down through the river bottom meadows of the glen to the west bank of Salt Creek. The streamside trail affords pleasant scenery as it follows the meander. Salt Creek is noted as a spawning ground for steelhead, brown trout, coho and chinook salmon and northern pike and the creek is a favorite with fishermen. Recently a 1,000 acre proposed area along the stream has been targeted for preservation and recreation to tie into the Little Calumet River and the National Lakeshore, a few miles downstream north. The Imagination Glen trail leads uphill to emerge at the ball fields.

The south spur leading from the parking area accesses the Iron Horse Heritage Trail, a rail-to-trail that was formerly the Wabash, Norfolk and Western right-of-way. Heading east 150 yards are excellent views overlooking Salt Creek from the trestle bridge. Currently the unpaved and undeveloped 62 linear acres ranges from US 20 east to Indiana 149, a total distance of five miles. The best natural portion is from Imagination Glen east to Indiana 149.

A second rail-to-trail, located 0.75 miles south of the Imagination Glen Park entrance on McCool Road is the Prairie Duneland Trail. The former Elgin, Joliet and Eastern railway is now a six mile long 74 acre greenway from County Line Road/US 6 east to Indiana 149. The best natural path portion is from McCool Road access east to Indiana 149, about two miles one-way. West of McCool Road, the Prairie Duneland Trail accesses the Portage city parks of Countryside Park at 5250 US 6 and Olson Park at Sunrise Avenue and Carmen Street. The rail-to-trail could eventually connect Chesterton and the Indiana Dunes National Lakeshore, and west to Lake County, connecting more rail-to-trail projects.

The Portage Parks and Recreation Department which owns and manages these exceptional urban parks is located at Woodland Park 2100 Willow Creek Road, phone (219) 762-1675.

To reach Imagination Glen Park from I-94 exit 19 south on Crisman Road/Indiana 249 and drive one mile to Portage Avenue and turn left/east. Continue on Portage Avenue about 1.5 miles to the park entrance at the intersection of Portage Avenue and McCool Road at 2275 North McCool Road in east Portage.

15. INDIANA DUNES NATIONAL LAKESHORE
Trip 9: Cowles Bog
USGS MAP(s): Dune Acres 1:24,000
TRAIL(s) DISTANCE: appx. 5.1 miles round trip
BEACH FRONTAGE: appx. 1 mile
ACREAGE: more than 600 acres
ACTIVITIES: hiking, nature study

A National Natural Landmark, the Cowles Bog is named for the former Dr. Henry C. Cowles, whose studies of plant succession made the Indiana Dunes famous as the birthplace of North American plant ecology. The little used area makes an excellent day hike, sampling such natural habitats as interdunal wetlands, oak savanna, dunal ridges and sand beach.

Two trailheads exist, a North and South entrance. The North entrance trailhead and parking area begin just east of the Dune Acres community entrance station on Mineral Springs Road. Park and walk west crossing the entry road. The foot path west follows a level wide path between the bog and the dunes for the first mile. A small portion is boardwalk. There are no vista breaks into the bog to the south or the beach to the north and although the shady path is walled in by vegetation and dune it is highly scenic with such trees as speckled alder, white, yellow and dwarf birch and an abundance of royal fern. The striking contrast between bog edge and dunal oak savanna is moving.

Near the northwest edge of the bog, the trail heads towards the beach, up and down dunes and along interdunal wetlands. There is a crossover 0.3 mile connecting spur at mid-point that forms a shorter loop of 2.7 miles. Arriving at the beach, the trail heads west 0.2 mile towards the looming NIPSCO and Bethlehem Steel monoliths and turns back into the dunes. The sandy trail heads updune along a ridge with industrial views to the west. The crossover connecting spur trail is 0.7 miles from the beach; the same trail encountered enroute. The trail descends and levels

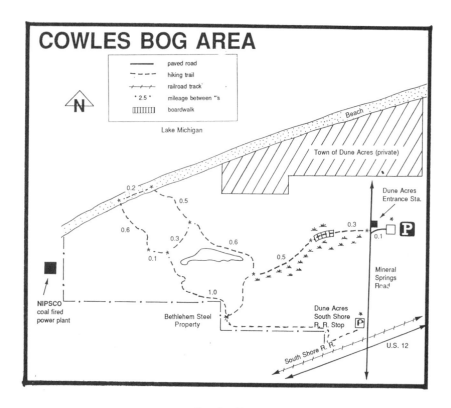

Cowles Bog

out returning to the edge of Cowles Bog, forming a complete loop. Continue back to the parking area along the already hiked bog edge-dune savanna segment across the boardwalk back to the trailhead.

To reach Cowles Bog from I-94 exit 26 north onto Indiana 49 and continue to US 12 and turn left/west. Continue on US 12 west about 1.5 miles to Mineral Springs Road and turn right/north. Proceed to the Dune Acres community entrance station and turn right/east into the parking area. Cowles Bog is about one mile north of the Bailly Homestead and Chellberg Farm.

16. INDIANA DUNES NATIONAL LAKESHORE
Trip 10: Inland Marsh Trails
USGS MAP(s): Portage 1:24,000
TRAIL(s) Distance: 2.5 miles of loops
ACTIVITIES: nature walks, nature study, picnicking, x-country skiing

Geologically, the trails that traverse the dune tops in the Inland Marsh area are of the older Tolleston Stage, formed 8,000 to 2,000 years ago when post glacial Lake Chicago (now Lake Michigan) was 25 feet higher at 605' elevation. These now stable oak wooded sand dunes are separated from the more recent dunes by the interdunal Great Marsh wetlands that ran for miles between the dunal ridges, now mostly filled or drained.

The Inland Marsh Trails begin and end at the south area of the parking lot adjacent to US 12, just west of the Ogden Dunes South Shore railroad station. The first 0.5 mile parallels the marsh to the west and Stagecoach Road to the east and is level easy walking. As the trail approaches the dunes, the sand base trail becomes more difficult. The first loop becomes a series of ups and downs as it skirts the wetland to the north the next 0.4 mile. A second loop is intersected and may be combined for a mile longer

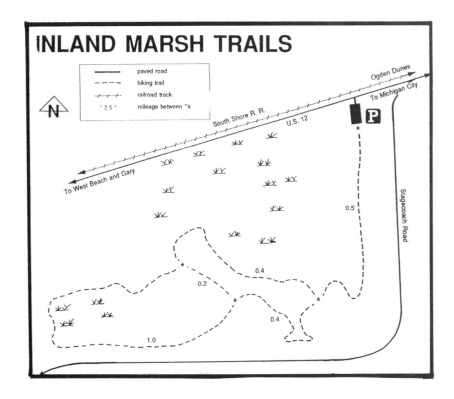

loop hike. There are several user side trails that veer off from the main marked trail, so it can become confusing but also interesting if you feel adventuresome. The trail continues to loop back to the original 0.5 mile linear entrance trail and the parking area. The first loop is color coded blue and the second loop is green.

To reach <u>Inland Marsh Trails</u> from I-94 exit 19 north onto Indiana 249 and drive just over two miles to US 12 and turn west. Continue on US 12 about two miles to the parking entrance on the south side of the highway.

Inland Marsh Trails, Indiana Dunes National Lakeshore

17. INDIANA DUNES NATIONAL LAKESHORE

Trip 11: West Beach Trails
USGS MAP(s): Portage 1:24,000
TRAIL(s) DISTANCE: 4 trails total appx. 7 miles
BEACH FRONTAGE: 3.5 miles
ACTIVITIES: nature hikes, nature study, beach swimming, lifeguards, beach house, visitor center, picnicking, shelters, x-country skiing, concessions
FEE(s): seasonal user fee

Bordering the Porter-Lake county line, the West Beach area is highly scenic despite the extensive sand mining that has created a man-made "valley" between dune ridges that the parking area now occupies. Beach, dunes, woods, prairie, marsh and lake comprise the natural attractions. The four hiking trails are as diverse as the surroundings.

The one mile self-guiding <u>Dune Succession Trail</u> loop begins/ends at the visitor center where a trail brochure may be obtained. From the visitor center the trail follows the paved service road to the bathhouse and beachfront. From here the identified trail becomes a boardwalk and moves from the beach inland, uphill to dune top. Along the stairway trail are eight numbered stations that correspond to the brochure; identifying the successional changes in plant life. An observation platform perches at the treetops of the wooded dune overlooking the lake. The wooden staircase

Dune Succession Trail

57

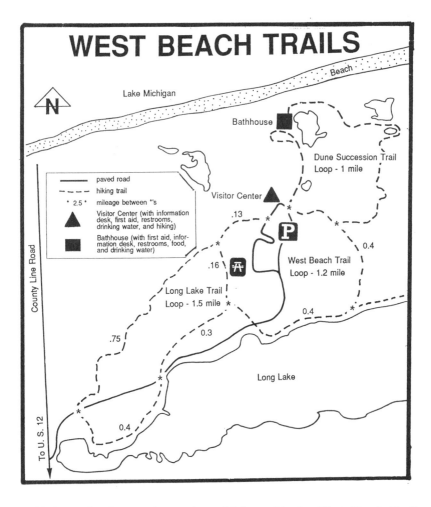

WEST BEACH TRAILS

Lake Michigan

Beach

Bathhouse

Dune Succession Trail
Loop - 1 mile

Visitor Center

——	paved road
– – –	hiking trail
• 2.5 •	mileage between •'s
▲	Visitor Center (with information desk, first aid, restrooms, drinking water, and hiking)
■	Bathhouse (with first aid, information desk, restrooms, food, and drinking water)

.13

P

0.4

.16

West Beach Trail
Loop - 1.2 mile

Long Lake Trail
Loop - 1.5 mile

0.4

.75

0.3

Long Lake

County Line Road

To U.S. 12

0.4

trail descends, intersecting and combining with the West Beach Trail enroute back to the visitor center and parking lot.

The 1.2 mile West Beach Trail loop also begins at the visitor center or from the parking area at Long Lake, adjacent to the main park entry road. The level trail encircles the sand-mined flats of the man-made "valley" and follows the north shore of Long Lake. The trail ascends the dunes at the west portion of the loop where the trail intersects with the 1.5 mile Long Lake loop.

To access the Long Lake Trail, park at the visitor center or at the entrance station lot, adjacent north. The trail follows the dunal ridges of the west property, skirts the northwest portion of Long Lake and moves through the re-colonizing flats. The loop trail crosses the park road twice.

The fourth trail is the linear <u>Marquette Trail</u> which is 3.27 miles one-way. The path begins west of the entrance station at the entry road curve, just west of the County Line Road overpass and is marked. A former railroad bed, the trail has been upgraded for bicycle use from West Beach to Grand Avenue. It is sandwiched between the cattail marsh wetlands of Long Lake and the oak-covered dunes to the north. The linear one-way path ends at Grand Avenue, not far from Miller Woods and the Paul H. Douglas Environmental Education Center but as yet there is no connecting trail. The <u>Marquette Trail</u> goes and returns on the same path.

To reach the <u>West Beach Trails</u> from I-94 exit 19 north onto Indiana 249 and drive about two miles to US 12 and turn left/west. Proceed west on US 12 to County Line Road and turn north and drive to the entrance road.

Another route from I-94 is exit 15 north onto Indiana 51, going north to US 20 and turning right/east. Go one mile on US 20 to County Line Road and turn left/north. Continue north on County Line Road two miles. West Beach is open 9 am to sunset.

18. MARQUETTE PARK
Gary, IN/Lake County
USGS MAP(s): Gary, Portage 1:24,000
TRAIL(s) DISTANCE: 1 mile exercise trail
BEACH FRONTAGE: 2.5 miles
ACREAGE: 241 acres
ACTIVITIES: nature walks, nature study, swimming beach, lifeguards, bathhouse, exercise trail, picnicking, tennis courts, concessions
FEE(s): beach parking

Situated in the residential Miller section of Gary, Marquette Park, owned by the city of Gary and managed by the municipal parks and recreation department, is tucked between the National Lakeshore property of Miller Woods Beach to the west and West Beach to the east. The city park came about from land donated to the city of Gary by U.S. Steel Corporation. The 241 acres of wooded backdunes, lagoons and sand beach are named for French Father Jacques Marquette who explored the south shore of Lake Michigan in 1675 and may have been the first European in duneland. A statue of Marquette greets visitors at the park entrance on Grand Boulevard.

The beach park is a popular spot in warm weather with swimmers and sunbathers but the sandy strand also provides foot access to a considerable amount of beach walking. Walking west, the beach connects Lake Street Beach and continues another mile along Miller Beach and the property boundary of U.S. Steel. To the east, the sandy trek skirts the residential lakefront homes of Oak Street as it makes its way unobscured about two miles to West Beach National Lakeshore.

Back away from the beach are wooded dunes surrounded by park roads and user trails weave through the shady black oaks. Immediately west of Grand Avenue are the picturesque lagoons of the Grand Calumet River, noted for birding. The former hey-day of the park is reflected in the Natatorium/beachhouse and recreation building to the west adjacent to the lagoons; architectural wonders of the Chicago's World's Fair.

To reach Marquette Park from I-94 exit 15 north onto Indiana 51 and drive to US 20 and turn left/west. Continue on US 20 to Lake Street and turn north/right. Follow Lake Street north a few blocks to Miller Avenue and turn right/east. Proceed on Miller Avenue to where the road curves and Grand Avenue and continue to the park entrance.

From West Beach National Lakeshore, go north on County Line Road to Oak Street and turn west/left and continue to Marquette Park.

19. INDIANA DUNES NATIONAL LAKESHORE
Trip 12: Miller Woods/Paul H. Douglas Center for Environmental Education/Lake Street Beach
USGS MAP(s): Portage, Gary 1:24,000
TRAIL(s) DISTANCE: 1.1 mile Beach Frontage: appx. 1.1 mile
BEACH FRONTAGE: appx. 1.1 mile
ACTIVITIES: nature walks, nature study, naturalist, environmental education center, picnicking

Situated at the west edge of Gary, Indiana in northeast Lake County, Miller Woods and the Paul H. Douglas Center for Environmental Education are at the western borders of the Indiana Dunes National Lakeshore. Miller Woods encompasses several noteworthy natural areas including oak savanna, interdunal ponds, marsh, high dunes, lagoons, and prime foredunes as well as beach. The land was acquired from various owners and a generous donation from neighboring U.S. Steel.

Access to Miller Woods is via an overpass foot bridge leading from the parking area adjacent to Lake Street to the Paul H. Douglas Center for Environmental Education. The Center has computers, media learning rooms, live animals, a bookstore and naturalists who lead scheduled hikes.

Miller Woods / Paul H. Douglas Center

There are two designated foot trails. A paved 0.1 mile trail begins and ends at the back door of the Center where a picnic area has been placed. The trail loops about an oak savanna woodland. The second hike double loops about the cattail swale adjacent to the Center. Near mid-point, a wooden foot bridge bisects the pond providing views of the wetlands and woods. The trail is about a mile long.

The mile-long beach, the southernmost extent of Lake Michigan, has excellent marram grass-covered foredunes and extends east to the city of Gary-owned Lake Street Beach and Marquette Park and west to the boundary of U.S. Steel. The wide beach makes for great birding. Miller Beach is also accessible by car from the parking area of Lake Street Beach, north of the Paul H. Douglas Center.

Miller Woods and the Paul H. Douglas Center for Environmental Education is open daily 8 am to 4:30 pm Monday through Friday. A small parking lot just north of the Center is open everyday for access to the trails.

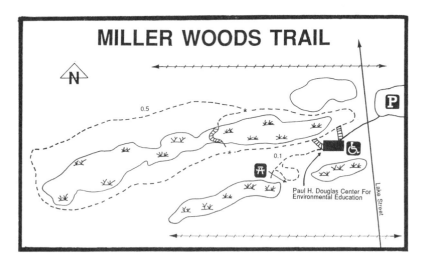

Miller Woods/Paul H. Douglas Center for Environmental Education

To reach the property from I-94 exit 15, go north on Indiana 51 and drive one mile to US 12 and turn left/west. Continue on US 12 west to Lake Street, just beyond the Miller railroad station and turn right/north. Go north on Lake Street about a mile to Miller Woods/Douglas Center parking area on the right/east side of the street. Lake Street Beach and Miller Beach at lakeside is about a mile north of Miller Woods and the Douglas Center on Lake Street.

Paul H. Douglas Center for Environmental Education

20. GIBSON WOODS NATURE PRESERVE
Hammond, IN/Lake County
USGS MAP(s): Highland 1:24,000
TRAIL(s) DISTANCE: 4 trails total appx. 4 miles
ACREAGE: 130 acres
ACTIVITIES: nature walks, nature study, nature center, naturalist, displays, programs, activities, lectures, gift shop

Outside of the Indiana Dunes National Lakeshore and Dunes State Park, Gibson Woods preserves the longest intact inland dunal ridge and marsh swale remnant in the Midwest. Located about one mile south from the lake, the preserve was acquired in 1980 by The Nature Conservancy from the Penn Central Railroad and is now owned and managed by the Lake County Parks and Recreation Department as a dedicated state nature preserve.

Four trails loop and interconnect in the narrow elongated band of land that parallels the Conrail Railroad to the north. There are several rare endangered plants and animals that reside in the urban sanctuary of savanna, prairie and wetlands including paper birch, orchids, dune goldenrod, Franklin's ground squirrel, Blanding's turtle and the Karner blue butterfly. The well-marked and color coded trails begin just east of the Environment Awareness Center at the north edge of the parking area. A trail brochure is available and a trail map sign is posted at the trailhead.

The one mile blue coded Nippising Lake Trail loops around the west end of the preserve. From the parking lot trailhead follow the boardwalk north to the "T" junction and go left. The narrow footpath winds along a dunal ridge and around a buttonbush swale.

The 0.5 mile red coded Short Trail goes right at the "T" from the parking area and traces a loop around a wetland.

The longest trail is the 2 mile green coded Prairie Dune Trail. The path continues east on the Short Trail through the dry and wet prairie to jog north and form a loop in the oak savanna of the extreme east property bordering Tennessee Avenue.

The fourth trail is the 0.5 mile Prairie Trail which is a linear connector trail between the Nippising Lake Trail and the Prairie Dune Trail. The path moves between the swell and swale in an open area of bluestem grasses and flowering prairie plants.

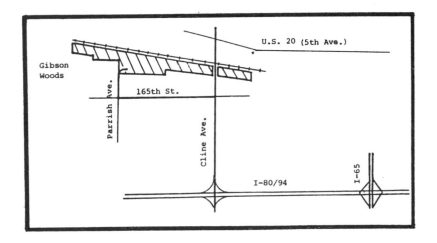

Gibson Woods Nature Preserve

Additional dune and swale nature preserves within Lake County include the 34 acre Ivanhoe Dune and Swale, the 42 acre Clark and Pine Dune and Swale, the 7.5 acre Lakewood Dune Forest and the 49 acre Tolleston Ridges Nature Preserve. All four properties were acquired by The Nature Conservancy and require their permission to visit the sites. Permission may also be obtained from the Indiana DNR Division of Nature Preserves or the Lake County Parks and Recreation Department.

Gibson Woods Nature Preserve is located at 6201 Parrish Avenue, at its dead end. The gate hours are 9 am to 5 pm. The Environmental Awareness Center is open from 11 am to 5 pm daily.

To reach the preserve which is located in the Hessville neighborhood of Hammond, from I-94 exit 3 north onto Kennedy Avenue and drive to 165th Street and turn right/east. Continue seven blocks to Parrish Avenue and turn left/north. Proceed north on Parrish Avenue to the preserve entrance just north of Harding School and Park. There are walk-in gates along 163rd Street at Grand Avenue, Tennessee Avenue, and California Avenue.

21. WHIHALA BEACH/WHITING PARK/MIGRANT TRAP
Whiting & Hammond, IN/Lake County
USGS MAP(s): Whiting, Lake Calumet 1:24,000
TRAIL(s) DISTANCE: 0.5 mile user paths at Migrant Trap
BEACH FRONTAGE: appx. 1.5 miles total
ACREAGE: 21 acres WB/25 acres WP/16 acres MT
ACTIVITIES: nature walks, nature study, swimming, lifeguards, beach
 house, picnicking, shelters, playgrounds, tennis courts, fishing, boat
 launch at Whihala, concessions
FEE(s): parking in summer, boat launch

Located west of the National Lakeshore and the industrial complex of
Gary and Indiana Harbor of East Chicago, these three northwest Lake
County lakefront nature places provide opportunities for outdoor
recreation and are combined into one for the sake of simplicity since they
are situated in close proximity.

Whihala Beach is a 21 acre Lake County Park that primarily serves
swimmers and boaters but nature walkers will find their niche at this
lakeside "pocket" park at the more natural west end. To reach Whihala

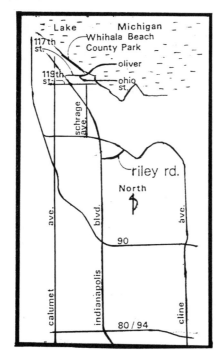

Whihala Beach County Park

Beach from I-94 in south Hammond exit 2 onto Indianapolis Boulevard/Indiana 152/US 12 & 20 and drive north to 117th Avenue and turn right/east. Continue on 117th Avenue to Park Road and turn left/north to Whihala Beach at 1561 Park Road.

Whiting Park, west of Whihala Beach County Park, is a municipal lakefront park. The small manicured park with shady paths and some natural area was constructed by the WPA during the 1930s. The recreational activities include swimming, boating with launch ramp, fishing, and tennis. The west section of the beach is natural and may be walked to the property line of the city filtration plant. The Whiting city park is noted for migratory birds.

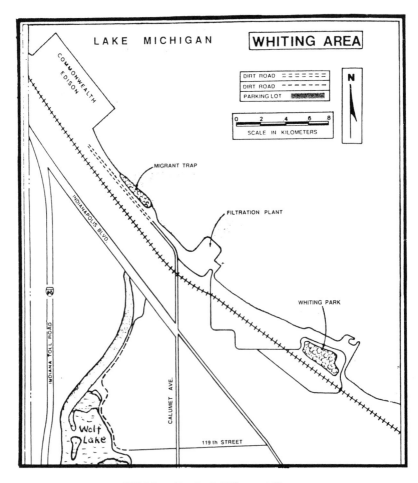

Whiting Park & Migrant Trap

Further west 1.25 miles is the <u>Migrant Trap</u>, just west of the Hammond Marina between the Commonwealth Edison power plant and the municipal filtration plant. Currently the 16 acre site is owned by NIPSCO but future plans are to annex the property with the adjoining Hammond Marina.

This small speck of young cottonwoods with weedy undergrowth surrounded by industry is the only island of green within eye-seeing distance. Yet during the height of bird migration vast numbers of different species of birds, especially warblers, funnel through enroute north and south. Parking is normally free after Labor Day in the Hammond Marina parking area. From the parking area walk west through the chain-link gate where there are conspicuous user paths that weave through the former dump site and along the shore. The Migrant Trap represents nature's will to survive amidst the desert landscape of industry. The cottonwood grove could easily be named, "Last Stand".

To reach the Migrant Trap and the Hammond Marina from I-94 exit 1 north onto Calumet Avenue/US 41 and drive to lakeside.

Herring Gulls, Whiting Area

PRAIRIE: OVERVIEW

*"For years the message of our great prairies had appealed
to me. Every leisure moment found me tramping through
unspoiled bits of these vast areas. I wanted to understand
their force, their enchantment that called on me"*

Siftings (1939), Chapter: "Compositions", pp. 81-82
Jens Jensen, prairie landscape designer and founding
member of the Prairie Club.

Except for isolated remnant patches, the prairie in northwest Indiana has
gone the way of the buffalo and prairie chicken but nature walkers will
discover the once vast "sea of grass" has worthwhile areas to explore.
Prior to settlement, thirteen per cent of the Indiana landscape was covered
by a complex ecosystem of tall grasses, broadleaf forbs and oak savannas
that required thousands of years to evolve; an area shaped by climate,
moisture, soils, geology, geography and fire. The Miami and other tribes
were known to hunt buffalo and other game by fire, which also served to
create and maintain areas of prairie by keeping the eastern forest from
invading. The "red buffalo" is still used today to restore preserves of
prairie and savanna in Indiana. After John Deere's steel plow was
invented in 1837, the prairie, once thought infertile, turned over into the
richest agricultural land in the world and by 1900 most of the Indiana
prairie was history. There was a failure to save anything of significance.

The "prairie peninsula" of northwest Indiana is the easternmost edge of
the "Grand Prairie" of Illinois. The boundary is not easy to draw on a
map since prairie also occurs in the Lake Plains, Wabash Valley and Till
Plain areas. The northwest Indiana prairie has distinct types such as wet,
dry and a mix between the two plus savanna or "forest islands" of open
oak and prairie grasses usually found along sandy ridges surrounded by
wet prairie.

Most of the trails in the parklands and preserves of the prairie area lead
to wet prairie. The Hoosier Prairie Nature Preserve in Griffith, Indiana
is an outstanding example of wet prairie and a walk through the preserve
is an experience that comes the closest to what the original tallgrass
prairie was like before settlement. Beaver Lake Nature Preserve in north
Newton County is a prime remnant of dry prairie where little bluestem
grass and herbaceous forbs are stunted by soil type and lack of moisture.
Oak savannas, a parkland setting where forest meets the prairie, have been
preserved and quality areas to visit include Conrad Savanna, Tefft
Savanna and Ober Savanna.

PRAIRIE LISTINGS

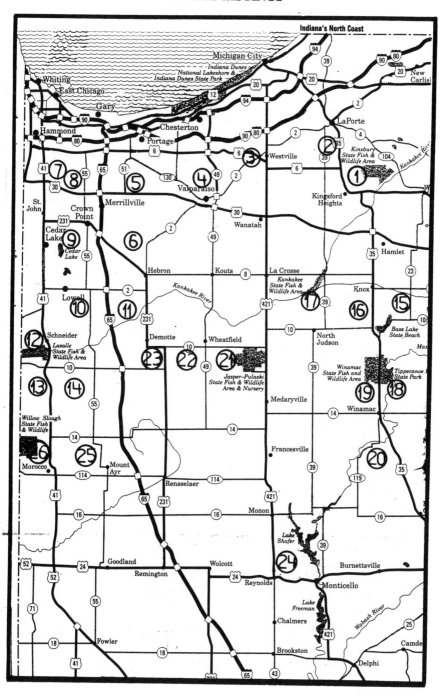

Ideally a 4,000 acre or more Prairie State Preserve or Park could be established; an expanse large enough for restoration of the diverse "Grand Prairie" ecosystem. Formerly the prairie reached its best development in Benton County and the area along Mt. Gilboa Ridge near Wadena, Indiana would be a choice setting. However obtaining the valuable agricultural land would not come easily.

Abandoned railroads and roadsides are potential areas that could become prairie preserves. The DNR's Division of Nature Preserves does manage small tracts of roadside prairie in northwest Indiana and the Department of Transportation has a program called the Roadside Prairie Project. The following sites are established and maintained roadside prairies:

Location	Prairie Types	Acreage
US 52 Fowler, south	Mesic/Wet	15
US 421 Monon, north	Mesic	18
US 24 Kentland, east	Mesic	20
I-65 MM 223	Sand Hill Savanna	109
I-65 Kankakee Rest Area	Savanna	13
I-80/94	Mesic/Wet	10
US 30 Grovertown, east	Dry	16

Sandhill Cranes, Jasper-Pulaski Fish & Wildlife Area
(photography by Jim Bergens, Francisville)

1. KINGSBURY FISH & WILDLIFE AREA
Kingsbury, IN/LaPorte County
USGS MAP(s): LaPorte East, Stillwell 1:24,000
TRAIL(s) DISTANCE: appx. 2 miles of levee, riverbank, service roads
ACREAGE: 5,062 acres
ACTIVITIES: nature walks, nature study, picnicking, fishing, canoeing, lake & river launch ramps, fish hatchery tour, hunting, archery range, Class C camping
FEE(s): camping

Prior to being deeded to the State of Indiana, Kingsbury Fish and Wildlife Area was once an ordnance depot producing shells, cartridges and mortar rounds during World War II and the Korean War conflict. The munition producing history of the area is still evident in the form of grass-covered bunkers and the thousand acres of contaminated disposal sites which are fenced and posted off limits in the west property, east of headquarters and the campground. However the east property beholds a remnant of the Grand Marsh of the Kankakee River, Tamarack lake, Mixsawbah Fish Hatchery and oak-hickory woodlands. Check with property headquarters to determine hunting seasons.

Along the River Road south from the intersection with Hupp Road is 450 acres of restored wetlands of the Grand Marsh. Parking in 5-F lot accesses the area along the levee. Wood ducks, teal, rails, geese, sandhill cranes and double-crested cormorants are often spotted in the marsh. Further south, River Road dead ends at the north bank of the Kankakee River where fishermen's paths line the shore. Another nature walk in the general area is east of the intersection of River Road and Nickle Road. Follow Nickle Road east to the 5-E parking lot. Walk south along a service road from the parking lot through the maturing oak-hickory forest to the Kankakee River and return along the original route.

At the dead end of Hupp Road is the west shore of 20 acre Tamarack Lake and parking lot 5-A. There is little area to explore on foot but the vistas and canoeing is great. Incidentally the name Tamarack is a misnomer since the lake and surrounding wetlands do not support the deciduous "evergreen" trees. Northwest a short distance of Tamarack Lake is Mixsawbah Fish Hatchery which is open to the public. Since 1974, the eight acre facility has reared and stocked salmon and trout to enhance Lake Michigan fishing. The small fish are released in Trail Creek and the Little Calumet River. Mixsawbah and Twin Branch (Bodine) on the St. Joseph River near Mishawaka are the only two coldwater fish hatcheries in the State of Indiana. The hours are 8 am to 3:30 pm Monday through Friday year around.

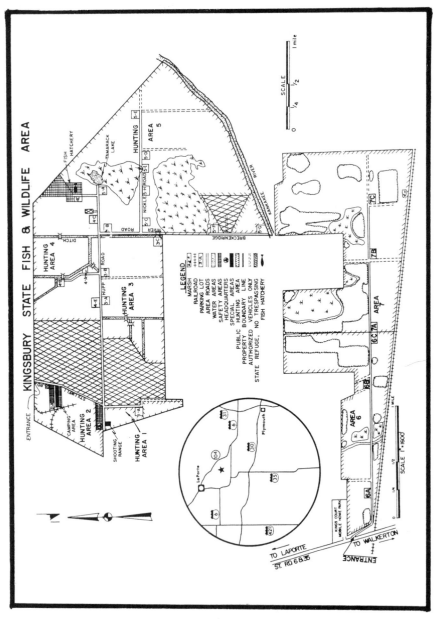

Kingsbury State Fish & Wildlife Area

Kingsbury Fish and Wildlife Area is located ten miles southeast of LaPorte, Indiana, five miles east of US 35. From US 35 turn east on CR 500S and drive to the "T" intersection with Hupp Road and turn right/south and proceed to the area.

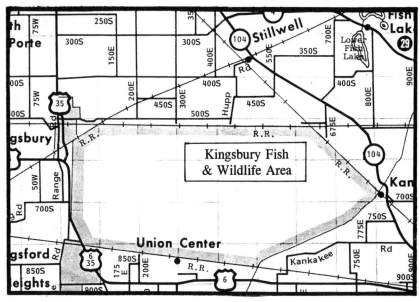

Kingsbury State Fish & Wildlife Area

2. LUHR COUNTY PARK
LaPorte, IN/LaPorte County
USGS MAP(s): LaPorte East 1:24,000
TRAILS(s) DISTANCE: 9 trails total 2.12 miles
ACREAGE: 73 acres
ACTIVITIES: nature walks, nature study, naturalist, nature center, picnicking, shelter, fishing, bicycling, amphitheatre, x-country skiing, year around programs, special events

Dedicated in 1987, the LaPorte County Park was a gift from the Clarence Luhr family to be developed as a nature study park. The natural area's habitats include level mixed forest, wetlands with a pond and some restored prairie. The nature center, adjacent north of the parking area, is the place to become oriented to the park by visiting with the naturalist, thumbing through the library, viewing the displays, and observing the wildlife through the observation window. A trail map is available.

There are nine short interwoven trails with catchy nature names that spread throughout the parkscape. Nearly half of the park's well marked trails are paved while the other half are wood chipped. A brief summary of the trails follows:

Trail 1: Autumn Run - 0.24 mile
        Paved asphalt, all weather, handicapped accessible trail leading

from the nature center northwest to the wetlands through maturing forest. Accesses Trails 2, 3, 5, 4 & 8.

Trail 2: Discovery Lane - 0.15 mile
Begins near nature center, spur trail from Trail 1 to Trail 3. Main feature is the Wildlife Discovery Patio.

Trail 3: Crabapple Corners - 0.20 mile
As the name suggest there are flowering crabs, begins at the northwest terminus of Trail 2, also accessible from Trail 1, accesses Trails 5,9,& 4.

Trail 4: Walkabout - 0.31 mile
Paved trail begins at the parking lot and goes west underneath power lines, past natural prairie restoration area leading to wetlands, accesses Trails 5, 6, 7, 8, 9, and 3.

Trail 5: Deer Trail Pass - 0 - 0.19 mile
North to south trail in woodland west of the nature center, accesses Trails 3, 1 & 4.

Trail 6: Hickory Hollow - 0.16 mile
Paved trail from parking lot, leads to amphitheatre south, accesses Trail 7 & 4.

Trail 7: Country Walk - 0.17 mile
Begins at either Trail 4 or 6, just west of the amphitheatre, abandoned succession meadow to young woodland.

Trail 8: Lumberjack Pass - 0.66 mile
Park's longest trail, begins and ends from Trail 4, loops through mature mixed woods in the west property, also serves as a x-country ski trail, and forestry management study area.

Trail 9: Boardwalk - 0.04 mile
Accessible from Trail 3, boardwalk leads out to observation tower and the wetland ecology study area.

To reach Luhr County Park which is located three miles south of LaPorte at 3178 South CR 15OW from US 35, drive west one mile on CR 250S and turn left/south on CR 15OW and continue about a mile to the parking lot. From IN 39 drive east on CR 250S one mile to CR 15OW and turn south, driving one mile to the parking area which is located underneath the power lines. The park is open daily from 8 am to dusk.

Luhr Park

A Multi-Purpose Nature Center

Scipio Twp., LaPorte County

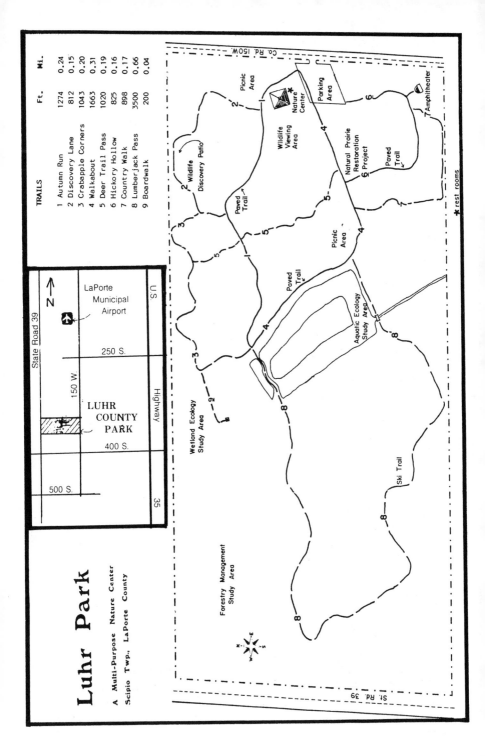

TRAILS	Ft.	Mi.
1 Autumn Run	1274	0.24
2 Discovery Lane	812	0.15
3 Crabapple Corners	1043	0.20
4 Walkabout	1663	0.31
5 Deer Trail Pass	1020	0.19
6 Hickory Hollow	825	0.16
7 Country Walk	898	0.17
8 Lumberjack Pass	3500	0.66
9 Boardwalk	200	0.04

State Road 39

LaPorte Municipal Airport

250 S.

150 W

LUHR COUNTY PARK

400 S.

500 S.

US

Highway

35

Co. Rd. 150W.

Picnic Area

Nature Center

Parking Area

Amphitheater

Wildlife Viewing Area

Natural Prairie Restoration Project

Paved Trail

Wildlife Discovery Patio

Paved Trail

Picnic Area

Paved Trail

Aquatic Ecology Study Area

Wetland Ecology Study Area

Forestry Management Study Area

Ski Trail

St. Rd. 39

★ rest rooms

3. BLUHM COUNTY PARK

Westville, IN/LaPorte County
USGS MAP(s): Westville 1:24,000
TRAIL(s) DISTANCE: two trails total 5.5 miles
ACREAGE: 83 acres
ACTIVITIES: hiking, nature study, x-country skiing, all terrain biking,
   equestrian trail

The LaPorte County park was established from a generous gift of Gayle and Lucille Bluhm who wanted to see their land preserved for posterity. The natural area is divided by CR 1100W into a 30 acre east tract and a 50 acre west tract. Both rolling forested tracts are surrounded by farm fields and from the parking area, the town of Westville can be seen.

The eastern tract has a 0.5 mile hiking only loop trail that leads from the parking area along the south edge of an old growth beech-maple forest to a vehicle wide path that penetrates the woods. The trail snakes through the forest, skirting wet depressions, then follows the east perimeter, leading to a small pond and an old windmill. The path continues along the forest-field edge back to the parking area. Across CR 1100W from the parking area is the Bluhm property west which is open to hikers, mountain bikes, horse riders, and cross country skiing. Cross the road and follow the broad grassy strip due west, past the wetland to the woods. There are five miles of unmarked, interconnecting narrow trails that wind and weave throughout the maturing woodland and around the wetlands. The trail network continues across the ditch that bisects the west woods.

The property is located just northwest of Westville. From the intersection of IN 6 and IN 2 drive west to the next road, CR 1100W and turn north. Continue north on South CR 1100W to the property.

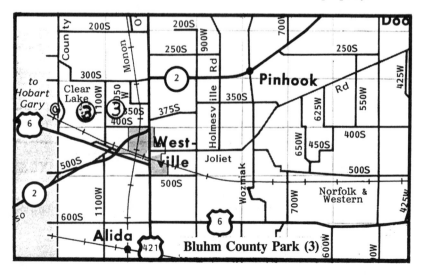

4. VALPARAISO NATURE PLACES

ACTIVITIES: nature walks, nature study, picnicking, shelters, playgrounds, gardens, beach, swimming, fishing, pier, boating, boat launch ramp, winter sports, park store, concessions, special events
FEE(s): seasonal entrance, shelter rental

Valparaiso's parklands contribute meaning to the Spanish-derived place name, "paradise valley". The city and county green spaces are located conveniently in close proximity to one another on the north side of the Porter County seat, about fifteen miles south of the Indiana dunes.

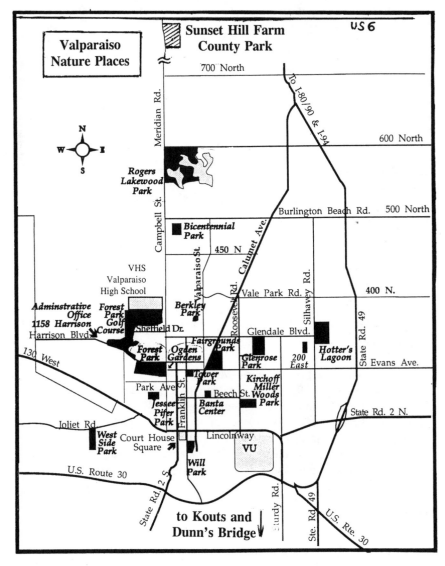

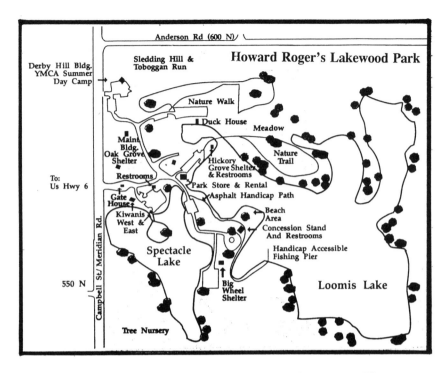

Howard Roger's Lakewood Park, Valparaiso Nature Places

The ten acre <u>Forest Park</u> is situated on a knoll covered with upland forest. It is a fine place to picnic and visit the adjoining <u>Ogden Gardens</u> which is a lovely setting with identified plantings. The city park and gardens are located just west of Harrison Boulevard and Campbell Street intersection on Harrison Boulevard. The Valparaiso Department of Parks and Recreation is located further west at 1158 Harrison Boulevard (219) 462-5144.

North on Campbell Street/North Meridian Road about two miles more or less is the 123 acre <u>Rogers-Lakewood Park</u>. Two designated short trails that total 1.5 miles loop about the north uplands above Loomis Lake and Spectacle Lake, the western extent of the Valparaiso Chain of Lakes. These self-guiding trails pass through forest and revegetating meadow and the lakeshores are strollable. A map is available at the gate or park store. The developed city park includes plenty of shaded picnicking areas and a swimming beach.

Further north on North Meridian Road near the junction with US 6 is the Sunset Hill Farm County Park which is currently under development. Recently opened in 1993, the former 235 acre dairy farm is Porter County's first park. The Hickory Grove picnic area is open and trails are being developed east of the farm. Future planned development includes picnic shelters, barn shelter, an outdoor amphitheatre, campground, nature interpretive center, and pond. The county park is the site of the annual Northern Indiana Historical Power Festival in September.

Further south on the Porter-Jasper county line, the Porter County Parks Department administers the three acre Dunn's Bridge site on the Kankakee River east of Kouts, Indiana. From Indiana 8 go east of Kouts three miles to CR 500E and drive south 6.6 miles.

Valparaiso is accessible from US 30, Indiana 2, 130, and 49.

5. DEEP RIVER COUNTY PARK
Hobart, IN/Lake County
USGS MAP(s): Palmer, Crown Point 1:24,000
TRAIL(s) DISTANCE: appx. 6 miles
ACREAGE: 960 acres
ACTIVITIES: nature walks, hiking, nature study, tree ID trail, historic grist & saw mills, picnicking, shelters, gardens, gazebo, fishing, canoe launch ramp, playground, fitness trail, bridle trail, x-country skiing, snowmobiling, hayrides, seasonal visitor center, gift shop, concessions, special programs, events, tours
FEE(s): admission to grist mill, shelter, ski equipment, recreational equipment & gazebo rentals

The majority of visitors to Deep River, a Lake County Park, come to tour the restored John Wood's 1876 gristmill, the first industry in a now heavily industrialized county. Originally built in 1838, the scenic old mill still grinds grains into flour for sale and features historic exhibits and displays on the second and third floors. The adjacent gift shop and visitor center is sheltered in a former church built in 1904. Wood's Historic Grist Mill is listed in the National Register of Historic Places. The Mill and Visitor Center are open daily 10 am to 5 pm May 1 to October 31. The nearby gardens and gazebo are a popular setting for weddings and a working sawmill is exhibited across Deep River via a foot bridge.

Downstream away from the gristmill/gift shop area, and from the activity along old Lincoln Highway 330, begins the park natural area which spans both sides of Deep River for four miles to Ainsworth Road.

John Wood's 1876 Gristmill, Deep River County Park

This natural area contains wooded upland forest that sharply slopes downhill to the floodplain forest. The hillside seeps nourish rare plants.

The wide linear hiking trail/service road follows the south bank of the river. There are open areas of prairie. Beyond the trestle of the Grand Trunk railroad the trail splits. The streamside trail enters an even more remote section of the park. The riparian trail goes and returns along the same pathway. The main trail or bridle trail continues on to the "sulky horse track". A longer hike can be made by combining the two trails. This will lead you back in the direction of the main entrance parking lot. Deep River flows north to eventually join the Little Calumet River. The trails appear to be compacted and tend to hold water in the low places for days after a rain or after high flood water.

To reach Deep River County Park from I-65 exit 253 onto US 30 and drive east about five miles to Randolph Street and turn north/ left. Follow Randolph Street north 0.25 mile to Old Lincoln Highway (CR 330) and turn right/east. Continue one mile east on Old Lincoln Highway 330 to the park entrance on the left/north side of the highway just west of the Lake and Porter county line. There is also parking on County Line Road, east and north of the main entrance.

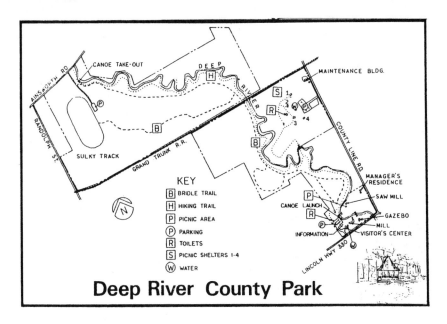

Deep River County Park

KEY

- B BRIDLE TRAIL
- H HIKING TRAIL
- P PICNIC AREA
- P PARKING
- R TOILETS
- S PICNIC SHELTERS 1-4
- W WATER

A third entrance is located on Ainsworth Road and is reached by continuing north on Randolph Street (instead of turning east on Old Lincoln Highway 330). Randolph Street intersects Ainsworth Road. Turn right/east and drive a short distance to the parking area next to the canoe launch and sulky track [See location #5 on Hoosier Prairie NP (#7) map]. This area also accesses the trails north of Ainsworth Road which lead to a scenic overlook.

The park hours are 7 am to dusk daily.

6. STONEY RUN COUNTY PARK
Leroy, IN/Lake County
USGS MAP(s): Leroy, Hebron 1:24,000
TRAIL(s) DISTANCE: appx. 6.75 miles
ACREAGE: 296 acres
ACTIVITIES: nature walks/hiking, nature study, bridle trails, x-country skiing, picnicking, shelters, playgrounds, fitness trail, fishing, ice skating, hayrides, primitive camping year around, annual events
FEE(s): seasonal entrance, fishing, ski rental, camping

Rural and somewhat remote, this Lake County park offers outdoor recreation facilities in a rustic setting. Woodlands, open grassy meadows and ponds comprise this natural passive parkland which borders the Lake and Porter county line.

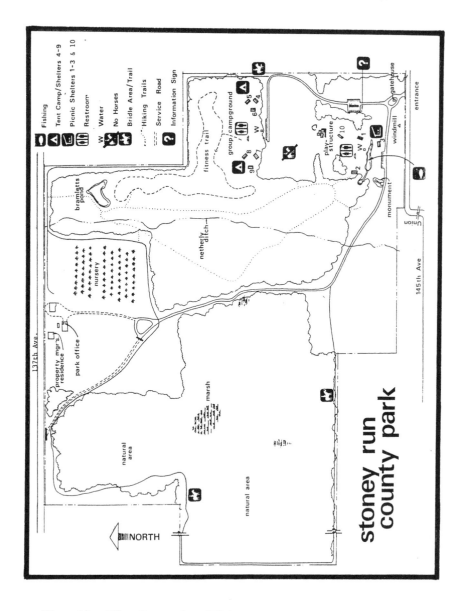

stoney run county park

Legend:
- Fishing
- Tent Camp/Shelters 4-9
- Picnic Shelters 1-3 & 10
- Restroom
- W Water
- No Horses
- Bridle Area/Trail
- Hiking Trails
- Service Road
- ? Information Sign

The self-guiding Stoney Run Hiking Trail begins at the picnic shelter north of the pond and Vietnam Memorial site. The trail leads north through the oak-hickory woodland crossing intermittent runs that contribute to Stoney Run, to Bramlett Pond, south of the Lake County nursery. There are several unmarked side spur trails that may prove confusing but all together they form an interconnecting trail network within the woodland including an exercise trail just north of the primitive campground. The clayish earth paths can be slick and muddy after a rain.

Horses also use these foot paths contributing to the soil compactness. Bridle trails which are not heavily used follow the west perimeter of the park and may be hiked but be advised the grassy trail has hoof depressions that can prove difficult walking especially during wet weather when they hold water. Feel free to ramble from the beaten path. All trails are open to cross country skiing.

Stoney Run County Park may be reached from I-65 exit 247 onto US 231 and driving east through Leroy, Indiana to the County Line Road at the Lake and Porter county line, turning left/ north. Continue north just over two miles to 142nd Avenue and turn left/west. The park entrance is at 142nd Avenue and Union Street. The park is situated between 137th Avenue and 142nd Avenue. Roadside directional signs will also lead you to the park from US 30 and Randolph Street in Merrillville, Indiana. The hours are 7 am to dusk year around

7. HOOSIER PRAIRIE NATURE PRESERVE
Griffith, IN/Lake County
USGS MAP(s): Highland 1:24,000
TRAIL(s) DISTANCE: 1 mile loop
ACREAGE: 548 acres
ACTIVITIES: nature walk, nature study

The Hoosier Prairie, now owned by the Indiana DNR Division of Nature Preserves, is a sizeable remnant of virgin prairie that represents such ecologically diverse habitats as savanna, sand prairie, wet prairie, marsh and sedge meadow. In fact this National Natural Landmark is the largest remnant prairie tract in Indiana and is often cited as the single most significant natural area in the state. The only negative about this special area is its location in the heart of the Calumet region (instead of rural Benton County, two counties south). Nonetheless the noteworthy natural experience outweighs the looming oil storage "farm" to the south and east and the Main Street traffic of Griffith which bisects the preserve.

The Hoosier Prairie trailhead and registration box are located in an old revegetating field adjacent east to the parking area where a self-guiding trail brochure is provided. The level narrow foot path enters the prairie via a portal of black oaks. There are eight numbered posts that correspond to the informative brochure that has been provided by the Indiana Dunes National Lakeshore (the preserve lies within the National Lakeshore boundaries). As many as 500 native species of plants thrive in this level landscape punctuated with seasonably wet depressions. Fire continues to preserve the prairie flora and savanna as it has for thousands of years.

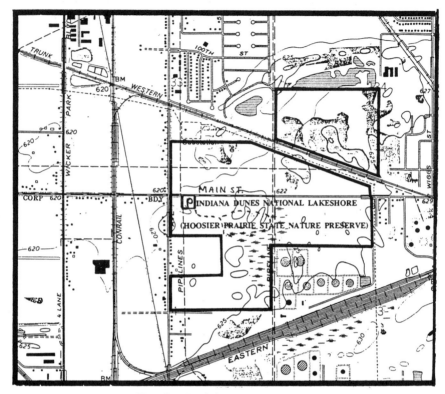

Hoosier Prairie Nature Preserve

The mosquitoes at times are prolific. Additional prairie trails are located in nearby Oak Ridge Prairie County Park located one mile east on Main Street to Colfax south 0.25 mile to the park entrance. Other prairie nature preserves within Lake County include Gibson Woods Nature Preserve, owned by Lake county parks.

To reach the Hoosier Prairie Nature Preserve from the I-65 and I-80-94 exchange in south Gary, Indiana, go west ten miles to the US 41/Wicker Park Boulevard exit south. Continue south 3.5 miles on US 41/Indianapolis Boulevard to Main Street in Griffith. Drive east on Main Street 0.7 miles to a parking lot on the south side of Main Street just beyond Kennedy Avenue where the trailhead and registration box are located.

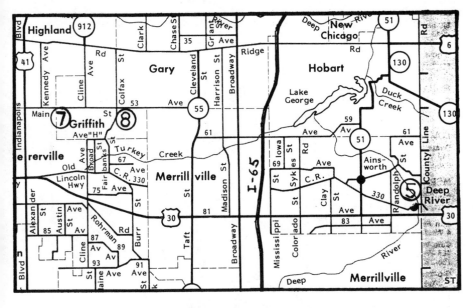

Deep River County Park (5)
Hoosier Prairie Nature Preserve (7)
& Oak Ridge Prairie County Park (8)

8. OAK RIDGE PRAIRIE COUNTY PARK
Griffith, IN/Lake County
USGS MAP(s): Highland, Gary 1:24,000
TRAIL(s) DISTANCE: 2 trails total approx. 3 miles
ACREAGE: nature trails, nature study, picnicking, shelters, fishing, pier,
  playfields, x-country skiing, sledding, ice skating, warming shelter
FEE(s): seasonal entrance, fishing, shelter, ski equipment rental

Due east of Hoosier Prairie Nature Preserve one mile is the Lake
County owned and managed Oak Ridge Prairie Park. Preserved within its
borders are significant areas of wet prairie, restored tallgrass prairie, oak
savanna and numerous wetlands. The green expanse is broken at midpoint
by recreational facilities and the parking area from where the two color
coded trails radiate. The trails can be seasonally wet in places and the
mosquitoes voracious.

The 1.5 mile linear and loop trail or Wetlands Trail explores the border
of the fishing lake, young aspen-sumac forest and a marsh at the eastern
edge of the park. The trail leads around the bulrush and cattail lined shore
of the lake, popular with local fishermen, to the east side where it enters
a young forest. The trail follows the woodland edge to the marsh where

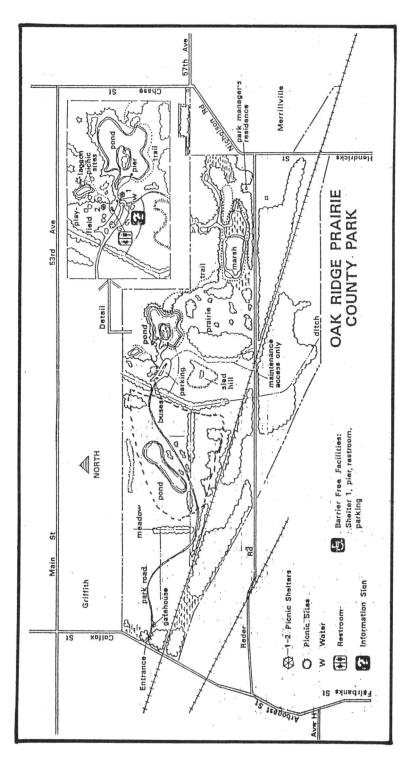

OAK RIDGE PRAIRIE
COUNTY · PARK

Barrier Free Facilities:
Shelter 1, pier, restroom,
parking

1-2: Picnic Shelters
Picnic Sites
Water
Restroom
Information Sign

the trail forks. One spur trail leads due east to end at the edge of the wetland where you must retrace your steps. The right fork leads around the marsh to an end loop. Again you must retrace your steps back.

The second loop trail heads west along the parking area entry road a short distance, across a ditch to the trailhead on the right/ north side of the park road. The 1.5 mile long green trail or Prairie Trail follows high ground leading through open prairie meadow adjacent to a airport on the north. The trail arrives at the park road and crosses in a young woodland of oaks, aspen and sumac paralleling a railroad and along a ditch back to the parking lot; a complete loop. The wooded oak grove northeast of the parking lot is a fine place to picnic.

To reach Oak Ridge Prairie County Park from US 30 in Schererville, exit US 41/Indianapolis Boulevard and drive north on US 41/Indianapolis Boulevard to Main Street (2nd right turn), turn right/east. Follow Main Street east past Hoosier Prairie Nature Preserve through downtown Griffith to Colfax Street and turn right/south. The park entrance is located 1,000 feet south of the intersection of Main Street and Colfax Street [see location #8 on Hoosier Prairie Nature Preserve (#7) map]. The address is 301 South Colfax Street.

Park hours are from 7 am to dusk daily.

9. LEMON LAKE COUNTY PARK
Crown Point, IN/Lake County
USGS MAP(s): Lowell 1:24,000
TRAIL(s) DISTANCE: appx. 2.5 miles
ACREAGE: 300 acres
ACTIVITIES: nature walks, hiking, nature study, fitness trail, x-country skiing, arboretum, picnicking, shelters, fishing, paddle boating, playground, playfields, ballfields, tennis courts, basketball courts, ice skating, sledding, hayrides, concessions
FEE(s): seasonal entrance, fishing, x-country ski and paddleboat rentals, picnic shelter rental

Lake County Park Department's first park offers a balanced mix of active and passive outdoor recreation in a suburban natural area. Nature walkers will discover the wooded ridges, open grassland, marsh and lake in the eastern portion of the property much to their liking as well as the facility-rich west property. Trailheads are located east of the parking area at Lemon Lake and north of the parking area at Lemon Lake Marsh.

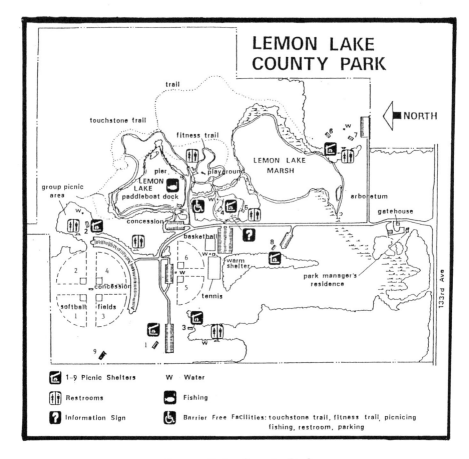

Lemon Lake County Park

A paved 0.5 mile trail encircles Lemon Lake which is popular with fishermen. Now in disrepair, a former audio interpretive network with several stops line the lakeside path. The mile long Touchstone Trail (one-way) branches off from the Lemon Lake Trail and heads uphill to follow the wooded ridge south to the east parking and picnic area trailhead. User paths veer off from the Touchstone Trail. One user path skirts the north shore of Lemon Lake Marsh which is a favored stopover for migratory waterfowl. Southeast of Lemon Lake, a covered bridge over a ravine leads to the playground where a 0.5 mile vita fitness course loops east. A small semi-formal arboretum is located at the southwest edge Lemon Lake Marsh where several of the trees are identified.

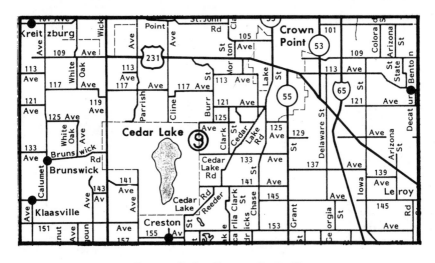

Lemon Lake County Park (9)

To reach Lemon Lake County Park from I-65 exit 247 onto US 231, turn, west/left toward Crown Point. Follow US 231 to State Rd. 55 (1st stop light), turn left/south to 133rd Ave. Turn right/west, continue 3 miles west to park entrance on right/north side of the road.

The park hours are from 7 am to dusk.

10. BUCKLEY HOMESTEAD COUNTY PARK

Lowell, IN/Lake County
USGS MAP(s): Lowell 1:24,000
TRAIL(s) DISTANCE: 1 mile loop
ACREAGE: 160 acres
ACTIVITIES: historic walk, historic sites, visitor center, gift shop, gardens, picnicking, group tours, special events
FEE(s): seasonal admission

Buckley Homestead, owned and operated by the Lake County Parks Department, is a living history farmstead that depicts three time periods in southern Lake County when life was more traditional and moved at a slower pace. First settled by the Irish immigrant Buckley family, the 1850's is represented by a restored pioneer farm that features a log cabin surrounded by field crops and store house amidst a prairie. The 1900 Buckley school is a reconstructed one room "3R" learning center at the turn of the century. The 1910 Buckley farm includes the original house, hired hand house, garden, orchard, hog barn, granary, milkhouse, silo, barn and tool shed. In its heyday the farm was a dairy which sold milk to

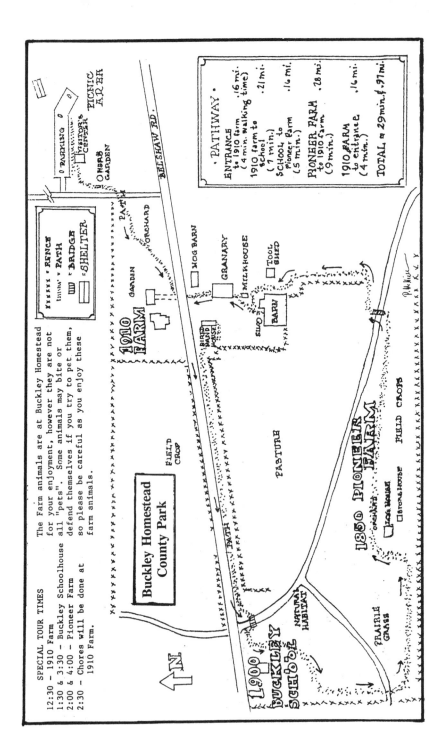

SPECIAL TOUR TIMES

12:30 - 1910 Farm
1:30 & 3:30 - Buckley Schoolhouse
2:00 & 4:00 - Pioneer Farm
2:30 - Chores will be done at
        1910 Farm.

The Farm animals are at Buckley Homestead for your enjoyment, however they are not all "pets". Some animals may bite or defend themselves if you try to pet them, so please be careful as you enjoy these farm animals.

Buckley Homestead County Park

PATHWAY

ENTRANCE
to 1910 farm   .16 mi.
(4 min. walking time)
1910 farm to
school   .21 mi.
(7 min.)
SCHOOL to
Pioneer Farm   .16 mi.
(5 min.)
PIONEER FARM   .28 mi.
to 1910 farm
(9 min.)
1910 FARM   .16 mi.
to entrance
(4 min.)

TOTAL = 29 min. & .97 mi.

XXXXX = FENCE
~~~~~ = PATH
IIIII = BRIDGE
☐ = SHELTER.

1910 FARM

GARDEN
ORCHARD
PATH
BELSHAW RD.
PARKING
VISITOR'S CENTER
PICNIC AREA
ONION GARDEN

HOG BARN
GRANARY
MILKHOUSE
TOOL SHED
BARN
BIRD HAND HOUSE
CROPS
PASTURE

1850 PIONEER FARM
FIELD CROPS
ORCHARD
HOG HOUSE
STONEHOUSE
P. White

1900 BUCKLEY SCHOOL
NATURAL HABITAT
PRAIRIE GRASS

N

FIELD CROP

1850 Log House, Buckley Homestead

Chicago markets. Horses may be seen working, pulling the farm equipment as was done years ago and which is still carried on by the Amish today in northeastern Indiana. "Residents" in historic dress portray life as it once was and the Homestead Days Festival is an annual event. All three time periods are connected by a one mile loop that begins and ends at the visitor center, picnic area and parking lot.

To reach Buckley Homestead from I-65 exit 240 onto Indiana 2 and drive west about four miles to Hendricks Road and turn left/south. Proceed 0.25 mile to the visitor center parking lot on the left/east side of Hendricks Road. The loop trail crosses Hendricks and Belshaw roads twice so exercise caution in crossing. From May to October the historic buildings are open weekends from 10 am to 5 pm and during weekdays by appointment and tours. The grounds and loop trail are open year around from 7 am to dusk.

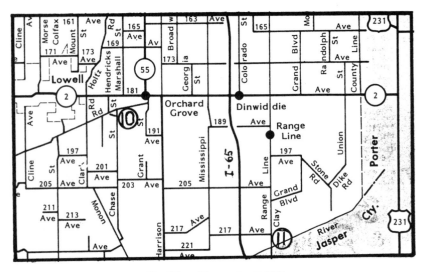

Buckley Homestead (10)
Grand Kankakee Marsh County Park (11)

11. GRAND KANKAKEE MARSH COUNTY PARK

Hebron, IN/Lake County
USGS MAP(s): Shelby, Demotte 1:24,000
TRAIL(s) DISTANCE: approx. 6 miles of service roads
ACREAGE: 1,900 acres
ACTIVITIES: hiking, nature study, picnicking, shelters, boating, boat
  launch ramp, fishing, photography blinds, seasonal fall hunting
FEE(s): shelter rental, hunting

The Lake County park is a remnant of the Grand Kankakee Marsh that once covered half a million acres in northwestern Indiana. Extending for three miles along the north bank of the dredged Kankakee River, the park was the first fish and wildlife county park in Indiana, originally purchased by The Nature Conservancy and Lake County Parks Department. The park is closed to the general public during hunting season from October through December when special permission is required to enter. Normally the best months for visitation are from January to May and later September when the abundant mosquito population is non-existent or low.

Service roads serve also as hiking trails. Nearly three miles of service road fronts the Kankakee River from west beyond the I-65 overpass, east to a drainage ditch and the property line. From the Range Line Road visitor center or boat launch ramp parking areas, walk either direction.

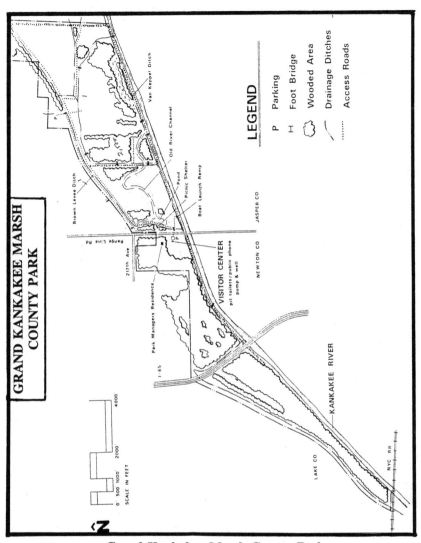

Grand Kankakee Marsh County Park

For a complete loop, walk east from the boat ramp to the property line and drainage ditch (1.6 mile), turn north and follow the ditch line 0.75 mile to the Brown Levee Ditch at the property's northeast corner. Go west along the Brown Levee Ditch just over two miles to return to the parking lot or boat launch ramp. There are two short-cut interconnecting service roads enroute of about 0.5 mile distance each that will reduce the walking distance from the Kankakee River to Brown Levee Ditch.

To reach Grand Kankakee County Park from I-65 exit 240 east on Indiana 2 and proceed 1.5 miles to Range Line Road and turn right/south. Continue about five miles south on Range Line Road to the parking lot and visitor center. The park manager resides near the visitor center (pit toilet, telephone, water). The hours are 7 am to dusk from January through September unless hunting.

12. LASALLE FISH & WILDLIFE AREA
Lake Village, IN/Newton & Lake Counties
USGS MAP(s): Schneider, Illiana Heights 1:24,000
TRAIL(s) DISTANCE: several miles of service roads
ACREAGE: 3,648 acres
ACTIVITIES: nature walks, nature study, picnicking, fishing, boat launch ramps, rifle range, hunting, Class C primitive camping (April through September)
FEE(s): camping

Formerly a state park, the fish and wildlife area is named in honor of the French explorer Robert Cavalier, Sieur de LaSalle who crossed northwest Indiana with his small expedition by way of the Kankakee River in the late 1600s in an attempt to find a water route to the Pacific Ocean. Nearly two and a half centuries later, the Grand Marsh of the Kankakee that LaSalle had explored, has lost its grandeur to dredging and channelization. It became practically non-existence by 1915. Today the Kankakee River flows four miles through the property that preserves a small remnant of the former Grand Marsh.

Several miles of service roads serve as trails. The one mile one-way gravel road from headquarters to the campground and picnic area crosses Beaver Lake Ditch and straddles the wetland and upland of the southwest property. A short distance east of the ditch stood the state's largest cottonwood, recently downed by a storm. The bayou in the campground has user paths along its banks. The longest hike on the property begins/ends at parking lot 3A along the Kankakee River. Most of this trail is closed for waterfowl hunting October first to December first. Service roads follow the south bank levee of the river east and west for about a mile in either direction. Enroute the walk is between the watery seemingly southern worlds of river and bayous, rich with waterfowl and wildlife. The service roads turn inland and head south 0.5 to 0.75 mile, then curve to connect the same property road. Walking an additional 0.75 to one mile, they join at parking lot 3 for a complete loop.

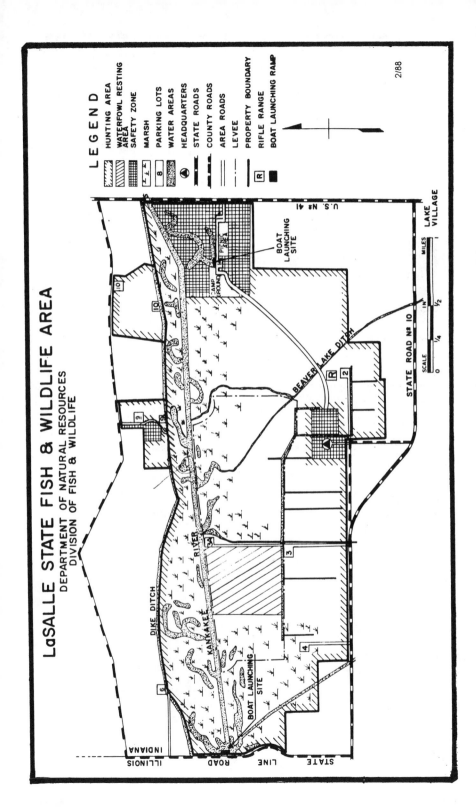

LaSALLE STATE FISH & WILDLIFE AREA

DEPARTMENT OF NATURAL RESOURCES
DIVISION OF FISH & WILDLIFE

LEGEND

- HUNTING AREA
- WATERFOWL RESTING AREA
- SAFETY ZONE
- MARSH
- PARKING LOTS
- WATER AREAS
- HEADQUARTERS
- STATE ROADS
- COUNTY ROADS
- AREA ROADS
- LEVEE
- PROPERTY BOUNDARY
- RIFLE RANGE
- BOAT LAUNCHING RAMP

2/88

SCALE
0   ¼   ½   1
MILES

LAKE VILLAGE

U.S. Nᵒ 41

STATE ROAD Nᵒ 10

BEAVER LAKE DITCH

BOAT LAUNCHING SITE

CAMP GROUND

PICNIC AREA

KANKAKEE RIVER

DIKE DITCH

BOAT LAUNCHING SITE

INDIANA

ILLINOIS

STATE LINE ROAD

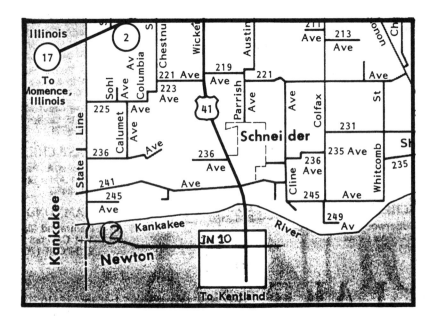

Lasalle Fish & Wildlife Area (12)

From parking lot 3 walk north on the property road to return to the Kankakee River and parking lot 3A. Heading north from parking lot 4 also accesses the west portion of the loop roads. A scenic drive along State Line Road at the west property boundary is scenic as the river takes a natural course as it makes its meandering way into Illinois.

To reach LaSalle Fish and Wildlife Area from I-65 exit 230 onto Indiana 10 and drive about 12 miles west to the property headquarters, about 2.5 miles beyond US 41. Follow the road signs. Be advised the Kankakee River can be very mosquitoey during warm weather. Consider visiting Conrad Savanna and Beaver Lake Nature Preserve while in the general area.

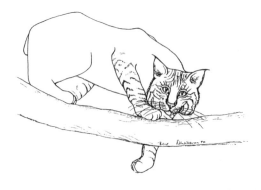

13. CONRAD SAVANNA

Lake Village, IN/Newton County
USGS MAP(s): Enos 1:24,000
TRAIL(s) DISTANCE: old farm lanes
ACREAGE: 313 acres
ACTIVITIES: hiking, nature study

Owned and managed by DNR's Division of Nature Preserves, Conrad Savanna is a large black oak savanna remnant set among a rolling landscape bordered by gravel roads, fields and Beaver Lake Creek/Ditch. Accessible from old farm lanes, the wooded grasslands make for easy walking beneath the scattered black, white and burr oaks. The month of June is an outstanding month to walk in this unique natural area. Pioneers called these parklands, "oak openings", since they were areas that were "open" compared to the dense, shady eastern deciduous forests. The term, "barrens" were also applied to these sparsely forested area because they usually were infertile due to droughty soils.

Easily accessed by road, the preserve may be reached from I-65 exit 230 west onto Indiana 10 and driving about nine miles to the junction of Indiana 10 and US 41 and turning south. From the intersection of SR 10 and US 41 near Lake Village, go south on US 41 for 2 miles. Since the bridge is out at US 41 and CR 700N, go west on CR 800N, south on CR 400W, then east on CR 700N. Continue to the gate and park. Follow the old farm lane into the property, a dedicated state nature preserve.

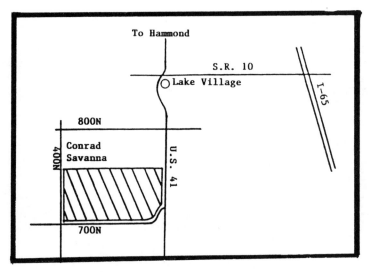

Conrad Savanna Nature Preserve

14. BEAVER LAKE NATURE PRESERVE
Enos, IN/Newton County
USGS MAP(s): Enos 1:24,000
TRAIL(s) DISTANCE: no est. trails
ACREAGE: 640 acres
ACTIVITIES: nature walk, nature study

Beaver Lake was secured in 1945 by the State of Indiana with financial help from the Isaac Walton League to establish a refuge for the prairie chicken but the noble effort proved fruitless even though the birds frequented the site as late as 1953. Actually the refuge was never known to have been used as a "booming ground" or "lek" by prairie chickens, a type of grouse that prefers undisturbed tall grass prairie. Last legally hunted in 1935, numerous reports find that the prairie chicken has not been seen in Indiana since 1970. Recent sightings report the birds do exist, although not confirmed, in Jasper County, Indiana. The prairie chicken's range today includes Wisconsin, Illinois, Michigan, Manitoba, Canada south on the Great Plains to Oklahoma.

Historically, the 640 acres was part of the 28,000 acre Beaver Lake and the Grand Marsh of the Kankakee River. The vast lake was seven miles long, five miles wide and nine feet at the deepest point. The first drainage attempt began in 1853 and ended after World War II. Beaver Lake Ditch and Mud Lake Ditch drain the property, flowing northwest to the Kankakee River.

Blazing Stars (Liatris), Beaver Lake Nature Preserve

Today the large expanse is now a nature preserve and is important in that the sandy level flats are a refuge for prairie plants. There are no established trails but the treeless plain allows for easy walking. Controlled burns maintain the prairie flowers and grasses. Permission must be obtained to visit the preserve from the property manager at LaSalle Fish and Wildlife Area, about eight miles northwest.

To reach Beaver Lake Nature Preserve from I-65 exit 230 and drive west on Indiana 10 nine miles to the junction with US 41 and turn south/left. Proceed about 4.5 miles on US 41 (about 3 miles north of Enos) and turn east/left on 400E and drive one mile and turn north on CR 200W. Continue about a mile to the preserve on the right/east side of CR 200W.

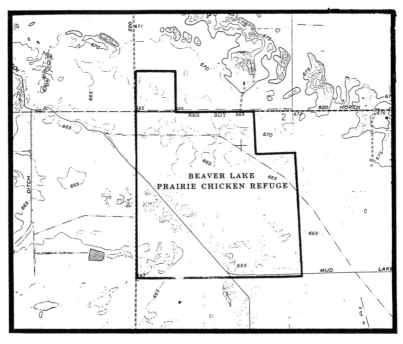

Beaver Lake Nature Preserve

15. OBER SAVANNA
Ober, IN/Starke County
USGS MAP(s): Knox East 1:24,000
TRAIL(s) DISTANCE: no est. trails
ACREAGE: 90 acres
ACTIVITIES: nature walk, nature study

Ober Savanna is one of several Nature Conservancy acquired properties in northwestern Indiana that preserves the rare black oak savanna that once covered nearly 30 million acres in the Middle West. In addition to savanna (from Spanish, Zavana, originally Taino Indian, Caribbean) the acreage includes an abandoned revegetating field that has prairie potential and a pin oak flat.

The preserve is bisected by an active railroad so caution should be exercised if deciding to visit the young savanna to the north. The south portion of the property is shaped like a right handed triangle and the upland eastern section has been recently burned to restored the savanna. Beneath the fire scarred oaks are yellow and white indigo, lupine, puccoon, flaxleaved asters, dwarf dandelion, prickly pear cactus, June, porcupine, bluestem and Indian grasses, shrubby St. Johnswort and low bush blueberry. Fame flower is the rarest plant of the preserve. There are no established trails but the openness of the savanna allows easy strolling. An old farm lane heads northwest from the property sign entrance to the abandoned prairie-like field.

To reach Ober Savanna from US 30 in north Starke County, exit south at Grovertown on Indiana 23 and drive about eight miles to Ober, just south of Indiana 8. Turn right/west at CR 200S at the old school and drive 0.5 mile (across the flashless railroad crossing) to the preserve entrance at the property sign where there is off-road parking for two cars.

Another approach from US 30 in north Starke County is to exit south onto US 35 and drive through Knox to the junction of US 35 and CR 200S at the south side of the city and turn left/east. Proceed on CR 200S 4.5 miles to the preserve on the left/north side of the road.

While travelling through Knox enroute to Ober Savanna, consider visiting the city park of Wythougan. The scenic community park is located along the south bank of the Yellow River with several user paths and a service road along the wooded floodplain. A man-made waterfall adds interest near the US 35 bridge. After crossing the Yellow River bridge on the north edge of Knox, turn right/west at the first residential street and drive one block to the park entrance, just north of the county courthouse.

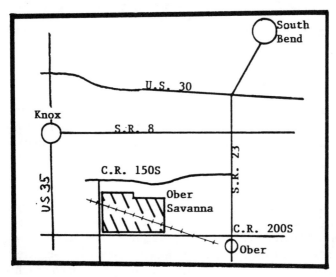

Ober Savanna Nature Preserve

16. ROUND LAKE WETLAND CONSERVATION AREA & NATURE PRESERVE

Toto, IN/Starke County
USGS MAP(s): Denham 1:24,000
TRAIL(s) DISTANCE: service road 0.5 mile
ACREAGE: 140 acres
ACTIVITIES: nature walk, nature study, canoeing, fishing, seasonal
   hunting, trapping

Aptly named, Round Lake is nearly circular in shape. The muck bottomed water body is ringed with cattail marsh (and some poison sumac) making foot access along the shoreline nearly impossible but the sandy upland portion on the southwest shore is explorable. Historically, the lake area was a habitation site utilized by native Americans during the Late Woodland mound-building cultural period about 1,200 years ago and reportedly the last historic Indian settlement in Starke County.

The best vantage point overlooking the lake and surrounding countryside is at the south shore site of a former farmhouse. From here the lake's round outline is visible and so are the transitional natural areas from lake, to marsh, wetland forest, upland forest and prairie. Wildlife food plots have been planted along the southwest property. The sandy service road doubles as a trail where New Jersey tea, shining sumac, oaks, and aspens thrive along the road edge. Round Lake is a favored wetland by waterfowl and goldfinches are numerous in summer. Canoeing is ideal.

To reach Round Lake from US 30 in north Starke County exit US 35 and drive south through Knox, Indiana about two miles from the intersection of US 35 and Indiana 8 to CR 300S/Toto Road, at the flashing yellow light and turn right/west. Continue on CR 300S/Toto Road west and drive approximately 2.5 miles to the junction with CR 150E and turn left/south. Proceed south on CR 150E past the Round Lake Church and Cemetery 1.6 miles to the property entrance which is marked. Turn left/east onto the entry road to the parking area overlooking Round Lake. Consider exploring by car and foot the north boundary of the area along CR 435S, the first road north and east of the entry road.

The nearby town of North Judson has nature trails in their community park. The short Sumac and Wild Plum Trails loop about in an old abandoned pasture where prickly pear cactus is abundant and very showy on a sunny June day. The trails are located south across the street from the picnicking and playground area, east of the community schools in southwest North Judson.

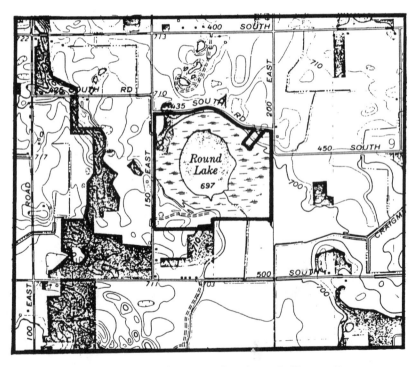

Round Lake Wetland Conservation Area & Nature Preserve

17. KANKAKEE FISH & WILDLIFE AREA
English Lake, IN/Starke & LaPorte Counties
USGS MAP(s): nature walk along Ten Mile Scenic Drive
ACREAGE: 4,095 acres
ACTIVITIES: nature walks, nature study, picnicking, shelter, boat launch
ramp, fishing, hunting, trapping

The name Kankakee may possibly be derived from the Potawatomi, teh-yak-ki-ki meaning "swampy country". If this is true, the name aptly describes this fish and wildlife area which lies in the floodplain of the Kankakee and Yellow rivers. The area represents only a tiny fraction of the former Grand Kankakee Marsh that once was home to one of the greatest concentrations of wildlife in North America (somewhat similar to the Everglades of south Florida). In Indiana, the 2,000 original river bends were dredged and straightened reducing the 250 miles of stream to 85 miles while in Illinois the river assumes a natural course as it flows to the Illinois River. Today the area is still popular with sportsmen and non-hunting birders and other nature seekers.

The Ten Mile Scenic Drive along the levee roads may also serve hikers. The Scenic Drive begins along Indiana 8 just before the Kankakee River bridge on the south side of the highway, 0.5 mile west of the junction of Indiana 8 and Indiana 39. Across from the drive entrance is the picnic shelter, canoe launch and check-in station where hunters are required to sign in. All other property use activities are not required to sign-in.

The drive follows the south bank of the Kankakee River to the near-confluence with the also channelled Yellow River (the rivers join near English Lake) and loops back east along the north bank of the Yellow River to end at Indiana 39, about 0.5 south of the Indiana 8 and Indiana 39 junction. Enroute there are two cross levee spur roads that short-cut the drive. There are several flooded marshy compartments between the rivers where waterfowl and other wildlife haunt. The floodplain forest of silver maple, ash, river birch, cottonwood and willow line the roadsides and fill the narrow wedge-shaped swampy bottomlands. Be advised the Ten Mile Scenic Drive is closed to non-hunters during the waterfowl hunting season from late October to early December.

To reach Kankakee Fish and Wildlife Area from US 30 in south central LaPorte County exit south on Indiana 39 and drive 6.2 miles to the junction of Indiana 39 and Indiana 8. Turn right/west on Indiana 8 and drive 0.5 miles to the entrance for the Ten Mile Scenic Drive on the south side of the highway.

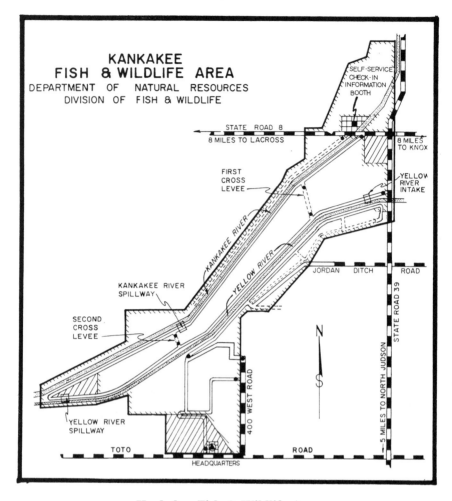

Kankakee Fish & Wildlife Area

To reach the property headquarters drive south from the Indiana 8 and Indiana 39 junction on Indiana 39 about four miles and turn right/west on CR 30OS/Toto Road. Proceed west on CR 30OS/ Toto Road about 2.3 miles to the property headquarters. The headquarter's office hours are 8 am to 3:30 pm, Monday through Friday, except Indiana State holidays.

18. TIPPECANOE RIVER STATE PARK

Winamac, IN/Pulaski County
USGS MAP(s): Winamac, Bass Lake 1:24,000
TRAIL(s) DISTANCE: 11 trails total appx. 22.5 miles
ACREAGE: 2,761 acres
ACTIVITIES: hiking, nature study, nature preserves, seasonal naturalist, equestrian trails, firetower, biking, playgrounds, picnicking, shelters, Tepicon Recreation Hall, fishing, canoe/boat launch, canoe camp, Class A campground, dumping station, group, youth, handicap, horsemen's, and rent-a-tent campground, cultural events, cross country skiing
FEE(s): entrance, camping, shelter reservations, boat launch fee, recreation building rental, bike rental

Tippecanoe River State Park is comprised of oak barrens, pineries, wet and dry prairie, marshes, timbered wetland bottoms, and of course, the river which forms seven miles of east park boundary. Primarily lake fed, the historic 166 miles long river begins at the outlet of Crooked Lake in Whitley County, flowing west and south to join the Wabash River near Americus, Tippecanoe County. The state park is about midway between these two points.

The park is a success story in secondary succession. The submarginal agricultural land was acquired by the Federal government during the 1930's and was developed by the Workers Program Administration WPA during the 1940s. Today the maturing natural landscape is more inviting than in its earlier agricultural days.

Hiking trails and horse trails wind and weave through the eight natural communities, some special such as the dry sand prairie preserve and the oxbow slough preserve. Formed by the Wisconsin glacial ice age, forty foot high sand dunes and blowouts are unique geological features along some trails that are reminiscent of Indiana Dunes National Lakeshore at Lake Michigan. River otters were recently introduced here.

Trail Summary:

Trail 1: Sand Ridge Trail - 2.2 mile

This sandy trail forms a loop between the fire tower and the waterfowl area with trail spurs leading to and from the main campground. Hikers and equestrians share the high sand dunal trails along the east to west ridges. Oak barrens exhibit a sparse understory.

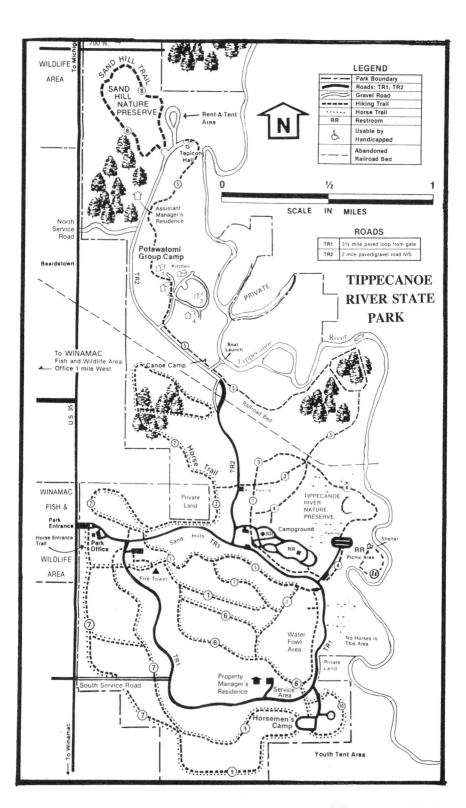

Park in the firetower and picnic area parking area at the junction of the TR 1 road loop. Go south from the picnic and playground area to the firetower. The over 100 foot high firetower at the top of 740 ft. Beard's Hill is climbable and safe. Views of the sand ridges, Bunker Hill, Tippecanoe River valley and surrounding towns are excellent. The trail's east terminus is at the parking lot for the waterfowl area. The adjacent 60 acre waterfowl area is great for birding. From the waterfowl parking lot head south along the levee next to the park TR 1 loop road.

The upland oak-hickory forest has three east-west ridge trails to explore. Noxious insects are less pesky along the sand ridge trails. This area is somewhat similar to the backdunes at Indiana Dunes State Park.

Trail 2: Pin Oak Trail - 3.7 miles

Begins/ends at the firetower/picnic parking area and ends/begins at TR 2 parking lot, north of the campground entrance. Trail is shared with equestrians and may be muddy in places. Across from the firetower parking lot and park road north, the trail enters a maturing oak-hickory forest. The trail forms a loop along the north side of TR 1 road and turns east and north skirting private land. The trail enters flat and wet pin oak and black gum woods. Near the abandoned hikeable railroad bed, the trail forms a second loop in a pine plantation. Trail 2 joins Trails 1,7 and 3.

Trail 3: Homestead Trail - 2.0 miles

Trail 3 forms a hour-long, loop trail hike. The hike begins/ends at TR 2 parking area north of the campground entrance. The earth path heads northeast through pine plantations towards an old railroad bed. The trail intersects at midpoint with Trails 4 & 5 and turns or loops back west to return to parking lot. Go west from the parking lot to access Trail 2.

Trail 4: Oxbow Trail - 1.7 miles

The most popular hiking path in the park forms a easy loop through a nature preserve. The trail begins in the picnic area north of the river shelter parking area and follows the floodplain forest trail through the 180 acre Tippecanoe River Nature Preserve. The oxbow sloughs (cut-off river channels), are wildlife rich communities.

Follow the river, curving northwest to Trail 3 and 5. Trail 4 continues south back to the campground and the park road through old fields, pines and woods. Continue the loop through the campground to TR 1 road and the river shelter parking area.

Tippecanoe River

Trail 5: River Bluff Trail - 4.5 miles

The longest hiking trail in the park. The trail follows the floodplain forest of the Tippecanoe River in the north area of the park, north of the abandoned railroad bed (for the adventuresome, the old railroad bed is hikeable from the Tippecanoe River northwest to Beardstown and beyond into the Winamac Fish & Wildlife Area.)

The north trail access begins/ends at the parking lot of the Sand Hill Nature Preserve and Tepicon Hall. Go east beyond Tepicon Hall down a service road where the trail begins adjacent to a private cabin.

Trail 5 follows the river bluff south through Potawatomi group camp, past the canoe camp/ramp (dry prairie habitat across the park road), floodplain forest and across the abandoned railroad bed to join with Trails 3 and 4. Parking is available at TR 2 lot north of the campground where Trail 3 leads to Trail head 5. Further trail extension is planned for the River Bluff Trail 5 in the north park area.

Trail 6: "The Barrens" Trail - 2.0 miles

A short loop trail designed for equestrians leads north from the horsemen's campground across TR 1 to the south boundary of the waterfowl area. The trail goes northwest through oak-hickory forest and "barrens" area of sparse understory vegetation. Forms a loop trail back along similar path to horsemen's camp.

Trail 7: White Pine Trail - 2.6 miles

Open to hikers and horsemen. Loop trail begins/ends at park office parking area and heads south close to US 35 through aging white pine plantations. Spur trail connects east loop side of Trail 7. Continue south across South Service Road to join with Trail 9. Loop back on Trail 7 east section and go north towards the firetower. Trail loops west to gate office parking.

Trail 8: Bluestem Trail - 1.9 miles

The Bluestem Trail loops through the 120 acre Sand Hill Nature Preserve. Park in the Tepicon Hall parking area west of the hall. Go north on the trail through pine plantations to the wet and dry sand prairie. (This section can be wet in spring). Continue on through the aspen edged prairie to a pine plantation and the upland oak-hickory forested sand hills. Trail skirts the rent-a-tent area and returns through an open prairie stand to the parking lot.

Trail 9: Black Oak Trail - 1.4 mile

Primarily a horse trail. Forms loop in the south property where trail leads from horsemen's camp to join with Trail 7. Travels through deciduous and coniferous forest and prairie amidst sand hills.

Trail 10: Sand Blowout Trail - 0.6 mile

Short loop trail adjacent east of the horsemen's camp, in the youth tent area. Worthwhile to see blowout, a denuded sandy area.

Trail 11: Riparian Trail - 0.7 mile

The park's most recent trail, the Riparian Trail 11 follows the west bank of the Tippecanoe River and the adjacent floodplain. The 0.7 mile loop features old growth floodplain forest, gravel bars, river vistas, river terrace, and a man made oxbow that was created by dredging a new channel, cutting off the old riverbed. Beaver, softshell turtles and swamp warblers may be seen. The easy trail begins at the river, south of the river shelter and nature center and ends at the playground. The trail may be underwater in the spring and mosquitoey during the summer months.

Be advised mosquitoes and deer flies are a nuisance during the warm and wet summer months. Hikers may want to reconsider hiking the well used horse trails during summer wet weather.

Bass Lake State Beach, eight miles north and east on SR 10 provides an opportunity to walk along a sandy northern Indiana lakeshore. Bass Lake is the fourth largest natural lake in Indiana. While in the area, the old Bass Lake Fish Hatchery, now Fisheries Station, may be explored. The historic facility lies on the northeast shore within the village of Winona at the road curve behind the restaurant. Follow directional signs.

The entrance to Tippecanoe River State Park is about 4.5 miles north of the Pulaski County Courthouse in downtown Winamac, Indiana located on the east side of US 35. From Logansport, Indiana the park entrance is located 30 miles north and west on US 35.

19. WINAMAC FISH & WILDLIFE AREA
Winamac, IN/Pulaski County
USGS MAP(s): Bass Lake, Denham, Ripley & Winamac 1:24,000
TRAIL(s) DISTANCE: 22 miles firelane service roads
ACREAGE: 4,650 acres
ACTIVITIES: hiking, nature study, picnicking, wild plant gathering, seasonal hunting, restricted trapping, shooting and archery ranges, bird dog field trials
FEE(s): Must have appropriate fishing, hunting, or fishing/hunting license for those activities. There is also a user fee for the put-take pheasant release and for field trials

Acquired in the 1930's from abandoned farm lands, Winamac Fish & Wildlife Area has become a managed haven for wild game and non-game animals. Formerly part of Tippecanoe River State Park, the nine square miles of the property provides a variety of oak-hickory woodlands, old fields, croplands, prairie and some wetlands to explore during the non-hunting months. Some wild fauna that may be seen include white-tailed deer, grouse, quail, songbirds, waterfowl and if you are fortunate, wild turkey, a recent introduction that is successfully adapting to the northwestern Indiana sandlands. The abundance of quaking and big tooth aspen and shining sumac in the open revegetating fields and along roadsides adds a charming quality to the property. The mosquito and deer fly can be a nuisance during the warm summer months however the absence of large water bodies keeps their numbers down.

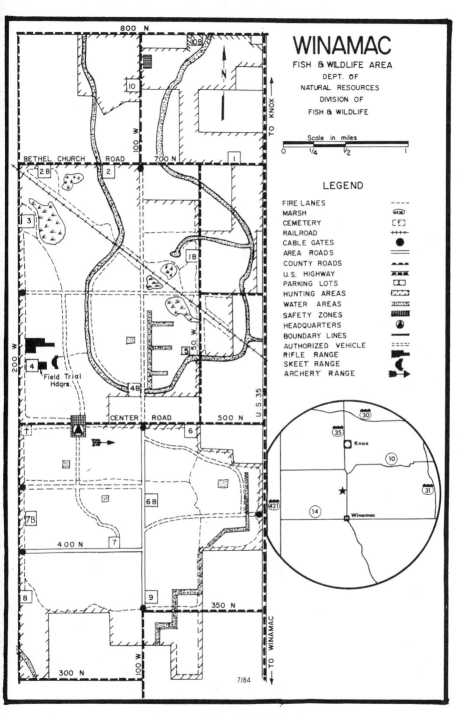

Winamac Fish & Wildlife Area

Best places to walk and explore are along the numerous grassy or sandy service lane roads as well as the grassy strips or firebreaks. Parking lots 2B, 3, 5, 6, 6B, 7, 9 and the property headquarters are choice places to park and walk.

Just south of the property check-in station/headquarters on Center Road/50ON is a developed wetland pond for wildlife. Follow the vehicle wide service lane 0.25 mile south to the first service lane heading west. The pond is another one hundred yards towards the clearing. Continue your walk south to parking lot 7 and 400N. Retrace your steps.

Southeast and east of the property headquarters a mile or so are parking lots 6 (Center Road) and 6B (100W) that are fine places to park and explore the highest sand dune ridge on the property. The sand dune is the western extension of the east-west ridge that extends across US 35 into the Tippecanoe State Park to the river. Re-established prairie is located northeast of parking lot 9 (100W), just south of 6B parking lot.

North and northeast of the property headquarters is the largest wetland and the oldest stand of forest on the property. Follow Center Road west to 200 W and turn north. Go north about 1.5 miles to parking lot 3. Walk the firebreak lane east about 100 yards to a large marsh divided by a levee.

Continuing north on 200W is an abandoned CSX railroad bed that is also walkable and heads southeast to Beardstown and Tippecanoe River State Park about 2 miles one-way.

Just beyond the abandoned railbed is Bethel Church Road CR 700N. Turn right/east and drive a few hundred yards to parking lot 2B and access via firelane the oldest second growth oak-hickory forest on the property. A small marsh lies to the southeast of parking lot 2B.

The area southwest of parking lot 1B and northwest of parking lot 5 on 50W is also marshland, woods and old fields. The abandoned railroad track divides the marsh. There are other areas to explore on the nearly 5,000 acres but the areas forementioned are the most scenic and wildlife rich.

North property parking lots and walks may be found by continuing west on Center Road from the property headquarters to the first crossroads and 200W. Turn right/north and drive to parking lot 3 and on to Bethel Church Road turning right/east to 2B. Continue east on Bethel Church Road to 1C parking lot and turn south on 50W to parking lots 1B and 5.

Continue south on 50W to Center Road, a complete country square (This is actually 2.5 sq. miles).

South property parking lots and walks begin along Center Road at parking lot 6 and also property headquarters. Turn south from Center Road onto 100W for parking lots 6B and 9. Road 400N and parking lot 7 may be accessed south of parking lot 6B enroute to 9.

To reach Winamac Fish & Wildlife Area drive north from Winamac, Indiana on US 35 about 5 miles (past the entrance of Tippecanoe River State Park). Turn left/west at the first road west past the state park entrance which is Center Road/500N.

Proceed about 1.5 miles to the property headquarters to obtain further information. Follow the directional signs.

20. BERNS-MEYER NATURE PRESERVE
Pulaski, IN/Pulaski County
USGS MAP(s): Buffalo, Star City 1:24,000
TRAIL(s) DISTANCE: 0.5 mile loop
ACREAGE: 20 acres
ACTIVITIES: nature walk, nature study

This rectangular block of old growth forest was donated to The Nature Conservancy by the Berns and Meyer families and was later transferred to the Indiana DNR Division of Nature Preserves who dedicated the property as a preserve in 1980. Spring wildflowers are prolific in the wet woods and mosquitoes are to be expected during the warm weather months. However a more relaxed walk during the normally dry autumn can be just as rewarding.

The trailhead and registration box is located near the mini-parking lot at the northeast corner of the property. A well illustrated pamphlet is available at the registration box that corresponds to the 44 numbered stations along the loop trail. In addition to the numerous native hardwood trees being identified, the pamphlet recognizes wildflowers, shrubs, ferns, wildlife, and woodland phenomena such as den trees, wet depressions, the wood's edge and annual growth rings. The level path follows the perimeter of the woodland weaving alongside stinging woodland nettle patches, underneath bladderpod shrubs and dogwoods, and beneath the shady canopies of maturing deciduous trees. A footbridge over a wooded wet depression is perfect habitat for wood ducks. Visitors can expect to have the seemingly remote woods to themselves.

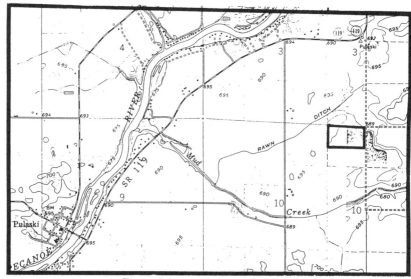

Berns-Meyer Nature Preserve

Berns-Meyer Nature Preserve is located south of Winamac, Indiana, south of Indiana 119 about 2.3 miles northeast of Pulaski, Indiana. From the Tippecanoe River bridge at Pulaski, north of the Catholic Church, travel north 2.3 miles on Indiana 119 to 100W at the road curve and turn right/south. Proceed past the farm and continue 0.6 mile to the preserve parking lot on the right/ west side of the road at the road junction with 500S. The preserve is open dawn to dusk. From the Indiana 119 approach, the woodlot stands out in size from any other woods nearby.

Berns-Meyer Nature Preserve

21. JASPER-PULASKI FISH & WILDLIFE AREA

Medaryville, IN/Jasper, Pulaski & Starke Counties
USGS MAP(s): San Pierre 1:24,000
TRAILS(s) DISTANCE: 2 trails total 1.5 miles one-way
  (several miles of service roads)
ACREAGE: 8,022 acres
ACTIVITIES: nature walks, nature study, nature preserve, sandhill crane observation, nursery, picnicking, shelters, playground, non-motorized boating, launch ramp, fishing, hunting, trapping, archery & shooting ranges, Class C camping

Straddling the county lines of northeast Jasper, northwest Pulaski and southwestern Starke, Jasper-Pulaski is the oldest managed fish and wildlife area in Indiana. Established in 1929 as a game farm and preserve, most of the property was acquired during the 1930s and 1940s from the purchase of marginal farm lands. The Civilian Conservation Corps played a major working role in the development of the property facilities. While the first and foremost mission of "JP" is to provide quality hunting and fishing opportunities, non-hunters will discover their share of outdoor recreation. All visitors, except picnickers, are asked to register at the self-service non-hunting check station adjacent to headquarters.

Due west of headquarters about 200 yards and along CR 1650W (the first road west of headquarters) is the 0.25 mile Sandhill Crane Observation Tower Trail that leads from the parking lot northwest to a observation tower that overlooks Goose Pasture. During the spring and especially fall migration, thousands of sandhill cranes converge in the pasture and nearby wetlands enroute to Georgia and Florida. Sunrise and sunset are the best times to witness the largest assemblage of sandhill cranes east of the Mississippi River; truly the most outstanding ornithological event in Indiana. Bring binoculars.

A second area to observe these close relatives of the whooping crane is the waterfowl resting area. Drive north on CR 1650W from the observation tower past the pheasant game farm, archery range and Ryan Ditch to the next crossroads CR 700N, turning right and parking at lot B. Heading west along CR 700N, the 1.3 mile one-way Marsh Observation Trail/Road is normally open to vehicular traffic but during the fall there is limited access. The posted hours during waterfowl hunting season vary from year to year. In the past it has been several days in mid October and the second week in November to early December with hours from 1 pm to sunset Saturday and Sunday, and 3 pm to sunset, Monday to Friday. The remainder of the year it is sunrise to sunset.

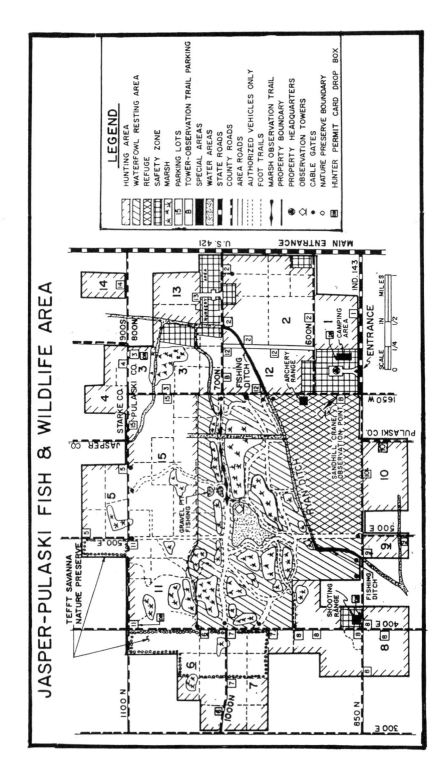

JASPER-PULASKI FISH & WILDLIFE AREA

LEGEND

HUNTING AREA	
WATERFOWL RESTING AREA	
REFUGE	
SAFETY ZONE	
MARSH	
PARKING LOTS	
TOWER-OBSERVATION TRAIL PARKING	
SPECIAL AREAS	
WATER AREAS	
STATE ROADS	
COUNTY ROADS	
AREA ROADS	
AUTHORIZED VEHICLES ONLY	
FOOT TRAILS	
MARSH OBSERVATION TRAIL	
PROPERTY BOUNDARY	
PROPERTY HEADQUARTERS	
OBSERVATION TOWERS	
CABLE GATES	
NATURE PRESERVE BOUNDARY	
HUNTER PERMIT CARD DROP BOX	

Jasper Pulaski Fish & Wildlife Area

The walk or drive along the Marsh Observation Trail/CR 700N has pin oak flats and marshlands. The road trail ends at a gravel pit and the trail continues to the observation overlook. The overlook perches above a vast waterfowl resting area marsh where numbers of the sandhills find nighttime refuge during the migratory stopover, the only major stopping point between their northern breeding grounds and their wintering grounds. Hikers will need to retrace their steps back along the county road.

Further east of parking lot B along CR 700N about a mile is the Jasper-Pulaski Tree Nursery. Founded in 1939 and operated by the Division of Forestry, the 150 acres encompasses seedbeds, transplant holding areas, seed orchards, a research area and windbreaks. The nursery grows 20-some tree and shrub species annually, totalling two million. The Vallonia Nursery near Vallonia, Indiana and Starve Hollow State Recreation Area is the only other state tree nursery. Feel free to walk the grounds and see what the nursery grows. The office hours are 8 am to 4 pm Monday through Friday. The entrance is 0.5 mile from US 421, 6.5 miles north of Medaryville and two miles south of Indiana 10.

The Tefft Savanna Nature Preserve located in the west and northwest portion of the area is a special place to hike about. From the Marsh Observation Trail head, travel north on CR 1650W to the "T" and CR

1100N. Turn left/west and go to the second road right/north or CR 500E. At the southwest corner of this junction is the first parking lot 11. Beginning west 1/4 mile from this parking lot and for another 1/4 mile marks the southern boundary of the northern part of the Tefft Savanna Nature Preserve. This Nature Conservancy 80 acre addition to Tefft Savanna is considered to be the best undisturbed example of black oak sand savanna within the present 480 acres. Continue west on CR 1100N to the junction with CR 400E and the second parking lot 11. The south 400 acre portion of the preserve lies west adjacent to CR 400E, south of the second parking lot 11. The south tract is accessible on foot from parking lots 6 and 7 which are south about one mile from CR 1100N on CR 400E. Sandy dune firebreaks serve as trails but feel free to wander. A brochure is available that describes the preserve in detail. Be advised hunting is allowed in the preserve during season.

Jasper-Pulaski Fish and Wildlife Area is located about 6.5 miles north and west of Medaryville, Indiana. Drive five miles north on US 421 and turn left/west on Indiana 143 and proceed 1.5 miles to the entrance.

22. STOUTSBURG SANDHILLS SAVANNA
Stoutsburg, IN/Jasper County
USGS MAP(s): Wheatfield 1:24,000
TRAIL(s) Distance: old farm lanes
ACREAGE: 240 acres
ACTIVITIES: hiking, nature study

Acquired by The Nature Conservancy in 1986, the property was purchased by the Indiana Nature Preserves Division of the DNR and dedicated as a nature preserve in 1990. The preserve is divided into two separate tracts less than 0.5 mile apart but the northwest tract is isolated and inaccessible. The larger southeast portion of the preserve is accessed along paved county roads at separate entrance gates along the south property however parking is confined along the roads.

The Stoutsburg Sandhills Savanna has spacious, open herbaceous covered areas that were former fields as well as forested sand dunal ridges. The widely spaced oaks contain an understory of low bush blueberry colonies, hoary puccoon, prairie phlox, rough blazingstar, western sunflower as well as prairie grasses and sedges. Controlled burns will prevent the shrubby undergrowth of the oaklands from evolving into dense forest, thereby preserving the savanna. The natural range of black oak savanna is restricted to the north central states. Old farm lanes and animal paths serve as trails in this sizeable preserve that sees few people.

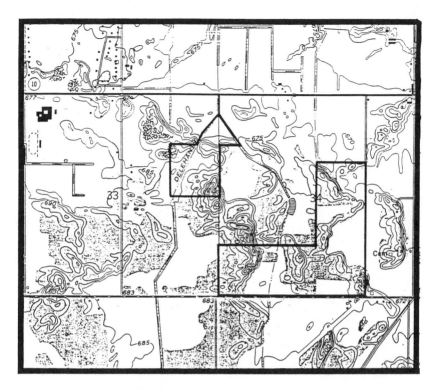

Stoutsburg Sandhills Savanna

To reach Stoutsburg Sandhills Savanna Nature Preserve from I-65 exit 230 and drive east on Indiana 10 to Indiana 110 and US 231 and turn left/north. Proceed north on US 231 three miles to Indiana 10 again and turn right/east. From the junction of Indiana 10 and US 231 continue east on Indiana 10 3.8 miles to CR 350W and turn right/south. Proceed one mile south on CR 350W to CR 1100N and turn left/east. Go 0.50 east on CR 1100N to the preserve's boundary on the left/north side of the road. The preserve continues east for about 0.75 mile and almost to CR 200W. Park in the available property gate entrances or along the road.

23. THOMAS CIURUS PARK NATURE PRESERVE

DeMotte, IN/Jasper County
USGS MAP(s): DeMotte 1:24,000
TRAIL(s) DISTANCE: appx. 2 miles
ACREAGE: 40 acres
ACTIVITIES: nature walk, nature study

This unique city park is also a dedicated state nature preserve. The square block of land was a gift to the town of DeMotte by Thomas Ciurus. From the roadside parking area, an old farm lane leads due west 0.25 mile to the marked property.

The rolling sand hills and flats support a remnant black oak savanna, the most threatened ecosystem in the United States today. Former three-wheeled motorized trails provide access to most of the preserve. Beneath the dominating oak canopy are prairie grasses and flowers including the rare cream wild indigo and bristly sarsaparilla as well as the more common cleft phlox, butterfly weed and bracken fern. Fire will play a major role in upgrading and preserving the savanna.

To reach Thomas Ciurus Park Nature Preserve from I-65 exit 230 east onto Indiana 10 and drive about 6.5 miles to US 231 (includes a few miles of Indiana 110) and turn left/north.

Proceed north on US 231 two miles to CR 1100N and turn left/west. Follow CR 1100N 0.5 mile to CR 600W and turn left/south. Continue south 0.5 mile and park along the west/right side of the road where the obvious footpath heads due west to the preserve.

Thomas Ciurus Park Nature Preserve

While in Jasper County, consider visiting the community parks of Rensselaer and Remington. Rensselaer city parks include Iroquois Park, located west of downtown along the Iroquois River at College and Austin Avenues. Iroquois River canoe access ramps are located along Washington Street, west of College Avenue. North and west of Iroquois Park is the larger Brookside Park at Clark Street/Indiana 114. The well landscaped campus of St. Joseph College features a reflecting pool and a wooded walk to a grotto. The campus is located west of US 231 in S. Rensselaer.

The recently established Remington City Park, located on the northwest side of town and US 24 features a graveled nature walk east of the ball field. Marked trees are identified along Carpenter Creek and the trail interconnects with the parking lot and spacious picnicking shelter.

Both Jasper County communities are accessible from I-65 exits 201, 205 and 215.

24. SPINN PRAIRIE
Reynolds, IN/White County
USGS MAP(s): Monticello North 1:24,000
TRAIL(s) DISTANCE: user paths only
ACREAGE: 29 acres
ACTIVITIES: nature walk, nature study

Tucked between a railroad and a gravel county road, Spinn Prairie, owned and managed by The Nature Conservancy as a dedicated state nature preserve, represents a surviving remnant of endangered bluestem-Indian tallgrass prairie community. This elongated patch of seemingly level ground features an open oak-hickory savanna at the north section of the property, gradually sloping south to a wet swale of prairie cordgrass and little bluestem. In the middle of the prairie, wildflowers thrive among the tallgrasses including cream wild indigo, prairie, ashy and sawtooth sunflowers and rattlesnake master, as known by botanist Charles Deam in his Flora of Indiana as button snakewort. There are no established trails as yet but user paths venture out from the property sign at the center of the preserve. Best time to visit is June to October.

To reach Spinn Prairie from I-65 exit 201 east onto US 24 and drive about 16 miles to Reynolds, Indiana and turn left/north on US 421. Drive two miles north on US 421 and turn right/east onto a paved country road. Go over the tracks and proceed 0.2 mile along the north edge of the preserve to the "T" and turn right/south. Continue south along the east edge of the preserve and the property sign. Park alongside the road.

While in White County consider visiting the Monon Town Park in Monon, Indiana, the next community north of Spinn Prairie, six miles. The park is a fine place to picnic under the large oaks and there is a short loop through an adjacent wooded area to the west at the south end of the park. To reach the Monon Town Park turn at the first residential street left/west beyond the Little Monon Creek bridge as your enter town on US 421 from the south.

Monticello, the county seat of White County, has two city parks worthy of visitation. The main city park is located on the community's south side next to US 421/Indiana 39 between Armory Road and Gordon Road. The level upland portion of the park is activity-based while nature walkers will appreciate the staircase that leads to a deep ravine in the lower park which is also accessible by car via Dodge Camp Road. The road dead ends at a small marina and the Lake Freeman portion of the Tippecanoe River. Blue Water Beach park is on the west bank of the Tippecanoe at the midtown section of Monticello just off Blue Water Drive via St. Marys Avenue and Main Street.

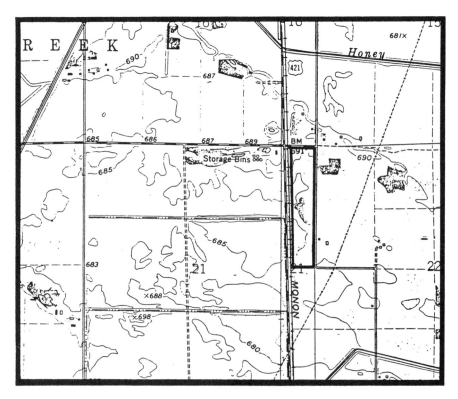

Spinn Prairie

Consider also driving alongside the Tippecanoe River along the Norway Road that leads to <u>Norway Dam</u> which retains Lake Shafer, a popular spot with fishermen. Norway Road begins at the intersection of Main Street and Rickey Road in north Monticello enroute to Indiana Beach.

25. HOLLEY SAVANNA
Mount Ayr, IN/Newton County
USGS MAP(s): Mount Ayr 1:24,000
TRAILS(s) DISTANCE: no est. trails
ACREAGE: 79 acres
ACTIVITIES: hiking, nature study

The Nature Conservancy property is an oak woodland and wet forest, portions which are managed to regenerate the former savanna. The forested, east to west rectangular-shaped property is drained by a small stream which draws wildlife. Hiking here is for the adventuresome since there are only deer trails and much of the forest is thicket due to previous logging making access slow and difficult. Nonetheless the sizeable preserve is one of the few in this part of farmed-out northwestern Indiana.

To reach Holley Savanna from I-65 in Jasper County west of Rensselaer, Indiana exit 215 west onto Indiana 114 and drive about seven miles to Newton CR 200E, two miles beyond Indiana 55. Turn right/north on CR 200E. Drive about 2.4 miles to 150S and turn right/east. Continue 1.3 miles on the winding gravel road to the cemetery and to where the road becomes 100S. Park on the east end of the cemetery. The preserve is marked with the yellow and green oak leaf signs.

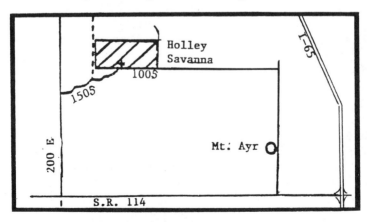

Holley Savanna

Another route taken is by turning north on Indiana 55 from Indiana 114 and driving north through Mount Ayr on Indiana 55 about three miles to CR 100S. Turn left/west and drive about 0.5 mile to the cemetery and the adjacent preserve. Holley Savanna lies about ten miles due east of Willow Slough Fish & Wildlife Area.

26. WILLOW SLOUGH FISH & WILDLIFE AREA
Morocco, IN/Newton County
USGS MAP(s): Morocco, Donovan, Enos, Leesville 1:24,000
TRAIL(s) DISTANCE: service roads, levees, user paths
ACREAGE: 9,956 acres
ACTIVITIES: hiking, nature study, nature preserve, picnicking, non-motorized boating, boat ramp, fishing, hunting, trapping, rifle target range, trap shoot, archery range, class B camping, concessions
FEE(s): camping, boat rental

Established in 1949 along the Indiana-Illinois state line in west central Newton County, Willow Slough is an area of sandy ridges, marshes and the 1,500 acre J.C. Murphey Lake, the centerpiece of the property. Although greatly altered by drainage and agriculture of the late 1800s and early to mid-1900s, an actual remnant of the former slough still exists at Goose Pond, an 18 acre swamp wetland south of J.C. Murphey Lake. According to Deam, a slough often is a shallow elongated water body or channel between two higher sand ridges, rarely over six feet in depth.

Hiking at Willow Slough is along service roads, levees and user paths. The adventuresome may tramp and wander. Due to insects and hunting, the best months for visitation is April, May and September. For birders, the property's wetlands make an ideal migratory waterfowl stopover. The best hiking places are the areas around J. C. Murphey Lake and adjacent wetlands and at Goose Pond east to Bill Barnes Nature Preserve. The southwest wooded shoreline of J. C. Murphey Lake is a fine place to stroll and become oriented. The site includes the property headquarters and the picnicking, fishing, campground and concession facilities.

North 0.75 mile of the headquarters entry road on State Line Road is parking lot 6A which provides immediate access to the Salisbury Levee which bisects Salisbury Rookery. Rookery Levee lies about 0.25 mile south along a service road and separates J. C. Murphey Lake from Salisbury Rookery. This area can be good birding. Another birding and natural area to visit is north on State Line Road 1.75 miles from the headquarters entry road to Pogue Road, turning right/east and driving about 0.5 mile to parking lot 4, just before the gate barrier (closed

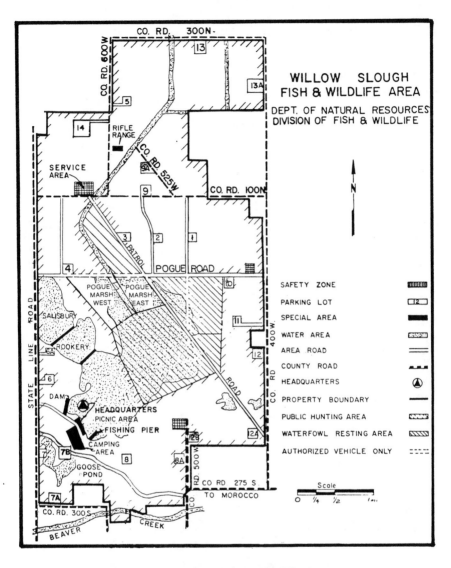

Willow Slough Fish & Wildlife Area

October 1 - December 31). Walk south on a service lane that parallels Pogue Marsh West. Mormon Hill, the highest point on the property, is in the vicinity. Walking east on Pogue Road leads to the waterfowl area, crossing the main outlet ditch for J. C. Murphey Lake, to Patrol Road. From the intersection of Pogue Road and Patrol Road, walk south along Patrol Road which divides the east portion of the lake and waterfowl resting area.

Goose Pond and Bill Barnes Nature Preserve is situated south of the property headquarters and J. C. Murphey Lake. From the entry road go south on State Line Road 0.5 mile to the first gravel road and turn left/east. Continue on to parking lot 7B at the north side of Goose Pond. There are several user paths fanning out along the edge of the wetland.

Further east on the gravel road one mile is parking lot 8 which provides access to Bill Barnes Nature Preserve, one of four separate tracts. There are no trails in the preserve. Walk across the road into the preserve which includes the best stand of oak savanna on the property. The L-shaped preserve also includes pin oak flats, sand prairie and sedge meadow. Even though it is a nature preserve, hunting is allowed. Bill Barnes, a wildlife biologist for the DNR, devoted years to the study of the prairie chicken in northwest Indiana.

Additional parking lots to set out on foot include #10 on east Pogue Road, east of the waterfowl area, #9A on CR 525W, a remote dead end that leads to Main Ditch, and #12B at the dead end of CR 500W, south of J. C. Murphey Lake.

To reach Willow Slough Fish and Wildlife Area from I-65 exit 215 onto Indiana 114 and drive west beyond US 41 and Morocco, Indiana to the Indiana-Illinois state line. Turn right/north on State Line Road and proceed about two miles to the headquarters and campground entry road and turn right/east. Continue another 0.5 mile to the headquarters on the southwest shore of Lake Murphey.

Consider visiting the nearby Iroquois County State Wildlife Area located about five miles due west of Willow Slough in neighboring Illinois where established trails loop through the 2,480 acre property.

Canada Geese, Willow Slough

LAKE PLAINS: OVERVIEW

*"What a loss it will be to the landscape of Indiana,
where the beech reigns supreme, when the last beech
woodlot has been destroyed. I wonder if the Hoosier State
will then create as many poets as it has heretofore?"*

Jens Jensen, Siftings, (1939)
Chapter: "Our Native Landscape"

By far, the most publicly accessible nature walks in northern Indiana lie in the lake plains of the north central and northeast counties. Advancing and retreating glaciers of the last ice age thousands of years ago have created a variety of geological landforms such as moraines, kames, kettles, eskers, outwash, till and lake plains. Today the post-glacial landscape is filled with lakes, marshes, bogs, fens, swamps, rivers, dry and wet prairie, savanna and deciduous forest. Three hundred plant species with northern affinities reach their southern limits. Hundreds of natural lakes punctuate the nearly level to gently rolling terrain although more have been drained than presently exist and several are designed by man. Their size ranges from a few pond acres to the state's largest natural lakes: Wawasee, James, and Maxinkuckee.

The majority of nature walks in the lake plains are in the hands of the DNR's Divisions of state park, fish and wildlife, nature preserves and state memorials; city and county parks; private colleges, trust foundations, religious organizations and individuals; The Nature Conservancy and ACRES, Inc. a "regional nature conservancy" of northeastern Indiana, headquartered in Ft. Wayne, Indiana.

The most outstanding lake experiences are found along the trails at Crooked Lake Nature Preserve, Olin Lake Nature Preserve, McKenny Nature Preserve and Ropchan Wildlife Refuge and Wetland Conservation Area. Shoreline development is minimal or non-existent and the natural areas retain original character. The state parks of Pokagon and Chain of Lakes provide the most trail mileage in one setting, as they move through a variety of lakescape habitats. These two state parks plus Potato Creek and Maplewood have noteworthy nature centers and naturalists. The most remarkable multi-lake wetland experience is the Tri-County Fish and Wildlife Area where 30 lakes, ponds and wetlands in close proximity of each other, dot the rolling topography.

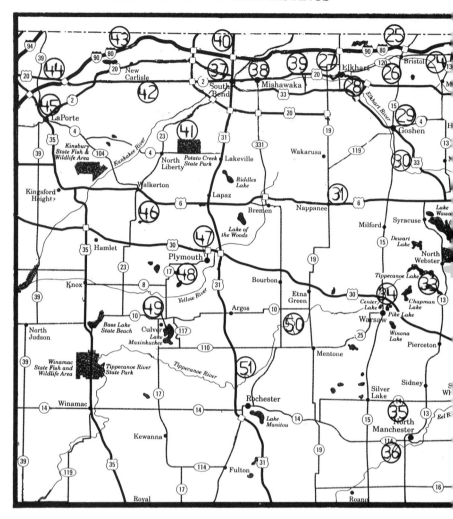

For vastness of wetland expanse but little foot access are the wetland conservation areas of Marsh Lake and Mallard Roost; where the eyes do the walking. The nature preserves of William L. Lieber, Koontz Lake, Ball Wetlands, Lonidaw, Laketon Bog, Beechwood and Wing Haven are outstanding for their scenic beauty and fine representation of the lake environments. Scott Mill County Park, River Preserve County Park, Douglas Woods and Pigeon River Fish and Wildlife Area are remarkable stream experiences. For a mixture of natural and social history visit Bonneyville Mill County Park, David Rogers County Park and the Gene Stratton Porter Memorial. Notable old growth forest are found at Edna W.

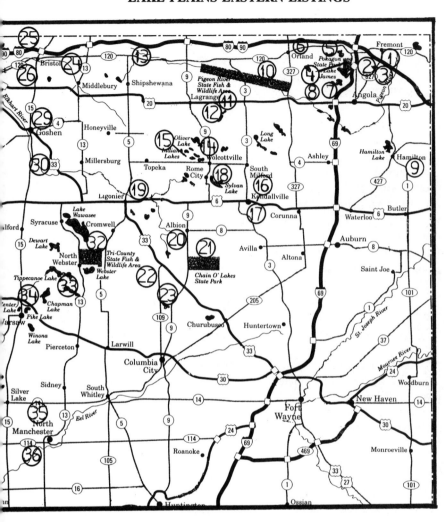

Spurgeon Woodland Reserve and Grider Woods Nature Preserve at Tri-County Fish and Wildlife Area. Fine examples of dry prairie thrive at Koontz Lake Nature Preserve, Conley Wildlife Refuge and Pigeon River Fish and Wildlife Area. Exceptional county parks systems include St. Joseph, Elkhart and Lagrange counties. Excellent urban parks are situated in the cities of LaPorte, South Bend, Mishawaka, Elkhart, Goshen, Plymouth and Warsaw and the smaller communities of Kendallville, Nappanee and Culver. The best nature experiences of the lake area that are privately-owned and managed are Merry Lea Environmental Learning Center, Potawatomi Wildlife Park and Wildwood.

1. ROPCHAN WILDLIFE REFUGE & WETLAND CONSERVATION AREA

Fremont, IN/Steuben County
USGS MAP(s): Angola East 1:24,000
TRAIL(s) DISTANCE: 1.5 mile one-way
ACREAGE: 184 acre refuge/90 acre WCA
ACTIVITIES: nature hike, nature study

The combination of the ACRES, Inc. refuge, a state dedicated nature preserve, and the DNR Fish and Wildlife Wetland Conservation Area has produced an outstanding natural sanctuary for day-use visitors. The property showcases a classic example of a glacial kettle hole lake and surrounding gravel and boulder kame knolls, so unique to the lake area of northeastern Indiana. The kettle and kame rolling landscape is covered by a green mantle of mature upland oak-hickory and mixed deciduous forest, evergreen pineries, revegetating fields, lowland red maple and tamarack forest, expansive cattail marsh and open water of Cemetery Lake. The looping trail traverses all this; an experience in northern exposure.

From the parking area adjacent to Indiana 827, the trail leads east past an old apple orchard, through the upland forest curving south around the wetlands and the Lakeside Cemetery. The foot path descends from the uplands to cross a foot bridge over an inlet stream to Cemetery Lake. From this point the trail skirts and passes through the low lying wetlands to gradually ascend an upland where the trail concludes in the forest near the south boundary not far from the Indiana Toll Road. A recent scout project has created an observation overlook, and a bridge over the stream to loop back to the parking lot.

At the trailhead parking area, a plaque honors Sam and Adeline Ropchan who donated the 180 acre refuge portion of the property in perpetuity under the stewardship of ACRES, Inc. There is also a quotation by Chief Seattle that has an ecological ring:

"What is man without beasts? If all beasts were gone men would die from a great loneliness of spirit, for what ever happens to beasts, soon happens to man, all things are connected."

To reach Ropchan Wildlife Refuge/Nature Preserve and Wetland Conservation Area from I-69 exit 154 and drive west on Indiana 127 a short distance and turn right/north on US 27. Follow US 27 north about two miles to Indiana 120 and turn right/east. Go east on Indiana 120 about three miles to Fremont and turn right/ south at the town center on Indiana

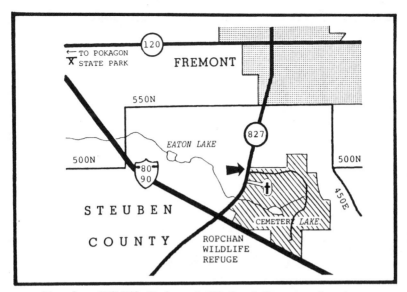

Ropchan Wildlife Refuge & Wetland Conservation Area

827. Continue south one mile on Indiana 827 and park on the left/east side of the highway.

Access may also be obtained from I-69 exit 148 east on US 20 to Angola, Indiana and turning north on Indiana 827, driving north just past the Indiana Toll Road/I-80-90.

2. WING HAVEN RESERVE
Angola, IN/Steuben County
USGS MAP(s): Angola East 1:24,000
TRAIL(s) DISTANCE: 3 trails total appx. 1 mile
ACREAGE: 159 acres
ACTIVITIES: nature study and walks, historic log cabin, special events

This ACRES, Inc. reserve proves as equally attractive as the uplifting place name, Wing Haven. The reserve was the former home and resort of the Swenson family who were sensitive to the land and its preservation. The glacially-carved kettle and kame landscape encompasses a significant share of the chain of Seven Sisters Lakes with pristine Little Gentian Lake being the most accessible. ACRES wants to increase protection and preserve the remaining areas of the Seven Sisters Lakes. The sanctuary is divided into three separate tracts but only the south tract along CR 400N is readily accessible. Three short interwoven trails weave through the varied terrain of the south tract.

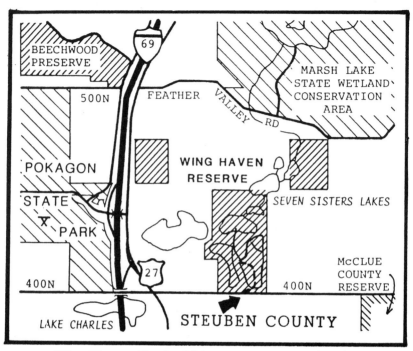

Wing Haven, Charles Mclue, and Beechwood Reserves

The trails begin/end from the two parking areas along CR 400N. From the parking area adjacent to the property's steward log cabin is the 0.33 mile long Meadow Loop Trail which encircles the east wildflower filled meadow where bluebirds frequent. The 0.25 mile Little Gentian Lake Trail is a linear path that begins west of the steward caretaker's cabin and leads from the upland to the lakeshore. Positioned upland along a ravine from the lake is a 19th century tulip log cabin which is open for visits on arrangement or the first Sunday of each month, 1 pm to 5 pm. Along the lakeshore rich aquatic plant life thrives. The 90 foot deep lake drains to the east, towards Marsh Lake. To the west, I-69 runs like a "concrete river", dividing Wing Haven Reserve and the Seven Sisters Lakes from Pokagon State Park; destroying much of the natural essence. The third trail, Trillium Wood Trail, connects with the Little Gentian Lake Trail near the wooded lakeshore. The 0.33 mile path forms a lakeside, ridge, ravine, old field loop leading to the second parking area along CR 400N.

Wing Haven Reserve may be reached from I-69 exit 154 onto Indiana 127 south to CR 400N and turning left/east. Travel 0.4 mile east on CR 400N and the two parking areas will be on the left/north side of the road. Further east a half mile or so is the Charles McClue County Reserve located on the right/south of CR 400N.

3. CHARLES McCLUE RESERVE
Angola, IN/Steuben County
USGS MAP(s): Angola East 1:24,000
TRAIL(s) DISTANCE: 3 trails total 2.5 miles
ACREAGE: 80 acres
ACTIVITIES: nature walks, nature study

Just east 0.5 mile of Wing Haven Reserve on CR 400N is another exceptional sanctuary that was a gift of Maurice McClue in memory of his father, Charles, to Steuben County. The reserve is supported by private donations and governed by a ten member Board of Directors who serve without compensation under the Steuben County Commissioners.

The reserve is rolling moraine carpeted with old forest, swamp and successionally advanced abandoned fields. Thirty acres of mature growth oak-hickory and mix deciduous woodland predominates in the northwest and west central section of the property while most of the remainder is open shrubby young woods of dogwoods, red cedar, aspen and sumac. There are three separate swampy depressions of about an acre each.

Three color coded loop trails interjoin throughout the reserve and there is a printed trail brochure available. The green 0.75 mile Tulip Trail begins/ends from the parking lot, leading through old growth forest, past a swamp, looping back via a young woods. The Tulip Trail intersects the Juniper Hill Trail twice in its course. The yellow blazed, 0.5 mile Juniper Hill Trail loop continues south through the old growth woods to enter an old field, curving back to ascend Juniper Hill where a poem by Edna C. Joll has been carved on a sign. The poem reads:

> *"Every child should know a hill*
> *and the clean joy of running*
> *down its long slope*
> *with the wind in his hair."*

The Juniper Hill continues down the slope, beads east, curving north past a swamp to rejoin the Tulip Trail. The Juniper Trail intersects the long Trail twice enroute.

The blue 1.25 mile Long Trail may be accessed either from the east edge of the parking lot or from the Juniper Hill Trail loop. Basically the trail skirts the east perimeter's young woods and the south perimeter of an abandoned field. The Long Trail connects the Juniper Hill Trail twice. A loop of varying lengths may be combined for a much longer hike.

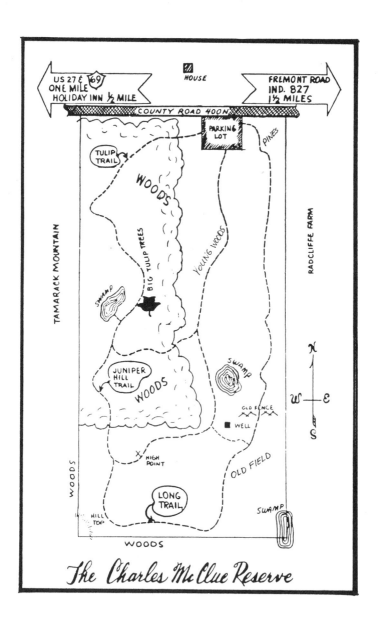

The Charles McClue Reserve

The reserve is open dawn to dusk. For more information contact the nature center at Pokagon State Park. To reach Charles McClue Reserve from I-69 exit 154 at the Fremont-Pokagon State Park ramp and drive south on Indiana 127 to the first road left/east or CR 400N and turn. Follow CR 400N east for mile (past Wing Haven Reserve) to the parking area on the right/south side of the road (see 2. Wing Haven Reserve map).

4. POKAGON STATE PARK

Angola, IN/Steuben County
USGS MAP(s): Angola West 1:24,000
TRAIL(s) DISTANCE: 7 foot trails total 10.5 miles
ACREAGE: 1,203 acres
ACTIVITIES: nature walks, nature study, nature center, naturalist, nature preserve, picnicking, shelters, playgrounds, playfields, tennis courts, two beaches, swimming, bathhouse, lifeguards, boating, fishing, waterskiing, saddle barn, equestrian trail, winter sports, x-country skiing, toboggan run, amphitheatre, cultural arts program, 142 room inn, restaurant, gift shop, cabins, Class A, B & C camping, youth & group camping, camp store
FEE(s): seasonal entrance, camping, horse and pony rides, hayrides, rentals include recreation building, shelters, row, pontoon, and paddle boats

Year around attractions make Pokagon State Park one of Indiana's most popular parklands. Probably most Hoosiers think of the state park as a "winter wonderland" with its picturesque inn, quarter mile long toboggan slides, ice fishing and cross country skiing. However with warm weather, the waters of adjoining Snow Lake and Lake James, Indiana's 2nd largest natural lake, are alive with swimmers, boaters, water skiers and campers.

Historically, the residents of Steuben County purchased 580 acres along the east shores of Lake James and Snow Lake and the land was presented to the state of Indiana as a Christmas gift; the state reciprocated, adding an additional 127 acres, creating the third largest state park in Indiana at that time. In 1927, Colonel Richard Lieber, "Father of Indiana State Parks", suggested naming the park, Pokagon, in honor of the Potawatomi Chief Simon Pokagon, who not so long ago, resided in northern Indiana. Most of the park's construction was carried out by the Civilian Conservation Corps (CCC) from 1934 to 1942.

Hiking the trails of Pokagon State Park is also a popular pursuit of visitors. If possible, plan your trip during the not-so-busy weekdays. To become informed of the natural history of the park's glaciated landscape and wildlife, stop and visit at the nature center and the naturalist year around. The easy and moderate seven nature trails are as follows:

Trail 1: The 1.5 mile linear trail begins along the Lake James shore, southwest of the Potawatomi Inn adjacent to the tennis court and cabins. The foot path heads west near the lakeshore to the nature center via a spur. Trail 1 continues south then curves north to conclude at the Apple Orchard picnic area. Trail 1 does connect the two mile long horse trail at

Pokagon State Park

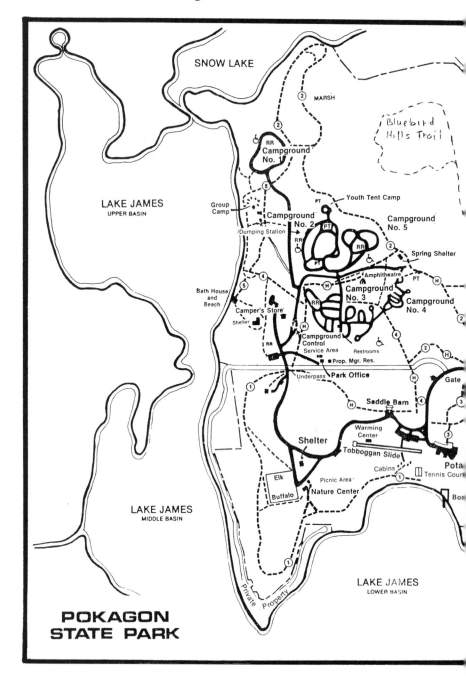

SNOW LAKE

MARSH

Bluebird Hills Trail

RR
Campground No. 1

LAKE JAMES
UPPER BASIN

Group Camp

Youth Tent Camp

Campground No. 2
Dumping Station
RR

PT
PT

Campground No. 5

Spring Shelter

Campground No. 3
Amphitheatre
PT

Bath House and Beach

Camper's Store
Shelter

RR

Campground No. 4

Campground Control
Service Area
RR

Restrooms
Prop. Mgr. Res.

Park Office
Underpass

Gate

Saddle Barn

Shelter

Warming Center
Tobboggan Slide

Cabins
Pota
Tennis Court

Elk
Buffalo

Picnic Area
Nature Center

Boa

LAKE JAMES
MIDDLE BASIN

LAKE JAMES
LOWER BASIN

Private Property

POKAGON STATE PARK

Pokagon State Park

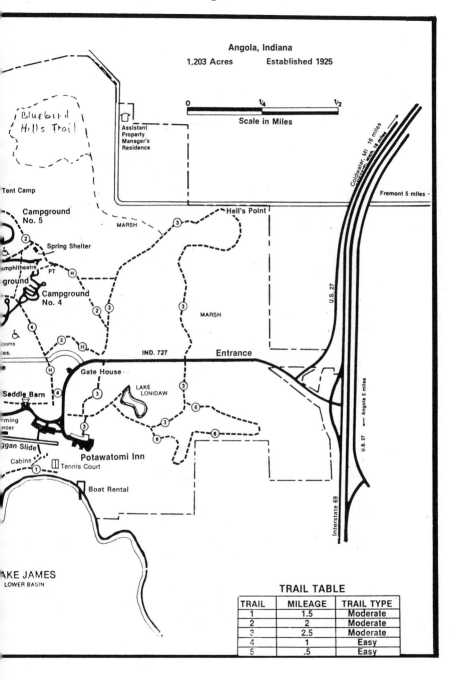

Angola, Indiana

1,203 Acres   Established 1925

0   ¼   ½

Scale in Miles

Bluebird Hills Trail

Assistant Property Manager's Residence

Tent Camp

Fremont 5 miles -

Campground No. 5

Hell's Point

MARSH

Spring Shelter

②

amphitheatre

PT   Ⓗ

ground

Campground No. 4

②   ③

③

MARSH

④

③

oms

es.

②   Ⓗ

IND. 727

Entrance

Ⓗ

Gate House

③

LAKE LONIDAW

③

Saddle Barn

④

③

⑥

rming nter

③

③

⑥

⑥

ggan Slide

Cabins

①

Potawatomi Inn

Tennis Court

Boat Rental

AKE JAMES
LOWER BASIN

U.S. 27

Coldwater, MI 16 miles

Angola 5 miles

U.S. 27

Interstate 69

TRAIL TABLE

TRAIL	MILEAGE	TRAIL TYPE
1	1.5	Moderate
2	2	Moderate
3	2.5	Moderate
4	1	Easy
5	.5	Easy

the underpass park road. There are side spur trails that crossover to the nature center enroute. Good trail for those with little time or inn guests.

Trail 2: Begins east of the gatehouse on the main park road and heads north combining with the horse trail and Trails 3 and 4. The trail forks and goes northwest past Spring Shelter picnic area, east of campground #3. The best natural portion of Trail 2 is north of campground #1, where the trail encircles a marsh and skirts along the high bluffs of Snow Lake. Trail 2 ends at campground #1. If returning to the gatehouse, follow connecting Trails 5 or 4 or walk the same route on Trail 2.

Trail 3: The 2.5 mile trail loop is the longest and one of the best hikes in the park. Trail 3 starts behind the Potawatomi Inn and leads north a short distance and forks east. East a short distance is the lovely Lonidaw Lake and the 208 acre Potawatomi Nature Preserve which encompasses most of the east and southeast section of the park. A spur of boardwalk extends out into the small lake, named for Simon Pokagon's wife. The preserve also features marsh, wet meadow, tamarack and yellow birch swamp, and forested deciduous uplands.

The trail loops through the preserve intersecting Trail 6, a side loop, twice. Trail 3 heads due north across the main park road to follow a wide path to the Hells Point overlook. Then Trail 3 loops southwest intersecting the Bluebird Hills Trail and continues southwesterly, connecting the horse trail and Trail 2, recrossing the park road and returning back to the Potawatomi Inn.

Trail 4: The linear one mile trail begins north of the gatehouse at the county road and connects and combines with Trail 2 and the horse trail and then leads through campground #3 west, across the park road to conclude at Trail 5, north of the beach and bathhouse.

Trail 5: The 0.5 mile loop trail begins near campground #1 and heads south around the group camp along the shore of the upper basin Lake James to connect the picnic area, beach, bathhouse, and camp store. Trail 5 returns along a parallel path back to campground #1.

Trail 6: A one mile loop trail extending from Trail 3, east of Lake Lonidaw. The loop trail encircles mature hardwood forest punctuated with swampy depressions. Trail 6 ends and begins from Trail 3 which it may be considered part of.

Bluebird Hills Trail, Pokagen State Park

Trail 7. <u>Bluebird Hills Trail</u>: The trail-with-a-name is the best in the park for remoteness and rolling morainal hills with vistas. The two mile path begins along <u>Trail 3</u> in the north border of the park, southwest of Hells Point overlook. The earth path loops along the glacial ridges and glen bottoms with wetlands and prairie-like areas. Excellent bluebird habitat.

<u>Horse Trail</u>: The two mile equestrian path is actually not the best for hikers especially during the busy summer season. The horse path begins at the Saddle Barn and heads west and north looping around campground #3 and connects and combines with <u>Trails 2, 3</u> and <u>4</u>.

To reach Pokagon State Park from I-69 exit 154 onto Indiana 727 west which leads directly to the park entrance. Unless camping or rooming at the inn or cabins, the park hours are 7 am to 11 pm daily.

5. BEECHWOOD NATURE RESERVE

Angola, IN/Steuben County
USGS MAP(s): Angola West 1:24,000
TRAIL(s) DISTANCE: 1.5 mile loop
ACREAGE: 89 acres
ACTIVITIES: nature walk, nature study

Beechwood Nature Reserve, an ACRES, Inc. sanctuary and dedicated state nature preserve, borders Pokagon State Park at the northeast property boundary near Hells Point. As the reserve's name suggests, there are beech-maple covered slopes and ridges as well as a tamarack bog, marsh, creek, old retired fields, a former apple orchard and a bit of lakeshore fronting Little Otter Lake.

The maintained and marked nature trail begins/ends at the gravel access road to Big and Little Otter lakes adjacent to US 27. From the small road corner parking area, the trail leads down to a bog, skirting its wet mucky shore along a boardwalk through a yellow birch grove. The trail continues west and ascends the rolling moraine ridges reaching an elevation of 1,050 feet. The openness of the former fields and orchard provides fine vistas

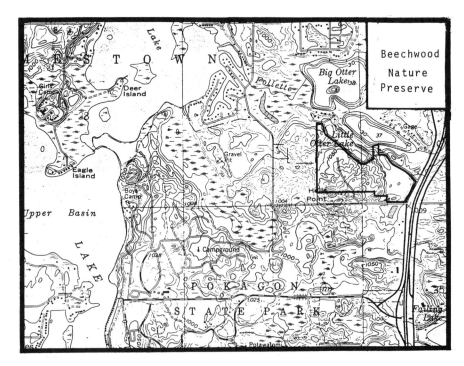

Beechwood Nature Preserve

of the lake country of Steuben County. White-tailed deer are very common, browsing on the apple twigs, buds and fallen fruit, giving the trees a pruned appearance. The trail loops about the uplands and reconnects the original entry trail to return across the boardwalk to the parking area.

To reach Beechwood Nature Reserve from I-69 exit 154 west on Indiana 127 towards Pokagon State Park. Turn right/north on US 27 from Indiana 127 and drive north less than a mile to the not-so-obvious gravel road, just beyond CR 500N. Park at the southwest corner adjacent to the gravel road (leads to Big and Little Otter lakes) and US 27. A property sign and a brown metal registration box identifies the trailhead parking area. I-69 is adjacent east, across US 27 and the fence. (See Winghaven Reserve Map #2).

6. ROPCHAN MEMORIAL NATURE RESERVE
Orland, IN/Steuben County
USGS MAP(s): Orland, Angola West 1:24,000
TRAIL(s) DISTANCE: one mile round trip
ACREAGE: 77 acres
ACTIVITIES: nature walk, nature study

The flavor of the north woods predominates at this ACRES, Inc. nature reserve, which is also a dedicated state nature preserve. The sanctuary exemplifies geological attractions, encompassing a tamarack bog, kettle hole lake, red maple swamp forest, and oak-hickory covered morainic sand ridges. The plant life that covers the varied terrain is just as diverse and interesting.

The linear foot path spans the half-mile wide, rectangular shaped reserve. From the parking area, the trail enters a mixture of young and old growth forest. After a short distance, the path arrives at the edge of the wetland and circumnavigates the north edge between the two contrasting habitats of lowland swamp and upland forest. Continuing eastward, the wetland breaks into an expanse of tamarack forest. The trail concludes at the east perimeter of the reserve near CR 700W. Retrace the original route, returning to the parking area.

The Ropchan Memorial Nature Reserve is located east of Orland, Indiana in northwest Steuben County. From Orland, drive two miles east on Indiana 120 to CR 750W and turn left/north. Continue on CR 750W north to the marked parking area on the right/east side of the road.

While in the Orland area, consider visiting the Fawn River Fish Hatchery at the north edge of town on both side of Indiana 327. The service roads accessing the hatchery's ponds may serve as walking trails. The state fish hatchery was developed by the WPA in the early 1940s. Fawn River flows along the north ends of both the east and west ponds. The Fawn River is an outstanding canoe stream.

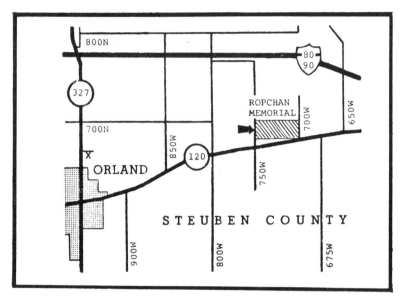

Ropchan Memorial Nature Reserve

7. LOON LAKE NATURE PRESERVE
Angola, IN/Steuben County
USGS MAP(s): Angola West 1:24,000
TRAIL(s) DISTANCE: 0.25 mile one-way
ACREAGE: 99 acres
ACTIVITIES: nature walk, nature study, canoeing, launch ramp

Tamarack bog, sedge meadow, marl prairie, open marsh and lake, and upland forest characterize the natural communities of Loon Lake Nature Preserve; home to several rare wetland plants. The preserve occupies the south and west shore of the seemingly untouched 138 acre shallow glacial lake. The preserve was purchased by The Nature Conservancy but is now owned and managed by the DNR Division of Nature Preserves.

The wetland communities restrict foot access to most of the preserve. However a marked linear 0.25 mile (one-way) trail leads from the roadside cable gate down a weedy service road, jogs right/south through the upland forest, re-emerges on the service road and heads straight north, gradually sloping to the lake's edge where open vistas of Loon Lake and surroundings appear. Retrace the path back to the parking area.

To reach Loon Lake Nature Preserve trailhead and parking area from I-69 exit 148 west onto US 20 and drive west 0.2 mile and turn right/north onto CR 325W, the first county road. Proceed north 0.6 mile on CR 325W to the road curve and park at the wire cable gate pullout which is the southwest boundary of the preserve.

Along the northeast shore of Loon Lake, south of CR 100N and the Landes Road intersection, is the DNR Division of Fish and Wildlife canoe/boat launch ramp that allows public access to the lake.

Adjacent west of the public access launch ramp is the 80 acre Anspaugh Wildlife Habitat Trust Area which preserves the west shore's wetlands, wet meadows and lowland woods. The area is open to the public on a limited basis. Check with the Angola Chamber of Commerce for access.

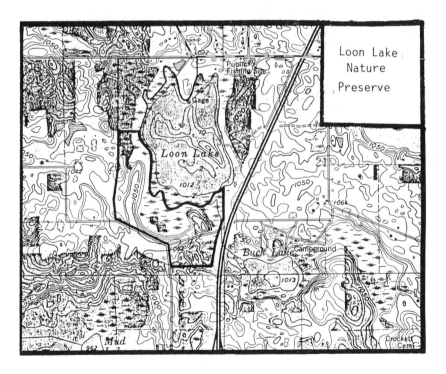

Loon Lake Nature Preserve

To reach the public access launch ramp and Anspaugh Wildlife Habitat Trust Area on the north and west shore of Loon Lake from I-69, exit 148 east onto US 20 and drive to the first road north CR 200W and turn left/north. Go north on CR 200W one mile to the crossroads of CR 100N and turn left/west. Drive west on CR 100N underneath the I-69 overpass to the public access site on the south/left side of CR 100N.

8. McKENNY NATURE PRESERVE
Angola, IN/Steuben County
USGS MAP(s): Angola West 1:24,000
TRAIL(s) DISTANCE: no est. trails
ACREAGE: 80 acres
ACTIVITIES: nature hike, nature study

The McKenny Nature Preserve lies on the northwest shore of scenic Cheeseboro Lake in west central Steuben County, one of five lakes of the so-named Grass Lake chain. The Nature Conservancy property, a gift of the Charles McKenny family, is divided about evenly between wetlands and uplands. The wetlands harbor a shallow sedge-bulrush marsh and a buttonbush swamp along the lakeshore, the eastern portion of the preserve. During late summer and autumn, when the water levels normally fall, the dry muck and mud flats provide an opportunity to explore for plants that are associated with the Atlantic Coastal Plain. White and black oak uplands perch high above the lake providing fine views. Birding is reported to be good. Further west, are abandoned fields filled with the early successional herbs and pioneering trees. There is no established trail system as yet, but the preserve is open for visitation. Currently deer "trails" may serve as footpaths. There is plenty of poison ivy and briars. An ideal trail would loop following the high bluff and along the lake edge.

To reach McKenny Nature Preserve from I-69 exit 148 and go west on US 20 about 2.8 miles to CR 600W and turn right/north. Follow CR 600W one mile north to CR 100N and turn right/east. Proceed about 0.5 mile on CR 100N to the boundary of the preserve which is marked. Park along the south side of the county road at the pullout across from the entrance to the Vulcan gravel pit at the rise. The north shore of Loon Lake is less than three miles east on CR 100N.

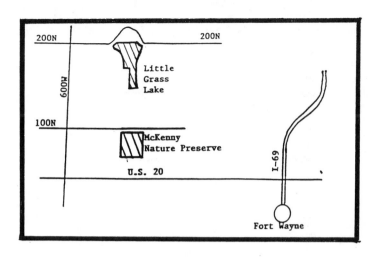

McKenny Nature Preserve

9. DOUGLAS WOODS
Hamilton, IN/Steuben & Dekalb Counties
USGS MAP(s): Hamilton, Edon 1:24,000
TRAIL(s) DISTANCE: old farm lanes
ACREAGE: 273 acres
ACTIVITIES: nature hike, nature study

Straddling the Steuben-Dekalb county line southeast of Hamilton, is The Nature Conservancy's preserve of Douglas Woods. The property has been in the Douglas family since 1926 and mostly undisturbed since the 1950s. The upland mixed forest is considered to be the largest old growth in the area. There are also wetlands and a pond habitat. Fish Creek, a tributary of the St. Joseph River, runs through the preserve for two miles. In the past, the purity of Fish Creek's healthy waters was seen by the diversity and quantity of mussels found on the stream bottom. There were some 30 different species of mussels found in Fish Creek including the northern riffleshell, clubshell, lady finger, and others. Unfortunately, an oil spill has damaged the creek and several species may be just hanging on. Dams, pollutants, and the invasion of the European Caspian Sea zebra mussel threaten the native freshwater mussel population of the eastern United States with extinction but hopefully not at Fish Creek. Fifty acres of the preserve is farm land and will continue to be farmed by conservation tillage practices to demonstrate erosion and chemical control. Near future plans call for a proper parking area and trailhead to access a trail network. Currently visitors are on their own to follow old farm lanes.

To reach Douglas Woods from I-69 exit 140 at the Dekalb-Steuben county line. Drive east on CR 800S 7.5 miles to Hamilton and Indiana 1. Turn right/south on Indiana 1 and drive southeast about 2.5 miles. Proceed east 0.4 miles on CR 4A, beyond the Fish Creek bridge and enter the old farm lane on the left/north side of the county road across from the Douglas farm and park. Follow the farm lane due north to the woods.

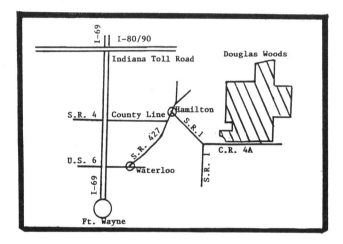

Douglas Woods Nature Preserve

Further Notes on Steuben County

Steuben County, "the Switzerland of Indiana", is exceptional in the fact it has more land set aside for recreation and preservation of any northern Indiana county, yet it is one of the smallest counties in the state. Visitors to this extreme northeastern corner of the Hoosier state are never far from one natural area to the next. There are several publicly accessible lands that are worthy of visitation although foot access may be limited due to fragility of site, wetlands, poor or restricted access and lack of foot trails.

The six acre Elizabeth Hanna Nature Preserve (USGS Map Clear Lake 1:24,000) is located on the east shore of 800 acre Clear lake, east of the Clear Lake Road. The Clear Lake Town Council dedicated the property to "Lib" Hanna in recognition of her dedication to the preservation of wildlife areas in Steuben County. Currently the marked preserve is trailless but trails will be developed.

Cedar Swamp Wetland Conservation Area (USGS Maps Angola East and California 1:24,000) consists of 450 acres of partially drained shallow lake which forms the headwaters of the Pigeon River. An old lane service road skirts the southeast side of the swamp along the lower base of an upland forest. The make-due trail leads to an embankment that bisects the swamp and heads northwest to an old farmhouse, one of two on the property. Remote birding and wildlife area. Retrace the route you arrived back to the first farmhouse at CR 600E.

To reach the parking area from Fremont, Indiana, go east on Indiana 120, 1.5 miles to CR 600F where Indiana 120 curves south and turn left/north. Continue 0.25 mile north to the old farm lane and park at the abandoned farmhouse. The old lane service road heads right/east.

The town of Fremont's Vistula Park (USGS Map Angola East 1:24,000) along the north side of Indiana 120 on the community's west side features a woodland Tree Trail, which was established by the Fremont Community Schools. The active park also includes a playground, playfields, picnic area and tennis courts.

The 700 acre Marsh Lake Wetland Conservation Area (USGS Map Angola East 1:24,000) is one of Indian's largest wetland systems. The 460 acre glacial basin lake is surrounded by extensive wetlands including swamps, fen, marsh and some upland forest primarily along the south boundary of Feather Valley Road. A portion of Marsh Lake WCA is a dedicated state nature preserve. The Indiana DNR Nature Preserves has a 27 acre preserve adjoining the northeast property.

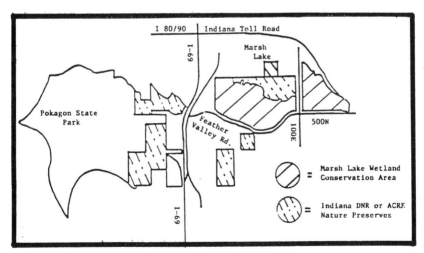

Marsh Lake Wetland Conservation Area

Marsh Lake WCA may be reached from I-69 exit 154, driving north on Indiana 127 to Feather Valley Road and turning right/east. Follow Feather Valley Road about seven miles to the marked entrance road and turn left/north. Proceed to the launch ramp for great views of the lake. Another outstanding view of the vast wetland is along CR 100E, the next road left/north on Feather Valley Road. Follow CR 100E north across the wetland and at the rise there is a small parking area on the right/east side of the country road. Walk west across the road to the upland overlook.

Jimmerson Lake Wetland Conservation Area is the smallest and least accessible of the four WCA's owned and managed by the DNR Division of Fish and Wildlife in Steuben County. The area is best accessed by canoe since the wetlands includes a 14 acre island and the northwest shoreline near Nevada Mills, Indiana.

From I-69 exit 148 at Angola, drive west on US 20 about 2.8 miles and turn right/north on CR 600W. Follow CR 600W, 2.5 miles to CR 200N and turn right/east. Continue on CR 200N 0.5 mile to the road curve and the preserve boundary (see: Little Grass Lake on 8. McKenny Nature Preserve map). Park alongside the road. There is no easy access down the slope to the lakeshore. Once down to the lake, follow the west shore. Scenic lake views south.

The Steuben County Park on the east side of Crooked Lake on CR 200N is an activity park and a summer campground. There is also a sandy beach, picnic area and playground.

Finally, at the Steuben-Lagrange county line on the south side of US 20 is the Prairie Heights Community School Outdoor Lab which includes a nature trail loop. The trail begins at the windmill and ponds next to US 20 and loops south covering a wide variety of educational stations. There are sections of boardwalk.

From I-69 exit 148, go west on US 20 about eight miles to the county line just south of the Pigeon River Fish and Wildlife Area.

10. PIGEON RIVER FISH & WILDLIFE AREA

Mongo, IN/Lagrange & Steuben Counties
USGS MAP(s): Mongo, Orland 1:24,000
TRAIL(s) DISTANCE: several miles of firelanes/service roads
ACREAGE: 11,500 acres
ACTIVITIES: hiking, nature study, nature preserves, fish hatchery,
    picnicking, x-country skiing, ice skating, canoeing, launch ramps,
    fishing, rifle range, hunting, Class C primitive camping
FEE(s): camping

From three NIPSCO donated hydroelectric impoundments in the 1950s,
Pigeon River has grown to be the largest fish and wildlife area in Indiana
today. The southeast to northwest property spans both sides of the Pigeon
River from western Steuben County, west to near Howe, Indiana in north
central Lagrange County. Mongo, Indiana is the near center of the area
and the old barn headquarters and campground are located about 0.5 mile
east of town on CR 300N.

Although popular as a hunting and fishing wildlife area, Pigeon River
has several natural attractions for the non-game seeking public. Restored
prairie, the largest tamarack swamp forest in Indiana, marsh, fen, muck
pockets, 19 lakes and ponds, coldwater streams, oak upland forests and
abandoned and cultivated fields encompass the vast area. Attracted to
these natural communities are a variety of birds (216), mammals (34), and
reptiles (32) species. Forty-one rare plants are also found and the property
has set aside two unique state dedicated nature preserves.

The east section of Pigeon River Fish and Wildlife Area includes dry
prairie, waterfowl observation points, Beaver Dam Lake, the property's
best old growth forest, and the Tamarack Bog Nature Preserve. North of
US 20 one mile on Indiana 327 in Steuben County at parking lot L-8 is
the ten acre Gannon/Stayner Lake, the most calcareous lake in Indiana.
Across the highway from the lake east is the Stayner Dry Prairie situated
between two slopes. The two waterfowl observation points overlooking the
waterfowl resting area are at a roadside pulloff on CR 300N, just east of
CR 1100 at an embankment along CR 1100, 0.5 mile south of CR 300N.
The shoreline of Beaver Dam Lake is a quality natural area. Lakeshore
access is at the launch ramp at the junction of CR 375N and CR 1150E.
The best old growth oak forest is east and south of the headquarters check
station along CR 900E and CR 150. Park in G-2, G-3 or G-4 lots. The
170 acre Tamarack Bog Nature Preserve is too wet for walking and is best
viewed from the camping area and launch ramp on the north shore of
Mongo Reservoir looking south. The nature preserve can be skirted in the
old growth oak forest north and west of parking lots G-2, G-3, and G-4.

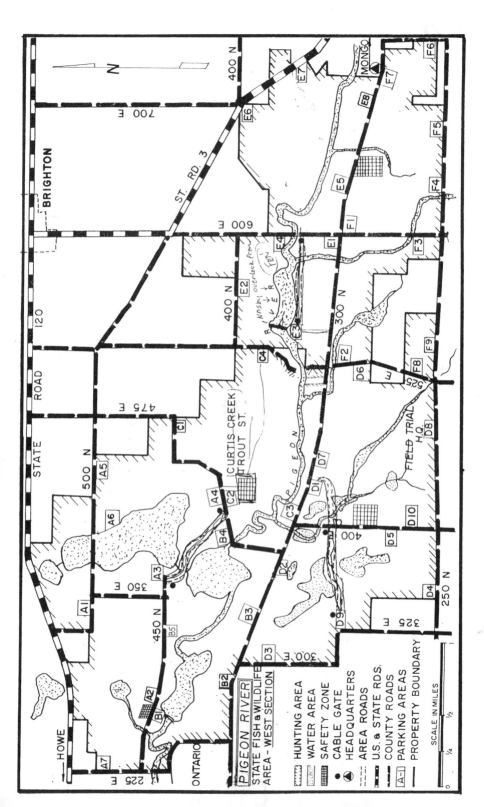

PIGEON RIVER
STATE FISH & WILDLIFE
AREA - WEST SECTION

⊞ HUNTING AREA
░ WATER AREA
▒ SAFETY ZONE
● CABLE GATE
◑ HEADQUARTERS
╍ AREA ROADS
━ U.S. & STATE RDS.
┅ COUNTY ROADS
A-1 PARKING AREAS
━ PROPERTY BOUNDARY

SCALE IN MILES
0   ¼   ½

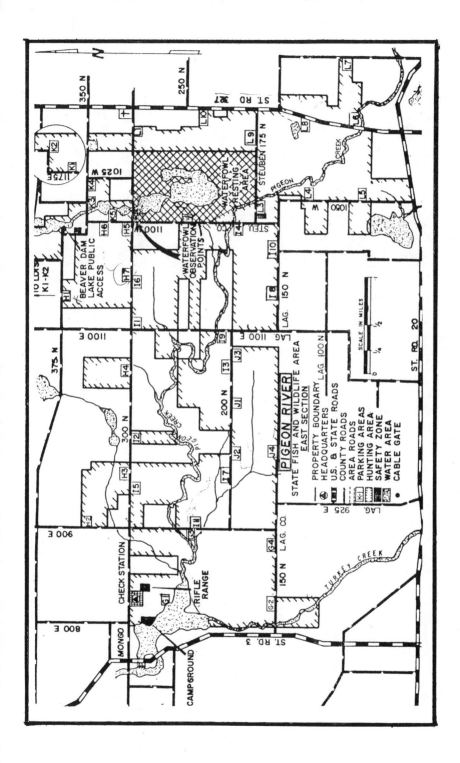

PIGEON RIVER
STATE FISH AND WILDLIFE AREA
EAST SECTION

PROPERTY BOUNDARY
HEADQUARTERS
U.S. & STATE ROADS
COUNTY ROADS
AREA ROADS
PARKING AREAS
HUNTING AREA
SAFETY ZONE
WATER AREA
CABLE GATE

SCALE IN MILES

WATERFOWL RESTING AREA

WATERFOWL OBSERVATION POINTS

BEAVER DAM LAKE PUBLIC ACCESS

CHECK STATION

RIFLE RANGE

MONGO

CAMPGROUND

TURKEY CREEK

PIGEON CREEK

ST. RD. 3

ST. RD. 20

ST. RD. 327

Fen at Pigeon River Fish & Wildlife Area

The west section of Pigeon River Fish and Wildlife Area features the Nasby Overlook Prairie, Mongoquinong Nature Preserve and the Curtis Creek Trout Station. The ten acre Nasby Overlook Prairie is a dry prairie similar in plant composition as the Stayner Dry Prairie near Gannon/Stayner Lake at the east property boundary. The upland prairie is north of the Mongoquinong Nature Preserve and overlooks the Nasby Reservoir and dam. The nature preserve lies alongside the reservoir and is primarily a fen or wet prairie that is kept in a marshy state by the bluffside seeps. The preserve is best viewed from the blufftop or from the adjacent CR 600E. Both the Nasby Overlook Prairie and Mongoquinong Nature Preserve are reached by driving 1.5 miles west of Mongo on CR 300N/Ontario Road to CR 600E and turning right/north. Go north on CR 600E and park in lot E-4 just north of the Pigeon River bridge crossing.

The Curtis Creek Trout Station is open to visitation from 8 am to 4 pm, Monday through Friday. Thousands of brown and rainbow trout are reared here. While at the hatchery, consider walking the service road that lies between parking lots B-4 and A-4 and head northwest about 0.75 mile between two large lake impoundments to parking lot A-3. Retrace your steps. Curtis Creek Trout Station is located three miles west from Mongo on CR 300N/Ontario Road and right/north one mile on CR 390E to parking lot C-2.

There are a number of other natural places to explore on both the east and west sections of the fish and wildlife area and all are easily accessible from the marked parking lots scattered throughout.

Pigeon River Fish and Wildlife Area is bordered by Indiana 120 on the north, US 20 on the south, Indiana 327 on the east, and Indiana 9 on the west. From I-69 exit 148, go west on US 20 to Indiana 3 north to Mongo and headquarters. From the Indiana Toll Road/I-80-90 at Howe, exit 120 south to Indiana 9 and east on Indiana 120 to Indiana 3 south to Mongo.

11. CLINE LAKE FEN
Plato, IN/Lagrange County
USGS MAP(s): Mongo 1:24,000
TRAIL(s) DISTANCE: no est. trails
ACREAGE: 64 acres
ACTIVITIES: nature hike, nature study

This wetland wonderland, only partly protected by The Nature Conservancy, includes the west shore of Weir Lake, marshes, a tributary of the Pigeon River and fens; low wet meadows covered partly or wholly by water. The fenlands are home to the rare northern leopard or meadow frog and the spotted "polka-dot" turtle which is more often seen in spring and are somewhat similar in appearance to the Blandings turtle. Plant life includes the rare purple or water avens, found only in a few northern counties in bogs and fens. The nodding flowers are usually in threes and are a brownish-purple. Also the wild smooth gooseberry shrub is found here and a few northern counties and is infrequent to rare. The east shore of Weir Lake has numerous tamaracks. There are no trails, however there is enough upland to wander about and view the wetlands and rich birdlife.

To reach Cline Lake Fen from I-69 exit 148 near Angola, Indiana and drive west on US 20 about 17.5 miles to Plato, Indiana; about four miles east of Lagrange, Indiana. Turn north/right on CR 475E and continue 0.3 miles. Follow CR 25N/CR 600E 0.7 miles to the property. Park along the pullout at the road curve where there is a 50 yard walk to the northwest shore of Weir Lake. The preserve lies to the south and is marked by yellow and green Nature Conservancy signs.

Maplewood Nature Center and Preserves is about three miles southwest of Cline Fen Preserve via CR 475E to CR 100S west.

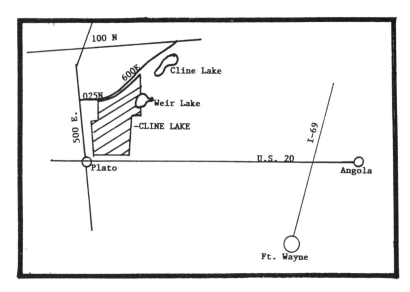

Cline Lake Fen

12. MAPLEWOOD NATURE CENTER & PRESERVES
Plato, IN/Lagrange County
USGS MAP(s): Wolcottville 1:24,000
TRAIL(s) DISTANCE: 4 trails total 2.3 miles
ACREAGE: 68 acres
ACTIVITIES: nature walks, nature study, nature center, naturalist, x-country skiing, maple sugar cabin, nature preserves, naturalist walks & programs year around
FEE(s): ski rental

This natural experience is the result of a joint cooperative effort between the Lagrange County Department of Parks and Recreation and ACRES, Inc. The seasonally wet upland mix deciduous woodlands are dominated by beech and maple trees. Spring wildflowers are outstanding. The Maplewood Nature Center is a modern but rustic spacious building that features displays, exhibits, a natural history library plus an entire wall of wildlife observation window. The county park naturalist schedules programs and guided walks for the visiting public. The nature center's hours are Wednesday 8 am to 4 pm, Saturday 9 am to 5 pm and Sunday noon to 5 pm. The trails are open daily dawn to dusk.

The four color coded loop trails begin/end at the east side of the nature center and maple sugar cabin and a trail map is available at a box by the center's entrance.

The 0.4 mile white square trail is the shortest loop that samples the woodland east of the parking, nature center, and maple sugar cabin complex. The white square trail also accesses a linear spur path to McNutt Ditch, which is more like a free flowing brooklet across gravel Road H. The white square trail forms a segment of the green circle trail.

The 0.35 mile yellow triangle trail is a side loop from the green circle trail. Head south from the nature center on the green circle trail across two foot bridges through wet low woods to a marked yellow loop on the west side of the property. The trail veers right and encircles the upland forest and reconnects with the green circle trail.

The 1.3 mile green circle trail traces a wide loop throughout the preserves. The mature trees are impressive and of special interest is the butternut walnut trees that have become rare in the wild in recent years. Orchids are also found on the forest floor.

The 0.25 mile red hexagon trail connects the yellow triangle and green circle trails. This section has unusual flowers such as squawroot, and numerous ferns. There are also mature tulip and sassafrass trees.

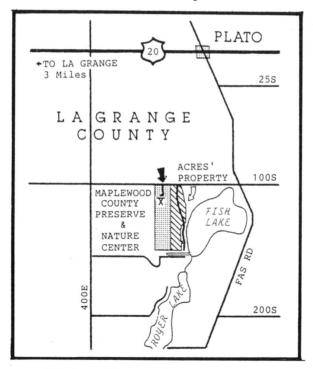

Maplewood Nature Center & Preserves

155

To reach Maplewood Nature Center and Preserves from Lagrange, the county seat of Lagrange County, go east from Lagrange on US 20 three miles to CR 400E and turn south/right. Continue one mile south on CR 400E to CR 100S and turn left/east. Proceed on CR 100S east about a half mile to the marked entrance on the right/south side of the road.

13. SCOTT MILL COUNTY PARK

Scott, IN/Lagrange County
USGS MAP(s): Shipshewana 1:24,000
TRAIL(s) DISTANCE: 1 mile loop
ACREAGE: 120 acres
ACTIVITIES: nature walk, nature study, picnicking, shelter, fishing, canoeing, launch ramp, playground, historic site

A large wooded island flanked by the forking Pigeon River is the main attraction of this Lagrange County Park, a former DNR Fish and Wildlife Public Fishing Area. From the parking area on the river south bank just south of Scott village, the trailhead of a mile long foot path begins by crossing a rustic covered foot bridge over the main fork of the Pigeon River. From the picnic shelter, the trail follows the perimeter of the island and forms a loop. The fast river current and the dense floodplain forest

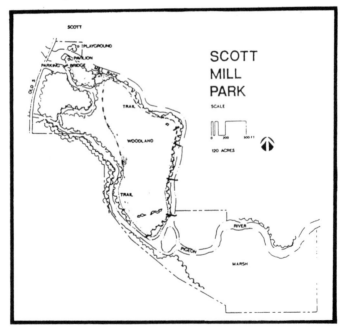

Scott Mill County Park

are the key features of the natural experience. The narrow trail can be overgrown in summer with lush riparian vegetation. Along the north fork just south of the picnic shelter, old mill race remains are still evident.

To reach Scott Mill County Park from the junction of Indiana 5 and Indiana 120, go east on Indiana 120 about a mile to CR 675W/ Old Indiana 5, where the road curves, and turn left/north. Follow CR 675W/Old Indiana 5 north about one mile to the parking area on the right/east side of the road at the public access site.

14. OLIN LAKE NATURE PRESERVE
Wolcottville, IN/Lagrange County
USGS MAP(s): Oliver Lake 1:24,000
TRAIL(s) DISTANCE: 1.5 mile loop
ACREAGE: 221 acres
ACTIVITIES: nature walk, nature study, canoe access from Oliver Lake

Due to the joint efforts of The Nature Conservancy, ACRES, Inc., the DNR's Division of Nature Preserves, and Oliver Lake Property Owners Association, the 100 acre Olin Lake, a significant undisturbed natural lake, and its surrounding shore, was saved from development and is now managed as a dedicated nature preserve.

Olin Lake is one of four glacial-gouged lakes connected by channel streams: Smith Hole, Martin Lake, Olin Lake and Oliver Lake. The low marshy shoreline supports a forest with northern affinities such as tamarack, yellow birch, skunk cabbage, winterberry, poison sumac, dwarf birch, and alder buckthorn. A quiet testimony to the lake's purity is the cisco, a deep freshwater fish that requires clean unpolluted waters for survival. The only high ground around the lake is located on the south shore where a loop trail penetrates mature beech-maple stands, formerly known as Browand Woods.

The foot path begins at the parking area adjacent to the junction of CR 125E and CR 550S. The marked path heads east and south through the forest upland following the preserve's perimeter and skirting the mushy shore. Besides mature beech and sugar maple, large trees include hackberry, red oak, basswood, tulip and walnut. At one point the trail spurs north to the lake edge and open views of the watery expanse and a island. The hour glass-shaped trail traces an intertwining double loop in the upland forest.

To reach Olin Lake Nature Preserve from Indiana 9 at Wolcottville, on the Lagrange-Noble county line, go north of Wolcottville about two miles on Indiana 9 and turn left/west on CR 660S. Follow CR 600S 1.7 miles to a "T" and CR 125E and turn right/north. Continue on CR 125E 0.5 mile to a marked parking lot on the right/ east side of the road at the CR 550S junction.

Access by canoe to Olin Lake is at the Oliver Lake public access site. From Indiana 9 at the CR 600S turnoff west, continue north on Indiana 9 another 1.5 mile to CR 450S and turn left/west. Follow CR 450S two miles west to the launch ramp. You will need to paddle across Oliver Lake to the channel to Olin Lake.

Olin Lake Nature Preserve

15. DALLAS LAKE/DELT CHURCH/ROGERS COUNTY PARK

Wolcottville, IN/Lagrange County
USGS MAP(s): Oliver Lake 1:24,000
TRAIL(s) DISTANCE: 2 m. DL/2.5 m. DC/ no trails RCPK
ACREAGE: 96 a. DL/119 a. DC/15 a. RCPK
ACTIVITIES: nature walks, nature study, picnicking, shelters, swimming beach, lifeguards, playgrounds, playfields, observation deck, observation tower, fishing, canoeing, x-country skiing, historic village site, special programs, festivals
FEE(s): shelter & lodge rentals

West and south of Olin Lake Nature Preserve are three Lagrange County parks within a few miles of each other with sizeable acreage for exploring on foot.

Dallas Lake Park, located on the south shore of Dallas lake, is a natural setting of woods, marsh, prairie, lake and open green grass spaces. The sand beach is nestled in a protected cove along the wooded shore. A group area is to the north of the beach where cabins and a lodge dot the open area. A scenic marsh observation deck overlooks the north portion of Pond Lil along the entry drive where pullout parking is available.

A two mile loop trail begins adjacent southwest near the entrance of the parking area. The narrow path at the time of visitation was overgrown and obscured by growth as it moved through the young mixed woods east, curving north to cross the service road wide trail to the beach from the parking area.

The trail improves as it follows the lakeshore west to the property boundary, curving south along the perimeter to the entry drive. Follow the park road south a short distance, to where the trail goes east, north of the caretakers residence. The path cuts through a prairie-like area to a loop junction and bears left, paralleling Pond Lil through a wooded area. The trail loop curves south and back west from the woodland to the prairie area back to the park drive. Either follow the original trail back or the park drive.

Dallas Lake Park is open daily at 8 am. The gate closes at 8 pm April to September and 6 pm October through March.

To reach Dallas Lake Park from Wolcottville, Indiana, go north on Indiana 9 one mile to CR 700S and turn left/west. Continue about three miles west on CR 700S around the southeast tip of Westler Lake to the signed park entrance.

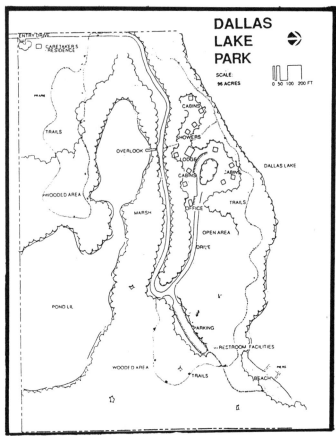

Dallas Lake Park, Lagrange County Parks

Atwood County Beach, on the north side of Atwood Lake, is also located on CR 700S enroute to Dallas Lake Park. The entrance is on the south side of CR 700S less than a mile east and Atwood Beach is open during the summer for swimming.

The next closest Lagrange County park is Delt Church, the largest Lagrange County recreational area. From the entrance road of Dallas Lake, go west on CR 700S about 1.5 miles to CR 200W and turn north/right. Continue north on CR 200W and drive 1.5 miles to the Delt Church entry drive on the right/east side of the road.

Bordering the north branch of the Elkhart River, the county park features floodplain, marsh, upland woods, prairie and open grassy areas. The park facilities such as the picnic shelters are artistically created with a rustic theme. Two nature trails traverse the natural areas of the park.

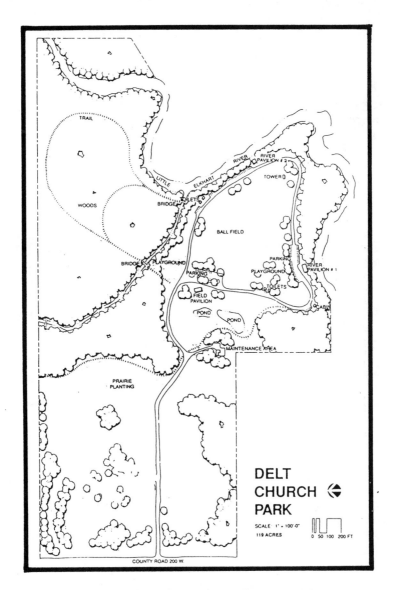

Delt Church Park, Lagrange County Parks

From the river shelter pavilion at the east end of the park, the 1.5 mile River Trail follows the bank upstream along the wooded floodplain, across a footbridge over an incoming channel. The earth path continues along the riparian plain then loops back in a horseshoe fashion to the main park. There is a crossover shortcut spur that cuts the distance in half. The trail can be wet and mosquitoey at times. The river is lake-fed mostly at this point.

161

The second trail, a one mile Prairie Trail, begins north of the second river shelter pavilion and heads north skirting a wooded area, a pond, and the maintenance area before crossing the main park drive. Cross the drive road north into an area that has been allowed to return to prairie. The linear path follows the edge between woods and prairie. Return along the same path. There is room for a loop trail in this prairie section of the park.

Besides nature paths, Delt Church Park facilities include picnicking, river shelter pavilions, playfields, playgrounds, river fishing, canoeing, observation tower and cross country skiing.

North and west of Delt Church Park is the David Rogers County Park. Unlike the Dallas Lake and Delt Church parks, 15 acre Rogers Park is much smaller and without natural areas. It is primarily a historic park with a reconstructed 19th century village, a park utilized for special programs and festivals. The park is a fine place to picnic atop the east to west ridge where there are open views of the Amish farms in the surrounding area.

From Delt Church Park entrance, drive north on CR 700S about 0.5 mile to CR 550S and turn left/west. The park will be on the right/north side of the country road.

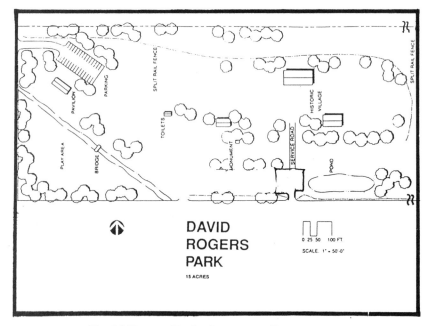

David Rogers Park, Lagrange County Parks

16. LONIDAW NATURE PRESERVE/DETERING NATURE PRESERVE

Kendallville, IN/Noble County
USGS MAP(s): Carina 1:24,000
TRAIL(s) DISTANCE: 1 mile loop LNP/old farm lanes DNP
ACREAGE: 25 a. LNP/50 a. DNP
ACTIVITIES: nature walks, nature study

These two ACRES, Inc. preserves are just over a mile apart by county road. Glaciers from the last ice have shaped the landscape of both of these preserves and so has human influence to some extent.

Lonidaw Nature Preserve is so-named for the legendary crystal clear lake somewhere in northern Indiana where Potawatomi Chief Simon Pokagon and his beloved wife, Lonidaw, built their wigwam home in a stately wood near its shore. Lonidaw is said to mean, "Spirit Queen of the Woods".

The one mile, moderately-easy loop trail begins at the limited parking pullout adjacent west of CR 1000E, northeast of Kendallville. The beech-maple forest path tops the crescent-shaped, narrow esker ridge, sloping gently northwest, past the lower trail fork, to conclude at the north property line. Enroute on return, follow the lower trail fork alongside the

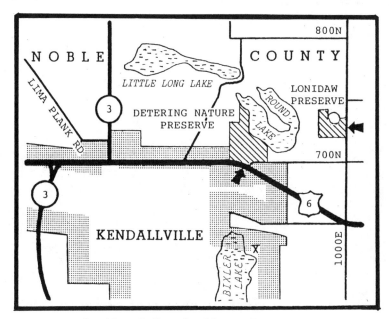

Lonidaw & Detering Nature Preserves

163

lush south edge of Little Whitford Lake, a five acre kettle-pot, glacially carved water body. Lonidaw is a fitting name for this pristine preserve where man's influence appears limited in recent years.

West of Lonidaw Nature Preserve on the south and west shores of Round Lake, is the twice-as-large <u>Detering Nature Preserve</u>. The former farm has rolling uplands of revegetating herbaceous forbs and pioneer trees. Below much of the shoreline is a cattail marsh wetland-shrub forest. A narrow wedge of upland extends to the shore of Round Lake, providing foot access near the southeast portion of the preserve.

The trailhead begins just west of the fine vehicle parking lot at the metal gate near the junction of US 6 and Kammerer road/CR 700N across the highway from the Fairview Center Mall. The 0.25 mile long linear trail is one-way as it makes its winding way to the shore of Round Lake. The trail can be a complete loop following the utility line service road south back to the parking lot.

To reach the ACRES, Inc. preserves, drive east on US 6 from the intersection with Indiana 3 to CR 700N, where US 6 curves southeast, and turn left/east. Detering Nature Preserve is on the left/north side of CR 700E. There is a parking area and a sign in box at the preserve.

Lonidaw Nature Preserve

To reach Lonidaw Nature Preserve, continue east on CR 700E from the junction with US 6 about 0.8 mile to the crossroads with CR 1000E and turn left/north. Follow CR 1000E about 0.3 mile to the preserve on the left/west side of CR 1000E. Be careful turning left on the rise of the road, to the grassy parking area north of the fenced entry gate.

Consider visiting <u>Bixler Lake Park</u> and <u>Wetlands Nature Area</u> in east Kendallville, a few miles south by road.

17. BIXLER LAKE PARK & WETLAND NATURE AREA
Kendallville, IN/Noble County
USGS MAP(s): Kendallville, Corunna 1:24,000
ACREAGE: 170 a. land, 117 a. lake, 75 a. nature area
ACTIVITIES: nature walks, nature study, nature area, herb garden, apiary, picnicking, shelters, beach, swimming, pier, fishing, boating, launch ramp, ballfield, ball courts, x-country skiing, camping, concessions
FEE(s): seasonal entrance, shelter rental, camping

For its size, natural attractions, and quality of facilities, this Kendallville community park is noteworthy; appearing more as if it were a regional county park. Ever since the days of settlement in the 1830s, Bixler Lake has been a popular place to gather among locals. After the Civil War, the scenic glacially-created lake became officially known as Sherman Park and its popularity continued to grow. At the turn of the 20th century, the city took more of an interest in development but it wasn't until the 1960s that a road was opened to the lake's natural east side where picnicking, a second beach and camping were provided. Several improvements have been made since including the dedication of a 75 acre Wetland Nature Area on the southeast shore.

The Kendallville Parks and Recreation Department has established three nature trails within Bixler Lake Park and Wetland Nature Area. The 1.5 mile long <u>Trail 1</u> treks over paved and gravel roads starting from the main park entry gate at Lake Park Drive and follows the north and east shore of the park to the campground. <u>Trail 2</u> is a 1.7 mile loop hike through the Wetland Nature Area. The trailhead begins east of the campground, near one of two observation platforms overlooking the marsh waterfowl area where there are 32 Canada geese nesting sites on the small islands.

Take time to look at the unique open air "nature center" which provides natural history information of Bixler Park's wetlands. At the trailhead, a tree and shrub identification booklet is available. Heading south and west,

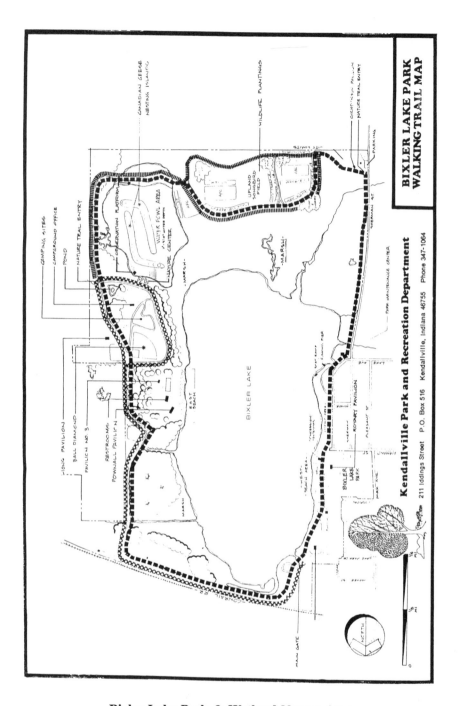

Bixler Lake Park & Wetland Nature Area

the trail moves through beech and sugar maple covered kame uplands, skirting the wetlands. The trail reaches an open area near the waterfowl area where a second observation platform rises out of the cattail-fringed marshland. West, beyond the marsh, the trail forms a loop about a field noted for songbirds and with wildlife plantings. If continuing west to Sherman Street and the southwest trailhead, hikers will discover a herb garden and apiary. The third trail is a 3.1 mile loop around Bixler Lake, combining both Trails 1 and 2. The developed west side of the lake is tame compared to the natural wilds of the opposite east and south shores.

To reach Bixler Park and Wetland Nature Area from US 6 in Kendallville, go south on Main Street, which is east one block of the intersection of Indiana 3 and US 6, to Diamond Street and turn left/east. Drive several blocks east on Diamond Street to Park Avenue and turn left/north. Follow Park Avenue to Lake Park Drive and turn right/east to the east shore of Bixler Lake.

While in the Kendallville area, considering visiting the ACRES, Inc. preserves of Detering Nature Preserve and Lonidaw Nature Preserve, northeast of the city.

18. GENE STRATTON PORTER HISTORIC SITE
Rome City, IN/Noble County
USGS MAP(s): Kendallville 1:24,000
TRAIL(s) DISTANCE: 0.75 mile of garden & woodland paths
ACREAGE: 20 acres
ACTIVITIES: nature walks, nature study, historic site, gardens, tours,
    picnicking, gift shop, special events

Nestled on the south shore of Sylvan Lake is the "Cabin in the Wildflower Woods", the second state memorial homesite of authoress, photographer and naturalist, Gene Stratton-Porter (1863-1924). The nationally acclaimed literary naturalist penned such well read books as Song of the Cardinal, A Girl of Limberlost and Freckles. In 1914, she and her husband moved from "Limberlost Cabin" in Geneva, Indiana (also a state memorial) to the two story white cedar log cabin surrounded by 150 wooded acres. Today visitors may tour the cabin home she designed which is still furnished with her personal memorabilia and library. The 16 room cabin is listed on the National Register of Historic Places.

Just as enjoyable are the adjacent gardens, arbor and woodland. The semi-formal garden is laced with gentle paths that weave among the flowers, herbs and fruit trees with places to rest and contemplate. There is a printed listing of 350 plants growing in the cultivated garden. The garden is listed in the National Gardens of America Register.

Inspirational scenic paths edge the lakeshore. The old large trees of "Wildflower Woods" are exceptional. Beech, sugar and black maples, red oak, white ash, tulip, black cherry, black walnut are found throughout the small but significant acreage. Scheduled wildflower and fall foliage walks are presented by the staff.

The woodland and lakeside trails and gardens are open daily dawn to dusk. Guided cabin tours are available Tuesday through Saturday from 9 am to 5 pm and Sunday 1 pm to 5 pm. Last tours start at 4:30 pm. The cabin is closed mid-December to mid-March, all Mondays and Easter, Thanksgiving and Christmas. Donations are appreciated.

To reach the Gene Stratton-Porter Memorial or "Limberlost North" at the southeast edge of Rome City in northeast Noble County, drive north on Indiana 9 from US 6, three miles to a marked road sign and CR 900N and turn right/east. Continue on CR 900N one mile to the marked property entrance.

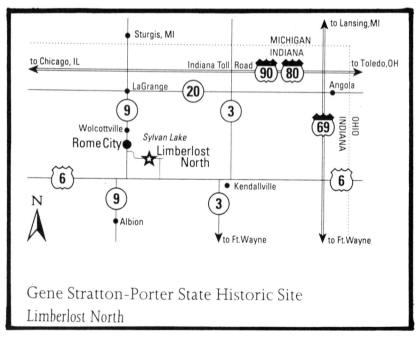

Gene Stratton-Porter State Historic Site
Limberlost North

Wildflower Woods, Gene Stratton Porter State Historic Site

19. EDNA W. SPURGEON WOODLAND RESERVE
Ligonier, IN/Noble County
USGS MAP(s): Ligonier 1:24,000
TRAIL(s) DISTANCE: 1.2 mile loop
ACREAGE: 65 acres
ACTIVITIES: nature walk, nature study

Locally known as "The Knobs", the Edna W. Spurgeon Reserve embraces a varied landscape of deep ravines and rolling uplands. Acquired by ACRES, Inc. from land donated from Mrs. Spurgeon, "The Knobs", unlike the sandstone rock, chestnut oak-covered high ridges of southern Indiana, are actually low glacial ridges of kame that are deeply carved by the erosive force of water. Oftentimes mined for its sand and gravel, kame is stratified or layered drift deposited by glacial meltwaters. This morainal topography make the hike interesting and slightly physically challenging.

The 1.2 mile loop trail exemplifies the geology and botanical features of the reserve. From the parking lot the trail heads east through a segment of bluegrass herbaceous field to enter the rich forest. The large second growth is predominately beech-sugar maple and also includes such deciduous trees as black cherry, red elm, basswood, green and white ash, red oak, hackberry, red maple, bitternut hickory and ironwood. Some oak-hickory and mixed forest occurs in the far eastern portion of the

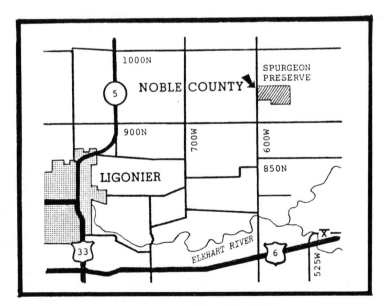

Edna W. Spurgeon Woodland Preserve

reserve. Nearly the largest in the state, tulip trees reach great heights and diameter in the lush moist ravines. Walking through the tall trees is a rare experience that brings a surge of joy to those who revere nature's natural wonders. Two foot bridges allow easy passage over the deepest ravines as the trail traces a loop through the reserve to return to the parking area. The reserve is also a dedicated state nature preserve.

To reach Edna W. Spurgeon Woodland Reserve from Ligonier in northwest Noble County, drive east of the junction of Indiana 33 and US 6, on US 6, 2.5 miles to CR 600W and turn left/north. Follow CR 600W north 2.2 miles to a signed parking area on the east side of the county road.

20. LLOYD W. BENDER MEMORIAL FOREST
Albion, IN/Noble County
USGS MAP(s): Albion 1:24,000
TRAIL(s) DISTANCE: 1 mile loop
ACREAGE: 116 acres, 60 acres dedicated
ACTIVITIES: nature walk, nature study

Positioned on the upper reaches of the South Branch of the Little Elkhart River, this ACRES, Inc. preserve yields a variety of plant communities including upland oak-hickory forest, old herbaceous fields, lowland forest and sedge meadow. Locally the meandering broad floodplain is known as "The Spreads". The outstanding natural feature of the sanctuary is the old growth lowland forest adjacent to the stream.

From the small parking area at River Road, the trail heads west along an old farm lane through abandoned fields undergoing various successional stages. The grassy path gives way to enter young oak-hickory forest where a sign outlines the loop trail.

The forest path continues west following the south perimeter of the property, skirting a wet immature wooded lowland. The upland trail follows the oak-hickory covered morainic ridge to gradually descend to the old growth floodplain forest and the river. Sizeable tree species include red and silver maples, green and black ashes, swamp white and bur oaks, red elm, cottonwood and black willow. Stinging wood nettle, poison ivy and swamp rose are also common in the rich alluvial soil as well as royal and cinnamon ferns. The Little Elkhart River marks the west and north boundary of the 60 acre dedicated state nature preserve portion of the memorial forest. The other inaccessible half of the memorial forest lies across the river.

The trail continues to follow the floodplain north and curves east to a second oak-hickory ridge that is about 20 feet higher than the floodplain. The high and dry trail continues east and then gradually slides south to cut through old woody fields along the east perimeter to return to the trail sign and the old farm lane back to the parking area.

Lloyd W. Bender Memorial Forest is located two miles southwest of Albion, Indiana, the county seat of Noble County. From Indiana 9, drive south of Albion and turn west/right onto River Road/ 250N. Continue on River Road following the winding road to a marked parking area on the right/west side of the road.

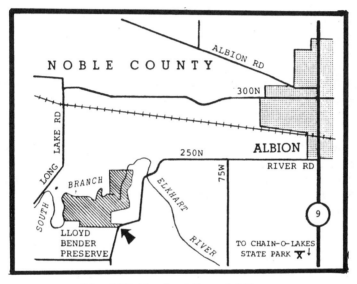

Lloyd W. Bender Memorial Forest

21. CHAIN O' LAKES STATE PARK

Albion, IN/Noble County
USGS MAP(s): Merriam, Ege 1:24,000
TRAIL(s) DISTANCE: 9 trails total 8.35 miles
ACREAGE: 2,678 acres
ACTIVITIES: nature walks, nature study, nature center, seasonal naturalist, cross country skiing, canoeing, launch ramps, picnicking, shelters, swimming beach, lifeguards, bathhouse, pier, fishing, playgrounds, playfields, winter sports, cultural arts programs, Class A, B, & C campground, canoe camp, youth & rally campground, family cabins, camp store, concessions
FEE(s): seasonal entrance, shelter, boat & canoe

True to the park's name, eleven glacially-carved kettle-hole lakes surrounded by upland kames form an east to west horizontal chain. Eight of the eleven water bodies are connected by ice carved channels: Long Lake, Dock Lake, Bowen Lake, Sand Lake, Weber Lake, Mud Lake, Rivir Lake and Miller Lake. When the water level is high, canoeists can easily glide from one lake to another. Several of the trails skirt or encircle these ancient lakes that were formed 10,000 years ago.

Recent improvements provide eight marked and maintained, easy to moderate nature trails that range in length from 0.5 to 2.5 miles. The 5.5 miles of cross country ski trails cover portions or all of Trails 1, 2, 3, 6 and 8 and the open area of the campground. A brief summary of the nameless numbered paths follows:

Trail 1: The 1.5 mile loop begins north of the main campground, across the park road, next to the fish cleaning station. The wide trail follows a young wooded ridge northeast, gradually sloping and curving north, before dropping down in a valley. It crosses two channels as it circles around the north side of Dock Lake, and returns to the campground.

Trail 2: This trail circles Bowen Lake. The 1.0 mile loop foot path begins at the parking lot on north shore of Bowen Lake. It follows the lake shore through the woods past a burial mound and returns to the parking lot.

Trail 3: The 0.5 mile linear trail also begins at the main campground entrance at the west edge. The path heads west and parallels the park road to end at the beach and concession area of Sand Lake. Trails 1 and 3 are basically campground connector trails to the main trail network and park facilities.

Trail 4: The one mile long linear, west to east trail leads through the more remote west area of the park. From the trailhead at Norman Lake, east of the youth and rally campground, walk southeast, crossing the park road, and continuing to the foot bridge over the channel connecting Mud and Rivir lakes. The canoe camp is just south of the channel crossing on the east shore of Rivir Lake. Proceed east on Trail 4 through the swampy lowland near the south shore of Mud Lake, crossing an inlet stream, to eventually conclude and connect with Trail 5 on the northwest shore of Sand Lake. Retrace Trail 4 back to the Norman Lake trailhead one mile.

Trail 5: The 1.3 mile loop trail encircles Sand Lake, the largest of the eleven lakes, and may be walked either direction. The easy lakeside path begins/ends at the boat rental or adjacent south beach and concession area. Along the north shore, the trail crosses two foot bridges over channels leading to Bowen and Weber lakes. Trail 5 intersects Trails 4, 3 and combines with Trail 7 on the north shore.

Trail 9, Chain O' Lakes State Park

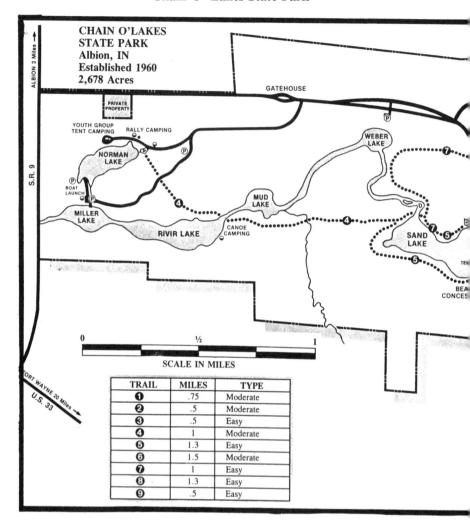

CHAIN O'LAKES
STATE PARK
Albion, IN
Established 1960
2,678 Acres

TRAIL	MILES	TYPE
❶	.75	Moderate
❷	.5	Moderate
❸	.5	Easy
❹	1	Moderate
❺	1.3	Easy
❻	1.5	Moderate
❼	1	Easy
❽	1.3	Easy
❾	.5	Easy

Trail 6: The longest and most remote trail in the park. Trail 6 may be accessed from Trail 1. From near the Dock Lake launch, Trail 6 follows the south shore of Dock Lake and continues east along the connecting channel between Dock Lake and Long Lake, accessing Trail 1 and crossing the park road enroute. The trail proceeds southeast along the shore of long Lake, past the cabin fishing pier and boat dock, skirting the cabin area. In the secluded southeast section of the park, the trail loops back to the Family Cabin playground area and terminates. If you prefer not to retrace Trail 6, follow the park road in the cabin area west, back to the main park road and the campground.

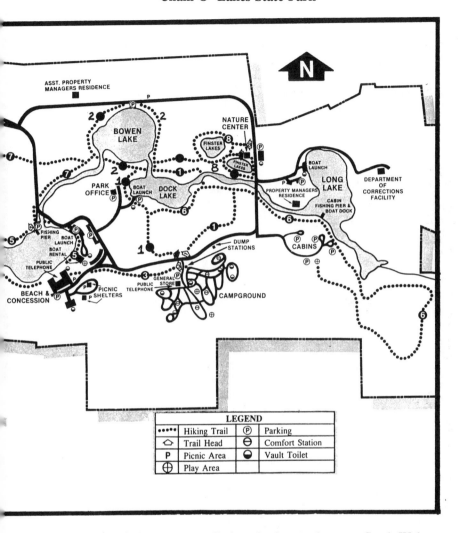

Trail 7: This trail forms a one mile loop in the area between Sand, Weber and Bowen lakes. Park at the fishing pier on Sand Lake's north shore or access Trail 7 via Trails 5 or 2. Trail 7 follows along the channel to Bowen Lake, then turns west to connect with Weber Lake and return along the channel to Sand Lake. It winds through lowlands, along two different channels, and through an upland forest.

Trail 8: Parking for Trail 8 is located at the Stanley Schoolhouse Nature Center. The 0.5 mile trail circles North Finster Lake, crossing a glacial kame, and returns to the Nature Center. Unlike Sand Lake and Trail 5, this lakeshore is undeveloped and natural. Trail 8 provides access to Trails 1, 2,and 7. This trail is also a self-guiding interpretive trail with 15 stations, looping around North Finister Lake adjacent to the Stanley Schoolhouse Nature Center. The flora, fauna, geology and forest ecology of the lake are described.

To reach the Chain O' Lakes State Park entrance, drive south on Indiana 9 from Albion, the county seat of Noble County, five miles to the entry road on the left/east side of the highway at 2355 East 75S. The park hours unless camping are 7 am to 11 pm.

22. MERRY LEA ENVIRONMENTAL LEARNING CENTER & NATURE PRESERVE
Wolf Lake, IN/Noble County
USGS MAP(s); Ormas 1:24,000
TRAIL(s) DISTANCE: 5.5 miles
ACREAGE: 1,150 acres
ACTIVITIES: nature walks, nature study, nature preserve, environmental learning center, picnicking, x-country skiing, hayrides, group tours, programs, events, membership
FEE(s): facility rental, programs

Merry Lea's extensive acreage was mostly acquired by The Nature Conservancy from private owners and was transferred to Goshen College, the present owners and managers, for environmental education purposes. The Merry Lea Nature Preserve is a 250 acre state dedicated nature preserve within the 1,150 acres and is accessible by permission only. Retired fields, meadows, forest, bogs, lakes and prairie comprise the natural communities visitors may experience along the level and easy trails which are open to the public daily 9 a.m. to 5 pm. The Environmental Learning Center's hours are 8 am to 5 pm, Monday through Friday.

Three miles of marked and maintained trails radiate out from the Environmental Learning Center and parking area in the direction of Bear and Cub Lakes and Kesling Farm. Nearly all of the melodious named paths loop and can be combined for longer or shorter hikes. Within the immediate area of the Center are Mary's Loop, Maple Bottom, Hickory Ridge, Walnut Trail, Luckey Lane, and Big Oak. Prairie Loop and Lee's Trace (some of the best hikes), pass through the alkaline prairie along the south shore of Bear Lake. Continuing east are the north and south trails of Cub Lake. The Wysong Trail leads through recently cultivated farm land and meadow, connecting the west property to the east property and Kesling Farm. The Kesling Loops are trails that encircle the rolling farmscape and wetlands in the area west of the Kesling Farm. During snowy winters, the foot trails become ski trails, open whenever people wish to ski. No fee is charged. Wildflower walks are given in April and May and in October there are Sunday fall color tours. For further information write or phone Merry Lea at Box 263, Wolf Lake, Indiana 46796 (219) 799-5869.

Merry Lea Environmental Learning Center is located in southwest Noble County (west of Chain O' Lakes State Park), 2.5 miles southwest of Wolf Lake, Indiana. Drive south from Wolf Lake on Indiana 109 about two miles and turn right/west onto CR 350S. Proceed one mile on CR 350S and turn right/north on CR 500W. Follow CR 500W about 0.5 mile north to the entrance. Continue north on the entrance drive to the parking area and the environmental learning center.

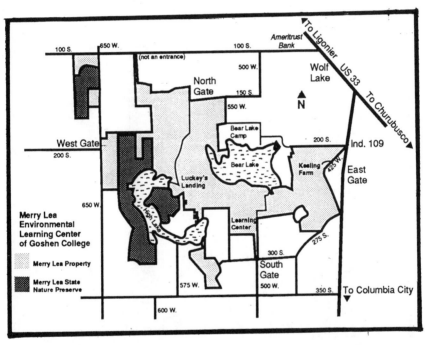

Merry Lea Environmental Learning Center & Nature Preserve

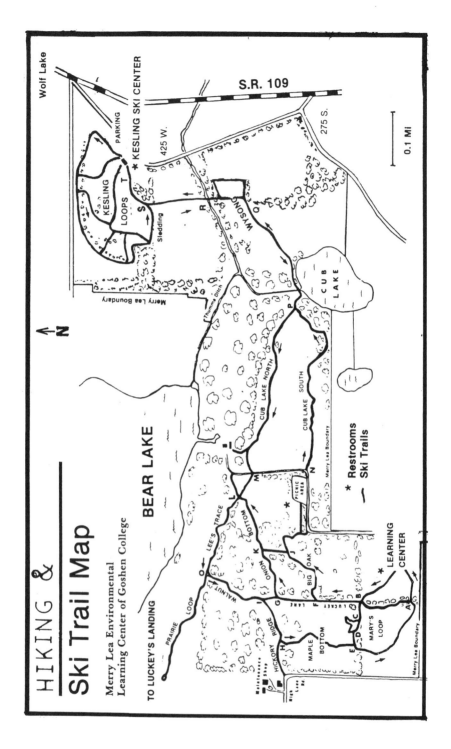

HIKING & Ski Trail Map

Merry Lea Environmental
Learning Center of Goshen College

BEAR LAKE

TO LUCKEY'S LANDING

Wolf Lake

PARKING

★ KESLING SKI CENTER

S.R. 109

425 W.

275 S.

0.1 Mi

N

KESLING LOOPS

Sledding

Merry Lea Boundary

Thumm Ditch

CUB LAKE

CUB LAKE NORTH

CUB LAKE SOUTH

Merry Lea Boundary

PICNIC AREA

★ Restrooms

— Ski Trails

LEE'S TRACE

ONION BOTTOM

PRAIRIE LOOP

WALNUT

HICKORY RIDGE

MAPLE BOTTOM

BIG OAK

LUCKEY LAKE

MARY'S LOOP

LEARNING CENTER

Merry Lea Boundary

178

23. CROOKED LAKE NATURE PRESERVE
Merriam, IN/Whitley & Noble Counties
USGS MAP(s): Merriam 1:24,000
TRAIL(s) DISTANCE: 2 loop trail total appx. 2.5 miles
ACREAGE: 101 acres
ACTIVITIES: nature walks, nature study

Crooked Lake Nature Preserve is among the most noteworthy natural experiences in the lake area of northern Indiana. The picturesque 206 acre glacial body of water is spring-fed and regarded by many limnologists as having the greatest depth (105 feet) and purity of waters of any natural lake in the state. Proof of purity lies in the fact that the state-endangered cisco fish or "lake herring", a member of the trout family, thrives in the lake bottoms; a freshwater fish dependent on clean water for survival. The preserve is located on the north and east shores and has 3,500 feet of lake frontage and nearly the same distance of shoreline trail. The upland forested slopes and bluffs protect the lake from erosive runoff. Cattail marsh, marl beach, meadow, abandoned field, lush ravines and an island are also found in the preserve. Lucky are those who live in the private homes overlooking the lake on the south and west shores, for they realize their preserve view will be permanent. This special area is the result of The Nature Conservancy, the DNR's Division of Nature Preserves, ACRES, Inc. and the Crooked Lake Property Owners working together for the common good of all.

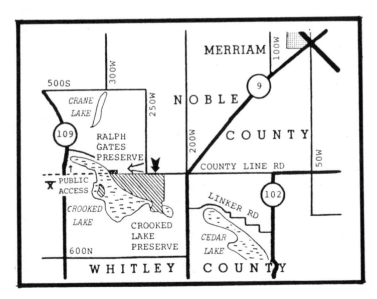

Crooked Lake Nature Preserve

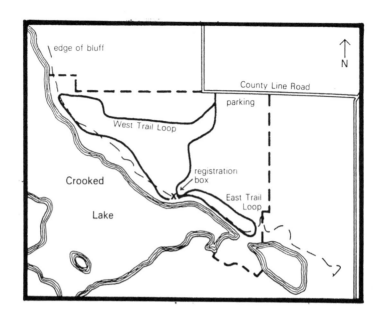

Crooked Lake Nature Preserve Trails

The two self-guiding and interconnecting trails are the East Loop and the West Loop. From the parking area at 250W and County Line Road, walk past the old barn and abandoned fields south down the farm lane towards the lake. Continue down the slope to the registration box where an interpretive trail map brochure may be obtained. The East Loop begins to the left and parallels the marshy lakeshore along a boardwalk and loops back to traverse the bluff top. A scenic ravine along this upper segment is dubbed the Tall Trees Memorial Grove and the pioneer Leaman family cemetery overlooks the lake. The loop trail descends the bluff curving closer to the lake and the registration box. The West Loop heads west/right of this spot. The forested shoreline path is higher and drier than the East Loop but there are wet segments with boardwalk. The trail continues up and down and curves back east at the pine plantation to top the upland and continues across the old field to the parking area. Further west of the nature preserve is the Indiana University Biological Station which monitors the life quality of the lake.

To reach Crooked Lake Nature Preserve from US 30 at Columbia City, drive north on Indiana 9 about 7 miles to the Noble-Whitley county line. Turn west/left on County Line Road and drive 0.5 mile to a marked parking area on the south side of the road, before the road curves north on CR 250W.

Further Notes on Noble County

Noble County, like several counties in the northeast lake region of Indiana, has a number of unique nature places to explore. Several wetlands were omitted from the main text since these watery realms made foot access nearly impossible. For the sake of being more comprehensive, they are included in these further notes.

The 94 acre <u>Swamp Angel Nature Preserve</u> (USGS Maps Wolcottville, Kendallville 1:24,000), owned and managed by The Nature Conservancy, is located on the shores of Needham and Grannis lakes in northeast Noble County. The preserve contains a marsh, fen, tamarack swamp forest and upland oak groves. The sanctuary also includes several rare plants and animals. Permission to enter the preserve must be obtained in advance to protect the fragile area.

The <u>Rome City Wetland Conservation Area</u>, also called the <u>North Branch of the Elkhart Wetlands</u> (USGS Map Oliver Lake 1:24,000) comprises 50 acres of extensive cattail floodplain, three miles west of Rome City and 0.5 mile west of Jones Lake on the north side of CR 1050N. Views are difficult to come by of the open wetland even from the road.

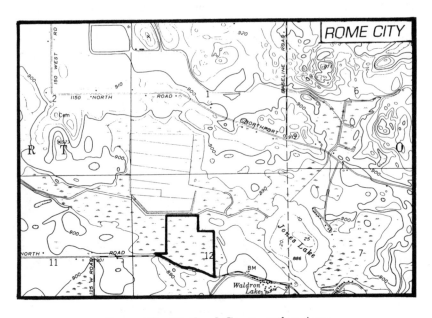

Rome City Wetland Conservation Area

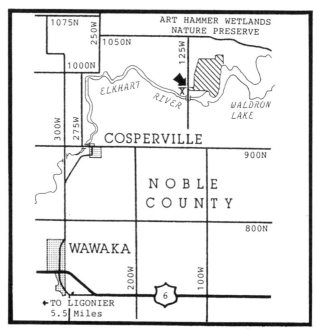

Art Hammer Wetlands nature Preserve

Further south about a mile or so along the North Branch of the Elkhart River is the Art Hammer Wetlands Nature Preserve (USGS Maps Albion, Oliver Lake 1:24,000), an ACRES, Inc. property that is a dedicated nature preserve. Attempts have been made to establish a trail through the 124 acre riparian and marsh wetlands but a boardwalk would be more in order. Best time to visit is during a dry autumn day. Park at the public access site at Dukes Bridge, CR 125W, four miles northeast of Wawaka.

Mallard Roost Wetland Conservation Area (USGS Maps Ligonier, Albion 1:24,000) is 760 acres of one of the most outstanding wetlands still found in Indiana. The area occupies a wide floodplain of the South Branch of the Elkhart River known as "The Spread". Rising above the flats is the 1,000 foot Diamond Hill to the west which adds to the scenery. One mile south from the CR 600N bridge at the Albion Road bridge is The Nature Conservancy's 145 addition to the Mallard Roost wetlands. Canoeing is the best way to explore the Mallard Roost expanse. A public access site is located at the CR 550 bridge, two miles southeast of Diamond Lake.

Just west of Mallard Roost wetlands and southwest of Diamond Lake is the Eagle Lake Wetland Conservation Area and Nature Preserve (USGS Map Ligonier 1:24,000). The 137 acre area completely envelopes the 59 acre Eagle Lake which is nearly undeveloped. There is a public access site

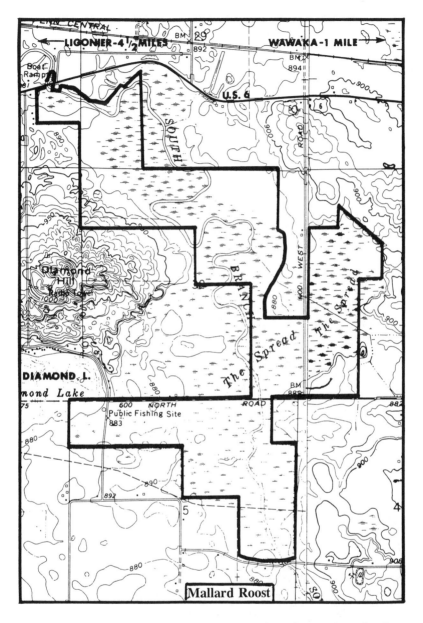

on the southwest shore at CR 500N. Fisherman's paths are along the shore near the launch ramp. A wedge of upland juts out into the lake at the southwest shore but access is difficult. Eagle Lake is another great canoeing opportunity. Eagle Lake is located two miles south of Ligonier on US 33 and two miles east on CR 500N. Be advised the wetland conservation areas allow hunting in season.

24. BONNEYVILLE MILL COUNTY PARK
Bristol, IN/Elkhart County
USGS MAP(s): Bristol 1:24,000
TRAIL(s) DISTANCE: appx. 5 miles of foot trails
ACREAGE: 223 acres
ACTIVITIES: nature walks, nature study, historic site, mill tours, picnicking, shelters, observation tower, playground, fishing, x-country skiing, sledding, snowmobile trail, special events
FEE(s): picnic shelter rental

Located on the Little Elkhart River, picturesque Bonneyville gristmill is the essence of this Elkhart County Park. Built in 1832 by Edward Bonney, the water-powered gristmill still stone grinds corn, wheat, rye and buckwheat and sells the fresh flour to the visiting public from May 1 - October 31, 10 am to 5 pm daily.

Surrounding the gristmill are natural areas of floodplain forest, marshy wetlands, old abandoned fields and upland forest to explore. The nature trails interwind and serve as winter cross country ski trails. The park is trisected by country roads.

To access the first area on the north and east portion of the park property, drive south from Indiana 120 on CR 131 about 0.10 mile to the parking lot on the left/east side of CR 131.

From the parking lot there are three directions to walk. A nature trail loops about the perimeter north of the parking lot. From the Kum Mol Rie picnic shelter a trail goes east into the 68 acre recent addition made possible by The Nature Conservancy. The trail forms a loop in the woods and wetlands along the Little Elkhart River. A third trail, the Alder Loop Nature Trail, leads south towards the old mill, and crosses several foot bridges and boardwalks over and along the scenic meandering river branch. The trail loops back to the original parking lot. During high water the trail would be difficult to traverse. In addition, the 62 mile Miami Snowmobile Trail begins at the parking lot and is open to snowmobilers during the winter months. These north and east property trails are also easily accessed from the old Bonneyville Mill main parking area located 0.5 mile south on CR 131 from Indiana 120.

The southern two-thirds of the park (south of the Little Elkhart River and old mill) is a combination of old fields, wetlands, and upland forest. The central portion between CR 131 and CR 8 is easily reached from the old mill main parking lot by walking south across CR 131. A loop trail skirts Valley Line picnic shelter and a small pond. Cross over CR 8 south

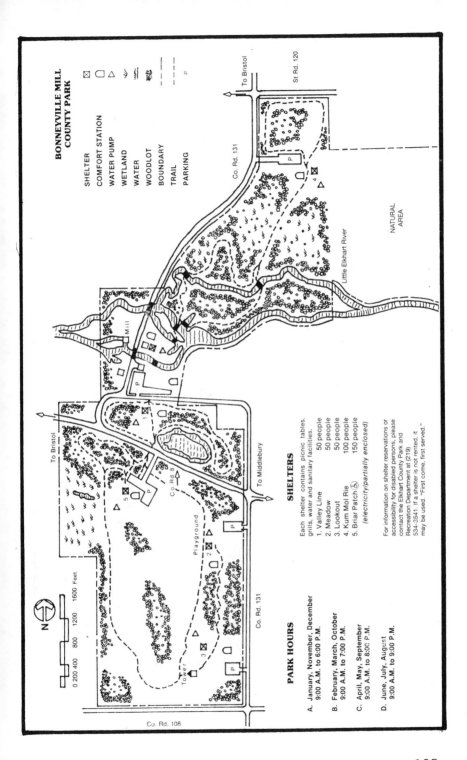

BONNEYVILLE MILL COUNTY PARK

SHELTER
COMFORT STATION
WATER PUMP
WETLAND
WATER
WOODLOT
BOUNDARY
TRAIL
PARKING

SHELTERS

Each shelter contains picnic tables, grills, water and sanitary facilities.

1. Valley Line — 50 people
2. Meadow — 50 people
3. Lookout — 50 people
4. Kum Mol Rie — 100 people
5. Briar Patch ♿ — 150 people

(electricity/partially enclosed)

For information on shelter reservations or accessibility for disabled persons, please contact the Elkhart County Park and Recreation Department at (219) 534-3541. If a shelter is not rented, it may be used. "First come, first served."

PARK HOURS

A. January, November, December
9:00 A.M. to 6:00 P.M.

B. February, March, October
9:00 A.M. to 7:00 P.M.

C. April, May, September
9:00 A.M. to 8:00 P.M.

D. June, July, August
9:00 A.M. to 9:00 P.M.

To Bristol
St. Rd. 120
Co. Rd. 131
NATURAL AREA
Little Elkhart River
Mill
To Middlebury
Co Rd 8
Playground
Tower
Co. Rd. 131
Co. Rd. 108
To Bristol

N
0 200 400 800 1200 1600 Feet

185

to access a longer loop trail in the southern third of the park. The trail follows the edge between marsh and field and forest. The observation tower near Lookout picnic shelter provides excellent views of the surrounding park and the rolling landscape beyond to the northwest. Parking lots are located along CR 8 and CR 131 that access the southern third.

The park is open at 9 am daily. The park closes at 6 pm November, December, and January; 7 pm February, March and October; 8 pm April, May and September; and 9 pm June, July and August. Bonneyville County Park is located east of Bristol on Indiana 120, 2.5 miles, turning south/right on CR 131 and driving 0.5 mile to the main parking area near the old mill.

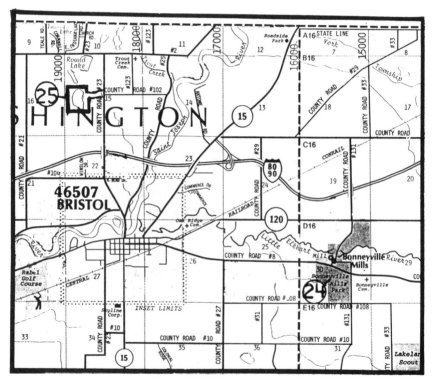

Bonneyville Mill County Park (24)
William L. Lieber Nature Preserve (25)

25. WILLIAM L. LIEBER NATURE PRESERVE
Bristol, IN/Elkhart County
USGS MAP(s): Bristol 1:24,000
TRAIL(s) DISTANCE: appx. 2 miles of user and deer paths
ACREAGE: 135 acres
ACTIVITIES: nature hike, nature study

For those who enjoy going afoot and afield and don't mind getting their feet wet, the William L. Lieber Nature Preserve is an experience well-suited for exploratory intrepid souls. Acquired by The Nature Conservancy, the preserve is now owned and managed by the DNR Division of Nature Preserves. The main highlight of the preserve is Pipewort Pond and the surrounding shoreline flats that harbor plants that normally thrive along the Atlantic Coastal seaboard such as the not-so-conspicuous sedges and rushes. A special botanical feature of the preserve is a cranberry bog. The best season to visit is late summer or early fall when the usually dry weather results in a drier shoreline providing easier access.

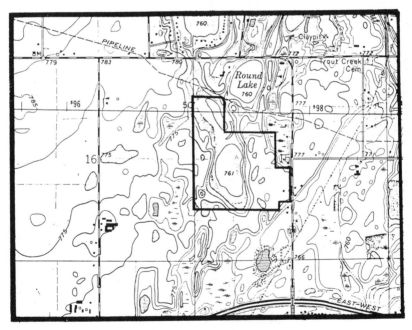

Pipewort Pond Nature Preserve
(William L. Lieber Nature Preserve)

From the small roadside parking lot near old farm buildings, follow the old farm lane due west to the woodland. Enter the woods continuing west to pondside. Follow the forested shore around the pond in a clockwise fashion. Deer and other wildlife have established their own trail network. The west shore affords the best woods and upland segment surrounding the pond. The north property is low, usually wet and mucky but it can be circumnavigated. Eventually you will arrive full circle. Walk east back along the farm lane to the parking area.

To reach William L. Lieber Nature Preserve and Pipewort Pond in extreme north central Elkhart County, go north from the intersection of Indiana 15 and Indiana 120 in Bristol, on the jog, crossing over the St. Joseph River and curving left/west at the fork on North Indiana Lake Road. Continue north out of Bristol and the road name becomes Division Road/CR 23. Cross over the Indiana Toll Road/I-80-90 and continue 0.5 mile to about where CR 23 intersects with CR 102. Park in the tiny lot on the west side of CR 23 and walk west (see No. 24 location map). A State Nature Preserve sign marks the preserve.

West of Pipewort Pond about five miles is the newly acquired Elkhart Bog by the DNR's Division of Nature Preserves. The 154 acre wetland is open for visitation but there are no trails except for old lanes. From the CR 23 parking lot, continue north on CR 23 about 0.5 mile to the "T" junction of CR 2. Turn west/left on CR 2 and continue a little over a mile to a second "T" junction and CR 19. Turn south/left on CR 19 and drive about one mile to CR 4 and turn right/west. Continue about 1.5 mile west on CR 4 to CR 15 and turn north. Follow CR 15 north 0.5 mile to a parking area at the southwest corner of Elkhart Bog.

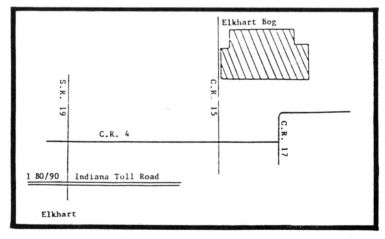

Elkhart Bog Nature Preserve

26. CONLEY WILDLIFE REFUGE

Bristol, IN/Elkhart County
USGS MAP(s): Bristol 1:24,000
TRAIL(s) DISTANCE: appx. 1 mile of user path & old farm lane
ACREAGE: 100 acres
ACTIVITIES: nature walk, nature study

The Conley Wildlife Refuge occupies high rolling glacial till and kame land that encompasses such natural attractions as oak-hickory forest, dry sand prairie, and several small ponds. Acquired in 1987, The Nature Conservancy property was a gift of the Lilian Conley estate.

Parking is currently limited to the roadside shoulder along CR 23. More specifically, park on the east roadside shoulder at the northeast edge of the refuge, just north of the electrical pylon towers that cross the property. An unmarked but conspicuous path along the west side of CR 23 enters a tree opening, leading up the slope to access the sunny open dry sand prairie. Continue to follow the narrow user path through the middle of the dry prairie to the forest where the trail becomes what was an old farm lane. Walking west through maturing deciduous forest, a pond will appear through the forest opening on the right/north. Eventually the old lane reaches the west boundary and bears left/south leading down ridge to emerge at a private residence. The point to point trail goes and returns along the same pathway however feel free to explore the 100 acre refuge.

To reach Conley Wildlife Refuge in north central Elkhart County, go south from Bristol on Indiana 15 two miles to CR 14 and turn right/west. Proceed on CR 14 0.75 miles to CR 23 and turn left/south. Drive 0.4 mile to the northeast property boundary.

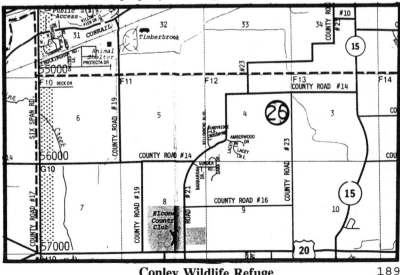

Conley Wildlife Refuge

27. ELKHART NATURE PLACES

ACTIVITIES: nature walks, nature study, environmental education center, canoeing, launch ramp, amphitheatre, picnicking, shelters, playfields, ballfields, playgrounds, fishing, bandstand, bandshell, fountains, sculpture, gazebo, gardens, observation tower, art league, historic sites, rivergreenway

Elkhart, the largest city in Elkhart County, is positioned at the confluence of the Elkhart River and the St. Joseph River in northwest Elkhart County. Nearly all of the best nature walks in this industrial city parallels these two rivers.

The 30 acre Elkhart Environmental Center (**E**) along the south bank of the Elkhart River in southwest Elkhart is uniquely different. In a cooperative effort by the city of Elkhart and the University of Notre Dame, the former landfill site is now an active recycling education center, teaching how to reuse "trash" and keep it out of future landfills. There are ten acres of model displays such as compost piles and a corn crop for ethanol and much more. The Center also includes a short trail along the Elkhart River that ties together wetlands-from-landfills, canoe launch ramp, amphitheatre, a waterfowl island and a log cabin environmental center. The EEC is located at the end of Lusher Avenue at 1717 Lusher Avenue, easily accessed from US 33. Plans are being made to connect the Center with Studebaker Park, downstream by trail.

A couple of river bends downstream is 39 acre Studebaker Park (**S**) located at 1020 McDonald Street. The city parkland of open spaces and large trees features a paved path along a north bend floodplain. A footbridge leads over the Elkhart River to Baker and F.O.P. Parks on the north bank where there are recreational facilities.

A few more bends downstream on the Elkhart River from Studebaker-- Baker-F.O.P. Parks is American Park (**A**), situated at the last big bend of the river before it joins the St. Joseph River at Island Park. By road, the wooded riparian park is just west from Goshen Avenue.

Island Park (**I**), at the mouth of the Elkhart River, gives the city of Elkhart its current nickname, "City with a Heart", and supposedly the origin of its place name, Elkhart, in reference to the elk heart-shaped island. The Conn Bandstand, park pavilion and an artesian fountain are the main attractions of the seven acre Island Park, which has been a literal "island of green" in downtown since 1887. There are three foot bridges to the island that in turn, connect four other city parks along the rivergreenway: Bicentennial, Pulaski, High Dive and Beardsley.

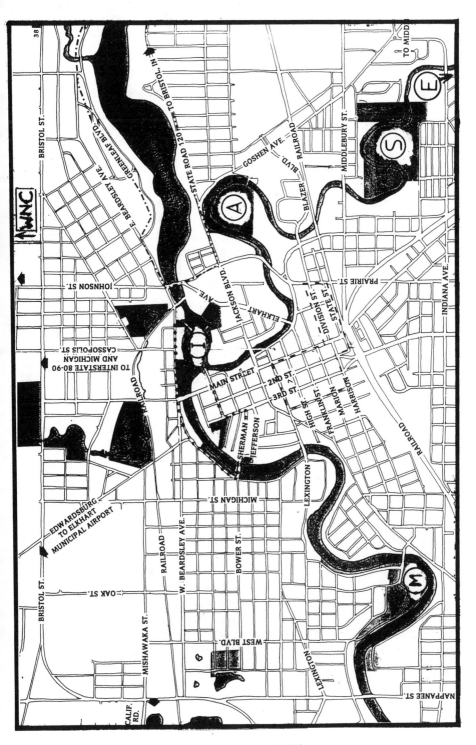

ELKHART PARKS

The annual Rhapsody in Green Festival held the second weekend in June is held at Island Park and draws over 30,000 Festival goers each year. Summer concerts are also held in Island and McNaughten Parks.

Across the south foot bridge over the St. Joseph River is Bicentennial Park which includes picnic sites, fishing area, playground and the YMCA-YWCA building. From Bicentennial Park west, a second footbridge spans the Elkhart Fiver and leads downtown. South along the east bank of the stream from the park is Waterfall Park, which is in the developmental stage.

Across the north foot bridge from Island Park over the St. Joseph River is Pulaski Park, the site of the former village of Pulaski with its historic "firsts" sites and picnicking area. Across Beardsley Avenue north is High Dive Park. This scenic urbane park comprises a footbridge over Christiana Creek, fountain ponds, outdoor sculpture, gazebo, fragrance gardens, pavilion, observation tower, and the Elkhart Art League center.

The third foot bridge from Island Park goes west towards downtown but turn right/north onto Main Street and crossover to the north bank of the St. Joseph River over the traffic bridge to Beardsley Park, the scene of summer concerts, picnicking and fishing. The park is so-named in honor of Elkhart's founder whose former home is "catty-corner" across Beardsley Avenue.

Three river bends downstream on the St. Joseph River from Island Park is McNaughton Park (M), at 701 Arcadia Avenue. The 25 acre river front park is fairly active with its ballfields and playfields, band shell, picnic areas, tennis courts, horseshoe courts, wading pool, boat launch ramp and more.

Away from the rivers to the north of the city on Johnson Street to Woodlawn west, north of High Dive Park about a dozen blocks, is the ten acre Woodlawn Nature Center (WNC). The natural history museum and nature center contains displays, dioramas and exhibits of seashells, Indian artifacts, fossils, an active beehive, wildlife viewing room and a library. There are special events and group tours. The little woods to the immediate east of the nature center has a 0.75 mile nature trail looping through the big trees. The Woodlawn Nature Center was privately established in 1965 by Dorothy Boynton, who loved nature and wanted to share it with others. The hours are Tuesday through Saturday, 9:30 am. to 4:30 pm. Call the Center for group tours by the naturalist director at (219) 264-0525. The address is 604 Woodlawn Avenue.

28. OX BOW COUNTY PARK

Dunlap, IN/Elkhart County
USGS MAP(s): Elkhart, Foraker 1:24,000
TRAIL(s) DISTANCE: appx. 5 miles
ACREAGE: 233
ACTIVITIES: nature walks, nature study, naturalist programs, picnicking, shelters, enclosed shelter, bicycling, fishing, canoeing, small boat launch ramp, playgrounds, observation tower, archery range, horseshoe pits, volleyball, disc golf, x-country skiing, sledding, open air chapel
FEE(s): entrance every day except Wednesday April-October, shelter rental, disc golf, archery range

Established in 1969 as the first Elkhart County park, Ox Bow Park is situated along the south bank of the Elkhart River midway between Elkhart and Goshen, Indiana. The place name, Ox Bow, is in reference to the U-shaped lagoons that formed when the river changed its meandering course, cutting off the old streambed. Originating with early settlers, an ox bow is a U-shaped frame that forms a collar on a ox's neck and supports the yoke that pulls the wagon. The ancient ox bow-shaped river channel of the Elkhart River is still evident in the park today.

The five miles of trails traverse several natural communities including floodplain forest, upland hardwood forest, meadows, prairie and marsh wetlands. All of these communities can be visited by hiking the park's three mile perimeter trail. An observation tower just off the trail provides hikers with a bird's eye view of the park and surrounding area. Several connecting trails allow hikers to link different trails, creating a variety of loops of varying distances.

The orange coded Witmer Trace National Recreation Trail forms a loop within the main park road loop. The mile long trail crosses several boardwalks and has 30 trees, shrubs and vines identified along the way. A self-guiding brochure is available at the trail head just west of the Ox Bow Haus Shelter. Witmer Trace is named after Dr. S. W. Witmer, who taught botany for many years at Goshen College. Dr. Witmer has also identified over 70 different species of trees at Ox Bow Park.

Ox Bow County Park is located east of Dunlap, Indiana. From US 33 about 1.5 mile south of Dunlap, turn north/left onto CR 15 and cross the Conrail railroad crossing and turn left/northwest onto CR 45/Hammond Street. Follow CR 45/Hammond Street to the park entrance on the right/north side of the road.

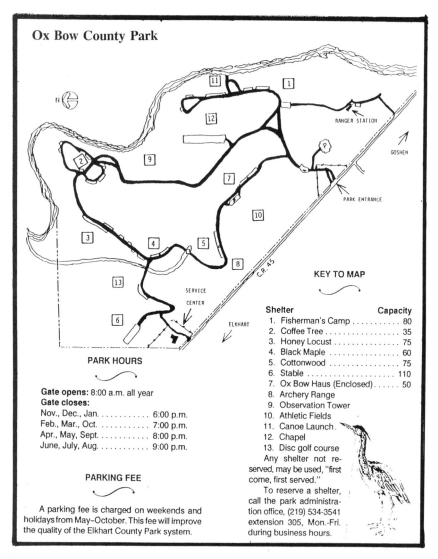

Ox Bow County Park

KEY TO MAP

Shelter	Capacity
1. Fisherman's Camp	80
2. Coffee Tree	35
3. Honey Locust	75
4. Black Maple	60
5. Cottonwood	75
6. Stable	110
7. Ox Bow Haus (Enclosed)	50
8. Archery Range	
9. Observation Tower	
10. Athletic Fields	
11. Canoe Launch	
12. Chapel	
13. Disc golf course	

Any shelter not reserved, may be used, "first come, first served."

To reserve a shelter, call the park administration office, (219) 534-3541 extension 305, Mon.-Fri. during business hours.

PARK HOURS

Gate opens: 8:00 a.m. all year
Gate closes:
Nov., Dec., Jan. . . . . 6:00 p.m.
Feb., Mar., Oct. . . . . 7:00 p.m.
Apr., May, Sept. . . . . 8:00 p.m.
June, July, Aug. . . . . 9:00 p.m.

PARKING FEE

A parking fee is charged on weekends and holidays from May–October. This fee will improve the quality of the Elkhart County Park system.

Ox Bow County Park

The park gate opens at 8 am all year around. The gate closes at 9 pm June, July and August; 8 pm April, May and September; 7 pm February, March and October; and 6 pm November, December, and January.

29. GOSHEN NATURE PLACES

ACTIVITIES: nature walks, nature study, nature preserve, arboretum, picnicking, shelters, boating, launch ramp, fishing, swimming pool, playgrounds, ballfields, ball courts, fitness trail

The "Maple City" of Goshen, the county seat and rural center of Elkhart County, has several nature places along the Elkhart River and adjoining millrace hydraulic canal; both providing a city watery greenbelt.

Witmer Woods, the Goshen College arboretum, has 18 acres of mostly native trees and shrubs that is open to the public to explore. Purchased in 1941, the arboretum was developed by Dr. S. W. Witmer and his botany and biology students who spent many hours transplanting plant materials. Dr. Witmer made Indiana botanical history when he discovered the Kankakee mallow (Iliamma remota), a rare plant found only in four other sites in the world. Witmer Woods consists of 101 varieties of plants and a guide booklet is available. Dr. Witmer also inventoried the plants at Ox Bow County Park near Dunlap, Indiana.

Witmer Woods (**W** on map) is located on the east bank of the Elkhart River/ Goshen Reservoir, west of Goshen College. In south Goshen, turn west on River Vista Drive from Indiana 15 and proceed to the first street, Reservoir Place, and turn left/south. Continue south on Reservoir Place to the parking area. There is a picnic area besides the reservoir.

In the same neighborhood a few blocks north and west of Witmer Woods parking area at the Goshen Dam site of the Elkhart River, is the Shoup-Parsons Swamp Nature Preserve [**C** on map] and the south terminus of the millrace hydraulic canal. From Witmer Woods, drive north on Reservoir Place to River Vista Drive and turn left/west. Follow River Vista Drive around the curve past the boat launch ramp to Westwood Street and turn left/west. Continue a short distance to the gravel parking area and follow the foot bridge over the millrace to the paved preserve trail next to the dam.

The all-weather 0.5 mile long path traces a loop in the 17 acre floodplain and upland forest between the millrace canal and the Elkhart River. There is a section of boardwalk that extends out into a two acre cattail marsh and shrub swamp with an observation pier at the end. Birding is reputed to be good at the preserve. The Nature Conservancy along with the city of Goshen acquired the preserve.

If walking you prefer, follow the east bank of the millrace north to Washington Street. Near the north end of the walk are the Goshen city

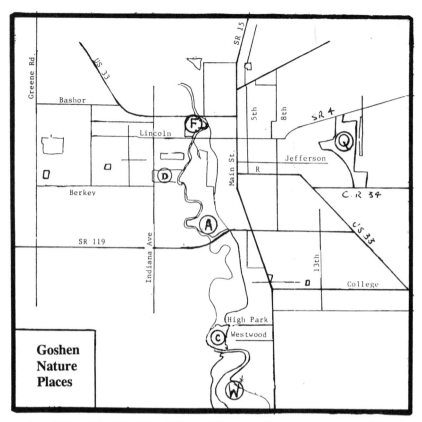

Goshen Nature Places

parks of Shanklin [A], New [D], and Rogers [F]; an approximate distance of two miles one-way. Shanklin Park [A] at West Plymouth Avenue is about a mile north of the Goshen Dam parking area. Situated between the millrace and the Elkhart River, the 90 acre park has one mile of nature trail, a swimming pool, ballfields, ball courts, playground, and picnic area. A foot bridge leads over the river to New Park, a 15 acre green space.

From New Park [D], walk north to Linway Lake and Plaza. Walk under the Lincoln Avenue bridge to access 12 acre Rogers Park [F] where there are several active facilities. Retrace your original route back to the Goshen Dam parking area. The 60 acre John 0. Abshire Park (Q) at East Lincoln and CR 34 on the city's east side, is currently under development as a nature park. In addition, the 26 mile Pumkinvine Nature Trail, a linear rail-to-trail, will connect the cities of Goshen, Middlebury and Shipshewana in the near future.

Goshen, Indiana is easily reached via the Indiana Toll Road/ I-80-90, US 33 and Indiana 15, 4, and 119.

196

30. RIVER PRESERVE COUNTY PARK
Benton, IN/Elkhart County
USGS MAP(s): Goshen, Milford 1:24,000
TRAIL(s) DISTANCE:
ACREAGE: 1,000 acres
ACTIVITIES: nature walks, nature study, historic sites, picnicking, shelters, canoeing, canoe launch ramp, fishing

Rich in history as well as in size, the 1,000 acre Elkhart County Park was acquired from donated land and is the largest of the three major parks. The River Preserve County Park is positioned along the Elkhart River between Benton, Indiana and the Goshen Dam in south Goshen, Indiana. Actually the park's name should be plural, River Preserves, since there are five unconsolidated tracts along the river corridor. Together the separate preserves total four miles of greenway along the Elkhart River.

Historically, the area was home to Potawatomi Chief Onaska, better known as Five Medals (?1750-1820). A granite boulder historical marker confirms his past presence at the historic Baintertown tract, located one mile east of Indiana 15 on CR 42 just northwest of Baintertown, Indiana. In 1830, the Wyland family came to the area from Ohio and were millers. They established a millrace, built a sawmill, a gristmill and later a woolen mill. Frederick Bainter bought the mills a few years later and named the village Baintertown. Eventually the mills were sold, resold and finally the surviving gristmill ceased operation in 1923. In the 1940's, the Interstate Public Service Company, now Northern Indiana Public Service Company (NIPSCO), acquired the mill site and constructed a hydroelectric power plant which still stands. The county naturalist leads scheduled historic hikes at the Baintertown tract and a historic interpretative trail is planned.

Access to the other River Preserve tracts are as follows:

Elkhart River canoe launch ramp and parking area is located on the north side of highway bridge on US 33 in Benton, Indiana. There are two undeveloped tracts just south of Benton, between US 33 and CR 31. The river flows through both tracts.

The Benton Dam and Spillway are located on CR 31, two miles south of US 33, southwest of Benton. Trails heading east and west begin at the covered bridge parking area on CR 31. On the south side of the bridge, follow the service road along the canal bank east about 0.4 miles to the dam and picnic area. A 0.25 mile trail loops through the riparian area along the Elkhart River just south of the dam. Return along the canal bank to the covered bridge parking area.

Benton Dam, River Preserve County Park

Heading west about 100 yards along the canal bank on the south side of the covered bridge leads to the spillway and picnic area. A footbridge crosses the spillway where the 0.4 mile Spillway Trail loop follows the north bank of the Elkhart River and enters an abandoned meadow woodland. The one mile, one-way Hydro Trail also begins at the spillway footbridge and heads north and west following the north bank of the canal, crossing CR 27, and continuing on to the site of the razed Benton hydro-electric site located near the confluence of the canal and the Elkhart River. Retrace your steps back to the spillway and covered bridge parking area.

The previously mentioned <u>Baintertown tract:</u> CR 42, one mile east of Indiana 15, northwest of Baintertown, Indiana.

<u>Goshen Dam</u> site in south Goshen, Indiana, west of Goshen College. From Indiana 15, drive 0.5 mile west on Westwood Road to a parking area adjacent to the millrace and dam. Site also accesses the city's 17 acre Shoup-Parsons Nature Preserve.

In addition, The Nature Conservancy has obtained a 21 acre tract along the Elkhart River's south bank, east of Benton 1.2 miles on CR 44. The <u>Leacock Woods</u> is open for visitation but is accessible only by crossing the river.

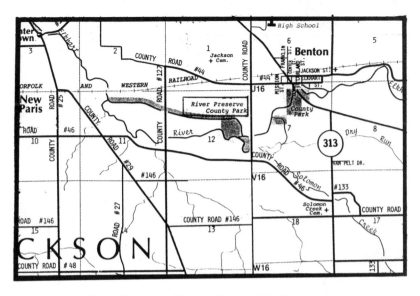

River Preserve County Park, (shaded areas)

31. BORKHOLDER ENVIRONMENTAL EDUCATION CENTER

Nappanee, IN/Elkhart County
USGS MAP(s): Nappanee East, Nappanee West 1:24,000
TRAIL(s) DISTANCE: 0.5 mile loop
ACREAGE: 35 acres
ACTIVITIES: nature walk, nature study, nature center, picnicking,
shelter, special programs

The recently established nature center is owned and managed by the
Nappanee Parks and Recreation Department. The property is situated in
the east suburban area of the community where the natural area adjoins
the Derksen golf course and Stauffer Park to the south and southwest.

The environmental education area includes prairie-like grassland, a
beech-maple woods and a wetland pond. The nature trail connects all three
habitats. Beginning at the center, the trail heads west through the
grassland curving north to enter the wet deciduous forest where large
specimens of beech trees are encountered. Going east through the forest,
the trail emerges at the cattail ringed pond where several bluebird houses
have been placed. The trail then loops back to the center.

To reach Borkholder Environmental Education Center and Area in east
Nappanee from US 6, turn north on CR 7 and drive 0.7 mile to the nature
center entry road and turn left/west (B on map). Continue 0.2 mile to the
parking area adjacent east of the attractive center.

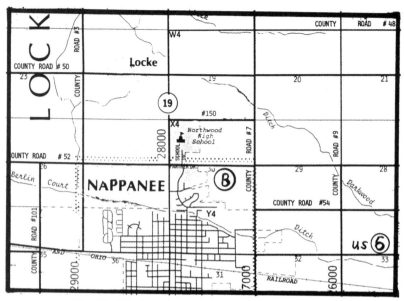

Borkholder Environmental Education Center

32. TRI-COUNTY FISH & WILDLIFE AREA
Syracuse, IN/Kosciusko & Noble Counties
USGS MAP(s); North Webster 1:24,000
TRAIL(s) DISTANCE: 0.4 mile est. trail, several miles of service roads, firelanes & fisherman's paths
ACREAGE: 3,486 acres
ACTIVITIES: nature hikes, nature study, nature preserve, canoeing, launch ramps, fishing, winter sports, rifle & archery ranges, hunting

Established in 1953, the Tri-County Fish and Wildlife Area occupies the locally known, "Hoss Hills", of northeast Kosciusko and southwest Noble counties. The third county of Tri-County is Whitley, where no property has yet been purchased. Of the sixteen existing DNR fish and wildlife areas statewide, Tri-County ranks fourteenth in size however the diverse landscape in the heart of lake country makes up for acreage with it quality and quantity of wetlands. Future plans call for the expansion of the property to 4,500 acres.

The rolling till plain uplands are punctuated with numerous natural lakes and man-made ponds and marsh wetlands. One out of every five acres is water, attracting a rich variety of waterfowl, songbirds and other wildlife. The area is located at a continental divide which separates the Great Lakes and Mississippi drainage systems. Parking lots are plentiful and provide easy access to the service roads, firelanes and fisherman's paths which vary widely in difficulty as well as length. The only designated foot path is the 0.4 mile Grider Woods Nature Preserve trail located south of Heron Pond and east of Spear Lake. The property headquarters is located on Hoss Hills Road. From Syracuse, drive south on Indiana 13 six miles to CR 900N and turn left/east. Proceed on CR 900N one mile to Hoss Hills Road and turn right/south. Continue on Hoss Hills Road to the property headquarters on the left/eastside of the county road. A property map and information about the current hunting season may be obtained.

The most outstanding natural areas to explore on foot are summarized as follows:

B-5 to B-4 parking lots: Waterfowl Resting Area. The walk follows service roads and embankments from Hoss Hills Road-B-5 parking lot east, between Hammond, Allen and Rothenberger natural lakes, across the embankment, upland through dense maturing hardwoods, turning left/north at the "T" to B-4 parking and Kohee Road. May walk in either direction. About 1 mile round trip.

Wyland Lake: A scenic five acre lake surrounded by mature trees. The 38 foot deep natural lake is stocked with trout. Consider a walk around its borders.

G-3 parking lot: Walk north to the country road junction and follow the service road northwest along the north shore of Bass Pond to Hoss Hills Road. Retrace steps.

F-3 parking lot: Follow fisherman's paths to and about Loon Pond.

A service road, located between F-3 and F-2 parking lot, curves north to Barrel and 1/2 Lake. Retrace linear route south.

G-2 parking lot: Accesses Goldeneye and Ruddy Ponds. Service road on the northwest shore of Goldeneye Pond serves as a trail.

I-1 parking lot: Accesses nine acre Bufflehead Pond which has reared pike, walleye and muskellunge. Across the county road is H-1 parking lot and a service road that runs north, paralleling Scaup Pond Wetlands.

Grider Woods Nature Preserve: Features a self-guiding trail with 25 stations, east of Spear Lake. The oak-hickory dominated woods has upland, ravines and forest stream. Located west from County Line Road and D-4 parking area, along gravel road to Spear lake.

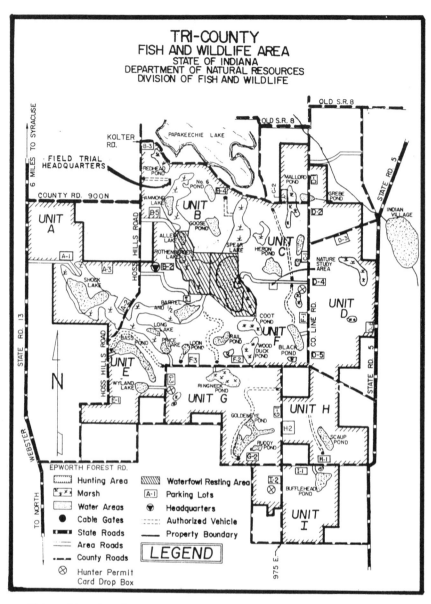

TRI-COUNTY
FISH AND WILDLIFE AREA
STATE OF INDIANA
DEPARTMENT OF NATURAL RESOURCES
DIVISION OF FISH AND WILDLIFE

LEGEND

Hunting Area		Waterfowl Resting Area	
Marsh		Parking Lots	A-1
Water Areas		Headquarters	
Cable Gates	●	Authorized Vehicle	
State Roads		Property Boundary	
Area Roads			
County Roads			
Hunter Permit Card Drop Box	⊗		

F-1 parking lot: Service road walk from Black Pond north to Mallard Storage Pond and Koher Road. Side spur trail leads around west side of Heron Pond to Grider Woods.

Tri-County Fish and Wildlife Area is bordered by Indiana 5 to the east, Indiana 13 to the west, Papakeechie Lake to the north, and Webster Lake and North Webster, Indiana to the south.

33. BALL WETLANDS NATURE PRESERVE

North Webster, IN/Kosciusko County
USGS MAP(s): North Webster 1:24,000
TRAIL(s) DISTANCE: appx. 2 miles of trail
ACREAGE: 249 acres
ACTIVITIES: nature walk, nature study

Beginning in 1980, The Nature Conservancy was instrumental in acquiring the Edmund and Virginia Ball Wetlands, which has since been dedicated as a state nature preserve. However the Ball Wetlands are owned and managed by the YMCA Camp Crosley, due east across James Lake from the preserve where permission to visit must be obtained; (219) 834-2331 summer or (317) 288-4448 the rest of the year.

Nature walking at the Ball Wetlands has an element of adventure. The vast wetlands nearly separate James Lake from Tippecanoe Lake and at one time did separate the two water bodies before dredging. Within the watery preserve are such wetland communities as open marsh, tall shrub swamp, red maple swamp forest and two upland islands covered with oak and hickory forest.

The nature trail begins from a small parking area at the northwest end of a subdivision suburb on the southwest shore of James Lake. The grassy path follows between a shrubby marsh and an agricultural field to lead to a boardwalk that spans an extensive cattail marsh. Following the boardwalk north, the wooden trail arrives at the first tree-covered island. The trail forks but go right and follow the loop around the island's perimeter. A boat dock landing and pier are located on the northeast portion of the isle and an outdoor education area is nearby. Continue to encircle the first island to arrive at a second fork and bear right again. This segment of the trail crosses over another marsh area to the second island and third trail fork. Bear right.

The undisturbed forest looms much larger on the larger second isle. Follow the trail loop along the eastern edge to the island's north tip, where the path becomes mushy, for a view of the open expanse. This point is the furthest extent of the trail. Return south along the west edge of the loop and recross the marsh to the first island. Continue to follow the west portion of the first island's loop to recross the first boardwalk and on to conclude at the parking area.

The trailhead and parking area may be reached from US 30, just north of Pierceton, Indiana, by driving north on Indiana 13 nine miles to CR 500N, just south of North Webster, Indiana. Turn left/west on CR 500N and travel 1.8 miles to Lakeside subdivision and Sharron Drive and turn right/north. Continue north on Sharron Drive to the road curve and park at the barrier straight ahead. The path northwest is conspicuous.

Of further interest is the YMCA Camp Crosley observatory which is open on clear Saturday nights from dusk to 11 pm, April to October. The observatory was built by the Warsaw Astronomical Society and has a rotating dome and a 7.5 foot long telescope. Call (219) 269-4145 for further information. In addition, the Camp Crosley lodge is open for families on Sundays year around for a small fee. It is especially nice in winter when cross country skiing, ice skating and sledding are available winter sports. There is also year around family camping. Call (219) 834-2331.

To reach Camp Crosley which is affiliated with the YMCA of Muncie, Indiana, turn west from Indiana 13 onto CR 500N and drive one mile to CR 675E and turn right/north. Follow CR 675E about a half mile to the marked entrance on the left/west side of CR 675E.

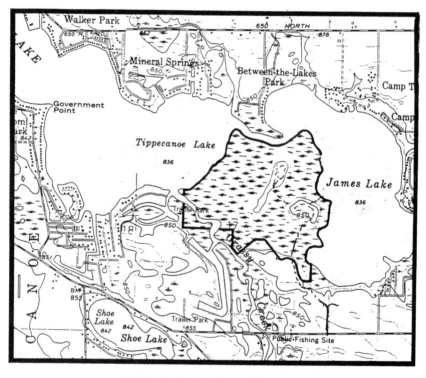

Ball Wetlands Nature Preserve

34. WARSAW BIBLICAL GARDENS

Warsaw, IN/Kosciusko County
USGS MAP(s): Warsaw 1:24,000
TRAIL(s) DISTANCE: 0.25 mile paved paths
ACREAGE: 0.75 acre
ACTIVITIES: nature walk, botanic gardens, city parks nearby

Located on the southeast shore of Center Lake at Levin Park is the Warsaw Biblical Gardens, one of the largest and finest botanical gardens of biblical plants in the United States. Surrounded by a field rock fence and tall trees, the enclosed gardens give a greater sense of calm from the busy Indiana 15 intersection to the east. A stroll along the garden's paved paths will reveal six areas representing the different environs described in the bible.

The Meadow in the garden's center is filled with flowers and a small brook flows. The Orchard is planted with fruit trees and shrubs of the bible and features a unique grape arbor. The Forest has large shade trees and herbaceous plants. The Brook area features water plants and fish. A Desert area provides a sampling of the dry environs and plants named in the bible. The Crops area contains over 25 types of vegetables, herbs and

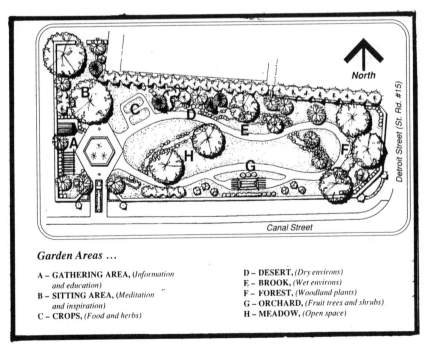

Garden Areas ...

A – GATHERING AREA, (*Information and education*)
B – SITTING AREA, (*Meditation and inspiration*)
C – CROPS, (*Food and herbs*)

D – DESERT, (*Dry environs*)
E – BROOK, (*Wet environs*)
F – FOREST, (*Woodland plants*)
G – ORCHARD, (*Fruit trees and shrubs*)
H – MEADOW, (*Open space*)

Warsaw Biblical Gardens

plants. In addition, a Gathering Area provides a place for information and assembly. For those desiring a place of solitude, a Sitting Area with benches under shady oaks is also provided.

The biblical gardens has been planned with every effort made to achieve botanical and historical accuracy. Each plant is labelled with a marker bearing its name. Frost sensitive plants are wintered over in greenhouses. The Warsaw Biblical Gardens are designed so all may browse, meditate and enjoy these living ties of Judeo-Christian scriptural heritage. The gardens are open dawn to dusk, April 15 through October 15.

Adjacent to both sides of the gardens are three Warsaw city parks to further add to the enjoyment of the day excursion: Bixler Park, Municipal Park and Nye Park. North and east of the gardens is Bixler Park which is well-suited for picnicking under the shady trees and shelters and other activities include swimming, boating, and fishing on Center Lake plus tennis and horseshoe courts. To the west of the gardens is the Municipal Park which is ideal for swimming, boating, fishing, picnicking, playground and ballfield. The 1930s pavilion is well suited for reunions. To the west of Municipal Park is Nye Park which features more picnic sites and an enclosed shelter. Actually, all three parklands and the gardens may be considered one big park. There is plenty of parking at streetside or at the north edge of Bixler Park. All parks and gardens are accessible from Indiana 15 and Canal Street in north Warsaw at Center Lake. Recently, the city of Warsaw has landscaped a large open area south of Center lake, "connecting" downtown to the lake.

East of Center Lake, Indiana 15 and Canal Street on Arthur Street to Pike Lake are several more city parks that include a seasonal campground. Pike Lake Park [7] and Pike Lake Campground [8] have a swimming beach, boat launch ramp, concessions, playground and a Class A campground that is open from April 15 - September 30. Lucerne Park, just north of Pike Lake beach park has cabins for rent overlooking Pike Lake.

The city of Warsaw, Indiana is easily accessible from US 30 and Indiana 15 and Indiana 25.

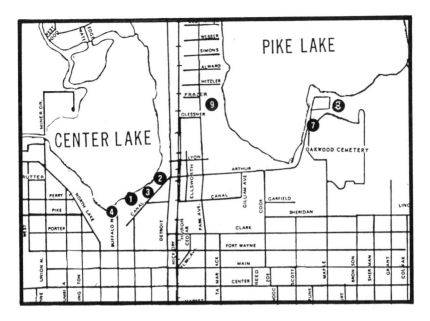

Warsaw City Parks

[1] Municipal park　　*[2] Bixler Park*　　*[3] Biblical Gardens*
[4] Nye Park　　*[7] Pike Lake Park*　*[9]Lucerne Park*

35. WILDWOOD
Silver Lake, IN/Kosciusko County
USGS MAP(s): Silver Lake, North Manchester North 1:24,000
TRAIL(s) DISTANCE: 2.75 miles
ACREAGE: 88 acres
ACTIVITIES: nature walks, nature study

This privately-owned woodland, grassy fields and marshy wetlands are not only home to wildlife but also to the owners, Robert and Alice Frantz, who enjoy sharing the heart of their family farm-turned-nature sanctuary with other nature lovers. A visit to Wildwood is an inspiration to any landowners who desire to return their property into a preserve and live more by nature's natural rhythms of the everchanging seasons.

Driving down the long lane from Indiana 14, visitors will arrive at the parking area and trailhead next to the Frantz's home which is nestled in a wooded area perched above a three acre pond. Guests to Wildwood are asked to register and a trail map is available. The interconnecting earth-based trails loop north and south throughout the rolling, glacially-designed landscape. The property is managed by the Frantzes under the DNR's Classified Forest and Wildlife Habitat Programs. A bird count has revealed 148 species and there are 43 species of trees. Respective visitors are asked to, "take nothing but pictures, leave nothing but footprints".

To reach Wildwood in south central Kosciusko County, drive east from Silver Lake, Indiana 3.4 miles on Indiana 14 to the property lane entrance and identified by the "Wildwood" sign on the south/right side of the highway. The address and telephone number is 409 E SR 14, Silver Lake 46982, (219) 352-2673.

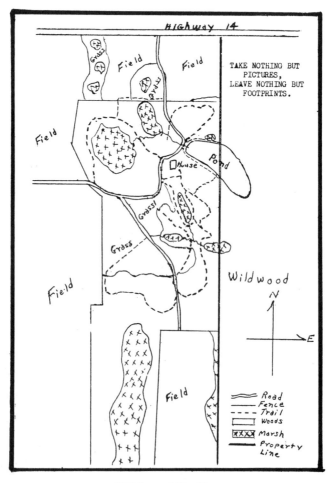

Wildwood Trails

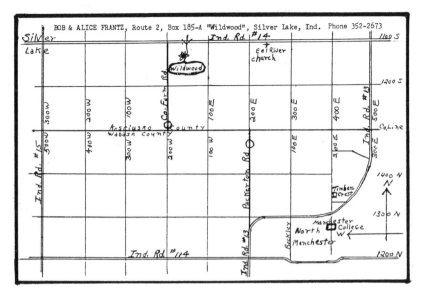

BOB & ALICE FRANTZ, Route 2, Box 185-A "Wildwood", Silver Lake, Ind. Phone 352-2673

Wildwood Location

36. LAKETON BOG NATURE PRESERVE

North Manchester, IN/Wabash County
USGS MAP(s): North Manchester South 1:24,000
TRAIL(s) DISTANCE: 2 mile loop
ACREAGE: 32 acres
ACTIVITIES: nature walk, nature study

Laketon Bog was obtained through efforts of The Nature Conservancy and is now owned and managed by the Indiana DNR's division of Nature Preserves. The most notable natural feature of Laketon Bog is the southernmost stand of tamarack trees in Indiana. This deciduous conifer is the northern counterpart of the southern bald cypress that is also a conifer found growing in wetlands, shedding its needles in autumn. Twice during the early 1900s around Laketon, nearly all the tamarack trees were cut and sold for railroad ties. In time, the tamarack at Laketon Bog will eventually die out as the bog fills in with organic matter.

The parking area and trailhead begins at the northwest upland edge of the bog adjacent to Ogden Road, just northeast of Laketon, Indiana. An interpretive trail brochure is available at the registration box that corresponds to the seven numbered posts along the trail. The self-guiding nature walk descends into the bog and onto the boardwalk which can be slippery during wet weather.

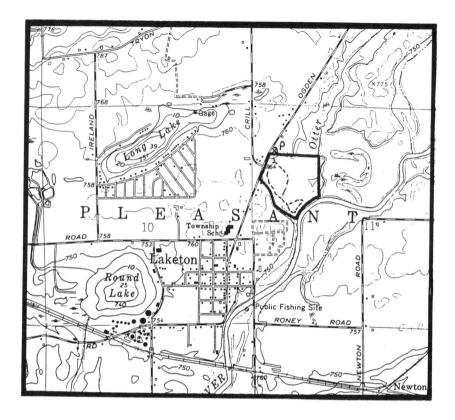

Laketon Bog Nature Preserve

The boardwalk cuts through the tree swamp and shrub fen where skunk cabbage, marsh marigold and cattail are prolific. The tamarack trees also line the wooden trail. Visitors may obtain a close-up look at the bark, needles and cones. The needles or leaves of the picturesque tamarack turn a golden yellow before dropping in the autumn. Willow, gray and red osier dogwoods, ninebark, poison sumac, shrubby cinquefoil and dwarf birch are also common. The peat soil of the bog is kept moist by groundwater seepage from the surrounding bluffs.

The trail soon arrives at a "T" and turns left/east and heads towards another major habitat of striking contrast compared to the bog; the floodplain of the Eel River. The floodplain includes such plants as sycamore, red and silver maples, stinging wood nettle, jewelweed, trilliums and wild ginger. The boardwalk through the floodplain loops back to the original segment of trail and continues west past the fork to follow the high ground between the bog and the bluff and back to the parking area.

To reach Laketon Bog Nature Preserve, go west 1.3 mile on Indiana 114 from the junction of Indiana 13 and Indiana 114 at North Manchester. Turn left/south onto Ogden Road/CR 200W and drive 1.4 miles to the small parking lot on the left/east side of Ogden Road.

While in the general area of North Manchester, consider visiting the city's eight acre Warvel Park at 901 North Market. The shaded rolling terrain is a fine place to picnic. The scenic 100 acre campus of Manchester College has several trees that are labelled with their common and scientific names and the college museum in the Communication Center in the heart of campus displays exhibits of geological specimens and historical artifacts. South of Main Street/Indiana 114, the only historic covered bridge in Wabash County is closed to motor traffic but open to foot traffic at South Mill Street and Singer Road over the Eel River.

Further Notes on Kosciusko County Nature Places:

Kosciusko County has over 100 lakes including Indiana's deepest, Tippecanoe Lake, and the largest, Lake Wawasee, plus numerous lesser-known or unheard of wetlands. These popular areas are often taken first for residential and commercial use and last for parklands and preserves. Despite the high population, farmland and substantial number of industries, Kosciusko County has nature places in addition to the main natural attractions described in the text not to be overlooked or go unmentioned.

The community of Syracuse on the northwest shore of 414 acre Syracuse Lake has a fine park system that includes the scenic but busy Lakeside Park on China Bay, just east of downtown. The tree-shaded pocket park features a swimming beach, picnic tables, shelter pavilion, gazebo, public docks, concessions, a cultural Music-in-the-Park series each summer, and a winter festival around Christmas. The Crosson Mill Park, along Indiana 13, west of Huntington Street and across from the Syracuse Town Hall, offers picnicking, fishing, a dam and labelled trees.

Neighboring Lake Wawasee, the state's largest natural lake of 2,618 acres, has a few nature sites along its shores (USGS Map Lake Wawasee 1:24,000). South of Syracuse in Conklin Bay's west side is one of three small wetland conservation areas found along Lake Wawasee's shores. The cattail marsh tract is too wet for walking as are the other two areas, located on the west side of Johnson Bay, just north of Ogden Island peninsula. There is also a 17 acre Wawasee Wetlands Nature Preserve sandwiched between the two WCA tracts at Ogden Island and access is by water only. At the extreme southeast area of Lake Wawasee near

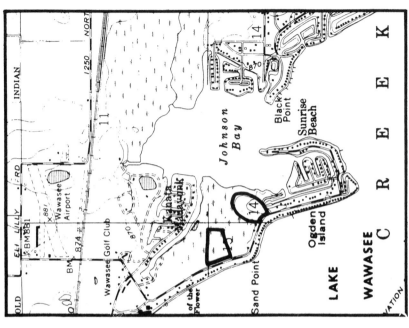

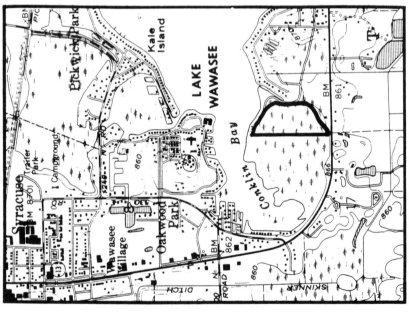

Buttermilk Point is the <u>Wawasee Lake Public Fishing Area</u>. The former fish hatchery site offers great open views of the expansive lake. The area is located four miles south of Syracuse on Indiana 13, then two miles east on Indiana 8.

The recently formed Wawasee Area Conservancy is helping to preserve natural habitats in the watershed by acquiring undeveloped lands.

The <u>Chapman Lake Wetlands</u> on the west shores of Big Chapman and Little Chapman lakes (USGS Map Leesburg 1:24,000) total 230 acres and are owned and managed by the DNR as nature preserves and as part of the non-game program. There are no parking areas, no trails and access is limited.

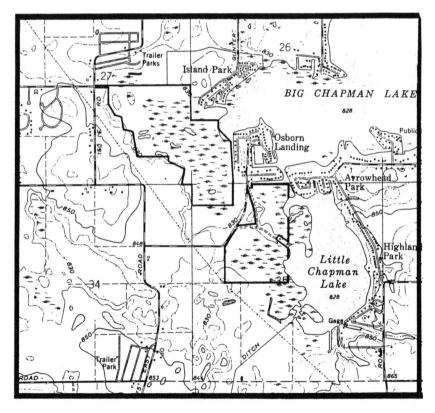

Big and Little Chapman Lakes Nature Preserves

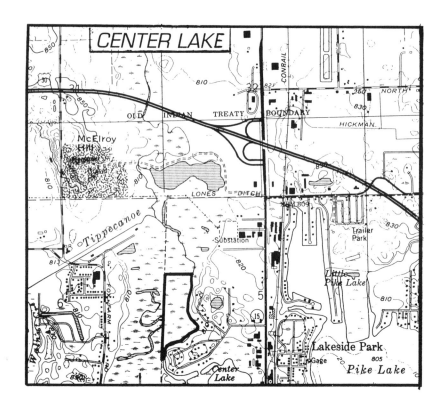

Center Lake Wetland Conservation Area

Center Lake Wetland Conservation Area (USGS Map Leesburg 1:24,000) is a 25 acre floodplain and upland mixed forest on the west side of the Tippecanoe River-Center Lake diversion canal, just north of Center Lake in Warsaw. Access is from Union Street. Subdivision encroachment on the natural area is to the east. There are nice community parks along the shores of Winona Lake, immediately south of Warsaw.

The eight acre Mentzer Memorial Park in west Mentone, Indiana is a fine place to stop enroute to another site and stretch your legs along the 0.5 mile gravel path that follows the park's perimeter. The town park includes a picnic and playground and lies adjacent west of the Lawrence D. Bell Aircraft Museum. Oak and Washington Streets.

37. SOUTH BEND NATURE PLACES

ACTIVITIES: nature walks, nature study, nature center, gardens, botanic conservatory, zoo, picnicking, shelters, kayaking, rafting, tubing, boating, launch ramps, playgrounds, ballfields & courts, historic sites, special events

South Bend, Indiana's fifth largest city and the regional center of Michiana, has nearly 1,400 acres of community parklands that range from the inner city to the suburban edges.

In the heart of downtown is the East Race Waterway (ERW on map) that extends from Jefferson Boulevard north to Hydralic Avenue. Once the site of a mill race, a paved foot path follows alongside the 2,000 foot waterway; a man-made channel that cuts across the south bend of the St. Joseph River. The race is one of three artificial whitewater raceways worldwide. Kayakers, rafters, and inner tubers "shoot the rapids" from June to September at scheduled hours and rentals are available. National and international kayak competitions are held at the East Race. A fish ladder allows chinook salmon and steelhead trout from Lake Michigan passage upstream. There are several provided rest benches and foot bridges to cross along the landscaped corridor.

Across the St. Joseph River from the East Race is Island Park (IP), just outside the Century Center's Great Hall. The ten acre island was built over the foundation footings of the former Indiana and Michigan hydro-electric power plant. From this open vantage point you can enjoy the man-made waterfall, the "Keepers of the Fire" sculpture, and perhaps see the reintroduced peregrine falcons cruising the South Bend skyline. Summertime on the island brings musical concerts. Entrance to Island Park is from Century Center.

Continuing upstream along the paved path from the East Race, go under the Jefferson Boulevard bridge to access Howard Park (HP). The riverway trail continues along the north bank. The cruise ship, Princess, one of four steamboats in Indiana, docks at Howard Park in summer and runs upstream to 100 Center in Mishawaka. Where Howard Park ends, walk south beside the stone wall to the old train footbridge which spans the river. From here the linear walk terminates. Retrace your route back to Howard Park and the East Race.

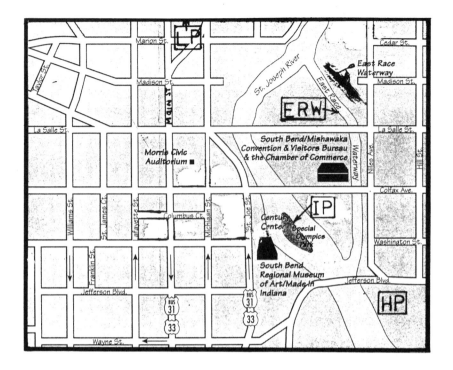

Downtown South Bend

Additional riverside parks to visit in South Bend include 26 acre <u>Leeper Park</u> (LP) with its fragrance and rose gardens at North Michigan and Riverside Drive, 43 acre <u>Pinhook Park</u> and <u>Pinhook Lake Lagoon</u> at 2800 Riverside Drive, and <u>Veterans Memorial Park</u> adjacent to Indiana University South Bend campus on Northside Boulevard.

East of downtown is the 62 acre <u>Potawatomi Park and Zoo</u>. Since 1917, the zoo has been a conservation, education, and recreation center. Over 250 animals representing five continents may be viewed and there is a petting zoo farm. In addition, the zoo includes a learning center, gardens, amphitheatre, tram, gift shop and concessions. The zoo is open daily 10 am to 5 pm except Thanksgiving, Christmas and New Year's Day and an entrance fee is charged. The entrance is at 500 South Greenlawn from Jefferson Boulevard. Also of interest in the southeast corner of Potawatomi Park along Mishawaka Avenue is the <u>Ella Morris Botanic Conservatory</u> which includes a tropical garden and Arizona Desert.

<u>Rum Village</u> is South Bend's best and largest nature park. Located at Ewing Avenue at Kemble Street, west of US 31/Michigan Avenue on the city's southwest side, the 160 acre parkland features a nature center and

center and 2.5 miles of trails in the southwest portion. The Rum Village Pathway adds four more miles of hiking and mountain bike trails. The nature center displays natural history exhibits, an observational beehive, a wildlife window, and a butterfly garden. Kaukema's courtyard, a play area, was recently constructed. Eight interconnecting foot trails weave through the 55 acre woodland. The nature center hours are from 8:30 am to 4:30 pm, Monday through Friday and 1 pm to 5 pm on Sunday.

On the northside of South Bend just east and west of North Michigan Avenue/US 31 Business, are the world renowned college campuses of Notre Dame and St. Mary's College. Both of these related Catholic institutions of higher learning have beautiful landscaped grounds that are open to visitors to tour. A guidebook to the Notre Dame campus identifies and locates several hundred trees and shrubs including some state champions. St. Mary's College campus features the George and Juanda Bick Nature Trail that moves along the riparian woodland adjacent to the St. Joseph River near the water tower.

38. MISHAWAKA NATURE PLACES
ACTIVITIES: nature walks, nature study, nature center, nature preserves, gardens, fish ladder, fish hatchery, picnicking, shelters, fishing, boating, launch ramps, ballfields, ball courts, playgrounds, playfields, swimming pool, winter sports, youth camp, river cruise

Mishawaka, "The Princess City", shares a common city limits with neighboring South Bend and like its "twin city" to the west, shares the St. Joseph River. Several of the best nature places in Mishawaka are found along the banks of the river and a few are located in the south suburbs.

The 16 acre Lincoln Park at, 1004 Lincoln Way West is the first city park located on the St. Joseph River going west to east. The active park has plenty packed in its green space with game courts, a ballfield, playground, picnic area and boat launch ramp plus a monument to the storybook Princess Mishawaka. The park adjoins 100 Center to the east where summer river cruises aboard the steamship, Princess, embarks to Howard Park downstream in South Bend. Within the river is Kamm Island Park, a nature sanctuary, which is accessible only by boat.

Northeast across the river is the 11 acre Battel Park located at 301 West Mishawaka Avenue. The main attraction is the terraced rock garden which is a popular place for summer weddings and the band shell is special. There is also room for other recreational pursuits in the handsome park such as ball courts and picnicking.

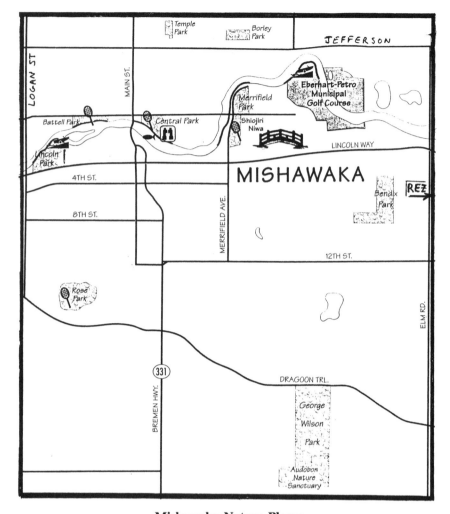

Mishawaka Nature Places

Further upstream on the north bank is <u>Central Park</u> at 295 East Mishawaka Avenue. The unique nature-oriented, man-made feature is the recently constructed DNR fish ladder at the southeast portion of the park adjacent to the dam. This concrete "ladder" permits Lake Michigan steelhead and salmon to bypass the dam and continue their annual migration upstream to spawn in early spring and late summer. There are other fish ladders on the St. Joseph River at the East Race Park in South Bend, Buchanan, Michigan and Berrien Springs, Michigan.

Shiojiri Grove, Mishawaka

Three miles or so upstream at 13200 East Jefferson Boulevard near Bittersweet Road is the <u>Twin Branch Fish Hatchery</u> which stocks the St. Joseph River with steelhead and chinook. The fish migrate downstream to Lake Michigan and return in three years as full grown gamefish. The 11 acre coldwater fish hatchery is open to tours 8 am to 3:30 pm weekdays.

Upstream from Central Park a few blocks is <u>Merrifield Park</u>, the largest of Mishawaka's river parks. The 35 acre riverside park is bisected by Mishawaka Avenue. North of the Avenue are the active facilities including an Olympic-sized swimming pool, ice rink, ballfields, boat launch ramp, Castle Manor Lodge and playgrounds. The park area south of the Avenue features the <u>Shiojiri Grove Japanese strolling garden</u> which symbolizes the sister-city relationship between Mishawaka and Shiojiri City, Nagano Prefecture Japan. The 1.3 acre garden beholds numerous manicured plantings, 200 large boulders, bridges, and a teahouse pavilion. In Shiojiri City, an American garden equivalent has been established representing the city of Mishawaka.

South of the St. Joseph River are two other noteworthy parks worthy of visitation. <u>The Res</u>, a former Boy Scout Camp, is a 30 acre privately endowed park located at 13950 Scout Lane, east of Capitol Avenue. The Res has three miles of interconnecting trails and the area along the winding swift stream is special. Within this seemingly remote area is the newly established Murraywood Nature Preserve which harbors a small nature center and self-guiding trail. The Res is popular with overnight camping youth groups. Within a short distance of The Res are the community parks of Laing, Bendix and Fred J. Hums.

The second natural park south of the St. Joseph River is the 54 acre George Wilson Park at Dragoon Trail between Fir and Clover Roads, east of Indiana 331. This outlying suburban park is well-suited for cross country skiing and snow tubing in the winter as well as nature walks along the trails in summer. The park also includes picnicking, a playground, an 18 hole disc golf course, and a location for star study and gazing.

39. FERRETTIE/BAUGO CREEK COUNTY PARK
Osceola, IN/St. Joseph County
USGS MAP(s): Osceola 1:24,000
TRAIL(s) DISTANCE: appx. 2 miles
ACREAGE: 180 acres
ACTIVITIES: nature walk, nature study, interpretive center, picnicking, shelters, swimming, lifeguards, playgrounds, snow tubing, sailing, canoeing, launch ramp, special events
FEE(s): seasonal weekend entrance, shelter & room rental, seasonal programs such as swimming, inner tubing, and canoe rental

The St. Joseph County Park is positioned at the confluence of Baugo Creek and the St. Joseph River on Baugo Bay, just west of the St. Joseph-Elkhart county line. The park reflects the French and Indian influence of the fur trading years prior to the 1830s. Several of the park's facilities are labelled with French words and a 34 foot replica, 20 passenger Voyageur canoe is occasionally launched on Baugo Creek to attest to its usefulness in the fur trade.

Beginning from Baugo Station, a nature trail follows the east bank of Baugo Creek upstream underneath the traffic bridges to the more remote area of the park. Historically, an Indian trail followed a similar path to a village site at the junction of Apple Road and Dragoon Trail. The present day trail crosses the stream via a foot bridge to the west bank where the trail traces a loop in an old meadow, returning along the same route back to Baugo Station. Additional trails loop south to Goshen road. The name Baugo is an abbreviated version of the Potawatomi word, Baw-baw-go, meaning "demon or devil stream". The 20 miles of creek is considered swift and dangerous during heavy rains. Ferrettie was a French fur trader.

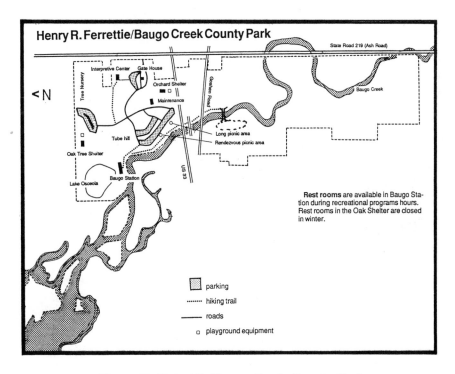

Henry R. Ferrettie/Baugo Creek County Park

To reach Ferrettie/Baugo Creek County Park from the US 20 bypass exit Indiana 19 and drive north to the intersection with US 33 and turn left/west. Continue on US 33 to Ash Road and turn right/north. The entrance is just north of the intersection of US 33 and Ash Road on the left/west side of the road at 57057 Ash. Canoes and small boats may be launched at Ferrettie/Baugo Bay property, located one mile northwest of the park entrance on Eastvue Drive via Neely Drive from Ash Road. The property hours are 7:30 am to sunset Monday through Friday and 10 am to sunset Saturday and Sunday.

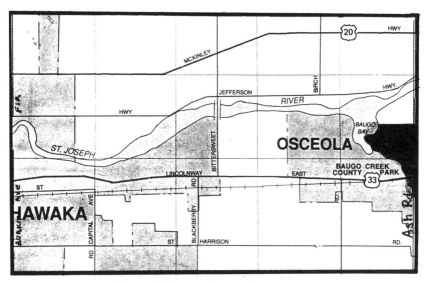

Ferrettie/Baugo Creek County Park

40. ST. PATRICK'S COUNTY PARK

South Bend, IN/St. Joseph County
USGS MAP(s): South Bend West, South Bend East 1:24,000
TRAIL(s) DISTANCE: 4 trails total 2 miles
ACREAGE: 100 acres
ACTIVITIES: nature walks, nature study, gardens, picnicking, shelters, outdoor fitness stations, playgrounds, fishing, piers wheelchair accessible, boating, launch ramp, docks, inner tubing, x-country skiing, Performing Arts Center, special events
FEE(s): weekend entrance, canoe & shelter rental, special events

St. Patrick's County Park is located to the immediate south of the Michigan-Indiana state line along one mile of the east bank of the St. Joseph River. The county park was acquired in 1976 from land belonging to the Sisters of the Holy Cross of St. Marys College. The park still has some flavor of the former working farm that occupied the site during the early 1900's. The white barn serves as the main administrative headquarters of the St. Joseph County Parks and Recreation Department and the red barn shelters the maintenance department. In addition to the herbaceous flowering plants, the Heritage Gardens has an orchard of pioneer grown varieties of apples and other fruit trees. Perhaps the most noteworthy aspect of the park is hikers may walk north along the river front trail into Michigan and the adjoining Berrien County Madeline Bertrand Park.

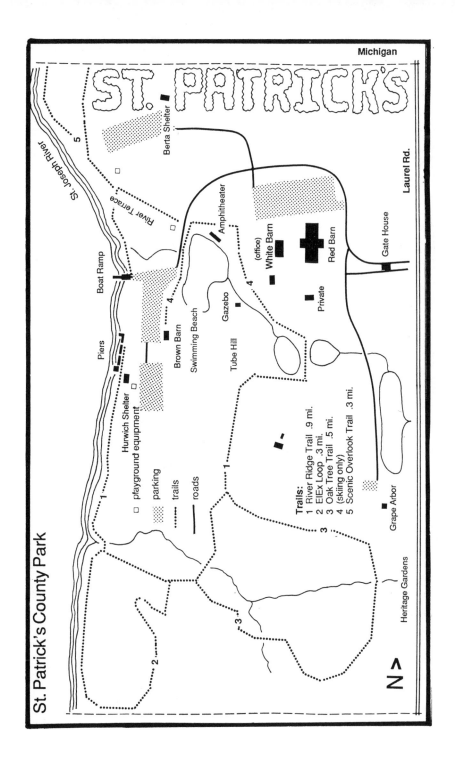

St. Patrick's County Park

ST. PATRICK'S

Michigan

Laurel Rd.

St. Joseph River

River Terrace

Berta Shelter

Amphitheater

White Barn

(office)

Red Barn

Private

Gate House

Boat Ramp

Piers

Brown Barn

Gazebo

Swimming Beach

Tube Hill

Hurwich Shelter

☐ playground equipment

⬚ parking

⋯ trails

━ roads

Trails:
1 River Ridge Trail .9 mi.
2 Elf Loop .3 mi.
3 Oak Tree Trail .5 mi.
4 (skiing only)
5 Scenic Overlook Trail .3 mi.

Grape Arbor

Heritage Gardens

N

The four level trails at St. Patricks are wide, short, easy, and loop about most of the property. Consider walking Trails 1, 2, and 3 all at once.

Trail 1 or the River Ridge Trail is 0.9 mile and the longest, connecting Trails 2 and 3 enroute. Beginning near the pier and Hurwich picnic shelter, Trail 1 follows the wooded bank of the St. Joseph River south crossing a small woodland creek and turning east connects Trail 2. Walking east through the woods the trail junctions Trail 2 again. Trail 1 continues east connecting Trail 3 and then turns north and continues, reconnecting Trail 3 once more. Trail 1 culminates near the tube hill, the ski Trail 4 and the park road.

Trail 2 or Horsetail Trace branches off of Trail 1 and may be considered a continuation as it follows the river south and curving east and north through maturing woodland to reconnect with Trail 1.

Trail 3, the Oak Tree Trail, and Trail 1 form a complete loop in the southeast portion of the park skirting the Heritage Gardens. Incorporate the Heritage Gardens in this 0.5 mile walk and see favorite varieties that the early settlers grew.

Trail 5 or the Scenic Overlook Trail follows the river north from the boat ramp 0.3 mile to the park boundary with Madeline Bertrand County Park. Continue the river bluff walk into Michigan and the Madeline Bertrand County Park along Trail 1. Feel free to explore the other inter-connecting trails. Being able to walk about is part of a shared bi-state agreement that works well for park visitors who want additional trail mileage.

To reach St. Patrick's County Park from the Indiana Toll Road/ I-80-90 exit 77 in north South Bend onto Business US 31-33/Michigan Street and drive north to Auten Road. Turn left/west on Auten Road and proceed 0.5 mile to Laurel Road and turn right/north. The park entrance is on the left/west side of the road at 50651 Laurel.

41. POTATO CREEK STATE PARK

North Liberty, IN/ST. Joseph County
USGS MAP(s): Lakeville & N. Liberty 1:24,000
TRAIL(s) DISTANCE: 5 foot trails total 8.5 miles
ACREAGE: 3,840 acres
ACTIVITIES: nature walks, nature study, nature center, naturalist, nature preserve, picnicking, shelters, bicycle trail, bridle trail, swimming beach, lifeguards, beachhouse, fishing, boating, launch ramps, playgrounds, playfields, winter sports, x-country skiing, Class A campground, family cabins, Class A horse camp, youth tent campground, concessions, camp store
FEE(s): entrance, shelter, boat rentals, camping

One of Indiana's most popular state parks which opened in 1977, Potato Creek's origins date back to the 1930s and the efforts of self-taught naturalist Darcy Worster, who advocated and persisted in creating a state park in southwest St. Joseph County. His namesake lives on at the park's 343 acre Worster Lake, formed from the creek waters of Potato Creek. Worster Lake, the central attraction of the state park, is surrounded by recreational facilities that includes a top notch nature center with naturalist programs, several picnic shelters with fine lake views, a 3.2 mile all weather bicycle trail, and a 1,100 foot swimming beach and bathhouse. Not far from the lakeshore are the modern campgrounds. The park headquarters is located at the entrance to the park along Indiana 4.

Within the six square miles of parkland there are three major hiking trails that are separate from the seven miles of horse trails. The 100 acre Swamp Rose Nature Preserve has no trail access but may be viewed from Steam Boat Hill along Trail 2. Additional foot trails will probably be designated in the future in the northwest undeveloped section of the park where a restored wetland now exists.

Trail 1 is a 2.5 mile loop that begins/ends at the nature center. The well used path follows the wooded northeast shoreline of Worster Lake, then turns north along an old lane/service road intersecting with Trail 2 twice before turning back west through old abandoned fields filled with bluebirds and other wildlife.

Trail 2 begins/ends from Trail 1 and enters the more remote northeast portion of the park. The trail continues through maturing woodland to slowly ascend, with the aid of stairs, Steam Boat Hill which overlooks 100 feet above Swamp Rose Nature Preserve. The trail then heads west along the ridge top to a second overlook at Vargo Hill with views of Worster Lake. This portion of the park lies roughly at the western edge of the

Potato Creek State Park

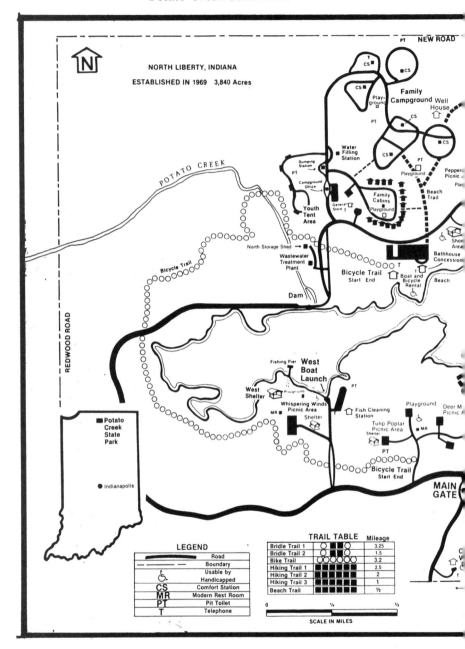

NORTH LIBERTY, INDIANA

ESTABLISHED IN 1969   3,840 Acres

NEW ROAD

Family Campground

Well House

Youth Tent Area

Water Filling Station

Campground Office

General Store

Family Cabins

Playground

Dumping Station

Peppermint Picnic

Beach Trail

POTATO CREEK

North Storage Shed

Wastewater Treatment Plant

Bicycle Trail

Dam

Shelter Area

Bathhouse Concession

Beach

Bicycle Trail
Start End

Boat and Bicycle Rental

REDWOOD ROAD

Fishing Pier

West Boat Launch

West Shelter

Whispering Winds Picnic Area
Shelter

Fish Cleaning Station

Playground

Deer Meadow Picnic Area

Tulip Poplar Picnic Area
Shelter

Bicycle Trail
Start End

MAIN GATE

■ Potato Creek State Park

● Indianapolis

LEGEND

	Road
	Boundary
♿	Usable by Handicapped
CS	Comfort Station
MR	Modern Rest Room
PT	Pit Toilet
T	Telephone

TRAIL TABLE

	Mileage
Bridle Trail 1	3.25
Bridle Trail 2	1.5
Bike Trail	3.2
Hiking Trail 1	2.5
Hiking Trail 2	2
Hiking Trail 3	1
Beach Trail	½

0   ¼   ½

SCALE IN MILES

226

Potato Creek State Park

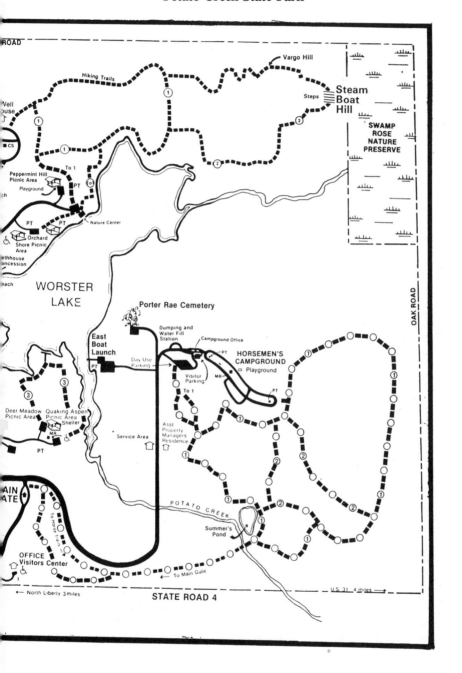

Maxinkuckee Moraine. The trail continues west to eventually descend a steep slope and reconnect to Trail 1. Both Trails 1 and 2 serve as a cross country ski trail in winter.

Trail 3. On the south central shore of Worster Lake is the one mile long Trail 3. The horseshoe-shaped trail begins at the east parking lot of Quaking Aspen picnic area and returns at the west parking lot. The trail enters an outstanding climax beech-maple forest where there are several ravines that descend to the lakeshore. In addition, the 0.5 mile Beach Trail is a connecting linear spur leading from the family campground to the beach-nature center.

To reach Potato Creek State Park from US 31, turn west on Indiana 4 north of Lakeville, Indiana and proceed to the park entrance on the right/north side of the highway. The park is located ten miles southwest of South Bend, Indiana.

42. BENDIX WOODS COUNTY PARK & NATURE PRESERVE
New Carlisle, IN/St. Joseph County
USGS MAP(s): Lydick 1:24,000
TRAIL(s) DISTANCE: 9 trails total 5.5 miles
ACREAGE: 195 acres
ACTIVITIES: nature walks, nature study, nature center, naturalist, picnicking, shelters, playground, volleyball, maple sugar house, winter sports, x-country skiing, gift shop, annual events
FEE(s): seasonal weekend entrance, shelter rentals

Little disturbed since the 1920s, Bendix Woods was donated in 1966 to the St. Joseph County Parks and Recreation Department by the Bendix Corporation, who had previously purchased the land from the Studebaker Corporation. Pine plantations and beech-maple deciduous forest cover the rolling uplands of which 27 acres is a dedicated state nature preserve. Nine short foot trails loop and interconnect throughout the property and vary in distance from 0.25 mile to 1.6 mile. A summary of the trails follows:

Trail 1 or Raccoon Run is the longest foot path stretching from the nature center west and south to the nature preserve and back to the nature center; a distance of 1.6 miles. Enroute through the forested area, the trail connects Trails 6, 8, 9, 5A, 5B, 2 and 3, crossing the park road five times.

Bendix Woods County Park

SR 2

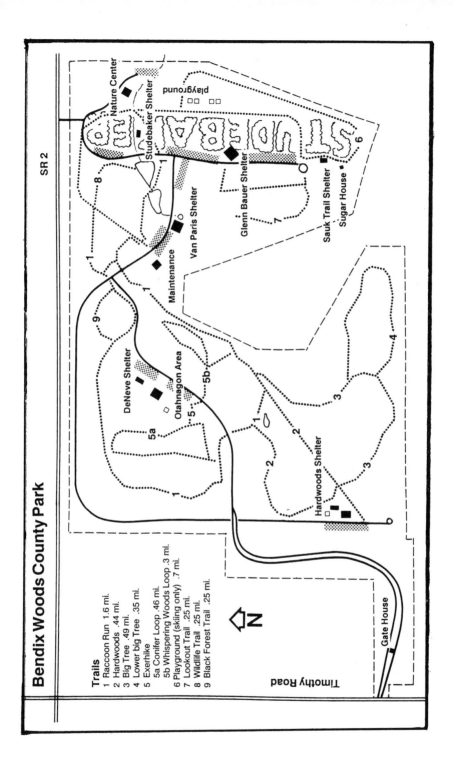

Trails
1 Raccoon Run 1.6 mi.
2 Hardwoods .44 mi.
3 Big Tree .49 mi.
4 Lower big Tree .35 mi.
5 Exerhike
5a Conifer Loop .46 mi.
5b Whispering Woods Loop .3 mi.
6 Playground (skiing only) .7 mi.
7 Lookout Trail .25 mi.
8 Wildlife Trail .25 mi.
9 Black Forest Trail .25 mi.

N

Nature Center
Studebaker Shelter
playground
Glenn Bauer Shelter
Van Paris Shelter
Maintenance
Sauk Trail Shelter
Sugar House
DeNeve Shelter
Otahnagon Area
Hardwoods Shelter
Timothy Road
Gate House

229

Trail 2 or the Hardwoods Trail is a 0.44 mile long path that loops about the old growth nature preserve where there are impressive beech, sugar maple, red elm and basswood trees. Trail 2 connects Trails 3 and 1. Closest trail access to the nature preserve is from the Hardwoods picnic shelter parking area.

Trail 3 or the Big Tree Trail is 0.49 mile long and also loops about the nature preserve. Showy white trilliums are outstanding in the spring. Connects Trails 1, 2 and 4.

Trail 4 or the Lower Big Tree Trail loops about 0.35 mile in the east portion of the nature preserve. Connect from Trail 3. The slopes and ravines in the preserve are covered with an understory of spicebush and paw paw.

Trail 5 includes two loops, 5A and 5B, that are bisected by the park road but are connected by the linear spur 5 in the Otahnagon picnic area. The Conifer Loop/5A is 0.46 mile and the Whispering Woods Loop/ 5B is 0.3 mile and the connecting 5 spur is 0.1. Trail 1 junctions with the Trail 5 network twice.

Trail 6 begins near the playground and parallels the park's east boundary at the base of the Studebaker pinery, looping back north near the maple sugar house and Sauk Trail picnic shelter for a total of 0.7 mile. This is the winter cross-country ski trail.

Trail 7 or the Lookout Trail is a 0.25 mile long non-loop that begins near the Glenn Bauer picnic shelter west of the ridgetop Studebaker pinery.

Trail 8 or Wildlife Trail is a 0.25 mile long linear trail that intersects with Trail 1 and leads to the pond west of the Studebaker Shelter, west of the pinery.

Trail 9 is the Black Forest Trail that forms a 0.25 mile loop with Trail 1 in the north central portion of the park.

Bendix Woods is located seven miles west of the US 31 South Bend bypass on Indiana 2 and three miles south of New Carlisle. The address is 32132 Indiana 2. The hours are 7 am to sunset daily except holidays. The nature center and gift shop are open 9 am to 5 pm Monday through Friday.

While in the general area, consider visiting Spicer Lake County Park and Nature Preserve. From Bendix Woods entrance, continue west on Indiana 2, 1.8 mile to County Line Road and turn right/north. Continue north on County Line Road 5.6 miles crossing US 20 to Spicer Lake, just north of Auten Road.

43. SPICER LAKE COUNTY PARK & NATURE PRESERVE
New Carlisle, IN/St. Joseph County
USGS MAP(s): New Carlisle 1:24,000
TRAIL(s) DISTANCE: appx. 2 miles total
ACREAGE: 240 acres
ACTIVITIES: nature walks, nature study, nature preserve, environmental education center, naturalist, wetlab

Located along the Michigan-Indiana state line, Spicer Lake is a dedicated nature preserve that is owned and managed by the St. Joseph County Park and Recreation Department. Geology-wise, Spicer Lake was formerly a 200 acre glacial-carved kettle or pothole lake that was created when a large ice block broke off from the retreating Wisconsinan ice field and melted thousands of years ago. Today the lake has been reduced to three to five acres of open water. Over time, succession has filled the lake with organic matter creating concentric rings of yellow pond lily marsh, buttonbush shrub swamp and red maple swamp forest. The area lies within the Valparaiso Moraine. Three centuries from now the lake may be bog.

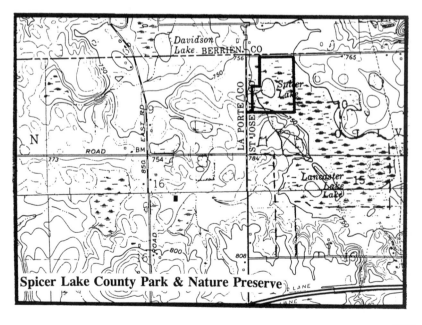

Spicer Lake County Park & Nature Preserve

Visitors to the property may learn about the natural history of Spicer Lake at the Schurz Environmental Education Center which is currently staffed by a naturalist on Sundays, 1 to 4 pm. Public nature programs are offered every Sunday (except holidays) at 2 pm.

Foot trails begin and end at the Schurz Center and the parking area to the near north along County Line Road. A boardwalk leads around the west edge where a pier extends out into Spicer Lake. East of the Schurz Center, a trail follows the edge between swamp forest and upland forest, looping back through the upland ridge and skirting the smaller Lancaster Lake. Crossover connecting spurs lie enroute.

To reach Spicer Lake in northwestern St. Joseph County from US 20, west of New Carlisle, turn right/north onto County Line Road and drive 3.7 miles to the parking areas.

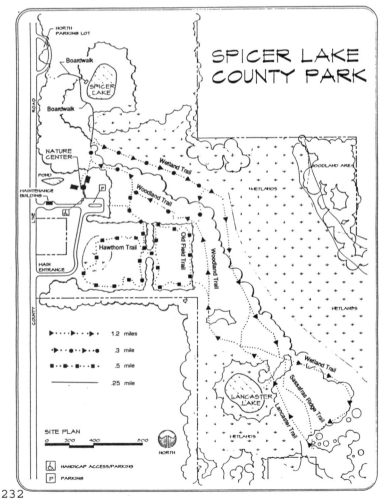

44. GALENA WETLAND CONSERVATION AREA/SPRINGFIELD FEN NATURE PRESERVE

Springville, IN/LaPorte County
USGS MAP(s): Springville 1:24,000
TRAIL(s) DISTANCE: no est. trails
ACREAGE: 165 acre WCA-45 acre NP
ACTIVITIES: hiking, nature study, seasonal trapping, fishing, canoeing

The Galena Wetland Conservation Area and the Springfield Fen Nature Preserve both occupy the same property at the headwaters of the Galena River, which is owned by the Department of Natural Resources but are managed separately by the Division of Fish and Wildlife and the Division of Nature Preserves. This combination of natural areas is also the management procedure at Round Lake and Koontz Lake in Starke County.

The 165 acre conservation area occupies the northern two thirds of this elongated narrow property. Scattered tree-covered islands rise above the marsh and shrub swamp. The diverse habitat is ideal for a variety of aquatic-seeking mammals such as beaver, muskrat and mink as well as waterfowl. Amazingly, migrating salmon and trout from Lake Michigan swim up the river to the headwaters to spawn. Although foot access is

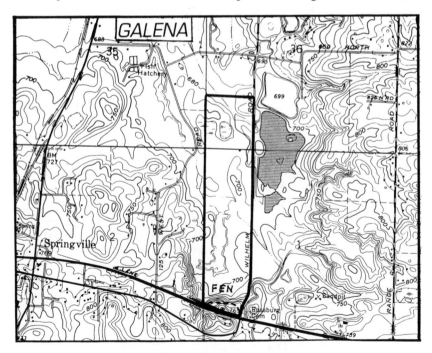

Galena Wetland Conservation Area

limited by the wetlands, the property provides excellent observation for nearly a mile along Wilhelm Road which forms the area's east boundary.

The 45 acre nature preserve at the south portion of the property is accessible on foot at the extreme southerly end where the property adjoins US 20. The wet prairie fen at the base of the beech-maple covered steep slope, 65 feet below, is kept moist by the hillside seeps.

Several prairie grasses and flowering forbs thrive in this restricted special habitat. Similar fens nearby include Trail Creek Fen and Yellow Birch Wetlands; all owned and managed by The Nature Conservancy.

To reach the property drive west 1.25 miles from the junction of Indiana 39 and US 20 at Springville, Indiana on US 20 to Wilhelm Road. Turn left/north on Wilhelm Road. The conservation area and nature preserve follows Wilhelm Road on the west side of the road for nearly 1.5 miles. A small parking lot is on the west side of the road one mile from the junction of Wilhelm Road and US 20.

45. LAPORTE NATURE PLACES

ACTIVITIES: nature walks, nature study, fitness trails, picnicking, shelters, swimming, lifeguards, playgrounds, fishing, boating, launch ramps, ballfields, tennis, basketball, handball, x-country skiing, winter sports, bandshell

FEE(s): summer weekend & holiday parking, shelter & ball rental

The community of LaPorte is often called the "City of Parks" and the larger parks are centered around the lakes of Stone, Pine, and Clear on the northwest side. Of the sixteen city public parks there are three that are nature-oriented and also activity oriented, plus of sizeable acreage: Soldiers Memorial Park, Fox Memorial Park and Kesling Park.

Soldiers Memorial Park, dedicated in 1928, contains 556 acres and is considered to be a regional park serving the people of northern Indiana and southern Michigan. It is LaPorte's largest park, known for its forested beauty, water sports and recreational activities. The park encompasses all of Stone Lake and all but 628 feet of shoreline.

Within its gently rolling terrain, the property is about 85% woodlands and water. A channel connects both Stone and Pine lakes. From the parking lot along Waverly Road, a foot bridge crosses over the channel and boat traffic to lead to the marked and maintained Soldier Memorial Nature Trails. Trail 1 is a 0.77 mile long loop and Trail 2, a 0.97 mile

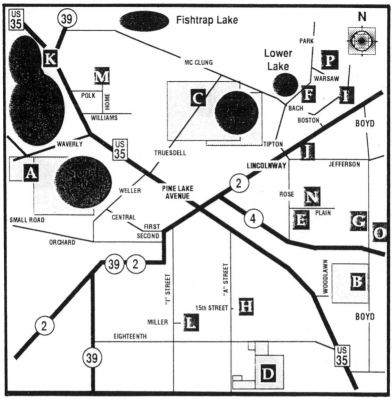

LaPorte Parks

[A] Soldiers Memorial
[B] Beechwood Golf Course
[C] Fox memorial Park
[D] Kesling Park
[E] Civic Auditorium
[F] City Park
[G] Allessee park

[I] Jaycee-Whirlpool Field
[J] Scott Field
[K] Kiwanis-Teledyne park
[L] Koomler Park
[M] Rumley park
[N] Rees park
[O] Monroe Tot Lot
[P] Warsaw Tot Lot

loop. The two interconnecting trails trace a loop around and along the densely wooded hill bluff and return across the foot bridge to the parking area. Soldiers Memorial Park is also the site of the administration offices of the LaPorte Parks and Recreation Department. The trailhead parking area is reached by turning west on Waverly Road from US 35/Indiana 39 at the city's northside. The Waverly Road parking area trailhead is located between Grangemouth Drive and Holton Road.

East a few block of Soldiers Memorial Park is the 170 acre Fox Memorial Park, located on the north shore of 100 acre Clear Lake, which is also included within the park's boundaries. Maurice and Herbert Fox commissioned the building of Fox Park in honor of their parents in 1911. The semi-formal landscaping compliments the beauty of the oak-covered uplands. Strolling paths weave throughout the park which is also home to ballfields, playgrounds, picnic shelters and the amphitheatre bandshell. The 0.5 mile fitness trail also doubles as a nature trail in the sylvan setting.

Fox Memorial Park is reached from US 35/Indiana 39 north, turning right/east on Truesdell Avenue and proceeding to Fox Park Drive north of Clear Lake near McClung Road.

Away from the lakes on the south suburban side of the city, is the 90 acre Kesling Park. The activity-oriented park lies adjacent to Kesling Middle School. The one mile paved fitness path and the one mile wood chipped nature trail follows the landscaped perimeter of the park along the edge of the recreational facilities. Students of the middle school have developed an outdoor education area in the park that is reputed to be one of the state's finest.

Kesling Park is easily reached from US 35 or Indiana 39 by turning on 18th Street and driving to the park entrance.

46. KOONTZ LAKE NATURE PRESERVE & WETLAND CONSERVATION AREA
Koontz Lake, IN/Starke County
USGS MAP(s): Walkerton 1:24,000
TRAIL(s) DISTANCE: appx. 1 mile old 3-wheeler trail
ACREAGE: 206 acres total
ACTIVITIES: nature walk, nature study. (hunting, trapping, and fishing
    in the WCA only)

The 206 acre combination of nature preserve and wetland conservation area (similar situation at Round Lake in southwest Starke County), at the north side of Koontz Lake provides a striking and scenic contrast of habitat diversity. Originally acquired by The Nature Conservancy, the DNR properties contain a flat to gently rolling sandy upland with a prairie-oak savanna mix while the adjacent lowland just a few yards away features a tamarack shrub bog and forested fen, the most sizeable marsh of its type in north central Indiana. The natural area helps maintain the ecological health of Koontz Lake, a 350 acre water body.

The nature walk follows an old three wheeler trail along the perimeter between the wetlands and the uplands. From the parking area (which is sandy and the possibility exists of becoming mired) the best long distance trek is made by walking west/right along the north property line to the oak forest edge, and going down the slope and turning left/southeast. Follow the obvious path along the natural edge between these two natural areas curving southeast. Near mid-point there is an old lane to the left/north that leads uphill back to the parking lot which makes for a short loop. If you continue to follow the edge the trail will end at a dead end turn around near CR 1200E. At this point retrace your steps back to either the old lane shortcut or continue to retrace your original path to the north boundary and back east to the parking lot.

Koontz Lake Nature Preserve

Koontz Lake is located in the extreme northeast corner of Starke County. The properties border Marshall County to the east and is one mile south of the St. Joseph county line. To reach Koontz Lake Nature Preserve and Wetland Conservation Area from US 30 exit north at Grovertown, Indiana on Indiana 23 and drive four miles to the town of Koontz Lake on the west shore. From the town center continue north on Indiana 23, 1.25 miles to CR 875N, 0.5 mile south of the Starke-St. Joseph county line, and turn right/east. Proceed on CR 875N one mile to the "T" intersection and CR 1150E. Turn right/south on CR 1150E and drive to the dead end and the parking lot.

47. PLYMOUTH NATURE PLACES
Plymouth,IN/Marshall County

ACTIVITIES: nature walks, nature study, historic sites, picnicking, shelters, fishing, playfields, playgrounds, swimming pool, lifeguards, ball fields, tennis, soccer, shuffle boards, basketball, winter sports, Blueberry Festival

FEE(s): shelter, x-country ski rentals, building rental

The city of Plymouth has two nature-oriented parks along the Yellow River located on the community's northside within a few blocks of each other. Future plans call for connecting the 100 acre Centennial Park and 16 acre Magnetic Park via a nature trail along the river corridor. Presently the one mile Pilgram Trail follows the Shuh-Baker tributary and Yellow River at Centennial Park.

Centennial Park, Plymouth Nature Places

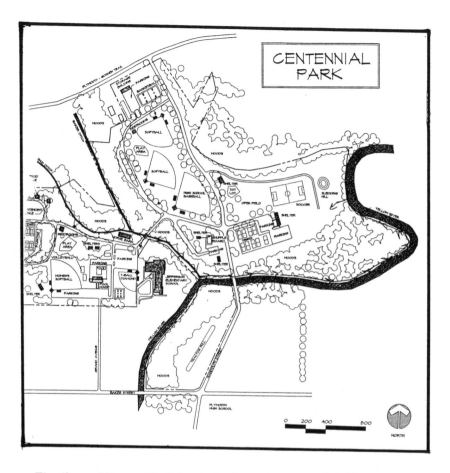

The linear Pilgram Trail begins/ends at the covered bridge over the Shuh-Baker tributary on the east bank. The floodplain path follows the stream south about 200 yards to where it merges with the Yellow River. The trail then jogs left/east upstream along the north bank and under the Randolph Street bridge. The shady and sometimes wet path continues upstream to end/begin at the sledding hill adjacent to the soccer field. Retrace the route back to the covered bridge. Mosquitoes can be annoying at various periods in warm weather. Occasionally there are scheduled nature hikes along the Pilgram Trail. Centennial Park was established in 1916 in celebration of 100 years of statehood and the city park was developed during the 1930s. The park is located on North Michigan Street/Old US 31, south of the US 30 exit one mile.

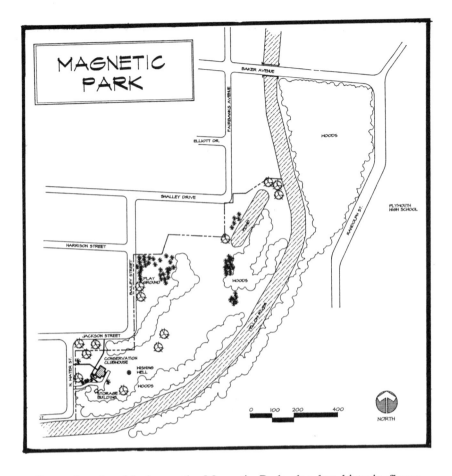

Located a few blocks south, Magnetic Park also has historic flavor. Prior to being a park, the site was once the location of a gristmill. Inspired by the spirit of the New Deal, the park was built by local conservationists of the 1930s. The field rock fence and arch is still intact and the Conservation Clubhouse is still used for recreational activities. The "magnetic" flowing wishing well's waters still flow and are reputed to have medicinal and curative properties. The well shelter house was constructed in 1875 and over 700,000 gallons flow every 24 hours. Further northeast of the well house along the floodplain is a small pond that is popular as a fishing site and ice skating area.

Magnetic Park is located east of North Michigan Avenue/Old US 31 at the end of Jackson Street in north Plymouth, Indiana.

48. MENOMINEE WETLAND CONSERVATION AREA
Plymouth, IN/Marshall County
USGS MAP(s): Plymouth, Donaldson 1:24,000
TRAIL(s) DISTANCE: no est. trails, old lanes
ACREAGE: 830 acres in 8 separate tracts
ACTIVITIES: hiking, nature study, canoeing, fishing, seasonal, hunting, trapping

The eight fragmented tracts that comprise the Menominee Wetlands are situated south of Plymouth, the Marshall county seat, and west within two miles of Starke County at Flat Lake. The topography and habitats are varied and include Yellow River floodplain forest, Maxinkuckee morainal kettle lakes and ponds, deep cattail marshes, dense shrub swamp, wet meadows, upland oak and hickory forest, pine plantations, and dry sandy revegetating fields. The eight tracts vary in acreage and few are readily accessible. The best two tracts to access are within one mile of each other and lie south and west of Indiana 17 about 5.5 miles west of Plymouth, south of the former West Township School and along CR 10B.

The first tract's north and west boundary follows Indiana 17 from east of the former West Township School south to Union Church and Cemetery at CR 10B. Park alongside the sandy roadside (at least ten feet) at the property sign on the east side of Indiana 17 just south of the bridge, south of the curve from the school. At this point there is a cabled gate which is the trailhead. Follow the old service road into the upland forest mix of pine and oak. The sandy wedge of upland extends into the wetlands and provides fine views of the deep water marsh. Numerous waterfowl and mammals nest or visit the wetland. Parking is also available adjacent east of the Union Church Cemetery on CR 10B, the next crossroad south on Indiana 17.

The second tract is east of Indiana 17 one mile on CR 10B. Follow the county paved road which turns to gravel to the upland pinery portion of the property where there is limited parking at a former homesite on the left/north side of CR 10B. This Menominee Wetland tract extends north about 0.5 mile and south across CR 10B about one mile, with about a 0.4 mile span east and west. This trek is for the adventuresome. Walking north on the upland veer east as you descend the slope into the lowland which can be mushy and under water during late winter and spring. Follow the edge as best as one can and continue upslope to a high wooded knoll. Further north is another low wet area and the property boundary. Return the same route. South across CR 10B, follow the upland pine plantation along the west perimeter above the wetland for some distance and return along the same route.

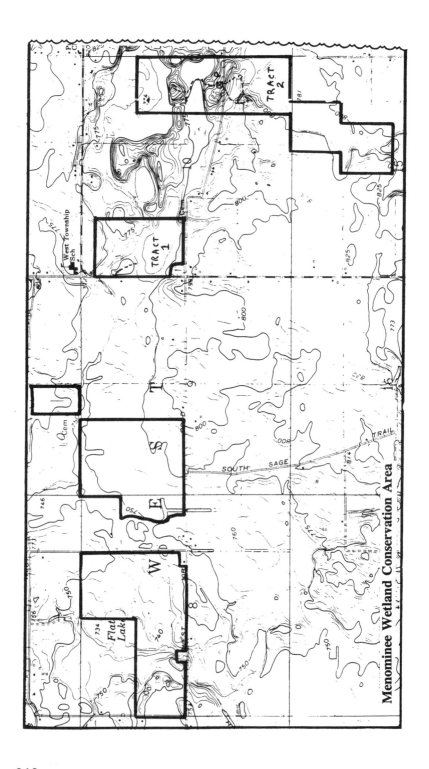

Menominee Wetland Conservation Area

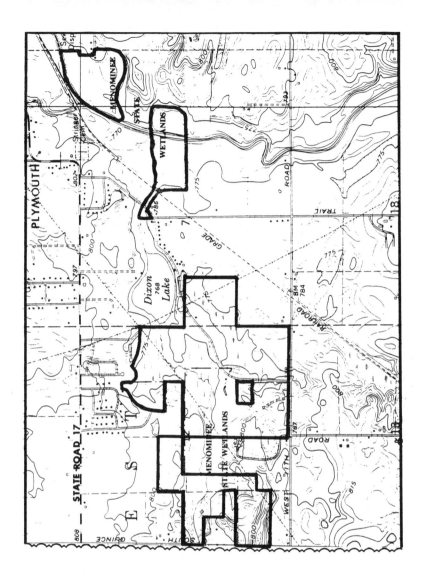

Menominee Wetland Conservation Area

The area is named for the Potawatomi Chief Menominee and his band who were marched west in the 1838 Trail of Death. A monument to Chief Menominee is located on South Peach Road, 6.5 miles southwest of Plymouth, just south of Twin Lakes.

While in the general area, consider walking the tree identification trail at <u>Mill Pond Public Fishing Site</u>. From the junction of Indiana 17 and CR

10B at the Union Church and Cemetery, drive south on Indiana 17 about 1.75 miles to the road curve, continuing straight a short distance to CR West 12th and turn left/east

Proceed east on CR West 12th about 0.2 mile to South Rose Road and turn right/south. Continue less than 0.5 mile to the Mill Pond Public Fishing Site on the left/east side of the road. The 0.5 mile loop trail begins near the sign at the wooded area south of the launch ramp. A prairie area is being developed. Canoeing is excellent on the 168 acre Mill Pond which has limited shoreline development.

49. CULVER NATURE PLACES
Culver, IN/Marshall County
USGS MAP(s): Culver 1:24,000
TRAIL(s) DISTANCE: 2 trail areas total appx. 2.5 miles
ACREAGE: 76 wca/ 10 acres Tpk & Indian trails
ACTIVITIES: nature walks, nature study, picnicking, playground, shelters, volleyball, basketball, beach, swimming, beachhouse, lifeguards, historic depot, concessions, fishing, WCA: hunting, trapping
FEE(s) seasonal parking, shelter rental at town park

Like most northern Indiana lakes, the shoreline of scenic Lake Maxinkuckee, the state's second largest natural lake, is consumed by private residences and other development and few natural areas remain. However there are two publicly accessible parklands; the Maxinkuckee Wetlands Conservation at the south inlet and the Culver Beach Park and adjoining Indian Trails area at the north shore.

The 76 acre Maxinkuckee Wetlands protect and serve as a biological "sponge" with its extensive cattail marsh along one the few inlets to the spring-fed 1,864 acre lake. Turtles, waterfowl, furbearers, deer and other wildlife are at home in the marsh. Geologically, the wetlands occupy a glacial outwash plain situated between two end moraines. A 0.25 mile trail traces a loop along the wooded upland west portion of the property following the edge of the wetlands, then looping back topping the open high point to the small parking lot. Across the inlet stream just a few yards east of the parking lot, a second trail could be negotiated along the levee, north towards the marina. The embankment provides open view south into the marsh.

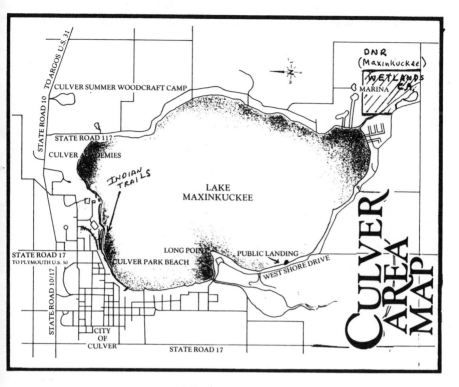

Culver Nature Places

To reach the area from US 31 and the junction of Indiana 110 at the Fulton-Marshall county line, drive west on Indiana 110 about eight miles to Indiana 117 and turn north/left. Follow Indiana 117 north nearly 0.5 mile and turn left/west on CR West 20B, the first road left. Continue another 0.5 mile to West Shore Drive, the next road, and turn right/north. Proceed along the west boundary of the wetlands to the parking lot on the right/west side of the Drive at the first curve. The trailhead begins adjacent east of the two-three car parking lot.

On the north shore along Lake Shore Drive near the town center is the Culver Beach Park and the adjoining Indian Trails natural area. The bluffs at the lakeside community park provide excellent views of the vast water body especially at the west portion of the park. The old turn of the century railroad depot awnings now serve as quaint picnic shelters. Paved paths line the shore and the bluff top. The popular park is busy in summer with water-related activities.

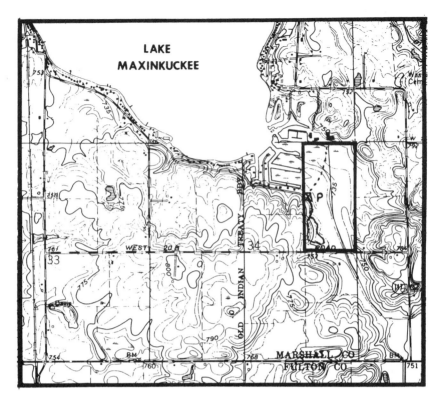

Maxinkukee Wetlands

The Indian Trails area, separating the town beach park from the nearby Culver Academies, begins at the east edge of the park. Several trails form an interconnecting network. Atop the oak-hickory wooded bluff there are three short linear trails that parallel the lake. The upper trail is paved asphalt and leads from the park to the academy. At mid-point the paved trail accesses a north to south spur that leads to a wood chipped rail-to-trail path. The 0.25 mile path follows the old railline of the Pennsylvania Railroad from the town park to Academy Road. Near Academy Road on the west side of the path, the lowland area has a loop trail with stairs and boardwalk through a wet area that once served as a fish hatchery.

To reach the Culver Beach Park and Indian Trails area continue north on Indiana 117 about 3.5 miles to Indiana 10 and turn left/west. Follow Indiana 10 west just over a mile to the junction with Indiana 17 and turn left/south onto Lake Shore Drive. Follow Lake Shore Drive about three blocks to the curve and the park.

50. POTAWATOMI WILDLIFE PARK

Tippecanoe, IN/Marshall County
USGS MAP(s): Mentone 1:24,000
TRAIL(s) DISTANCE: appx. 5 miles of loop trails
ACREAGE: 203 acres
ACTIVITIES: nature walks, nature study, picnicking, x-country skiing,
reference library, group tours, youth group camping by reservations,
youth group fishing, group amphitheatre, nature center
FEE(s): youth group camp

Ponds, marsh wetlands, creeks, old fields and bottomland along the Tippecanoe River comprise Potawatomi Wildlife Park, a privately endowed nature sanctuary maintained and managed by five area service clubs. Located in an area of extensive flat farm fields, the park is a welcome watery oasis. The well maintained trails loop about the five ponds and floodplain forest and are open daily from sunrise to sunset. Visitors are asked to register at the trailhead parking area before walking the trails. All camping and fishing is reserved for youth groups only.

In addition to three miles of unnamed trails, there are two self-guiding interpretive trails that total two miles and both are named for Potawatomi leaders of the early to mid-19th century. The Pe-ash-way Trail is a 0.5 mile loop that leads through old growth forest on the property's west portion. The available brochure identifies plants and discusses the role of beaver who have established a lodge at one of the ponds. The trail is named in honor of John Pe-ash-way, an elder of the village which existed on the property. The 1.5 mile Chief Stephen Ben-nack Interpretive Trail is named in honor of the chief whose village was on the property until 1854. Following the floodplain, the loop trail features ten stations which correspond to the interpretive brochure that describes the ecological diversity of the river, floodplain, creeks, ponds, and upland habitats. The trail may be wet and muddy at times and stinging wood nettle is a common forest plant of the floodplain.

Potawatomi Wildlife Park is located at 16998 Indiana 331, one mile north of Tippecanoe, Indiana. From US 31 at Argos, Indiana, drive east on Indiana 10 about 7.5 miles to its junction with Indiana 331. Turn south on Indiana 331 and continue about one mile to the park's entry lane on the left/east side of the highway. A colorful sign marks the entrance.

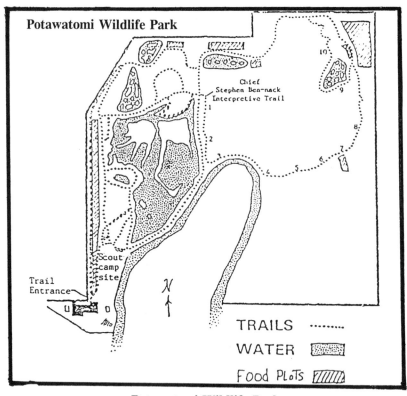

Potawatomi Wildlife Park

TRAILS ·········
WATER
Food Plots

Potawatomi Wildlife Park

51. GENEVA CENTER
Rochester, IN/Fulton County
USGS MAP(s): Rochester, Argos 1:24,000
TRAIL(s) DISTANCE: appx. 2 miles
ACREAGE: 185 acres
ACTIVITIES: nature walks, nature study

Occupying some of the highest ground in Fulton County is Geneva Center, a christian camp and conference retreat center, owned and managed by the Presbytery of Wabash Valley. The 185 rolling acres of glacial kame and moraine are covered with conifer plantations and deciduous forest. A buttonbush shrub swamp exists on the northwest portion of the property. Although Geneva Center's primary mission is to accommodate church and other non-profit organizations, the nature trails are generously open to the general public during the daylight operating hours. Visitors are asked to check in prior to walking the trails and obtain a trail and property map at the conference center office next to the parking area.

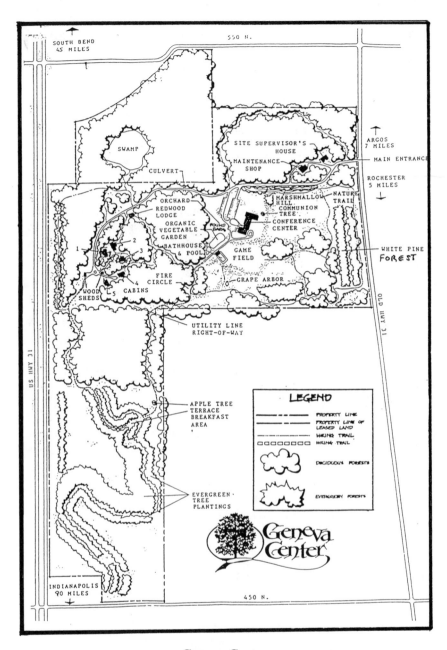

Geneva Center

The wide maintained trails radiate out in all directions from the parking area and conference center. Most of the paths may be accessed from the entry drive. The closest trail begins north of the parking area across the entry drive, west of the maintenance building. The forest trail traces a half-loop or arch through dense hardwoods to emerge near the property entrance. Cross over the entry road south and pick up the trail through the white pine forest that parallels old US 31. The trail loops about in the pinery and adjacent west pioneer deciduous forest. Head west and follow the trail along the perimeter upland just north of the gravel pit beyond the south boundary. The trail curves past the fire circle to access the conifer plantations of the southwest property, looping back north to parallel new US 31 and to end at the cabin area. Follow the park road north and near Butler Lodge, a spur linear trail heads north through maturing mixed forest to a buttonbush shrub swamp. Retrace your steps back to the park road and go left/east back to the parking area.

To reach Geneva Center from old US 31 in north central Fulton County, drive 4.7 miles north of Rochester, the county seat, crossing the Tippecanoe River, to the signed entrance on the left/west side of old US 31. From new US 31 go north of Rochester, across the Tippecanoe River, and turn left/north at the second road, CR 450N. Continue east on CR 450N one mile to old US 31 and turn right/south. Proceed to the entrance on the left/west side of the highway. For more information telephone Geneva Center at (219) 223-6915.

South of Geneva Center on old US 31 and left/east on CR 350N about 0.3 mile is the Menominee Public Fishing Area, accessing the Tippecanoe River. A user made fisherman's path leads visitors along this lake-fed stream about 0.25 mile one-way. The floodplain forest is dense and the understory is thick with stinging wood nettle and poison ivy but the trail provides a natural section of river where silver maple, basswood, redbud and sycamore are prolific. Plenty of parking. A nice nature spot.

The Menominee Public Fishing Area is located 2.7 miles north of the Rochester Courthouse on old US 31. The path is west of the boat ramp.

UPPER WABASH RIVER: OVERVIEW

"The trees are numerous along the Wabash and in the woods,
so that - blooming before leafage and almost first,
and seemingly to commingle with the mist and haze of
early spring - they touch the horizon with a faint purple
that melts into the blue of the sky and the lazy white clouds. "

Gene Stratton Porter (1863-1924)
from: Music of the Wilds, Chapter:
Song of the Fields, pg. 108

The natural and social history rich upper Wabash River valley is revealed in the parklands that line its banks, ranging from the urban green spaces of Lafayette, Indiana to the more remote nature preserves of Acres Along the Wabash and Portland Arch. Nature walks along the upper stretches of Indiana's best known river includes the tributaries such as the Salamonie, Mississinewa, and Wildcat and the Little (Wabash) River whose headwaters are near Fort Wayne.

In regard to physical geography, the upper Wabash River valley is basically a dividing line between the Grand Prairie and Northern Lake natural regions and the vast central Till Plain. Actually, Fort Wayne and much of Allen County belongs to the Black Swamp natural region of northwest Ohio but the area is placed in this section to simplify. Geologically young at 16,000 years, the Wabash River valley train and outwash plain run aside and cut through the Wabash and Mississinewa Moraines, as it makes its widening way west and south along the vast central Till Plain.

As of late, all levels of government, private organizations and individuals have been involved in creating the Wabash Heritage Corridor; a recreational, cultural and natural resource corridor of preservation. Indiana is showing a new wave of pride for its State river.

The most scenic nature walks within the Wabash valley include Limberlost County Park, Acres Along the Wabash nature preserve, Forks of the Wabash, Hanging Rock, and Ross Hills County Park. "Pure" Wabash areas include the Gene Stratton Porter Limberlost home at Geneva, Indiana, the Bluffton Rivergreenway, Ouabache State Park, the Delphi Trailhead Park & Towpath Trail.

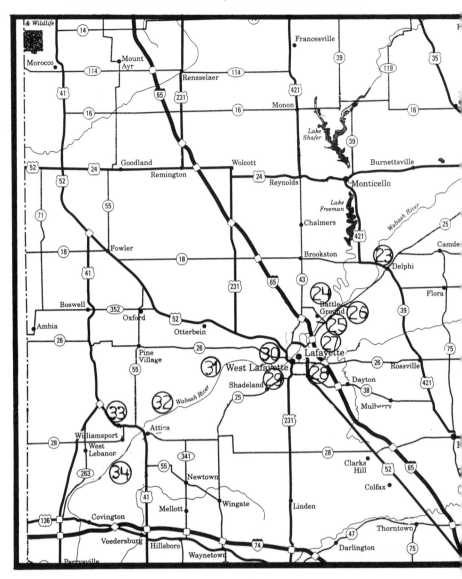

History is the glue that bonds Indiana's close ties to the Wabash and the historical parks include the Forks of the Wabash, Seven Pillars of the Mississinewa, Tippecanoe Battlefield, Fort Ouiatenon and Zachariah Cicott County Park. The most outstanding nature preserves are Vandolah, Fox Island, Fall Creek Gorge, and Portland Arch. The Purdue Campus walks are uniquely urbane.

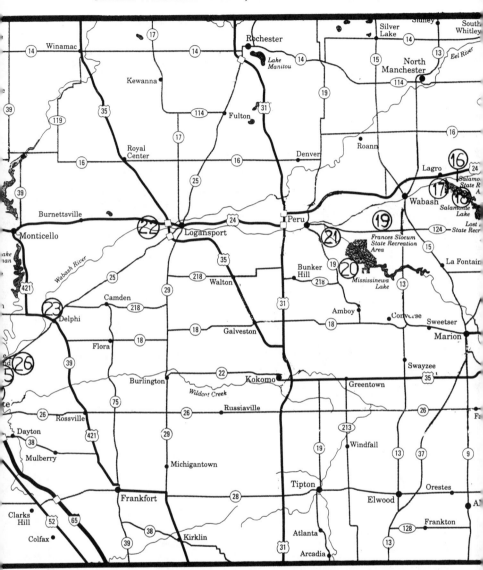

In addition to natural wildlife, there is contained wildlife to view at Ouabache State Park, the Fort Wayne Zoo, Wolf Park and the Lafayette Columbian Park Zoo. Ravine Park at Attica, Indiana is a special small town park. For cultivated gardens, visit the Foellinger-Freimann Botanical Conservatory and the Clegg Botanic Gardens. Waterfalls are always inspiring and may be seen at the Markle Town Park, Wabash River

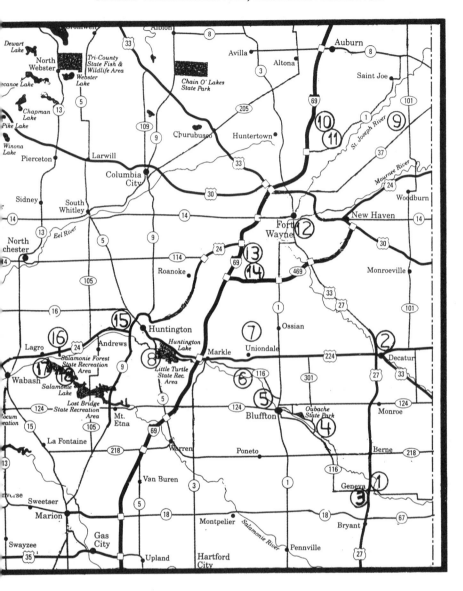

spillway, France Park, Ross Hills, Ravine Park, Fall Creek Gorge and Portland Arch. Geologically speaking the best nature walks are at Hanging Rock, Seven Pillars of the Mississinewa, France Park, Fall Creek Gorge and Portland Arch.

1. LIMBERLOST STATE HISTORIC SITE

Geneva, IN/Adams County
USGS MAP(s): Geneva 1:24,000
TRAIL(s): DISTANCE: landscaped grounds, appx. 3 miles of trails at nearby Fields Park & Limberlost County Park
ACREAGE: 2 a. gsphs, 12 a. fpk, 53 a. llcp
ACTIVITIES: nature walks, nature study, historic sites, garden, tours, gift shop, special events, picnicking, covered bridge

Limberlost Historic Site is the home where Gene Stratton Porter (1863-1924) began her career as a world-renowned naturalist and author. She was born and raised at the Stratton family farm at Hopewell, Indiana, a small community east of Wabash, Indiana, into a family that loved nature. In 1886 at age 23, Gene Stratton married Charles Darwin Porter of Decatur, Indiana, a druggist and banker; together they raised a daughter, Jeannette. Eleven years later in 1895, they built a cabin-styled home in south Geneva, Indiana near Limberlost Creek and Swamp, where she found the stuff of her novels in tramps through the 13,000 acre wetlands. Mrs. Porter named the rustic white cedar, fourteen room house she designed, for the nearby wilds that were supposedly named after "Limber" Jim McDowell, who went hunting and became lost for three days. Current efforts are being made to establish a nature reserve in the former swamp which has been entirely drained and only 100 acres is woodlots.

Gene Stratton Porter was a prolific writer and most of her best acclaimed works such as The Harvester, Freckles and The Girl of the Limberlost were written during her Geneva years (1895-1913). The shores of Sylvan Lake became their family home upon leaving Geneva and the Limberlost that was fast becoming drained farmlands. She named her new cabin-styled home, "Wildflower Woods", and it is also a state memorial historic site owned and managed by the DNR Division of the Indiana State Museum and Historic Sites.

Limberlost Historic Site is open for tours from mid-March through mid-December. The hours are 9 am to 5 pm, Tuesday to Saturday, 1 pm to 5 pm on Sunday, and closed major holidays. The historic site is located in Geneva, one block east of US 27 (Main Street), south of Line Street at 200 East 6th Street.

Fields Park, located two blocks east of US 27 and one block south of 6th Street, provides picnicking and nature trails. The 12 acre Adams County park was a gift from the Harold Fields family. The "farm field turned forest" started in the 1920s when Charles Field planted the trees.

The wooded park is close to Limberlost Creek and its confluence with the Wabash River, where, in the words of Mrs. Porter,

"goes laughing on the way
gathering force in a last rush
hurrying to merge with
the Wabash".

Just north of Geneva at Ceylon, Indiana is the 53 acre <u>Limberlost County Park</u> (**A**) that showcases the 126 foot long Ceylon Covered Bridge, built in 1862; the last covered bridge spanning the Wabash River. Actually, the covered bridge straddles an old river channel that locals call Rainbow Bottom. The 0.75 mile Gene Stratton Porter Trail loops a restored prairie to the northwest of the bridge. There are also picnic tables and a shelter. This is the heart of Amish farmlands. To reach the Adams County Park, drive north on US 27 about a mile from the intersection of US 27 and Indiana 116 in Geneva, to CR 950S and turn right/east. Follow CR 950S northwest along the curving route another 0.5 mile to the Wabash River covered bridge and the county park.

While in the south Adams County-Wabash River area, consider visiting the 15 acre <u>Linn Grove County Park</u> (**B**), downstream from Geneva, just north of Indiana 116 on the north bank of the Wabash. This is the best point of launching for a canoe to begin a journey on the river and at times can be too shallow. Many canoeists of the Wabash believe the Forks of the Wabash is the best place to begin a fluvual canoe journey. There is also picnicking in the riverside park. Also, visit the <u>Munro Nature Preserve</u> (**C**), just west of Geneva.

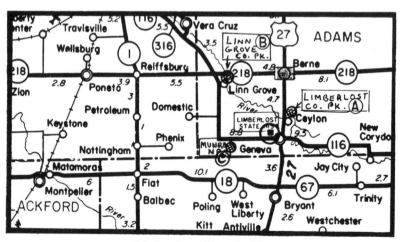

Limberlost Historic Site

2. DECATUR NATURE PLACES

ACTIVITIES: nature walks, nature study, naturalist, picnicking, shelters, gazebo, gardens, nature refuge, bicycling, playground, playfields, ballfields, ballcourts, fishing, canoeing, canoe launch ramp, recreation center

Decatur, the county seat of Adams County, is located on the St. Marys River in the Black Swamp Natural Region that is found primarily in northwest Ohio. By road, Decatur is located about 20 miles southeast of Ft. Wayne and is accessed via Indiana 101, US 27, US 33 and US 224. The St. Marys River provides the setting for the paved 0.75 mile linear rivergreenway walk along the floodplain fringe and the Hanna Nuttman Park encompasses a green segment of Borum Run where a 0.25 mile riparian trail follows the curving stream.

Decatur, like Anderson, Ft. Wayne, Marion, South Bend and other Indiana river cities, has utilized the floodplain corridor as a pedestrian pathway for walkers joggers and bicyclists. The path begins/ends at the Jackson Street Commons, the north terminus, along the east bank of the river, north of the Riverside Recreation Center at Monroe Street/US 224. The Recreation Center is the main office for the Decatur Parks Department and the Adams County Park Department, which oversees the county parks of Linn Grove, Limberlost and Fields Park along or near the Wabash River in the south county. A county naturalist occasionally leads nature walks at the various parks.

The trail heads south along the wooded edge, crossing the river on an abandoned railroad bridge, and on to Kekionga Park, an activity park in a natural floodplain setting. Access to the St. Marys River at the canoe launch ramp is a good starting point for a float to Ft. Wayne. There is also a natural area being restored to prairie.

Away from the St. Marys River west, on Washington Street from US 33 in northwest Decatur is the 45 acre Hanna Nuttman city park. A 15 acre wooded wildlife refuge is located in the northwest portion of the park adjacent to Washington Street. A fine stand of prairie dock, a sunflower type that blooms in late summer, along with closed bottle gentian with its bright blue bottle-shaped flowers are found here. The earth based path follows both wooded banks of the natural meandering Borum Run.

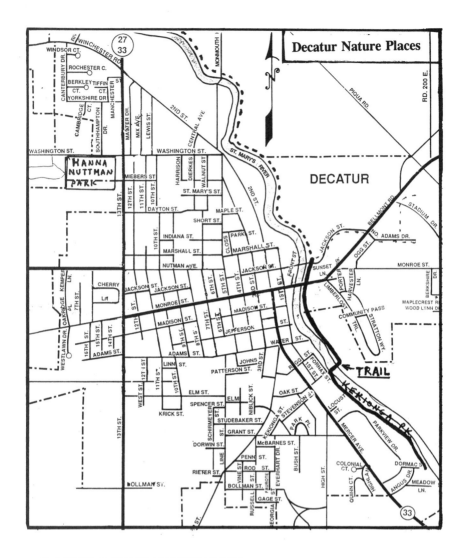

Decatur Nature Places

DECATUR

3. MUNRO NATURE PRESERVE
Geneva, IN/Adams County
USGS MAP(s): Geneva 1:24,000
TRAIL(s) DISTANCE: 0.5 mile loop
ACREAGE: 25 acres
ACTIVITIES: nature walks, nature study, historic site

Located on the northern edge of what was once the Limberlost Swamp, the Munro Nature Preserve is a mixed deciduous woodland owned and managed by ACRES, Inc. Also located at the site is the Brushwood schoolhouse, written about in Gene Stratton Porter's, <u>Girl of the</u>

<u>Limberlost.</u> The 0.5 mile perimeter loop trail through the woods begins and ends at the old school which was built at the turn of the 20th century. The low flat woods can be wet and muddy after heavy rains. Attempts to purchase additional Limberlost Swamplands is being supported by ACRES, Inc.

To reach Munro Nature Preserve drive west from Geneva in south Adams County, on Indiana 116 about 2.5 miles to CR 400W and turn left/ south. Continue one mile south on CR 400W to the preserve and the old school at the northeast corner of CR 400W and CR 1100S. Park along the roadside.

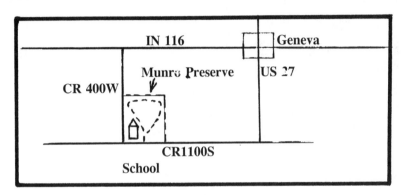

Munro Nature Preserve

4. OUABACHE STATE PARK
Bluffton, IN/Wells County
USGS MAP(s): Bluffton, Linn Grove 1:24,000
TRAIL(s) DISTANCE: 5 foot trails total 13 miles
ACREAGE: 1,100 acres
ACTIVITIES: nature walks, nature study, seasonal naturalist, wildlife buffalo exhibit, exercise trail, picnicking, shelters, swimming pool, waterslide, lake boating, lake boat launch, river & lake fishing, playgrounds, playfields, observation tower, x-country skiing, Class A & B camping, youth camping, cultural arts programs
FEE(s): seasonal entrance, camping, shelter rental, paddleboat & canoe rental, recreation, building rental

Ouabache (O-bah-chee) State Park occupies the north bank of the Wabash River, east of Bluffton in Wells County. Prior to becoming a state recreation area and later a state park in 1983, the property was known as Wells County State Forest and Game Preserve which began in the 1930s.

OUABACHE STATE PARK

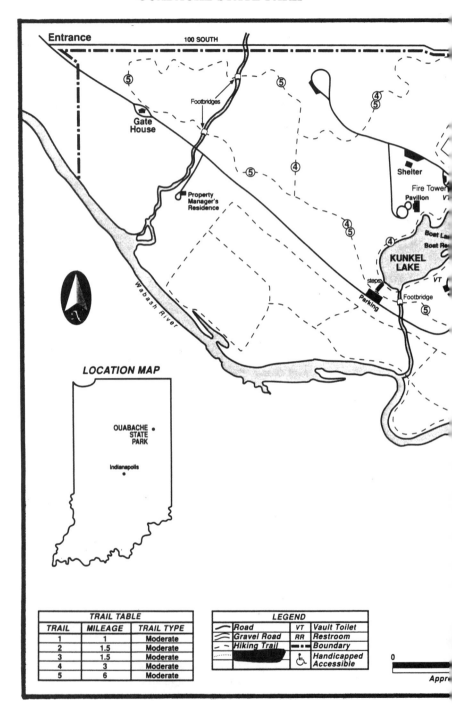

Entrance   100 SOUTH

Footbridges

Gate House

Property Manager's Residence

Shelter

Fire Tower

Pavilion   VT

Boat Lac

Boat Re

KUNKEL LAKE

steps

Parking   VT

Footbridge

Wabash River

LOCATION MAP

OUABACHE STATE PARK

Indianapolis

TRAIL TABLE		
TRAIL	MILEAGE	TRAIL TYPE
1	1	Moderate
2	1.5	Moderate
3	1.5	Moderate
4	3	Moderate
5	6	Moderate

LEGEND		
Road	VT	Vault Toilet
Gravel Road	RR	Restroom
Hiking Trail	‑ ‑	Boundary
	♿	Handicapped Accessible

0

Appr

OUABACHE STATE PARK

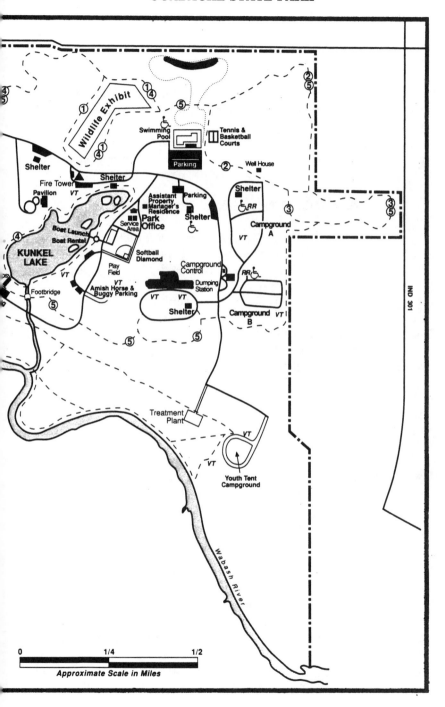

Wildlife Exhibit

Swimming Pool

Tennis & Basketball Courts

Parking

Shelter

Well House

Fire Tower

VT

Shelter

Pavilion

Assistant Property Manager's Residence

Parking

Shelter

RR

Service Area

Park Office

Shelter

Campground A

Boat Launch

Boat Rental

KUNKEL LAKE

Softball Diamond

VT

Play Field

VT

VT

Campground Control

RR

Footbridge

Amish Horse & Buggy Parking

Dumping Station

VT

VT

Shelter

Campground B

VT

IND 301

Treatment Plant

VT

VT

Youth Tent Campground

Wabash River

0   1/4   1/2

Approximate Scale in Miles

At one time the preserve was a major hatchery of pheasant, quail and even raccoon. The property was developed by the Works Projects Administration (WPA) and the Civilian Conservation Corps (CCC) during the Great Depression, when the state and federal governments built a solid park system that we enjoy today.

All five of the foot trails are north of the Wabash River. There are several miles of moderately difficult paths that vary in distance from one to six miles over level terrain. There are several miles of looping trails (previously bridle trails) along the river floodplain that can be difficult to negotiate after heavy rains. A canoe launch could be made from a short portage south to the Wabash River from the youth tent campground.

The five trails are briefly summarized as follows:

Trail 1: Encircles the fenced wildlife exhibit of buffalo or bison, (by some Hoosiers, the unofficial state animal of Indiana). The one mile long trail loop also combines and forms a segment of Trail 4. A popular walk.

Trail 2: The 1.5 mile trails begins at the north end of campground A near the Well House or accessed from the swimming pool parking area. The loop trail intersects with Trail 3 and combines and forms part of Trail 5. Trail 2 leads through planted pineries and hardwood forest in the northeast section of the park.

Trail 3 : Begins near Trail 2 trailhead, northeast of campground A. Goes east tracing a loop in the dense wet forest of the east central property, skirting Indiana 301. Trail 5 combines with and forms a trail segment.

Trail 4: The three mile loop begins at the wildlife bison exhibit and runs north and west through conifer and deciduous forest plantations into remote portions of the park. Trail turns south and then east to Kunkel Lake, encircling the lake. Climb the old firetower. Portions of Trail 4 are also parts of Trail 1 and Trail 5.

Trail 5: The six mile Ouabacbe Trail is the longest in the park. Encircles the park's perimeter that is bounded by Indiana 301 and CR 100 South, and includes a variety of habitats. Trail begins at wildlife exhibit area adjacent north of the parking area and includes many access points. Accesses all the foot trails and the exercise trail, north of the swimming pool.

Ouabache State Park entrance is on Indiana 201, four miles east of Bluffton at 4930 East State Road 201. Follow the roadside signs.

5. BLUFFTON RIVERGREENWAY

Bluffton, IN/Wells County
USGS Map(s): Bluffton 1:24,000
TRAIL(s) DISTANCE: 1.5 miles linear trail
ACTIVITIES: nature walk, nature study, exercise path, bicycling, arboretum, amphitheatre, special events, picnicking, shelters
FEE(s): shelter rentals

Bluffton, "The Parlor City", was established on the bluff rises perched above the Wabash River. The rivergreenway follows the south bank of the 30 yard-wide stream from CR 400E downtown to Kehoe Park and amphitheatre; a distance of 1.5 mile one-way and future plans will extend the rivergreenway east upstream to Ouabache State Park. The linear, paved all-weather wide path is popular with joggers, bikers and hikers. Benches, shelters, picnic tables and a covered walking bridge line the greenway.

Located in the residential neighborhood near downtown is the former home and gardens of Hoosier botanist, Charles L. Deam, author of Flora of Indiana. The current private garden, a site listed on the Indiana Historic Register, is located at the corner of 305 Wayne Street across River Road from the rivergreenway of the Wabash River. A tribute to Charles Deam is the State of Indiana's smallest park containing the unique Deam Oak located northwest of Bluffton near Murray, Indiana on Indiana 116 at the north side of the highway. The oak is a hybrid crossed between the white and chinquapin oaks. The 0.5 acre preserve is known as the Deam Oak Monument, three miles northwest of Bluffton on the right side of Indiana 116 (for map see Acres Along the Wabash Nature Preserve).

Just west of the Indiana 1/Main Street bridge is Kehoe Park and amphitheatre, and gazebo, a modern-styled urban riverfront green space designed for live entertainment from May to September. It is also a fine place to stroll, weather-permitting. The park and amphitheatre are adjacent south of the Dutch Mill Restaurant. Call the Bluffton Parks and Recreation Department at (219) 824- 2200 for further information.

Bluffton, Indiana, the country seat of Wells County, may be reached via Indiana 1, 124 and 116.

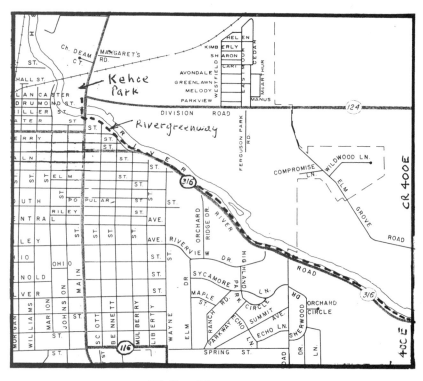

Blufton Rivergreenway

6. ACRES ALONG the WABASH NATURE PRESERVE
Murray, IN/Wells County
USGS MAP(s): Uniondale 1:24,000
TRAIL(s) DISTANCE: I mile loop trails
ACREAGE: 27 acres
ACTIVITIES: nature hike, nature study

This nature preserve showcases some of the best upland and riparian forest along the upper reaches of the Wabash River, rivalled only by Ouabache State Park. The 15 acres of old growth forest is positioned on a fine bluff above the Wabash River. Several acres run along the bluff southeast, upstream on the north bank towards Murray. There is a marked trail but at the time of visit was overgrown.

Acres Along the Wabash lies adjacent south of Indiana 116, about 1.5 miles northwest of the river community of Murray. A roadside pullout on the south side of Indiana 116 offers the best parking at this time, so be careful coming and going onto the state highway.

264

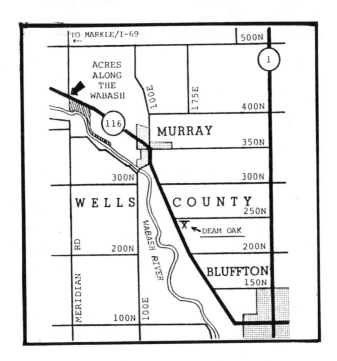

Acres Along the Wabash Nature Preserve

There is noticeable habitat contrast between the upland and lowland type forests along the Wabash River. Ravines descend to the stream on a scenic bend (0.75 mile of frontage). There is a colony of shooting stars. The loop trail follows the perimeter though woods leading along the river. You may see canoeists. The preserve is owned by ACRES, Inc. and is a dedicated state nature preserve. It is bordered by Indiana 116, fields, and the Wabash River.

Boiling Springs, located on the Wabash River near the former Cover Covered Bridge at Haiflich Ford near Murray, was historically a popular recreational site during America's "Golden Years" (1890 - 1914) for picnicking and Sunday School outings.

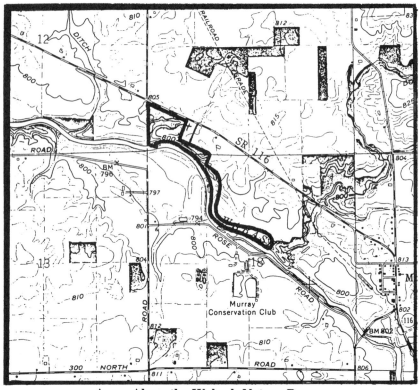

Acres Along the Wabash Nature Preserve

7. ANNA BRAND HAMMER NATURE PRESERVE
Uniondale, IN/Wells County
USGS MAP(S): Uniondale 1:24,000
TRAIL(s) DISTANCE: 0.75 mile
ACREAGE: 20 acres
ACTIVITIES: nature walk, nature study

   North and west a few miles from Acres Along the Wabash Nature
Preserve is another ACRES, Inc. owned and managed sanctuary; Anna
Brand Hammer Woods, a mixed hardwood forest noted for its spring
wildflowers. The forested oasis is enveloped by miles of fields. The
property is divided into fourteen acres of upland mixed forest and six
acres of pioneering abandoned fields. The small parking lot for three to
six cars and trailhead are situated at the southeast corner of the property.
The conspicuous but slightly overgrown narrow path can be like a deer
trail in places. A segment of trail follows the seasonally flowing woodland
run. The trail traces a loop in the shape of a crescent.

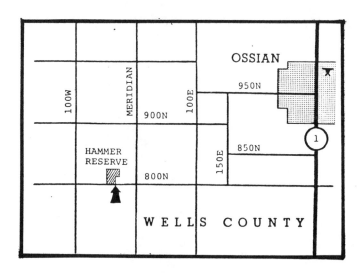

Anna Brand Hammer Nature Preserve

From Uniondale, Indiana and US 224, go north on CR 100W, two miles and turn east on CR 800N. Continue 0.5 mile on CR 800N to the preserve's parking area and trailhead on the north side of the road. Please sign the trailhead register at the metal brown registration box.

8. HUNTINGTON RESERVOIR
Huntington, IN/Huntington & Wells Counties
USGS MAP(s): Majenica, Markle 1:24,000
TRAIL(s) DISTANCE: 4 trails total 14.3 mile
ACREAGE: 8,322 acres
ACTIVITIES: hiking, nature walks, nature study, seasonal naturalist, picnicking, shelters, beach swimming, bathhouse, boating, launch ramps, fishing, playgrounds, model airport, exercise course, archery & shooting ranges, hunting, Class C & Youth camping, programs
FEE(s): seasonal entrance at Little Turtle SRA, camping

Since 1970, the Huntington Reservoir has been the only dam of significance on the Wabash River. The 870 acre reservoir provides flood control, water and recreation on the upper Wabash. Most of the activity centers near the dam where there are basically three areas: Arrowhead North, adjacent west of the dam outlet, Kilsoquah SRA and Little Turtle SRA. A special outlying natural area is at Markle, the "Wabash Rapids". Huntington Reservoir has one of the largest public land accesses on both sides of the Wabash of any area along the river.

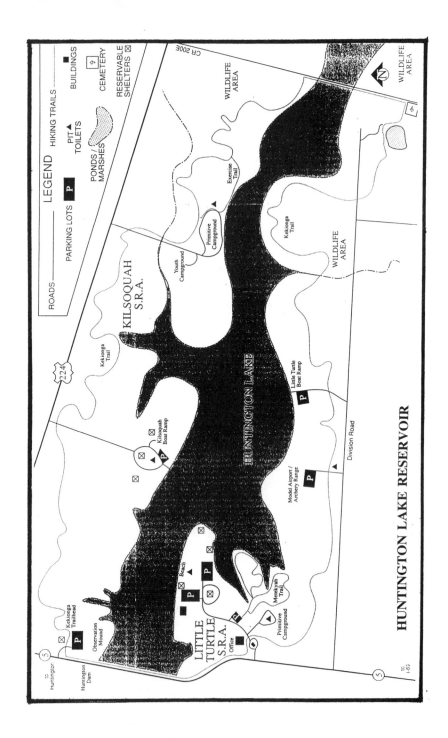

HUNTINGTON LAKE RESERVOIR

LEGEND

ROADS ——————

PARKING LOTS [P]

HIKING TRAILS ·······

PIT TOILETS ▲

BUILDINGS ■

CEMETERY ⚲

RESERVABLE SHELTERS ⊠

PONDS / MARSHES

HUNTINGTON LAKE

KILSOQUAH S.R.A.

LITTLE TURTLE S.R.A.

WILDLIFE AREA

Wildlife Area

CR 200E

Division Road

Kekionga Trail

Exercise Trail

Primitive Campground

Youth Campground

Kilsoquah Boat Ramp

Little Turtle Boat Ramp

Model Airport / Archery Range

Beach

Office

Primitive Campground

Meehyah Trail

Observation Mound

Kekionga Trailhead

Huntington Dam

224

to Huntington

to I-69

The longest trail on the property is the ten mile long <u>Kekionga Trail</u>, established by the Boy Scouts in cooperation with the IDNR. Basically the path follows the perimeter of the lake along the high overlooking bluffs and is blazed in both directions. The trailhead is located at the Observation Mound parking area on Indiana 5, just north of the dam.

From the Observation Mound, walk south across the dam, past the Corps of Engineers office and the DNR property office, then east across two access roads to CR 200E, north of the cemetery. Walk north on CR 200E across the Wabash River/Huntington Reservoir and turn west. Proceed walking west past the <u>Exercise Trail</u> forks and Kilsoquah Campground, back to the Observation Mound. Lake vistas, dense forest and lush ravines are the natural amenities of this long distance hike. There is a trail brochure available that describes the natural and social history of the area. This trail is also being used as a test mountain bike trail for a short period. It is suggested to wear bright clothing during the hunting season when walking. The north shore property is the safety zone.

A much shorter trail is the <u>Me-tek-yah</u> or <u>Forest trail</u>. The 1.25 mile self-guiding wildlife management trail begins and ends at the parking area just beyond the entry station at Little Turtle SRA, adjacent to Indiana 5. There are 15 interpretive stations that correspond to the trail brochure, available at the trailhead. The emphasis is on different types of habitat and habitat management practices. The boardwalk segments through marshy areas are of interest. There is an additional interconnecting <u>Lakeview Trail</u> loop that extends the trail another mile and the views are impressive of the man-made vast lake and the surrounding timber bluffs.

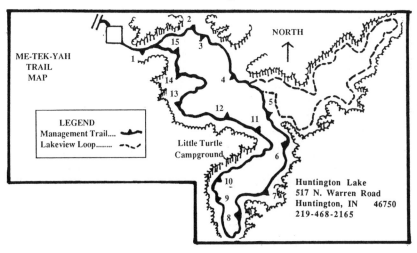

Me-Tek-Yah Trail, Huntington Reservoir

Wabash Rapids, Markle Town Park

An Exercise Trail begins and ends at the Kilsoquah campground on the north property shore of the Huntington Reservoir. The wood chipped path intersects and combines with the Kekionga Trail, following the ravines along Tecumwah Creek, looping back to the campground through dense woodlands. A trail brochure is available at the campground trailhead. Kilsoquah SRA is located six miles west of I-69 exit 86, on US 224.

To reach the Huntington Lake reservoir property office and Little Turtle SRA, continue west on US 224 at Kilsoquah SRA entrance to the intersection of US 224 and Indiana 5 and turn left/south on Indiana 5. Proceed south on Indiana 5 over the dam, past the Army Corps of Engineers office to the next left, and the DNR property office and Little Turtle SRA.

One of the best nature walks at Huntington Lake begins and ends at the Markle Town Park, north of the levee. The park entrance is on the west side of Indiana 3, just south of the intersection with Indiana 116 in Markle. Park at the entrance and walk west along the service road or follow the wooded area along the old Wabash channel west to a user path over the levee to the confluence of the spillway and the old river channel. The whitewater rapids over the limestone ledges are spectacular especially during high water. Retrace your steps for a mile long walk back to the trailhead parking area.

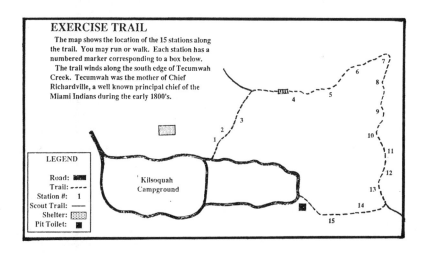

EXERCISE TRAIL

The map shows the location of the 15 stations along the trail. You may run or walk. Each station has a numbered marker corresponding to a box below.

The trail winds along the south edge of Tecumwah Creek. Tecumwah was the mother of Chief Richardville, a well known principal chief of the Miami Indians during the early 1800's.

LEGEND

Road:
Trail: ----
Station #: 1
Scout Trail: ——
Shelter:
Pit Toilet:

Kilsoquah Campground

Exercise Trail, Huntington Reservoir

9. HERMAN F. HAMMER WALD NATURE PRESERVE

Halls Corner, IN/Allen County
USGS MAP(s): St. Joe 1:24,000
TRAIL(s) DISTANCE: user paths & deer runs
ACREAGE: 42 acres
ACTIVITIES: nature hike, nature study

The woodlot "island" forest is located in a seemingly-remote farming area in northeast Allen County. The ACRES, Inc. owned preserve lies in different successional stages of woodland; an encouraging draw for a diversity of wildlife. The mature stand of mixed trees includes beech, maple, tulip, cherry, oak and hickory.

From the roadside parking area adjacent west of Rupert Road, the grassy trail heads west down an old farm lane to the square block of young and old forest and field. A trail system has not been developed but user paths and deer runs access the preserve for the adventuresome.

To reach Herman F. Hammer Wald Preserve from I-69 exit 109, east onto Indiana 37. Continue east from Ft. Wayne to Rupert Road, located about a mile from the junction of Indiana 37 and 101. Turn left/north on CR Rupert Road and drive north about 1.5 miles or so to the parking area on the left/west side of Rupert Road. The wooded preserve stands out among the adjacent fields.

271

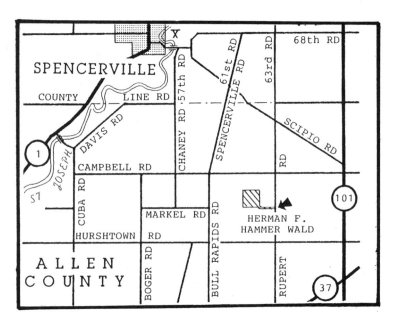

Herman F. Hammer Wald Nature Preserve

Nearby is the 195 acre McNabb/Walter Nature Preserve near Spencerville, along the St. Joseph River, however permission from ACRES, Inc. is required for visitation. Call or write ACRES at 2000 North Wells Street, Fort Wayne, Indiana 46808 (219) 422-1004.

10. VANDOLAH NATURE PRESERVE/FOXFIRE WOODS NATURE PRESERVE

Leo, IN/Allen County
USGS MAP(s): Cedarville, Auburn 1:24,000
TRAIL(s) DISTANCE: 1.5 mile vnp/wood ramble, old lanes fnp
ACREAGE: 47 a. vnp/8 a. fnp
ACTIVITIES: nature walks, nature study

These two ACRES preserves are in close proximity of a few miles of each other but the nature walks differ considerably. Vandolah is riparian, blufftop forest and regenerating old field while Foxfire is a well-drained upland forest and flowering edge.

Vandolah is an easy hike, moving through contrasting habitats and the best segment is the wooded blufftop trail overlooking the wide floodplain of Cedar Creek, 80 feet below. The trail begins at a roadside pullout beneath a few pines on Tother Road on the right/west roadside. The sounds of I-69 are in the air and sometimes in sight. The foot path follows the abandoned pasture edge curving around the wooded ravine to lead into the oak-hickory forest, then following the slope. A linear spur segment of the trail shoots off down an old lane to the Cedar Creek bottoms where there are colonies of horsetail and trillium wildflowers beneath the sycamores and black willows. Cedar Creek is included in the Indiana Natural Rivers system.

West of the I-69 overpass over Cedar Creek, the western portion of the Vandolah Nature Preserve borders the Cedar Creek/Rodenbeck Nature Preserve, that is managed by the Isaac Walton League and from whom permission must be obtained to access the preserve. IWL, 17100 Griffin Road, Hunterstown, IN 46748, (219) 637-6735.

Retrace your steps back from the bottoms back to the main loop and continue along the old meadow perimeter adjacent to the I-69 fence, back to the parking area. Further upstream near the DeKalb/Allen county line northeast of Huntertown, is the ACRES Cedar Creek Bottoms Nature Preserve. The 11 acre floodplain forest preserve is open by permission only.

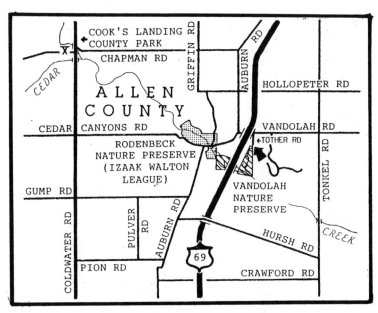

Vandolah Nature Preserve

To reach Vandolah Nature Preserve from I-69 exit 116 onto Dupont Road, north of Fort Wayne, and drive east 1.5 miles to the junction with Tonkel Road, just west of the intersection of Indiana 1. Turn left/north onto Tonkel Road and drive about four miles to Vandolah Road and turn left/west. Continue about a mile on Vandolah Road to just before the road goes under I-69 and turn left/south on Tother Road. Go south on Tother Road a short distance to the roadside pullout parking and trailhead brown metal registration box.

ACRES Foxfire Woods Nature Preserve is also in the vicinity about four miles northeast of Vandolah Nature Preserve. The nearly eight acres of second growth oak-hickory forest has an old farm lane meandering through the middle portion but there are no established trails at this time.

To reach Foxfire Woods from Vandolah Nature Preserve, drive east one mile on Vandolah Road to Tonkel Road. Turn north on Tonkel Road and drive 0.5 mile to Hollopeter Road and go right/east. Continue east on Hollopeter Road two miles to Hull Road and turn left/north. Drive 0.25 mile on Hull Road to the metal gate and trailhead on the right/east side of the road. Park at the gate and follow the field edge path past the house, east to the woods.

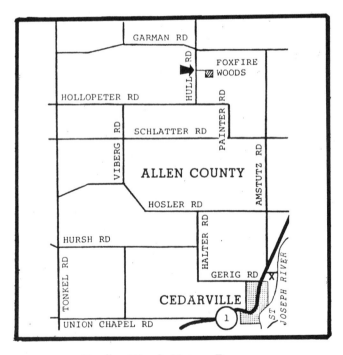

Foxfire Woods Nature Preserve

11. METEA COUNTY PARK

Cedarville, IN/Allen County
USGS MAP(s): Cedarville 1:24,000
TRAIL(s) DISTANCE: 2 trails total appx. 2 miles
ACREAGE: 450 acres
ACTIVITIES: nature trails, nature study, picnicking, shelter, playfields, sledding, x-country skiing, pond swimming, river fishing, primitive camping
FEE(s): seasonal entrance, shelter rental, primitive camping

Bordering Cedar Creek, this north central Allen County park features a natural area with a historic woodland Indian theme. Metea or Me-taw-wa, for whom the park is named, was a renowned and respected Potawatomi War Chief who lived downstream at the Cedar Creek and St. Joseph River confluence.

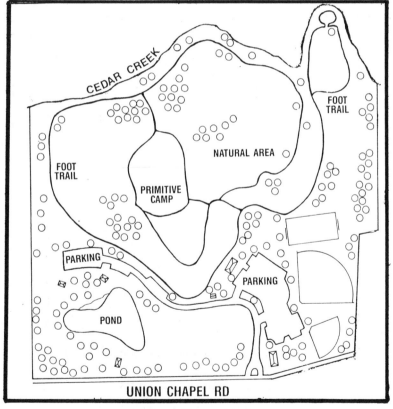

Metea County Park

Most of the park is retired fields in various stages of succession and the wooded fringe along Cedar Creek proves interesting. The E-se-bun and Mi-kan Trails, loop about and along the level old fields and floodplain forest. Connecting spur trails lead to the wooded aspen "island" camping area in the old field floodplain.

A large portion of the property lies north of Cedar Creek and is currently inaccessible until a foot bridge is built. The parkland northwest of Cedar Creek has a state designated nature preserve of hillside dry prairie, located on an old farmstead. Cedar Creek is a state designated scenic stream. The planned completion of the park facilities will occur over the next few years and will include an Indian Heritage Museum.

To reach Metea County Park from I-69 exit 116, east on Dupont Road, north of Fort Wayne. Drive about one mile on Dupont Road to the junction with Indiana 1/Leo Road. Turn northeast on Indiana 1/Leo Road and continue to Union Chapel Road, just before Cedarville, Indiana, and turn left/west. The park entrance will be on the immediate right/north side of the county road.

Metea County Park Access

276

12. FORT WAYNE NATURE PLACES

ACTIVITIES: nature walks, nature study, nature preserves, rivergreenway, gardens, zoo, museum, botanical conservatory, gift shops, picnicking, shelters, bicycling, playgrounds, playfields, ballfields, ball courts, winter sports, rentals, special events

Fort Wayne is Indiana's second largest city with first rate parklands; these being among the finest in the nation. There are nearly 70 public parks with a total acreage of over 2,000. The Rivergreenway, a superb zoo and botanical conservatory, the emphasis on flower gardens and landscaping, even nature preserves, has made urbane Fort Wayne, "The City of Three Rivers", a choice urban area for residents and visitors alike.

First planned in 1910, today, the Rivergreenway forms 12 miles of all weather paths along the banks of the St. Mary's and St. Joseph rivers, with emphasis towards extending the trail along the Maumee River. From north to south along a 3.5 mile stretch of the St. Joseph River is Johnny Appleseed Park and Griswold Park. Johnny "Appleseed" Chapman, a national folk hero, is buried in Archer's Graveyard within the 43 acre park named in his honor.

From the confluence of the Three Rivers, the Rivergreenway follows the St. Mary's River, where the trail connects Historic Fort Wayne, Lawton Park (1), Bloomingdale Park (2), Swinney Park (3), Foster Park and Tillman Park, a total of 8.5 miles and numerous acres of green spaces. Lawton Park is adeck with color in fall in the chrysanthemum gardens. Swinney and Foster parks both include attractive formal gardens. The Jaenecke Gardens in West Swinney Park are especially attractive in May. The Swinney Homestead features a herb garden at 1424 West Jefferson. The Foster Park gardens include the Diver Perennial Garden and the Allen Bridal Glen which features a delicate heart-shaped trellis, an All-American Selection Display Garden. Located between Hartmann Road and the St. Mary's River, the 250 acre Foster Park is named in honor of Col. David Foster, the "Father of Fort Wayne's Parks".

Downtown in Fort Wayne at 1100 South Calhoun is the 4.7 acre Foellinger-Freemann Botanical Conservatory (4), the 10,000 square feet make it the largest passive solar conservatory in the Middle West. The city-block square, "garden under glass" has three areas: the Showcase, which features six seasonal flower displays; the Tropical House, a forest of palms, orchids, cycads and a waterfall; and the Arid House, a 4,500 square foot Sonoran Desert of palo verde, acacia, barrel and saguaro cacti and more. There is also a gift shop and scheduled programs all year long. Outside is the Terrace Gardens, a favorite place to picnic.

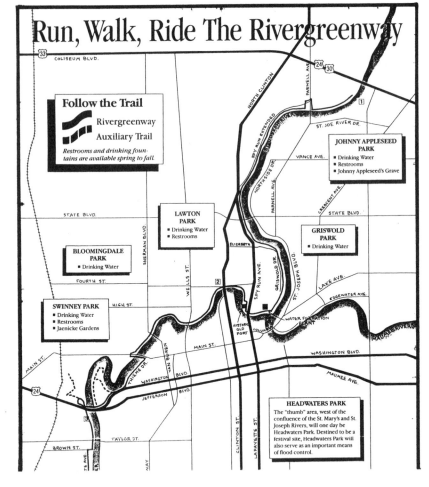

Run, Walk, Ride The Rivergreenway

Follow the Trail

Rivergreenway

Auxiliary Trail

Restrooms and drinking fountains are available spring to fall.

JOHNNY APPLESEED PARK
- Drinking Water
- Restrooms
- Johnny Appleseed's Grave

LAWTON PARK
- Drinking Water
- Restrooms

GRISWOLD PARK
- Drinking Water

BLOOMINGDALE PARK
- Drinking Water

SWINNEY PARK
- Drinking Water
- Restrooms
- Jaenicke Gardens

HEADWATERS PARK
The "thumb" area, west of the confluence of the St. Mary's and St. Joseph Rivers, will one day be Headwaters Park. Destined to be a festival site, Headwaters Park will also serve as an important means of flood control.

Fort Wayne River Greenway

There is an entrance fee to the conservatory, open 10 am to 5 pm, Monday through Saturday and Sunday 12 pm to 4 pm. In the same neighborhood, a few blocks east is the 0.2 acre Japanese Friendship Garden, presented from Fort Wayne's sister city Takaoka, in Japan.

Across the Maumee River on Lake Avenue is the 24 acre Lakeside Park (5) which features the 3.2 acre Lakeside Rose Garden, the largest rose garden in Indiana and one of the nation's largest. Over 2,000 roses form the All-American Rose Display Garden and includes such landscaping items as pergolas, trellises, reflecting pools, a floral sun dial and sunken gardens. The annual Fort Wayne Rose Festival is held in June.

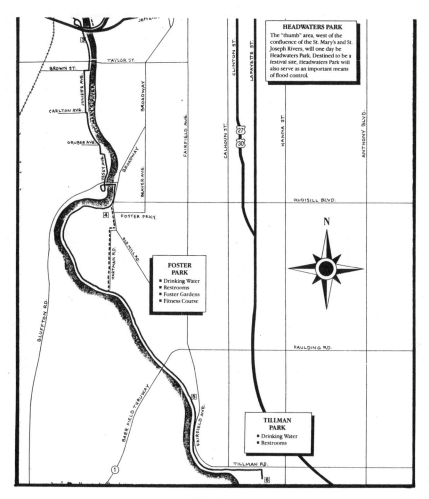

Fort Wayne Nature Places

The 42 acre <u>Fort Wayne Zoological Gardens (6)</u> is located in 282 acre Franke Park along Harvard and Sherman boulevards. Hundreds of exotic and native animals and plants may be viewed from late April to mid-October. The 22 acre East African Veldt is a simulated Kenya safari where visitors ride enclosed through a African grassland or savanna or walk along the elevated boardwalk. Giraffes, ostrich, cheetahs, antelope, gazelles, cranes and storks "inhabit" the created grasslands. The 5 acre Australian Adventure area is one of the largest and most complete Australian exhibits outside of "down under". The zoo hours are 9 am to 5 pm daily and 9 am to 6 pm on Sunday, during the warm months.

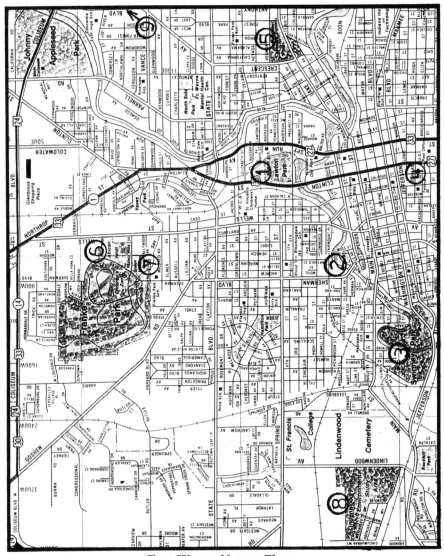

Fort Wayne Nature Places

Within eyesight is the <u>Diehm Museum of Natural History (7)</u> at 600 Franke Park Drive. The mounted fauna dioramas are exhibited in authentic natural habitats of North American animals. There is a nominal entrance fee and the museum is open from late April to mid-October, noon to 5 pm on weekends.

The two nature preserves are the 110 acre <u>Lindenwood Park Environmental Study Area (8)</u> and the 36 acre <u>Mengerson Nature Reserve</u>

(9). The Lindenwood Park, a dedicated state nature preserve, has four walking trails that lead through upland forest and prairie openings, a seasonal naturalist and nature center. Birdwatching and picnicking are also popular pastimes in this sanctuary in the city. The nature preserve is open from April to mid-November from 9 am to 6 pm Tuesday through Saturday and noon to 6 pm on Sunday. Winter visitation occurs for cross country skiing if there is four to six inches of snow cover. Lindenwood is located two miles west of downtown at 600 Lindenwood, adjacent west of the Lindenwood Cemetery.

Mengerson Nature Reserve (9), owned and managed by ACRES, Inc., is also a dedicated state nature preserve. The narrow rectangular 36 acre property is located in a suburban neighborhood of northeast Fort Wayne bordered by Northwood Shopping Plaza and subdivisions. There is an unmarked but obvious well used trail that loops about the wet hardwoods and open field. The easiest access is from Steelhorn Road, between Reed and Maplecrest roads. Go north on Schnucker Drive, one block to Leeds Lane and turn right. Park at the cul de sac and enter the open field.

Additional parklands with open green spaces being developed in the Fort Wayne area include the 144 acre Buckner Farm, west of I-69 and the 110 acre Maumee Park along the Maumee River.

13. FOX ISLAND COUNTY PARK & NATURE PRESERVE
Fort Wayne, IN/Allen County
USCS MAP(s): Fort Wayne West 1:24,000
TRAIL(s) DISTANCE: 8 trails total appx. 6 miles
ACREAGE: 605 acres
ACTIVITIES: nature walks, nature study, naturalist, nature center, nature preserver geogarden, astronomy observatory, x-country skiing, picnicking, shelters, playground, fishing, educational building, guided hikes, gift shop, primitive camping
FEE(s): summer entrance, camping, ski rental

Fox Island is the most extensive natural area in Allen County. The state dedicated nature preserve within the Allen County Park system comprises 270 acres of marsh and swamp swale bordered on the south by a black oak dune; the most outstanding southeast of the Indiana Dunes. The largest expanse of forest in Allen County includes climax beech-maple forest, bogs, pine plantations, and old fields. A listing of the flora and fauna, trail guides and other nature-related materials are available at the nature center and gift shop adjacent east of the parking area. Clustered around the nature center is the astronomical dome, the Alliance Education

Building, and a unique geogarden, comprised of Indiana glacial till boulders. Bowman Lake, a borrow pit, is to the west of the parking area.

Eight interconnecting loop trails wind about the property. The posted alphabetical letters denote trail junctions. The trail names are descriptive of what you may expect to experience. Near the nature center is the self-guiding 0.33 mile <u>Foxwood Trail</u> with ten interpretive stations and the <u>Hiker's Winter Trail</u>.

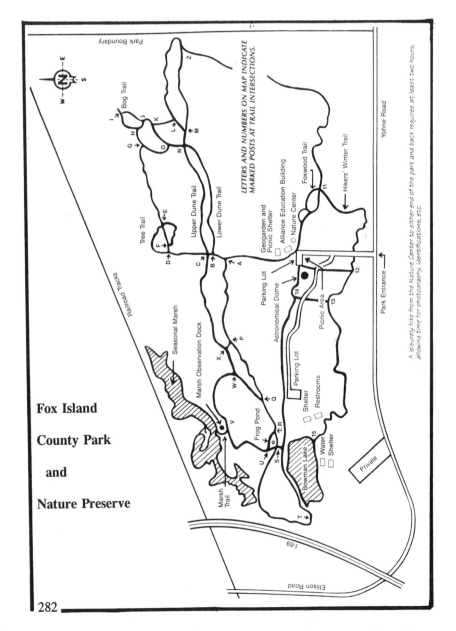

Fox Island

County Park

and

Nature Preserve

North of the nature center are a series of trails that explore the real nature of the dune and swale preserve: <u>Upper Dune Trail</u>, <u>Lower Dune Trail</u>, <u>Tree Trail</u>, <u>Skunk Cabbage Trail</u> and <u>Bog Trail</u>.

Further west is the two mile <u>Marsh Trail</u>, where a marsh observation dock and deck overlook the seasonal wetland; a remnant of an old glacial sluice. A leisurely hike from the nature center to either end of the park and back requires about two hours. Be advised the mosquito population can be voracious at times. The gate hours are 9 am to 7 pm Tuesday through Sunday in summer and winter hours are 9 am to 5 pm. Fox Island is closed Mondays.

To reach Fox Island, located about six miles southwest of Fort Wayne, from I-69 exit 105 and drive west on US 24 about 0.2 mile to Ellison Road and turn left/south. Continue about 1.4 miles to Yohne Road and turn left/east. Proceed 0.5 mile to the marked entrance at 7324 Yohne Road. There are directional signs along the highway. Fox Island is just north of the Little (Wabash) River. Consider visiting Fogwell Forest, an ACRES, Inc. nature preserver a mile or so south of Fox Island.

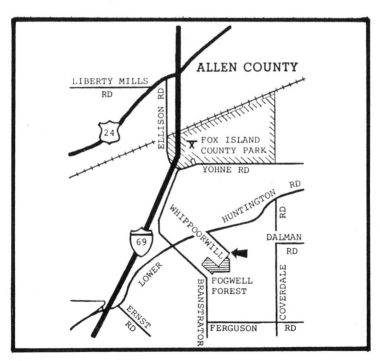

Fogwell Forest and Fox Island County Park

14. FOGWELL FOREST
Fort Wayne, IN/Allen County
USGS MAP(s): Ossian, Fort Wayne West 1:24,000
TRAIL(s) DISTANCE: no est. trails
ACREAGE: 28 acres
ACTIVITIES: nature hike, nature study

Fogwell Forest is located just over a mile south "as the crow flies" from Fox Island. This ACRES, Inc. nature property preserves a mixed deciduous forest with sections of low-lying areas that harbor buttonbush, swamp white oak and swamp red maple. The preserve is noted for its spring wildflowers. The sanctuary occupies the edge of an ancient glacial sluiceway or river bed where the Little (Wabash) River now flows between Fort Wayne and Huntington, merging with the Wabash River.

Currently there are no established trails, so hikers are on their own to ramble through the forest. The access begins at the cul de sac parking area and heads south and then west following the edge of the subdivision and the field, which is becoming another wetland. Fogwell Forest will increase to 60 acres in size with restoration. Be prepared for muddy feet.

To reach Fogwell Forest from I-69 exit 105 and drive west on US 24, 0.2 mile to Ellison Road and turn south/left. Continue on Ellison Road and drive under the I-69 overpass and turn right/ south on Branstrator Road (continuing on the other route becomes Yohne Road, leading to Fox Island). Follow Branstrator Road south to Lower Huntington Road and turn left/east. Drive about a half mile on Lower Huntington Road east to Whippoorwill Drive and turn right/south and park at the cul de sac. There is a forest sign and a brown metal registration box, as will be found at most ACRES, Inc. preserves. (For map see Fox Island County Park).

15. FORKS OF THE WABASH HISTORIC PARK
Huntington, IN/Huntington County
USGS MAP(S): Bippus, Andrews 1:24,000
TRAIL(S) DISTANCE: 0.5 mile riverwalk
ACREAGE: 110 acres
ACTIVITIES: nature walks, historic sites, visitor center, tours, museum,
  gift shop, picnicking, special events
FEE(s) entrance to museum

This historical interpretive park at the Forks of the Wabash River showcases the natural and social history of the upper valley. Long before statehood, the Forks served as a passageway linking two North American watersheds; the Great Lakes and the Mississippi to commerce and conquest. Accessing the Wabash River, which connected the watery continental divide, was made possible by a 20 mile "Long Portage through the Golden Gate". When the water was up, a nine mile shorter portage was possible from the St. Marys River, floating southwest to the Little River (the north fork), or downstream to the Forks of the Wabash, where there was usually enough water to carry heavily-ladened canoes.

The liquid highway allowed the Miami, French, British and later-day Americans to move with fair ease through the wilderness wilds, occasionally building outposts and small settlements. To the Miami, and other tribes, the forks were a spiritual landmark near a source of superior flint. It was not until the 1790s that the Miami made villages near the Forks, that were later razed during the War of 1812, and re-established in the 1820s, when Chief Richardville or Pin-je-wah built a home at the Forks (1814-1841). To the French, the Forks were a place of trade and not a permanent outpost like Ft. Ouiatenon. To the British, the Forks were a staging area to move troops between Detroit and Vincennes during the Revolution and the War of 1812. To the Americans, the forks were the site of three significant U.S. and Indian treaties in the 1830s and 1840s, whereby they acquired new lands for settlement and constructed the Wabash and Erie Canal.

Short riverside trails connect the restored Chief Richardville house and the Joseph Nuck pioneer house that are separated by the visitor center, museum and gift shop. A linear path heads north from the Nuck house along the Wabash River, past an island, and limestone silurian reef outcrops on the opposite shore, to conclude after 0.25 mile. Retrace your path back along the old canal trail to the visitor center, where visitors should begin their visit. A short trail leads upstream under the bridge to the forks. The visitor center's hours are 12 noon to 5 pm Saturday and Sunday, June 1 to Ocober 1. The historic park is owned and operated by the Historic Forks of the Wabash, Inc. and is located at the intersection of US 24 and Indiana 9 at the southwest corner, just west of Huntington, Indiana.

While near Huntington, consider visiting the Sunken Gardens, a former limestone quarry converted into a landscape wonder of a city park. Paved trails and foot bridges lead to the quarry bottom and ponds, plantings and extensive fieldstone works.

Sunken Gardens is located east of the US 24 and Indiana 9 intersection on Business US 24. Continue east on US 24 across the intersection about a mile to the city park office and the parking area to the gardens, along the south side of the highway. The park is bordered by West Park Drive, Diamond, Orchard Hill and Bartlett streets. Business US 24 highway bridge crosses the south corner of the Sunken Gardens park.

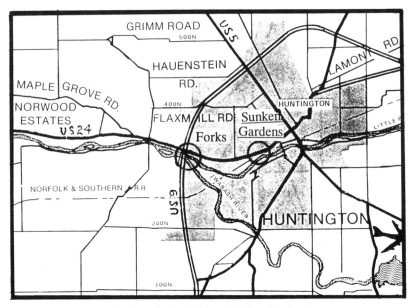

Forks of the Wabash Historic Park

16. HANGING ROCK NATURAL AREA
Lagro, IN/Wabash County
USGS MAP(S): Lagro 1:24,000
TRAIL(S) Distance: 0.2 mile
ACREAGE: 1.5 acre
ACTIVITIES: natural landmark, nature study

Downstream from the Forks of the Wabash and upstream from Lagro, near the confluence with the Salamonie River, is the best known National Natural Landmark on the upper Wabash, where geological rock formations are rare. Towering 84 feet, the ancient limestone pinnacle is climbable along a well worn path. The vistas of the river and adjoining valley are worth the climb. Summer sunrises are exceptional. The north facing riverside of the rock has been undercut by the stream, giving the massive monolith a "hanging" appearance. Geologically, the rock is a Silurian limestone coral reef. Botanically, unique plants seemingly grow out of the rock. The preserve is leased by ACRES, Inc., a nature preserving non-profit organization based in Ft. Wayne.

Hanging Rock at Sunrise

To reach Hanging Rock from Wabash, Indiana, drive east on US 24 to Lagro, Indiana and turn right/south on Indiana 524. Cross the Wabash River bridge and continue on Indiana 524 to the riverside Division Road. Follow the river road to Hanging Rock on the left/north side of the paved road. Roadside pullout parking. Watch the rise when parking or leaving.

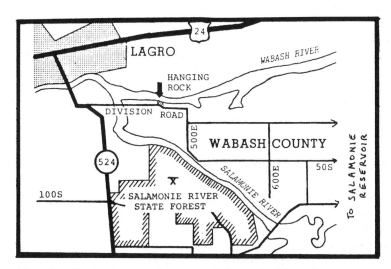

Hanging Rock Natural Area and Salamonie River State Forest

17. SALAMONIE RIVER STATE FOREST

Lagro, IN/Wabash County
USGS MAP(s): Lagro 1:24,000
TRAIL(s) Distance: 19 miles firelanes & bridle trails
ACREAGE: 780 acres
ACTIVITIES: nature hikes, nature study, picnicking, shelter playground, fishing, non-motorized boating, launch ramp (lake), x-country skiing, Class C camping, horse camp, bridle trails, youth tent, hunting
FEE(s); camping

The Salamonie State Forest is situated along the south bank of the Salamonie River, between the Salamonie Reservoir dam and the Wabash River. The Division of Forestry manages the 621 acre forest, one of two state forests in northern Indiana; the other being the Frances Slocum State Forest located northwest of the Mississinewa River. Today's densely wooded river bluffs were acquired in the 1930s from eroded farmlands. Geologically, the property is mostly outwash or till plain but borders on the Mississinewa Moraine to the south. The Civilian Conservation Corps (CCC) developed the forest facilities that are still in use.

Although there are no designated trails for hikers, there are miles of firelanes and bridle trails laced throughout the forest that are open to those on foot. One of the more popular areas to walk is an unmarked bridle trail that follows the riverside from Hominy Ridge northwest several miles. At times, the combination of steep seeping bluffsides, floodplain and horse impact can leave the trail rather muddy. Erosion continues to be a problem from overuse. The area around Hominy Ridge Lake is popular with hikers and horses, who are overusing the site. From parking lots 2 and 3, the firelanes head north to the river and the foundation of an old gristmill. From parking lot one, walk south to a remote area of the forest along a square-shaped firelane of a few miles. From parking lot 7, the firelane leads directly to the river following the bluff ridge along a seasonal brook. Across the park road, the firelanes in the campground one area are handy for overnight campers. Some of the more interesting walks are through the forest using a compass.

To reach Salamonie State Forest from Wabash, Indiana, go east eight miles on US 24 to Lagro, Indiana and turn right/south on Indiana 524. Follow Indiana 524 south two miles to the forest entrance (for location map see Hanging Rock Natural Area). Consider visiting Hanging Rock on the Wabash River just east of Indiana 524 along the river road. The Salamonie River makes an exciting trip in a canoe or raft when water is being discharged from the Salamonie dam.

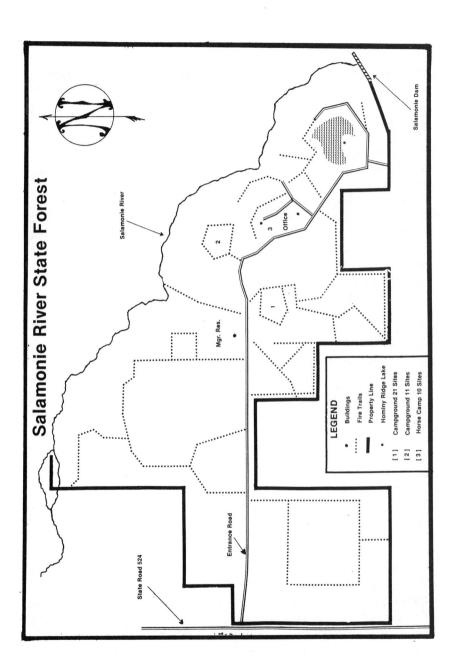

Salamonie River State Forest

LEGEND
- • Buildings
- ··· Fire Trails
- ▬ Property Line
- ▨ Hominy Ridge Lake
- [1] Campground 21 Sites
- [2] Campground 11 Sites
- [3] Horse Camp 10 Sites

Salamonie River
Salamonie Dam
State Road 524
Entrance Road
Mgr. Res.
Office

18. SALAMONIE RESERVOIR

Andrews, IN/Wabash & Huntington Counties
USGS MAP(s): Lagro, Andrews, Mt. Etna 1:24,000
TRAIL(s) DISTANCE: 7 trails total appx. 27.50 miles
ACREAGE: 11,506 a. land, 2,855 lake reservoir
ACTIVITIES: nature walks, hikes and study, naturalist, interpretive programs, nature center, picnicking, shelters, playgrounds, amphitheatre playfields, basketball, horseshoes, beach, swimming, bathhouse, fishing, boating, launch ramps, waterskiing, marina, cultural arts program, winter sports, x-country skiing, snowmobiling, hunting, bridle trails, horsemen's camp, Class A & C camping, youth tent, concessions
FEE(s): seasonal entrance at Lost Bridge West SRA, camping

Located three miles upstream on the Salamonie River from the confluence with the Wabash River near Lagro, Indiana is the Salamonie Lake Reservoir, the first of three US Army Corps of Engineer dam projects on the upper Wabash River, completed 1967. The property is operated and maintained by the Indiana Department of Natural Resources (DNR), under a lease arrangement with the US Army Corps of Engineers, as are Huntington and Mississinewa Reservoirs.

There are five state recreational areas surrounding the vast water body but nearly all the nature trails including the visitor's center, nature center, beach, marina, picnic area and campgrounds are located at Lost Bridge West SRA and Lost Bridge East SRA. The visitor's center is located at Lost Bridge West SRA, west of Indiana 105 on CR 400S and is open daily at 8 pm.

The nature trails located at Lost Bridge West SRA are summarized as follows:

Switchgrass Marsh Trail: A 0.25 mile linear out-and-back trail that leads to 11 acres of marsh and open water ponds. The wildlife viewing area is just west of the visitor's center but access is south of the Apple Orchard primitive campground. Follow the binocular signs.

Bridle Trail: The 12 mile (one-way) horse trail may be use by hikers but the high use impact may make the trail a trial in places. The bridle trail travels west, south and northwest from the horsemen's campground through hunting areas and the Dora-New Holland SRA, to the south side of the dam. Hikers may pick the trail up at Dora-New Holland SRA. The equestrian path extends into Salamonie State Forest.

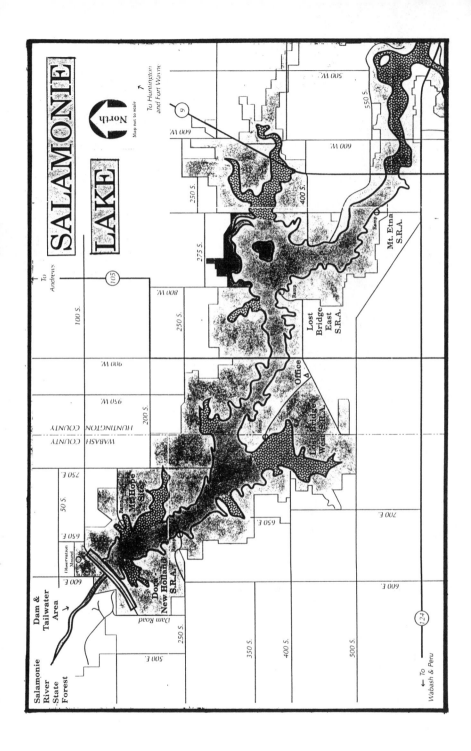

SALAMONIE LAKE

North
Map not to scale

To Huntington
and Fort Wayne

To Andrews

9

500 W.

550 S.

600 W.

600 W.

250 S.

400 S.

105

275 S.

Ramp

Mt. Etna S.R.A.

100 S.

800 W.

250 S.

Lost Bridge East S.R.A.

Ramp

900 W.

950 W.

200 S.

Office

HUNTINGTON COUNTY

WABASH COUNTY

Ramp

Lost Bridge West S.R.A.

750 E.

50 S.

Ramp

Mt. Hope Site

Ramp

650 E.

200 E.

Observation Mound

600 E.

Dora New Holland S.R.A.

Dam Road

250 S.

600 E.

124

Salamonie River State Forest

Dam & Tailwater Area

500 E.

350 S.

400 S.

500 S.

To Wabash & Peru

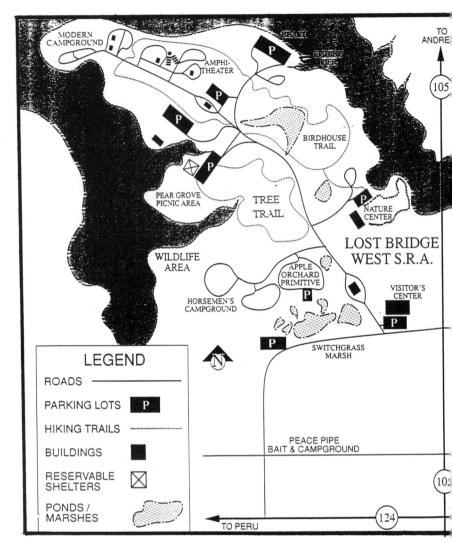

<u>Tree Trail</u>: There are over 50 trees identified with signs along this 1.25 mile self-guiding loop. Identification stations are found along the path that begins and ends at the Pear Grove picnic area, just south of the marina. Forest ecology and silviculture are the main topics.

<u>Birdhouse Trail</u>: The 1.5 mile loop features several types of birdhouses and their occupants. From the nature center, the trail encircles the modern campground. Fourteen numbered stations correspond to the trail brochure. There are plenty of bird house tips to attract avians.

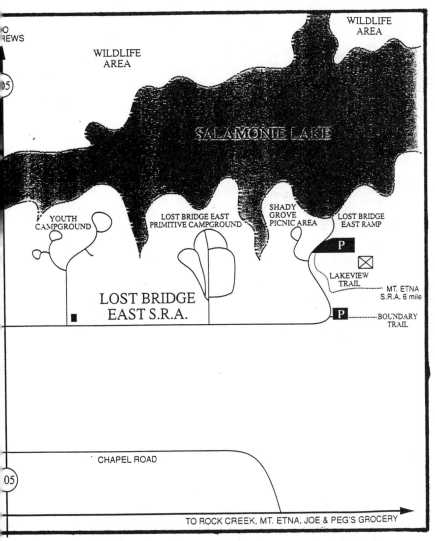

In addition, the nine miles of designated <u>cross country ski trails</u> are within the Lost Bridge West SRA and a trail map is available. Across Indiana 105 at Lost Bridge East SRA are two trails that actually interconnect and form a loop, making a fine day hike. The <u>Lakeview</u> and <u>Boundary trails</u> form a part of the 22 mile <u>Salamonie Snowmobile Trail</u>. A trail brochure and map are available.

<u>Lakeview Trail</u>: As the name implies, the level to rolling path follows the dense wooded uplands adjacent to the Salamonie Lake Reservoir,

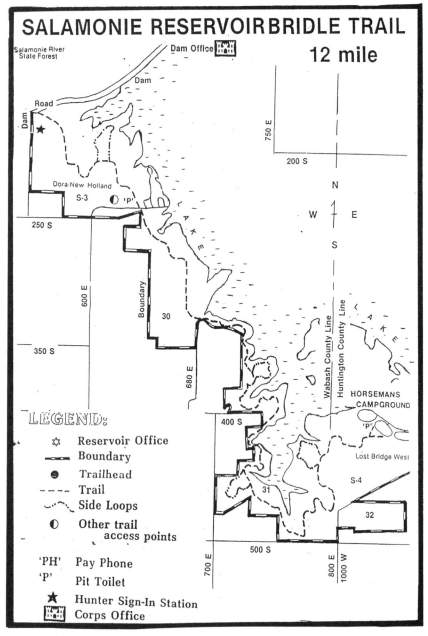

Salamonie Reservoir Bridle Trail

south about six miles to Mt. Etna SRA. There is one good open vista of the lake and Monument Island enroute. The trail is blazed in orange.

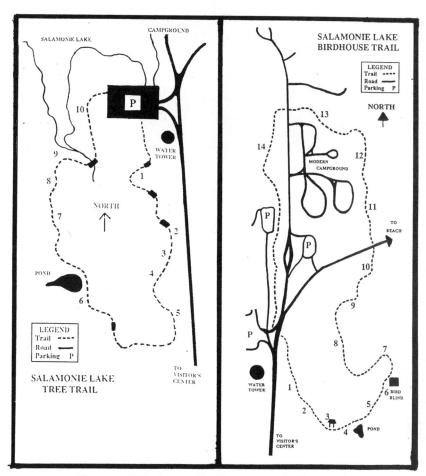

Tree and Birdhouse Trail, Salamonie Reservoir

Boundary Trail: The six mile trail begins at Mt. Etna SRA and ends at Lost Bridge East SRA, paralleling and at times interconnecting with the Lakeview Trail. The Boundary Trail is basically out-of-the-woods and moves through old pasture and open agricultural lands.

Turkey Cove Nature Trail: This short four tenths of a mile trail begins and ends at the Nature Center. It is ideal for children.

The area near the dam and tailwater are also worthy of visitation. Adjacent to the U.S. Army Corps of Engineers office is the 0.5 mile Visitors Center Trail. The self-guiding trail is mostly tree id. with 19 stations that correspond to a interpretive brochure available at the office. Northwest of the dam is an observation Mound overlook that provides vistas of the reservoir, the Salamonie State Forest and the Salamonie River

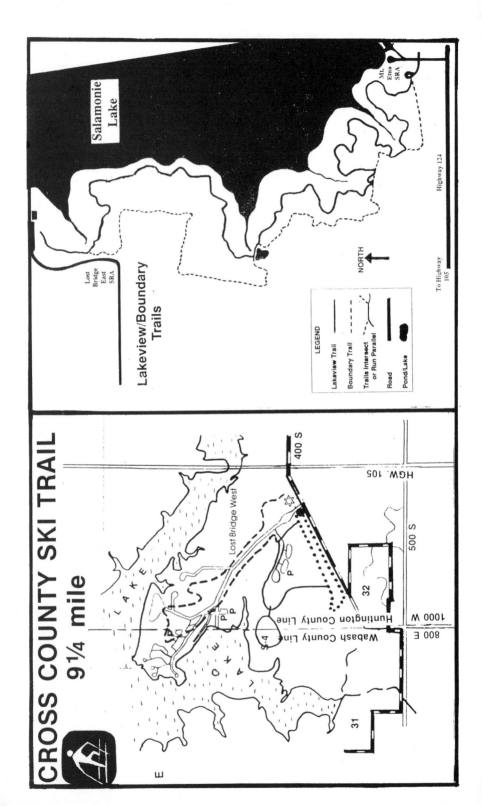

CROSS COUNTY SKI TRAIL
9¼ mile

Lost Bridge West

LAKE

400 S

HGW 105

500 S

Huntington County Line

Wabash County Line

1000 W

800 E

32

31

Salamonie Lake

Lakeview/Boundary Trails

Lost Bridge East SRA

Mt. Etma SRA

Highway 124

To Highway 105

NORTH

LEGEND

Lakeview Trail

Boundary Trail

Trails Intersect or Run Parallel

Road

Pond/Lake

below. A trail leads down to the tailwater or dam outlet which is scenic. Additional sites include <u>Mt. Hope SRA</u> which has several user paths leading to the lake, the <u>Majenica Marsh</u> overlook west of Indiana 9 on CR 400S, and the <u>headwaters mud flats</u> north of Indiana 124 and east of Indiana 9, via county roads 400W and 550S.

Salamonie lake Reservoir is accessed via Indiana 124, 105, 9, and 37 and US 24. From I-69 exit 78, north on Indiana 5 and drive one mile to Indiana 124 and turn left/west. Follow Indiana 124 west to the reservoir.

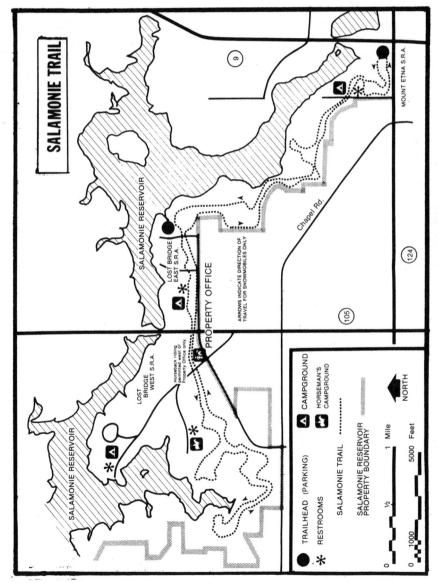

19. ASHERWOOD ENVIRONMENTAL LEARNING CENTER & NATURE PRESERVE

Rich Valley, IN/Wabash County
USGS MAP(s): Peoria 1:24,000
TRAIL(s) DISTANCE: 4 trails total appx. 3.6 miles
ACREAGE: 160 acres
ACTIVITIES: nature trails, nature center, picnicking, aviary, maple sugar house, weather station, amphitheatre, nature preserve, primitive camping, special events

Visitors are welcomed to hike the trails at the Asherwood Environmental Learning Center and Nature Preserve. The 160 acre rolling woodlands are owned and managed by the Marion Community Schools of adjoining Grant County. A director and staff live on the property. Asherwood is situated about three miles north of the Mississinewa Lake reservoir and Francis Slocum State Forest and about the same distance from the Wabash River south.

The four trails of varying lengths all begin near the parking area and property facilities. Deer Trail and Prairie Trail begin/ end near the aviary that is designed for recovering-injured birds-of-prey. The 1.5 mile Deer Trail features Asher Creek, Wood Duck Pond, beech-maple forest-covered ridges and ravines; part of a dedicated state nature preserve. The shorter 0.20 mile Prairie Trail leads from the aviary, moving through a re-established tallgrass prairie to end at the sugar maple house. The Rabbit Trail is a loop, 0.40 mile long trail that leads north from the nature center, looping ridges and ravines along Asher Creek. The Tulip Tree Trail is a 1.5 mile trail that begins at the nature center and follows the Deer Trail in reverse, ending at the Prairie Area and restrooms. Individuals are welcome on a drop-in basis but groups need to schedule by calling (219) 563-8148 or by writing 7496 West State Road 124, Wabash, IN 46992.

Asherwood Environmental Learning Center is located five miles west of Indiana 13 on Indiana 124 near the Wabash and Miami county line.

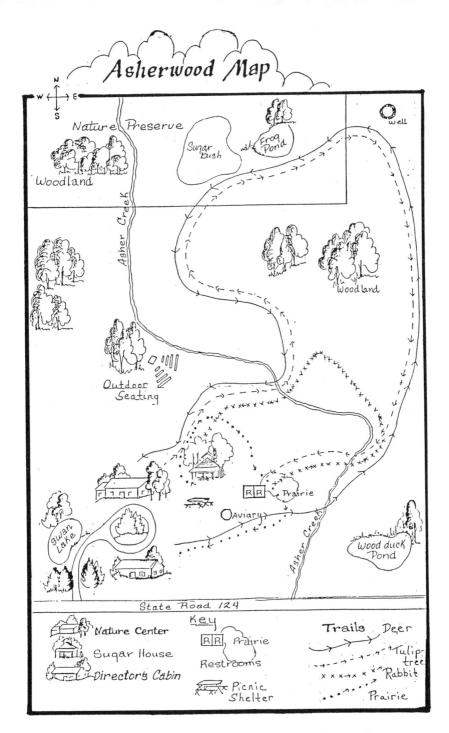

Asherwood Map

N
W · E
S

Nature Preserve

Sugar Bush

Frog Pond

Well

Woodland

Asher Creek

Woodland

Outdoor Seating

R R Prairie

Aviary

Swan Lake

Asher Creek

Wood duck Pond

State Road 124

Key

Nature Center

Sugar House

Director's Cabin

R R Prairie

Restrooms

Picnic Shelter

Trails   Deer

Tulip-tree

Rabbit

Prairie

Asherwood Environmental Learning Center & Nature Preserve

299

20. MISSISSINEWA RESERVOIR

Peru, IN/Miami, Wabash & Grant Counties
USGS MAP(s): Peoria, Somerset, LaFontaine 1:24,000
TRAIL(s) DISTANCE: 6 trails total appx. 14.1 miles
ACREAGE: 14,386 acres, 3,210 acre lake
ACTIVITIES: nature walks, hikes, and nature study, naturalist and interpretive program, historic sites, picnicking, shelters, playgrounds, play fields, beach, swimming, lifeguards, fishing, boating, launch ramps, waterskiing, frisbee golf course, model airplane field, cultural arts program, Class AA, A, B, & C camping, hunting
FEE(s); seasonal entrance to Miami SRA, boat launch fee, camping at Miami and Frances Slocum SRAs

Established in 1967, the Mississinewa flood control reservoir is the largest of the three upper Wabash River reservoirs; Salamonie and Huntington being the other two. The 20 mile long lake reservoir extends from the dam and tailwater area, east to the Trails End area near Indiana 15. The property is rich in Miami history, legend, and lore, reflected in the property's names and historical sites such as Frances Slocum and the 1812 Battle of the Mississinewa. Most of the designated nature walks are situated just north and south of the dam and tailwater area at Frances Slocum State Recreation Area and State Forest and the Miami State Recreational Area. The Reservoir and the surrounding lands are administered by the U.S. Army Corps of Engineers and the Indiana Department of Natural Resources.

There are five established trails that are marked and maintained, nearly all having trail brochures with maps and information to enhance your walks. These five trails are briefly summarized:

Easy Access Trail: The 0.4 mile level paved nature walk encircles the parking area of the Frances Slocum day-use picnic area on the north shore, north of the dam and the observation pavilion. The trail brochure identifies 12 stations, with themes of natural resource conservation.

Lost Sister Trail: The 1.5 mile loop begins at the same area as the Easy Access Trail; the Frances Slocum picnic/parking area at the south end towards the lake. The 22 station, self-guiding trail follows the cove ridges between the picnic area, east to the launching ramp, near the spillway. The trail crosses six roads so exercise caution. Great day-hike.

Shepoconah Trail: This trail begins in the lower Miama SRA, has three loops, 0.5 - 1.0 miles, total 2.5 miles, that wander through open meadows and young forest. Look for deer, nesting birds, and summer wildflowers.

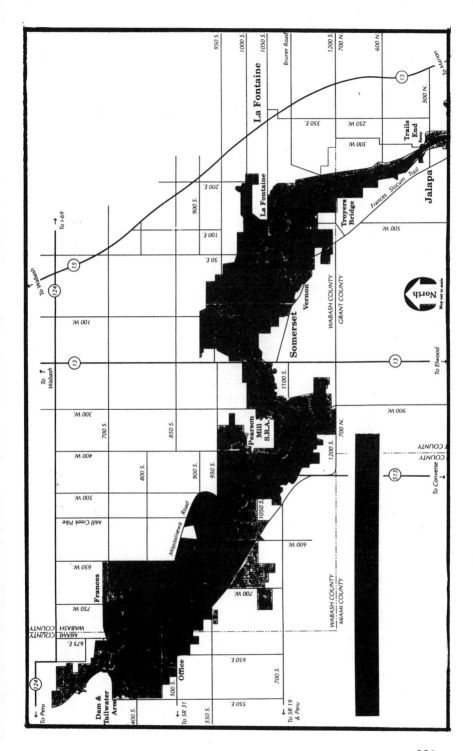

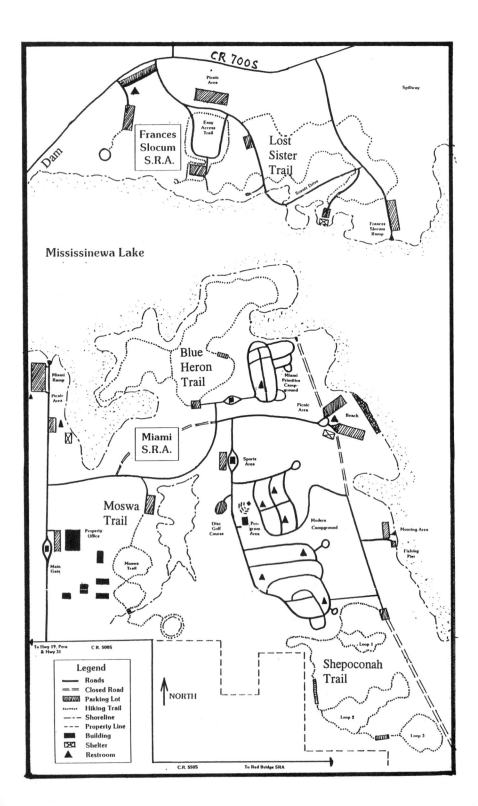

Blue Heron Trail: A 2.5 mile loop located between the entry office station and the campgrounds and beach at Miami SRA just south of the dam. The trailhead begins and ends next to the butterfly garden and parking area. The trail traces a loop through old fields and young forest alongside the reservoir. Good chance of possibly seeing great blue heron and possibly double-crested cormorants in summer and bald eagles in winter.

Moswa Trail: The Miami word for deer is Moswa and there is also a possibility of seeing the white-tailed. The 1.2 mile loop begins and ends in the fishing lake parking area on the main road through the Miami SRA. The trail traverses creek banks, pond borders, pasture open spaces, young woodlands.

Mississinewa Trail: The six mile trail was established by the Boy Scouts in the Frances Slocum State Forest northwest of the dam at the tailwater. The trailhead for the three loop trail begins at the Peoria fishing site parking area at the base of the dam on the north bank. Access to parking/trailhead area is a service paved road via CR 700S that crosses the dam. Yellow blazes mark the trail. Hikers be aware that the gorges and ravines of the forest are open to horse riders and the trail can be muddy, overgrown and confusing in places. Hunters also hunt here. This is a great trail for the adventuresome. The first loop is 1.2 miles of ravines and hills; loop 2 is 0.8 mile long between two ravines and hillock; loop 3 is along the Mississinewa River, a country road and the uplands. There are plans to close this area entirely and leave it as an open hiking area.

East of the dam area are several spots worth visitation such as Red Bridge SRA on the Old Frances Slocum Trail road, Pearson Mill SRA at the lake end of CR 300W, and especially the Trails End area near Jalapa, Indiana. The Trails End area was the scene of the last Miami-U.S. armed conflict in 1812. Historic markers and memorials identify the battlefield site and the village of Metocinah; the location of the annual Battle of Mississinewa re-enactment. There are plenty of old roads and user paths in the area to explore. The Mississinewa River appears as a river and not a reservoir, "sloping" or "slanting" over the rocky ledge enroute to the Wabash River; the source of its Miami place name. Trails End is reached from Indiana 15 south of LaFontaine, Indiana by turning west on CR 600N to CR 300W and south, following the river road northwest.

Mississinewa Reservoir is located seven miles southeast of Peru, Indiana. From US 31 one mile south of Grissom near Bunker Hill, turn east on CR 500S and drive a few miles to the brown property sign entrance to the property headquarters and the Miami SRA. The scenic

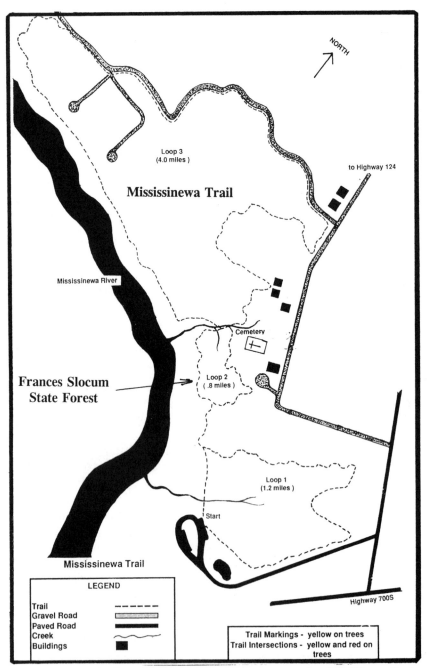

NORTH

Loop 3
(4.0 miles)

Mississinewa Trail

to Highway 124

Mississinewa River

Cemetery

**Frances Slocum
State Forest**

Loop 2
(.8 miles)

Loop 1
(1.2 miles)

Start

Mississinewa Trail

LEGEND	
Trail	
Gravel Road	
Paved Road	
Creek	
Buildings	

Trail Markings - yellow on trees
Trail Intersections - yellow and red on trees

Highway 700S

route is from Indiana 124 following the country roads of 675E, south, to 700S, west, to 550E, south, to 500S, east, to 625E, north to headquarters. Follow the directional signs.

21. SEVEN PILLARS LANDMARK & NATURE PRESERVE

Peru, IN/Miami County
USGS MAP(s): Peoria 1:24,000
TRAIL(s) DISTANCE: trails being developed
ACREAGE: appx. 150 acres
ACTIVITIES: nature walks, nature study, historic site, fishing

The Seven Pillars of the Mississinewa River have long been a geological wonder. The area has a cultural and spiritual significance to the Miami, who have historically gathered here. The 25 foot high limestone cliffs have been stream carved by the river, leaving alcove-like rooms. The pillars and cornices are especially unique. Above, the bluffs sport red cedar and juneberry, adding to the beauty. The formations are easily admired from the south bank of the river and the Seven Pillars Nature Preserve.

The 150 acre preserve was at one time the Miami Wappa-Pin-Sah Reserve. Trails are being developed in the open meadow and forested upland. The property is managed by ACRES, Inc. To reach the Seven Pillars Landmark and Nature Preserve from the Peru courthouse, drive south on Indiana 19 to CR 440S and turn left/east. Follow CR 400S just over a mile to CR 400E and turn left/north.

Seven Pillars of the Mississinewa River

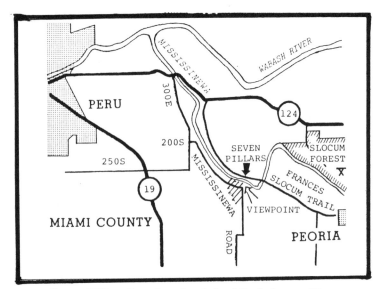

Seven Pillars Landmark of the Mississinewa River

Continue on CR 400E north about 0.75 mile to the roadside pullout to the right at the road curve by the river. Seven Pillars are about mid point between the Mississinewa dam and the confluence with the Wabash River.

Another route from Peru, is to drive southeast on Indiana 124 to the Mississinewa River valley and CR 300E and turn right/south. Follow CR 300E to CR 200W and turn left/east. Continue on CR 200E alongside the swift moving river to the Seven Pillar Nature Preserve.

22. FRANCE PARK
Logansport, IN/Cass County
USGS MAP(s): Lucerne 1:24,000
TRAIL(s) DISTANCE; 7 trails total appx. 6 miles
ACREAGE: 520 a. land/1 mile Wabash River frontage/35 a. quarries
ACTIVITIES: nature walks, nature study, nature center, historic sites, picnicking, shelters, swimming, bathhouse, lifeguards, SCUBA diving, water slide, mini-golf, playground, playfields, ball fields, fishing, canoeing, launch ramps, rappelling, winter sports, Class A camping, rent-a-tent, primitive camping, concessions, camp store
FEE(s): seasonal entrance, water slide, mini-golf, picnic shelter rental, SCUBA diving fee, camping, mountain biking, rock climbing

France Park, since 1967, has been owned and managed by the Cass County Park and Recreation Department. The county park has strong regional appeal due primarily to its natural and man-made attractions:

306

quarries, the Wabash River, a waterfall, springs, rolling forest and old fields, and the old historic Wabash and Erie Canal segment. It is a popular camping park , SCUBA dive and swimming quarry but hiking the seven interconnecting trails is a draw for many visitors.

Historically, France Park was a limestone quarry for over a century. The land was first quarried in 1835 by the Casparis Stone Company and about the same time the Wabash and Erie Canal was carved east and west through the park, less than a half mile from the Wabash River. In time, the camp grew and became a town known as Kenneth, Indiana and a post office was established in 1892. France Stone of Toledo, Ohio purchased the quarry in 1927, operating until 1943. For the next quarter century, the land was at rest and revegetating and was at last purchased as a Cass County park.

The seven trails are yellow blazed both ways and are also marked by hiking symbols. Although trailhead markers are absent, overall the paths are well maintained and move through quiet natural areas. The alphabetical labelled trails are identified A-G and are summarized as follows:

Trail A: Begins/ends at the entry gatehouse. Trail heads southwest to cross Paw Paw Creek and the 20 foot high spring-fed waterfall, and continues west paralleling the stream, leading to the Fish Pond Quarry, looping the west shore, connecting Trail B. The 0.5 mile linear trail returns to the gatehouse along the same route.

Trail B: Loop woodland trail of 0.25 mile on west shore of Frog Pond Quarry that connects Trails A, C and F. Good hike for picnickers and campers who use the area.

Trail C: Could easily be named the Wabash and Erie Canal Towpath Trail since the linear path skirts the old canal bed northside. The path can be mushy at times since the area is natural swale. Connects Trails G and close to Trail E and D. West trailhead located at parking turn-around at Fish Pond Quarry. About 0.4 mile distance.

Trail D: 0.4 mile long loop trail that passes through the wooded rent-a-tent and primitive camping area, skirting an abandoned field and the south side of the Wabash and Erie Canal. Connects E and F Trails.

Trail E: Most visitors would agree that this mile long trail is the most scenic in the park. The easy-to-rugged trail encircles the high scenic limestone bluffs of Swim Pond Quarry. Good vistas along the rocky trail on the quarry's south and east sides. Exercise caution when close to the cliff edges. A five acre portion of an old field on the east side of the pond is being restored to prairie. Access trail from the east side of the beach area.

Trail F: A west property trail. Connects Trail A, B and D and close to Trail C. The most remote trail. From A, B and F Trails head south across a ditch via a foot bridge, skirting Paw Paw Creek and fields on the edge of the forest. Cuts through pine plantation. Leads to drinking water sulphur spring and the Wabash River access ramp and picnic shelter across the Georgetown Road. Trail F heads north along Paw Paw Creek to Trail D.

Trail G: Located in the northeast section of France Park. Leads from Class A campground south to the Swim Pond Quarry parking area. Skirts the east side of Dry Quarry, where a baseball field has been situated. 0.25 mile trail one-way.

A plan to establish a hiking trail from France Park to the Little Turtle Waterway in Logansport has been proposed, and if completed, would be a vital link in the Wabash Heritage Corridor hiking trail.

The entrance to France Park is located four miles west of Logansport on US 24 on the left/south side of the highway. Unless camping, the park hours are from 7 am to 9 pm.

While in the area, consider visiting Logansport's nature-oriented parks. The four Eel River parks are small but are orientated to the stream. Popular Spencer Park is the furtherest upstream at the riverside junction of High Street and Plaza Drive. The scenic spot north of the main portion of the park features river views, a gazebo and flower beds. Next park downstream is Dunwoody Park, a riparian "pocket park" just off of High Street at the cul de sac of First Street. The small river frontage is natural and may be overgrown. Good place to fish and picnic, little area to walk. Further downstream is Riverside Park, an active park with more urban views but which has one of the finest restored carousels in the Midwest. North of High Street between 11th and 15th Streets. Front Street Park is located near the confluence of the Eel River and the Wabash River. Scenic views of the "rapids of the Eel River" and old Logansport. Turn onto Wheatland Avenue from North 3rd/Indiana 17N near downtown. Along the Wabash River is the Little Turtle Waterway at East Melbourne Avenue where the annual Iron Horse Festival is held. The Waterway will be a plaza showcase park geared to the river and hopefully the plan to build a hiking trail to France Park will be fulfilled.

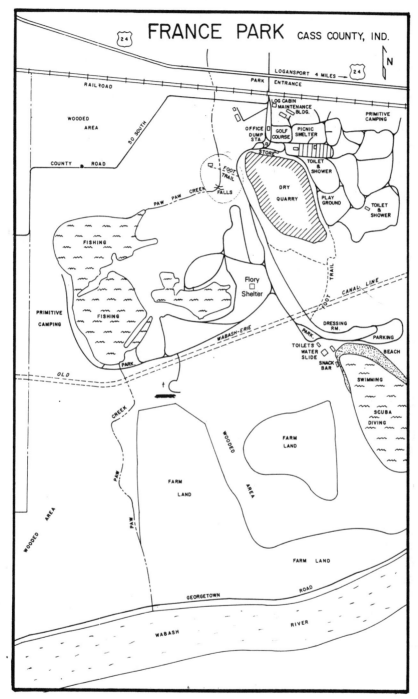

France Park

Away from the river at opposite sides of the city of Logansport are three natural parks: Dykeman, Wilmer Flory, and Woodland Acres. On the northwest side, Dykeman Park features a forest loop path adjacent to a wooded ravine at the cul de sac picnic area, west of the golf course. From North 3rd Street/Indiana 17N at College Hill, turn left/northwest onto Royal Center Pike at the hilltop. Go one block more and turn left on Eberts Road and the park entrance. Follow the scenic drive through the golf course to the picnic area. User paths lead to the ravine floor. The Wilmer Flory Nature Preserve is a small natural wooded area that has short unmarked and unmaintained linear and loop trails but the preserve is signed. From Indiana 435 in south Logansport, turn right at Hamilton Street and drive to the south end where parking is on the left/east side of the street. The 60 acre Woodland Acres Wildlife Area, a Cass County park, is located at the northeast edge of the city. Old overgrown trails lead from the parking and picnic area through the young woods to a woodland stream. To reach the area from downtown Logansport, go east on East Market, 1.3 miles to 24th Street and turn left/north. Go three blocks north to High Street and turn right/east. Turn north on Davis Street and cross the Eel River. Continue 0.5 mile to the Perrysburg Road and turn east. Drive 1.1 mile to CR 300N and turn north. Proceed one mile to the entrance. The gravel access road is 0.2 mile long and culminates at the parking and picnic area. The hours are 9 am to 7 pm.

23. TRAILHEAD PARK & TOWPATH TRAIL
Delphi, IN/Carroll County
USGS MAP(s): Delphi 1:24,000
ACREAGE: 20 acres
ACTIVITIES: nature walks, historic walks, nature study, picnicking, shelters, bicycling, fishing, canoeing, special events

Trailhead Park, just southwest 0.5 mile of Delphi adjacent north to Indiana 25, provides foot access via a suspension bridge over Deer Creek, to Towpath Vanscoy Trail, the former towpath of the historic Wabash and Erie Canal. Hopefully, the recreational trail will be extended upstream and downstream to form the proposed Wabash Heritage Corridor Trail.

At one point where the Wabash and Deer Creek merge, an old dam allowed barges and boats to cross Deer Creek on the Wabash and Erie Canal. Most of the trail follows the linear, vehicle-wide path alongside the old canal bed within the Wabash River floodplain. The trail extends 1.25 miles east to Bicycle Bridge Road near US 421 and the intersection with Indiana 25. Recently the trail has been extended up Deer Creek to Riley Park. The park and trail were developed from grants from the Wabash

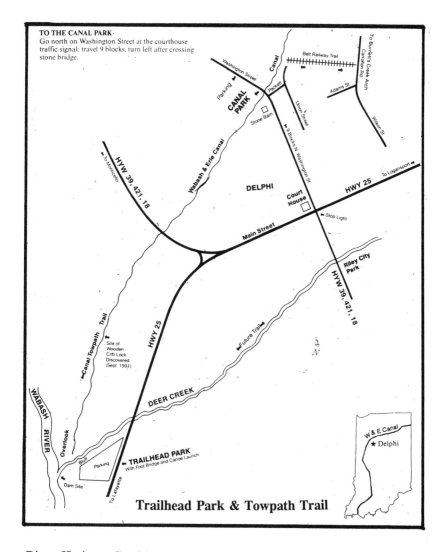

TO THE CANAL PARK·
Go north on Washington Street at the courthouse traffic signal; travel 9 blocks, turn left after crossing stone bridge.

Belt Railway Trail

To Burnett's Creek Arch
Carrolton Rd.

Washington Street

Canal

Packet

Adams St.

Wilson St.

Parking

CANAL PARK

Stone Barn

Union Street

9 Blocks N Washington St.

To Monticello

HYW 39, 421, 18

Wabash & Erie Canal

DELPHI

Court House

HWY 25

To Logansport

Main Street

Stop Light

Riley City Park

HYW 39, 421, 18

Canal Towpath Trail

HWY 25

Site of Wooden Crib Lock Discovered (Sept. 1993)

Future Trail

N

DEER CREEK

WABASH RIVER

Overlook

Bluff

Parking

TRAILHEAD PARK
With Foot Bridge and Canoe Launch

Dam Site

To Lafayette

W & E Canal

★ Delphi

Trailhead Park & Towpath Trail

River Heritage Corridor Fund. Not yet acquired, the old towpath runs downstream, between the river and the canal for some distance from Trailhead Park.

Another preserved segment of the old Wabash and Erie Canal and Towpath is in <u>Canal Park</u>, across from the <u>Stone Barn Park</u>, in north central Delphi. A canal-era village lines the towpath above the restored canal. An inn, trappers cabin, blacksmith and the Reed Case House Museum, which houses the Wabash and Erie Canal Association make up the village of the 1840s. The village comes alive during Canal Days and other special events.

311

To reach Canal Park, go north from the courthouse on Washington Street about nine blocks to the stone bridge, turning left upon crossing.

Another suspension bridge crossing Deer Creek is at <u>James Whitcomb Riley Park</u>. The scenic park occupies the level floodplain of Deer Creek and is flanked on the south by a wooded slope. There is a section of elevated boardwalk along the stream. From the courthouse, go south on Washington Street/Indiana 39 and turn left/east after crossing the Deer Creek bridge into <u>Riley Park</u>. Future plans call for connecting all three Delphi parks via streamside trails. The parks and trail are owned and managed by the Delphi Park and Recreation Department and the Wabash and Erie Canal Association.

Another park worth mentioning is the <u>French Post Park</u> at Lockport, Indiana, along the south bank of the Wabash River. The Carroll County park occupies the former site of an old French trading post at the confluence of Rock Creek and the Wabash. The small park offers sheltered picnicking and primitive canoe camping. Across the Wabash River bridge at Lockport is the old Wabash and Erie Canal aqueduct site that carried the canal waters over Burnetts Creek, along Towpath Road.

Lockport, Indiana is reached from Delphi via Wilson Street by following the Carollton Road/Towpath Road north and east along the Wabash River for about six miles or so.

24. WOLF PARK

Battle Ground, IN/Tippecanoe County
USGS MAP(s): Brookston 1:24,000
TRAIL(s) DISTANCE: 0.25 old farm lane
ACREAGE: 100 acres
ACTIVITIES: nature walk tours, lectures, wolf refuge, Howl Night,
  Wolf-Bison Demonstration, gift shop
FEE(s): entrance (members, sponsors, children under 13 free)

Founded in 1972 by Purdue ethology professor Erich Klinghammer, Wolf Park is the place to visit to know more about the North American timber gray wolf; the same wolf that was exterminated in Indiana around 1908. Visitors receive a close up view of this long-legged ancestor of the domestic dog. The non-profit educational and research wildlife park explains the unique role of this magnificent predator.

Once roaming the entire North American continent, the largest wolf population today in the lower forty-eight states is in Minnesota with about

2,000 wolves, while Canada has an estimated number of 45,000 to 60,000. The stereotype of the "cruel wolf" is not founded in fact, but is still believed. The wolf represents the wild and cannot be truly tamed. Wolf Park tries to eliminate false ideas about the wolf through education programs. The Park has eighteen adult wolves, plus two coyotes, two red foxes, sheep and a herd of bison. The bison, commonly called buffalo, are used in the Wolf-Bison demonstration on Sunday afternoons at 1 pm from May to November. The demonstration reveals how wolves test the bison, and how bison react by protecting themselves and their calves, with no animals getting harmed in the process.

Howl Night is Friday and Saturday evenings at 7:30 pm from May to November, and on Saturdays year round. Wolves howl not at a full moon but to communicate with the pack for social reasons. Wolves in the wild live in small pack families of two or more animals and cover a territory that depends on the availability of prey. In Minnesota it is about 10 square miles per wolf. The pack is led by a dominant male and female. Wolves eat mostly ungulates, sometimes smaller animals, and occasionaly wild fruit and fish. Normally, four to six pups are born in April or May after a sixty one day gestation period. Their life span in the wild is 10 to 18 years, though only about half the pups survive the first year. Wolves as being a threat to domestic livestock has been highly questioned.

Buffalo Wolf Encounter, Wolf Park

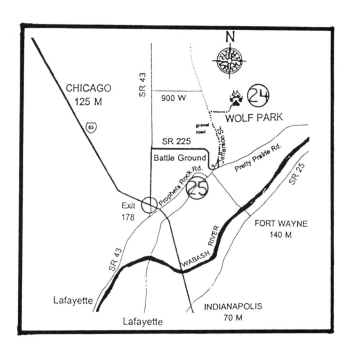

Wolf Park (24) and Tippecanoe Battlefield (25)

Wolf Park is open daily May 1 to November 30 from 1 to 5 pm and closed on holidays. Weather permitting, Howl night is offered year round on Saturdays at 7:30 pm, as well as Fridays during the open season. Lectures and tours are offered Monday to Friday, with special lectures and handling demonstrations also on Saturdays. Tours and the Wolf-Bison demonstration are offered on Sundays. Wolf Park members and children 13 and under are admitted free. Wolf Park has a wolf sponsoring program which allows sponsors to meet a wolf first hand. For more information, please call (317) 567-2265.

Wolf Park is located seven miles northeast of Lafayette. From Indiana 43 go east on Indiana 225 to Battle Ground, Indiana. In Battle Ground, cross the railroad tracks and stay left. Then take your first left, on Jefferson Street north out of town, and follow it for 1.5 miles until you see the Wolf Park sign on the right/north side of the road.

25. TIPPECANOE BATTLEFIELD
Battle Ground, IN/Tippecanoe County
USGS MAP(s): Brookston 1:24,000
TRAIL(s) DISTANCE: east terminus 7.5 m. Wabash Heritage Trail, 0.25 mile Tree Trail, 1 mile Prophet's Rock Trail
ACREAGE: 104 acres
ACTIVITIES: nature walks, nature bike, nature study, nature center, seasonal naturalist, historic sites, picnicking, shelters, swimming pool, interpretive center, museum, gift shop, retreat center, guided tours, special events
FEE(s): museum, shelter & retreat center rentals

Tippecanoe Battlefield, a National Historic Landmark, is the northeast terminus of the 7.5 mile one way Wabash Heritage Trail, one of the longest and most scenic hikes in the Wabash Valley. The Wah-ba-shik-a Nature Center is special and small but big on information. The nature center is open daily 10 am to 5 pm, April 17 through November 7. The interpretive center features a historic museum and gift shop which is open year around from 10 am to 5 pm and until 4 pm during winter months. The grounds are open year around, dawn to dusk, and includes the Battlefield, Burnetts Creek, Prophets Rock and the Wabash Heritage Trail.

Wabash Heritage Trail.(see trip 26) - A 7-1/2 mile linear trail (does not loop) that extends from the Tippecanoe Battlefield to the Harrison Bridge (State Road 231) in Lafayette. Terrain ranges from easy to moderate. parking and trail access also at Davis Ferry Park (3-1/2 miles south) and at Lafayette Municipal Golf Course (6-1/2 miles south).

Tree Trail. The 0.25 mile tree trail is near the Nature Center, Monument, and Battlefield encampment area.

Prophet's Rock Trail. - A one mile round trip loop trail from the Nature Center and back through the hills and woodlands above the Prophet's rock outcrop. According to legend, Tenskwautawa, the brother of Tecumseh, encouraged his warriers from this point during the battle of Tippecanoe. Across the meadow west and across Prophet's Rock Road is Prophet's Rock, a rock outcrop and overhang shelter, supposedly where the Shawnee prophet of "Prophetstown" prayed for victory against the American "Yellow Jackets" commandeered by Harrison. The American victory at Tippecanoe was just as significant as Fallen Timbers, Ohio, in breaking Indian resistance and open the frontier to settlement. One year later, the last Indian-U.S. battle in Indiana occurred at the Battle of the Mississinewa in 1812. In the future, the county park will form the nucleus of Prophetstown State Park.

Stairs and footbridge lead to and across scenic Burnetts Creek. Across the bridge west is the east terminus of the Wabash Heritage Trail that follows the creek downstream to the Wabash River and Lafayette's Digby Park, for now. Short hikes down a mile or so and back are also invigorating. Plans are being acted on to extend the trail downstream to Fort Ouiatenon, and upstream to Delphi's Trailhead Park.

To reach Tippecanoe Battlefield at Battle Ground, Indiana from I-65 exit 175 onto Indiana 25 and drive to Indiana 225 and turn left/north. Continue on Indiana 225 across the Wabash River (stop at the Prophetstown historic marker on the left side of the bridge) and on to Battle Ground, Indiana. Go across the railroad tracks and make a sharp left/south and drive to the south side of town and the county park entrance and parking area.

Also from I-65 exit 178, drive north on Indiana 43 to Indiana 225 and turn right/east. Follow Indiana 225 to Battle Ground. Turn south on the street before the railroad track crossing. Go four blocks to the entrance.

Wolf Park and Clegg Botanic Garden are nearby excursions.

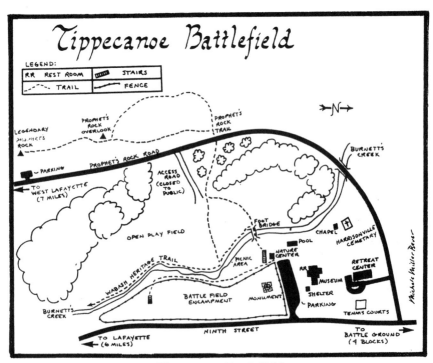

Tippecanoe Battlefield

26. WABASH HERITAGE TRAIL
Lafayette, IN/Tippecanoe County
USGS MAP(s): Brookston, Lafayette East, Lafayette West 1:24,000
TRAIL(s) Distance: 7.5 miles one-way
ACTIVITIES: hiking, nature study, nature center, historic sites, picnicking, fishing, boat launch, boating, city parks

The Wabash Heritage Trail is the premier hiking path in the Wabash River valley; longest in distance and the most historic. The point to point foot trail is a working example of the proposed state-long trail that would parallel the official State river from the headwaters to the confluence with the Ohio River.

Basically the Wabash Heritage Trail begins/ends at Tippecanoe Battlefield on Burnetts Creek, heads south on Burnetts Creek to the confluence with the Wabash at Davis Ferry, continuing downstream to conclude at Digby Park and Tapawingo Park for the time being. Plans are to expand the trail south 5.5 miles more to Fort Ouiatenon and upstream about ten miles to Delphi's Trailhead Park. Eventually, from Covington to Fort Wayne and Geneva and Fort Recovery are potential trail possibilities in the upper Wabash River valley.

A car shuttle or hiking short segments both ways are solutions to hiking 15 miles in one day, down and up. The best segment is along the 3.5 mile section of Burnetts Creek. There is one creek crossing and several foot bridges from Tippecanoe Battlefield to Davis Ferry County Park at the confluence of the two streams. A good day hike.

The trail from Davis Ferry follows the southeast bank of the Wabash to Lafayette's city parks of Digby and McAllister at Harrison bridge and Tapawingo Park. Three trailheads and parking areas are located at Tippecanoe Battlefield at Battle Ground, Davis Ferry Park at Davis Ferry Road at the southeast side of the Wabash, and Digby and McAllister parks on the Wabash River and Canal Road in Lafayette. Portions of the trail may be muddy and under water during rains and floods. The trail is well marked and interpretive signs line the trail enroute. Heron Island is a 12 acre Tippecanoe County wildlife preserve. For more information about the Wabash Heritage Trail call the Tippecanoe County Park and Recreation Department at (317) 463-2306 or 567-2993.

The trailheads and parking areas are easily accessed from I-65 exits 178, Indiana 43, and exit 175, Indiana 25; both travel to Indiana 225 and Battle Ground, the east terminus. Indiana 25 west of I-65 exit 175, leads to Digby Park and the riverfront Canal Street.

317

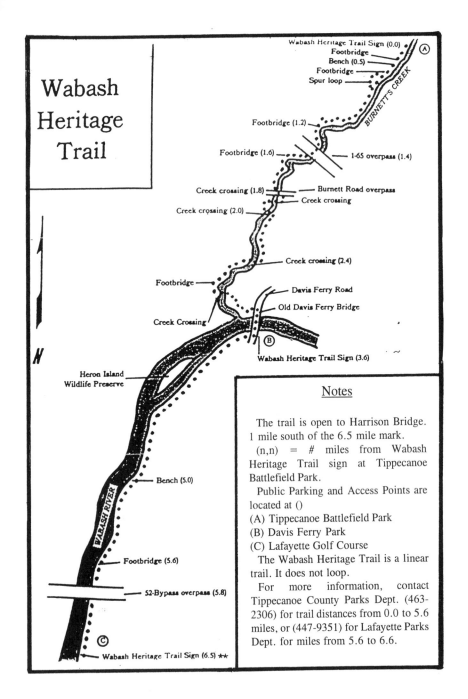

Wabash Heritage Trail

Wabash Heritage Trail Sign (0.0) Ⓐ
Footbridge
Bench (0.5)
Footbridge
Spur loop

BURNETT'S CREEK

Footbridge (1.2)

Footbridge (1.6)
I-65 overpass (1.4)

Creek crossing (1.8)
Burnett Road overpass
Creek crossing

Creek crossing (2.0)

Creek crossing (2.4)

Footbridge
Davis Ferry Road

Old Davis Ferry Bridge

Creek Crossing
Ⓑ
Wabash Heritage Trail Sign (3.6)

Heron Island
Wildlife Preserve

N

WABASH RIVER

Bench (5.0)

Footbridge (5.6)

52-Bypass overpass (5.8)

Ⓒ
Wabash Heritage Trail Sign (6.5) ★★

Notes

The trail is open to Harrison Bridge. 1 mile south of the 6.5 mile mark.

(n,n) = # miles from Wabash Heritage Trail sign at Tippecanoe Battlefield Park.

Public Parking and Access Points are located at ()
(A) Tippecanoe Battlefield Park
(B) Davis Ferry Park
(C) Lafayette Golf Course

The Wabash Heritage Trail is a linear trail. It does not loop.

For more information, contact Tippecanoe County Parks Dept. (463-2306) for trail distances from 0.0 to 5.6 miles, or (447-9351) for Lafayette Parks Dept. for miles from 5.6 to 6.6.

Wabash Heritage Trail

27. JERRY E. CLEGG BOTANIC GARDEN

Lafayette, IN/Tippecanoe County
USGS MAP(s): Lafayette East 1:24,000
TRAIL(s) DISTANCE: 1.5 mile
ACREAGE: 15 acres
ACTIVITIES: nature walks, nature study, botanic garden, guided tours
FEE(s): donations accepted, membership available

Fine old growth oaks cover the lush coves and ridges of this riverside sanctuary, perched high above on the bluffs of Wildcat Creek, not far from its confluence with the Wabash River in east Lafayette. There are lookout vistas of the Wildcat valley. Five acres near the road front and parking area are cultivated flower gardens that are easily seen along the Garden Path loop. Shooting stars are prolific and 250 plants and 44 trees have been labelled for easy identification. There are boardwalks, staircases and foot bridges, ascending and descending, the steep ravine slopes along Trails 2, 3, 4, and 5, all looping and interconnect. A trail map is available at the entrance visitor station.

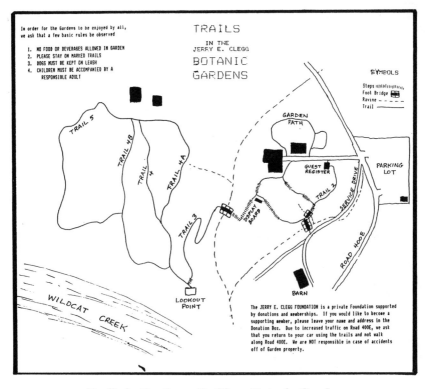

Trails in the Jerry E. Clegg Botanic Gardens

The garden first opened on Easter Sunday, 1965, in memory of Jerry E. Clegg by his family. The home and grounds was the summer residence of the Clegg family during their son's youth. The nature reserve is maintained by a privately funded foundation.

To reach Jerry E. Clegg Botanic Garden from I-65 exit 175, northeast on Indiana 25 and drive 0.5 mile to CR 300N, the first right/east road from Indiana 25. Go right/east on CR 300N, past the Aretz Airport, 0.5 mile to CR 400E and turn right/south. Follow CR 400E, 1.25 miles to the parking area on the left/east side of the road, across from the garden entrance. Please exercise caution crossing the wooded bend in CR 400E. The hours are 10 am to sunset every day. For further information call (317) 423-1325.

Three miles south of the Clegg Botanic Garden on winding Eisenhower Road is the 53 acre Wildcat Park. This Tippecanoe County park is at the junction of the north and south forks of Wildcat Creek. A short nature trail loop leads through a hardwood and pine tree plantation at the west end of the parking area. The streambanks and gravel bars are accessible on foot. Also picnicking, shelters, canoe launch and fishing pier.

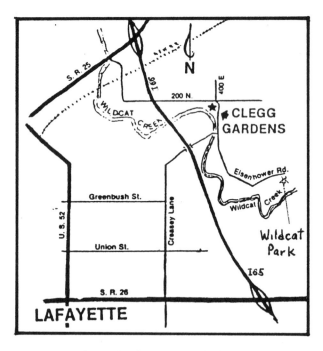

Jerry E. Clegg Botanic Garden

28. LAFEYETTE NATURE PLACES

ACTVITIES: nature walks, nature study, zoo, picnicking, shelters, playgrounds, playfields, ballfields, ball courts, swimming pool, lifeguards, amusement rides, paddleboats, mini-golf, lagoon, fishing, boating, launch ramp, outdoor theater, winter sports, disc-golf, programs camping, hiking

FEE(s): shelter & building rentals

Positioned along and above the Wabash River, the county seat of Tippecanoe County, the city of Lafayette has several nature-oriented parks to explore afoot and afield.

The 63 acre <u>Columbian Park and Zoo (A)</u> is a favorite of many residents and visitors alike. The park is filled with many recreational attractions with children in mind. For the nature-oriented, the zoo holds the major interest. It is Indiana's oldest established zoo. Sixty-four species of animals reside in the four areas: Main Animal House, Monkey Island, Big Barn Area and the Children's Petting Zoo. The Main Animal House is the residence for the big cats and the winter quarters for the monkeys. Monkey Island and the Petting Zoo are closed during the winter months. The Main Animal House and the Big Barn Area are open during the winter season from noon to 4:30 pm daily. Summer hours are noon to 8:30 pm. Admission is free and there are educational programs and membership available for the zoo.

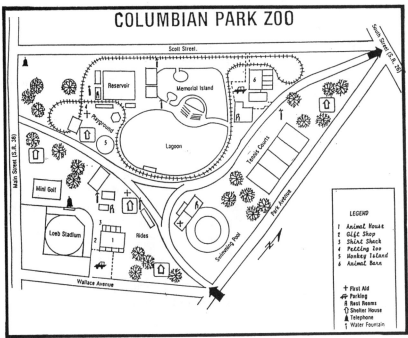

COLUMBIAN PARK ZOO

LEGEND

1 Animal House
2 Gift Shop
3 Shirt Shack
4 Petting Zoo
5 Monkey Island
6 Animal Barn

+ First Aid
Parking
R Rest Rooms
Shelter House
Telephone
Water Fountain

Lafayette and West Lafayette Nature Places

The Columbian Park and Zoo are located at South and Main Streets between Scott Street, Park Avenue and Wallace Avenue.

Murdock Park (B) is a 55 acre rolling wooded parkland located a few city blocks north and west of Columbian Park and Zoo, at 18th and Carson streets between Union and Ferry streets. The green space is a fine place to walkabout and there is a short nature trail at the north end through a remnant oak forest. There are also picnic areas, playfields, playgrounds, a winter sled run and summer concessions.

The Wabash River parks (C) of Digby, Lyboult Sports Complex and McAlister, north of the Harrison Bridge and south of the Sagamore

Parkway/US 52, offer over 400 acres of open spaces and even though they are active parks there is the riverfront and the south terminus of the Wabash Heritage Trail; a trail that is 7.5 miles long and stretches north to Tippecanoe Battlefield Park in Battle Ground, Indiana.

South of downtown at Beck Lane and 9th Avenue are two city parks situated adjacent to each other, bisected only by Beck Lane. Bishop Woods (D) is the largest of the two (55 acres) and is the most natural and undeveloped. Neil Armstrong Park (D) (26 acres) has playfields, ball fields and ball courts.

Further south of Lafayette, located on Wea Creek is Mar Len County Park. A short trail follows the north bank of Wea Creek where primitive camping sites are established. The park also offers picnicking, shelterhouse, fishing and a lighted ball diamond.

Mar Len Park is five miles south of Lafayette at South 18tb Street/CR 150E and Wea School Road.

It may be of interest to visit the Tippecanoe County Public Library (E) on South Street near downtown, where the surrounding grounds have been landscaped with native trees and shrubs.

29. WEST LAFAYETTE NATURE PLACES

ACTIVITIES: nature walks, nature study, nature preserves, historic sites, amphitheatre, picnicking, shelters, fitness course, playgrounds, playfields, ball fields, ball courts, fishing, boating, launch ramp, swimming pool, lifeguards, winter sports, gift shop, museum, special events

FEE(s): shelter rental, special events

As a general rule, "college towns" also have quality park systems and West Lafayette is no exception with its open spaces, parks and recreation facilities available. Several of the parks are related to the out-of-doors, beautification and ecology such as Happy Hollow Park, Cumberland Park, Celery Bog Park plus the riverside parks of Mascouten, Waterfront, Tapawingo and Ft. Ouiatenon.

The 81 acre Happy Hollow Park (5) is the largest and most popular city park. The long and wide hollow has open playfields, picnicking shelters, playgrounds, rimmed with forested slopes and ridges. A short rocky tributary flows to the Wabash River. Well worn nature trails follow the north slopes.

Entrance to Happy Hollow Park by road is from North River Road/ Indiana 443 to Happy Hollow Road. There is also a pedestrian entrance on North Salisbury Street between Grant Street and Highland Drive.

The 62 acre Cumberland Park (3) is part play and ball fields and part Michaud-Sinninger Woods Nature Preserve. The 16 acre woodlot is evident and obviously the only forest remnant surviving in this level expanse of grass. A curving trail loops through the wet woods (purchased by The Nature Conservancy but now part of the city park). The forest entrance is marked.

From North Salisbury Street, drive north from US 52/Sagamore Parkway, 0.7 mile to the parking area for Cumberland Park on the left/west side of North Salisbury Street. Cumberland Park is located along North Salisbury and Kalberer Road/CR 350N.

West of Happy Hollow and Cumberland Parks is the recently acquired 36 acre Celery Bog Park, which is being restored as an urban wetland. It contains a nature trail running through woods and along a marsh. The park is planned for expansion to be the city's largest park. Entrance to the park is north off Lindberg Road, 0.7 miles west of Northwestern Avenue.

Along North River Road/Indiana 43, south of I-65 and CR 500N, is the Tippecanoe County amphitheatre (F) where summer performances are held. The site is the headquarters of the Tippecanoe County Park and Recreation Department. South of the amphitheatre and across North River Road from the Indiana Veteran's Home is the 18 acre Tecumseh Trails roadside park (G) which allows visitors close contact with the Wabash River via fisherman's paths, and there are picnicking shelters. The Indiana Veteran's Home features the Commandant's Residence, a State designated memorial, and the 61 acre Indiana Veteran's Home Nature Preserve which is nearly inaccessible by foot due to the steep ravine slopes.

Further downstream along the river and North River Road is the 18 acre Mascouten Park (6) where there is fishing, a launch ramp, boating, picnicking and nature walks along the forested banks. Adjacent is Waterfront Park (10). Happy Hollow Park is nearby to the west.

The 19 acre Tapawingo Park (8), along Tapawingo Drive, between State Street and Brown Street, is along the sandy shores of the Wabash River. The active park features lighted basketball, volleyball, tennis courts, fishing, playground and picnic areas. A segment of the Wabash Heritage Trail is open to the public in the park and crosses the river on the Main Street Bridge, renovated for pedestrians/bicyclists and festival plazas.

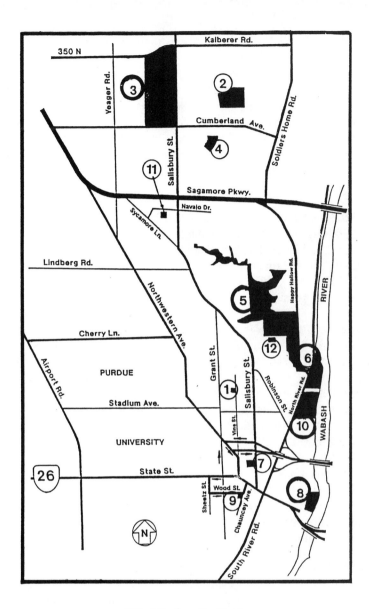

West Lafayette Parks

1. *Centennial Neighborhood Park*
2. *W. Lafayette Baseball complex*
3. *Cumberland Park*
4. *George E. Lommel Park*
5. *Happy Hollow Park*
6. *Mascouten Park*
7. *Morton Community Center*
8. *Tapawingo Park*
9. *Tommy Johnston Neighborhood P.*
10. *Waterfront Park*
11. *Parks and Recreation Office, City Hall*
12. *W. Lafayette Municipal Pool*

Downstream along the Wabash River, three miles southwest of West Lafayette on South River Road, is <u>Fort Ouiatenon (H)</u>, a 30 acre historical county park. A reconstructed replica of the original blockhouse fort built by the French in 1777 is open daily from April to October as a museum and gift shop. There are picnic shelter areas, fishing, boating, launch ramp and plenty of open space to wander. The park is also the site of the Feast of the Hunter's Moon Festival held in early autumn. The festival is sponsored by the Tippecanoe County Historical Association in cooperation with the Tippecanoe County Park and Recreation Department.

30. PURDUE UNIVERSITY CAMPUS WALK
West Lafayette, IN/Tippecanoe County
WALKING DISTANCE: appx. 7 miles of loops
ACREAGE: 627 main campus/1,500 total campus
ACTIVITIES: self-guiding campus tree tours, horticulture garden & park, nature trails, picnicking, shelters

Founded in 1869, the Purdue University campus in West Lafayette is beautiful and is best appreciated up close on foot. There are also fountains, statuary and sculpture that add to the beauty of the grounds. There are three tree trails, designed and established by the Purdue Grounds Department in cooperation with the Purdue's Department of Forestry and Natural Resources. For a more informal natural setting, try walking Purdue's Horticulture Park and adjoining Stewart's Woodlands at West Campus.

All three tree trails are loops and are color-coded: blue, gold and green. Two of the trails begin and end at the visitor center/parking garage at 504 Northwestern Avenue, where a trail map and other information are available. The numbered posts at the base of the trees corresponds to the trail map as follows:

Trail 1: The <u>Blue Trail</u> starts/ends at the visitor center and explores the north part of campus bounded by Stadium Avenue, University Street and State Street. There are 29 trees id. on this 1.75 mile walk. Some unique species on this walk include American yellowwood, golden rain tree, hican (hybrid pecan & shellbark hickory), Katsura tree and paperbark maple.

Trail 2: The <u>Gold Trail</u> guides the visitor through the center of campus. Thirty five trees are found along the 1.5 mile walk, and may require an hour. Interesting trees along this segment include Serbian spruce, sycamore maple, homestead elm, hedge maple, and Swiss stone pine.

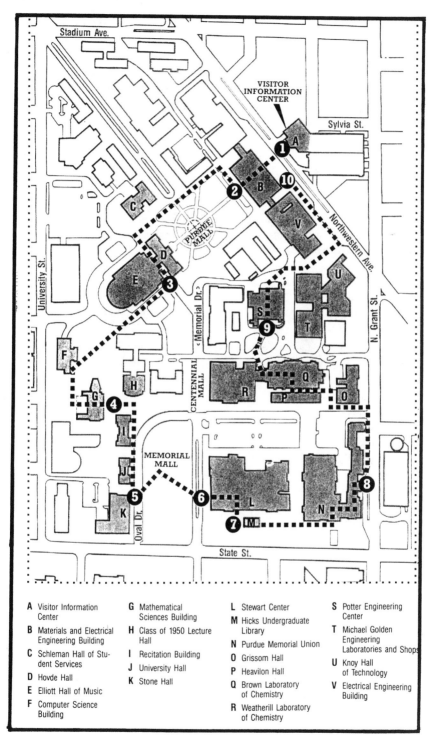

VISITOR INFORMATION CENTER

Stadium Ave.

Sylvia St.

University St.

Northwestern Ave.

N. Grant St.

PURDUE MALL

Memorial Dr.

CENTENNIAL MALL

MEMORIAL MALL

Oval Dr.

State St.

A Visitor Information Center
B Materials and Electrical Engineering Building
C Schleman Hall of Student Services
D Hovde Hall
E Elliott Hall of Music
F Computer Science Building

G Mathematical Sciences Building
H Class of 1950 Lecture Hall
I Recitation Building
J University Hall
K Stone Hall

L Stewart Center
M Hicks Undergraduate Library
N Purdue Memorial Union
O Grissom Hall
P Heavilon Hall
Q Brown Laboratory of Chemistry
R Weatherill Laboratory of Chemistry

S Potter Engineering Center
T Michael Golden Engineering Laboratories and Shops
U Knoy Hall of Technology
V Electrical Engineering Building

Trail 3: Across State Street south from the Blue and Gold Trails is the Green Trail which actually starts at the Ground Services Building, just west of Lilly Hall, leading through the south campus. There are 30 trees identified and described along the 1.5 mile long walk. Outstanding trees include the Amur corktree, "Shuttle" gum (sweet gum tree that germinated August, 1984 aboard the space shuttle Discovery), Japanese pagoda trees, Cedar of Lebanon, and the Shumard oak. Along the Green Trail, south of the Horticulture Building between Horticulture Drive and Marsteller Street, are the Horticulture Gardens. Self-guided tours may be taken of the ornamental and vegetable garden displays. Guided tours are also given with prior arrangements.

West of main campus is Horticulture Park and Stewart's Woods, open dawn to dusk. The 40 acres is about half semi-formal gardens and half natural forest. Horticulture Park has plenty of open space to roam about the evergreens, flowering crabs and flower beds.

At the north end of Horticulture Park, north of the shelter/maintenance facility, is the trailhead for the forest trails. The somewhat marked but obvious paths that total about two miles, trace interweaving loops in the old growth forest: Westwood Trail, Ecology Trail and Timber Trail. When wet, the trails can be slick clay and muddy along the small brooks that bisect the property. Purdue's Department of Forestry oversees the trails.

The west entrance to Horticulture Park is along Indiana 26, just west of the intersection of Airport Road/McCormick Road and Indiana 26/State Street. The east entrance is adjacent to McCormick Road, just north of the Indiana 26/State Street intersection, west of the Purdue West shopping center and north of the Purdue airport.

Further west of Horticulture Park/Stewart Woods a few miles is Purdue's Horticulture Research Farm where the public may purchase fresh apples and peaches in season. The address is 555 Sharon Chapel Road, just off Indiana 26 west.

Purdue and West Lafayette are easily accessed from I-69, US 52 and US 231, and Indiana State Roads 25, 38, 26, and 443/43/421.

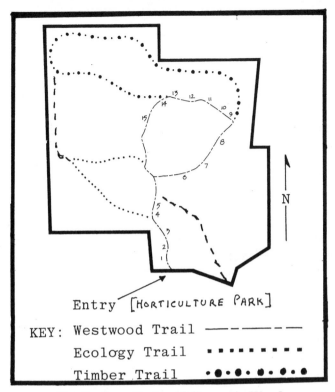

Horticulture Park and Stewart's Woods

Westwood Trail is the 1/2 mile , 30 minute loop trail. Posts 1-15 are keyed to the guidebook. *Timber Trail* is a 1/2 mile spinoff with a different guidebook. It starts near the Presidents home. You rejoin *Westwood Trail* after 20-30 minutes. *Ecology Trail* has signs on its 10 minute loop.

31. ROSS HILLS COUNTY PARK
Granville, IN/Tippecanoe County
USGS MAP(s): Otterbein 1:24,000
TRAIL(s) Distance: appx. 2 miles unmarked trails
ACREAGE: 170 acres
ACTIVITIES: nature walks, nature study, picnicking, shelters, playfields, playgrounds

The Tippecanoe County park of Ross Hills is situated on the north scenic bank of the Wabash River between Ross Camp and Ross Biological Reserve. The county park was formerly the Purdue faculty recreation area and all three properties are named in honor of David Ross (1871-1943), a Hoosier inventor, manufacturer and Purdue University benefactor. The park and adjacent properties are part of his former dairy farm and summer house, which is now available to groups of 50. The Ross Biological Reserve of 50 acres to the east is a botanical and biological laboratory for graduate student projects.

The upland glacial drift of Ross Hills is covered with oak hickory forest, grassy openings, vegetated slopes and ravines, and Wabash River valley floodplain. The waterfall at the east boundary is charming. The Bat "condo" shelter is special and hopefully it's occupied. Foot trails follow the ravine ridges from the level grassy upland picnic area to the Wabash bottoms where service roads serve as trails.

Ross Hills County Park is located about eight miles from the Purdue campus. Follow South River Road west past Fort Ouiatenon and continue west where the road changes names to Division Road to a "T" and CR 875W. Turn left/south and follow CR 875W to the entrance, near the Tippecanoe and Warren county line.

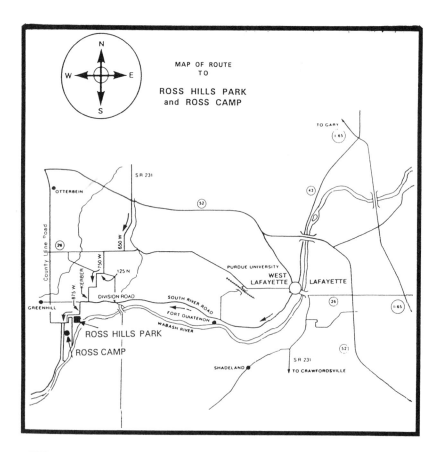

32. ZACHARIAH CICOTT COUNTY PARK/ ATTICA RAVINE PARK

Independence, IN/Warren County
USGS MAP(s): Attica 1:24,000
TRAIL(s) DISTANCE: 1.2 m. zccp/0.5 m. arp
ACREAGE: 70 a. zccp/40 a. arp
ACTIVITIES: nature walks, nature study, historic sites, picnicking, special events, swimming pool, pavilion, ballfields, ball courts

Zachariah Cicott, a French-Canadian, was a trader with the Potawatomi and Kickapoo at present day Independence, a town he founded around the early 1800s. Cicott was a scout to General William Harrison and participated in the Battle of Tippecanoe in 1811. After the War of 1812, Cicott settled with his Potawatomi wife and son just west of Independence until his death about 1850, continuing to trade with the Indians. He is buried in the Independence cemetery. The former trading post and homesite at the county park has been excavated and a large number of small trading post items have been discovered.

The Warren County features two self-guiding trails that lead through floodplain and upland forest and retired old fields. The 0.5 mile Upper Trail and the 0.4 mile Lower Trail begin east of the parking area at the visitor center. The trails loop and interconnect but neither trail goes near the river and both can be wet and mushy from the sloping hillside seeps. Views of the river are scarce through the dense forest. A granite boulder historic marker sits near the entrance, commemorating the 800 Potawatomi who camped here on September 14, 1838 during the forced march, "Trail of Death" to Kansas.

To reach the Cicott Trading Post Park at the east edge of Independence, on the north bank of the Wabash River, go east on Indiana 28 from Attica, Indiana to CR 500E and turn left/north. Follow CR 500E north to Riverside, Indiana and cross the Wabash River to Independence. At the first crossroads, turn right/east on Independence Road and drive about a half mile to the parking entrance on the right/south side of Independence Road.

Another approach from Attica is to go north on Indiana 55 from the intersection with US 41/Indiana 28, and turn right/east at the curve on Independence Road which parallels the Wabash. Follow Independence Road about five miles to Independence and continue east a short distance past the four way stop of Independence Road and Independence-Pine Village Road to the entrance of Cicott County Park.

Between the Independence Cemetery and Independence School is the Potawatomi Big Spring which still provides good drinking water. Located on the west side of the Independence-Pine Village Road, just north of the four way stop and the Wabash River.

A fine nature walk is found at the rolling river landscape of Ravine Park in Attica, downriver from Independence. The picturesque ravine is about six town blocks long as it snakes through an old residential neighborhood in east Attica. Happy Hollow Park in West Lafayette is somewhat similar. Historically, the main attraction of the ravine has been the hillside springs. It has long been known as a gathering place by historic Indian tribes and early American settlers.

Nature walkers will appreciate the artistic touches such as fountains and markers in the Turkey Run-like ravine, along the Beaker Trail. Picnicking, shelters, swimming pool, playgrounds, ballfields and ball courts are other activities and facilities at Ravine Park. From Main Street/Indiana 28 at the east edge of Attica, turn north on Ravine Park Drive or turn north on Canada Street, and drive to Park Avenue and Ravine Park Drive. There are pullouts along the ravine drive or park at the swimming pool parking area near 6th Avenue. The park hours are 6:30 am to 9 pm daily.

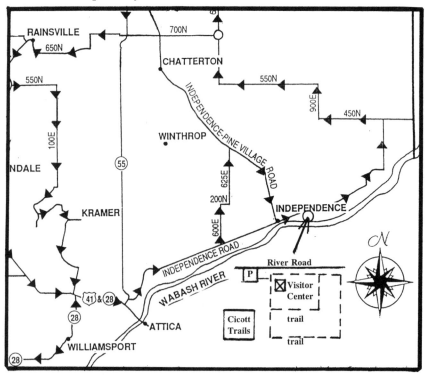

33. FALL CREEK GORGE/WILLIAMSPORT FALLS
Williamsport, IN/Warren County
USGS MAP(s): Williamsport 1:24,000
TRAIL(S) DISTANCE: 1.5 m. fcg/observation overlook wf
ACREAGE: 163 a. fcg/6 a. wf
ACTIVITIES: nature walk, nature study, waterfalls

Fall Creek Gorge, northwest of Williamsport, is a scenic Nature Conservancy owned sanctuary and a dedicated state nature preserve. The preserve is oftentimes called the "Potholes", for the large water-carved smooth basins in the bed of Fall Creek, a short tributary of Big Pine Creek. Charles Deam believed the best spring wildflowers in Indiana were found in the Big Pine Creek area such as snow trillium. Red cedar and white pine mix among the oak-hickory forest preserve, a beauty spot year around. A linear trail follows the narrow ridge above the sandstone canyon and allows the best views of these pothole pools. The trail returns along the same route it arrived on. Be advised the bedrock in the stream is very slick with algae. Fall Creek Gorge has the same jewel-quality as Portland Arch and Turkey Run, where geological and botanical features come together artistically.

"Potholes", Falls Creek Gorge

Williamsport Falls, Williamsport

To reach Fall Creek Gorge Nature Preserve from the highway junction of Indiana 28 and US 41, two miles west of Attica, take US 41, 1.8 miles west and turn right/north onto a gravel road locally known as Five Points Road. Drive 1.5 miles to a small marked parking area on the left/west side of the road, just before the Copeland Hill Road. The trailhead begins/ends at the parking area.

A few miles south in the center of Williamsport, the county seat of Warren County, is <u>Williamsport Falls</u>; Indiana's highest waterfall. It is a 100 foot drop from the lip of Fall Branch, a short tributary of the Wabash River, to the amphitheatre of rock below. It is sometimes called "Dry Falls" (especially in late summer and early fall). A ring of forest around the rim of the falls would add to the postcard scene. The observation overlook provides safe viewing but there is too much fence. A walk to the base of the falls is possible along an old path east of the overlook shelter.

The parking area and observation overlook is located behind the Warren County Historical Museum and fire station on Monroe Street, near the railroad tracks. Williamsport is accessed from Indiana 28 via US 41 south.

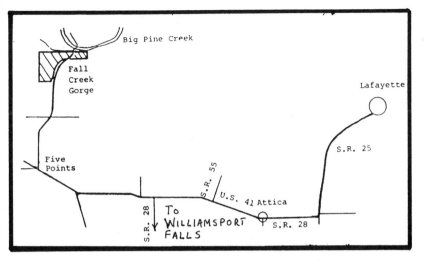

Fall Creek Gorge

34. PORTLAND ARCH NATURE PRESERVE
Fountain, IN/Fountain County
USGS MAP(s): Stone Bluff 1:24,000
TRAIL(s) DISTANCE: 2 trails total 1.7 miles
ACREAGE: 292 acres
ACTIVITIES: nature walks, nature study

Portland Arch, owned and managed by the DNR, Division of Nature Preserves, is a small ten foot high sandstone natural bridge, a rare geological phenomenon in Indiana. The North Trail passes through the archway of the National Natural Landmark, which is situated in scenic Bear Creek Canyon. The natural bridge was carved by Bear Creek, a tributary of the Wabash River. Additional natural attractions include talus slopes, 90 foot high sandstone canyon cliffs, occasional waterfalls, deep ravines and a floodplain. There is a rich mix of plants including a northern white pine community. According to local legend, Tecumseh sought refuge in Bear Creek Canyon after the Battle of Tippecanoe.

Portland Arch

A self-guiding nature trail called the North Trail traces a loop of 0.8 mile. Twenty-five marked stations correspond to the trail brochure available at the trailhead registration box. The marked earth path follows the forested ridge down into the canyon, passing through the arch, continuing up the scenic canyon to ascend the oak-hickory ridge back to the parking area.

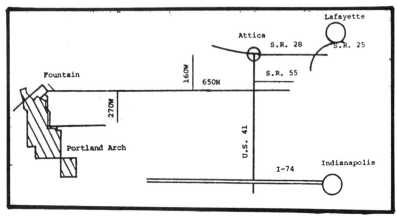

Portland Arch

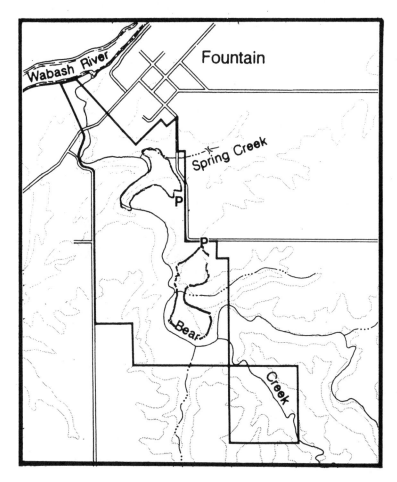

Portland Arch Nature Preserve Trails

A second trail at a second trailhead, the South Nature Trail begins 0.3 mile south and east on the country road from the Portland Arch parking lot. The 0.9 mile South Nature Trail loops counterclockwise and there are nine interpretive stations that correspond to a trail brochure available from the trailhead registration box. The trail leads through young woodland and successional field and along Bear Creek. Songbirds are plentiful due to the stream, open areas, and cover.

To reach Portland Arch Nature Preserve from Attica, Indiana, drive south on US 41, one mile south of the junction with Indiana 55, and turn west/right on CR 650N. Follow CR 650N a few miles west to Fountain, Indiana, turning left/south at the edge of the village onto a gravel road south to the preserve and the north and south tracts. Follow the signs.

TILL PLAIN: OVERVIEW

*"I have found wildflowers for more than a month now.
I gathered a handful a mile and a half from town this
morning before breakfast. When I first entered the woods
and stood among the beautiful flower and trees of God's
own garden...I could not help shedding tears of joy.*

John Muir, founder of the Sierra Club, May, 1866
from Indianapolis, A Letter to his sister, Sarah

Once nearly forested with American beech and sugar maple, the central
Till Plain of Indiana's midriff is now a corn belt that is home to the state's
largest population. Buried by glacial till overburden thousands of years
ago, the featureless vast expanse of 12,000 square miles has few sizeable
natural recreational areas that are available to the outdoor-seeking public
for feet first exploring. However efforts are being made by various levels
of government, private organizations and dedicated individuals to establish
more parklands particularly along the stream corridors such as Anderson's
Indian Trails and Marion's Mississinewa Riverway and from abandoned
railroads such as Zionsville's Nancy Burton Memorial Path and the yet to
be developed Cardinal Trail from Gaston to Richmond, Indiana.

Surprisingly, the state's highest elevation and most scenic areas are
found in this quilt-work of agricultural lands. In the western area of the
Till Plain where the glacial till drift is thin, streams have cut through,
exposing the scenic sandstone canyons of Pine Hills Nature Preserve,
Shades, and Turkey Run State Parks. A classic example of the Till Plain
is the Eunice Hamilton Bryan Nature Preserve; an outstanding woodlot
surrounded by farmland "plain". Since the rural outlying areas have little
to offer in recreational areas, cities have established trails in their nature
oriented parks such as Hartford City's Wilderness Park, Portland's Weiler
Wilson Park and Zionsville's Starkey Nature Park. Christy Woods at Ball
State University offers a unique natural setting within suburban Muncie.

Natural lakes are now non-existent on the Till Plain and multipurpose
reservoir "lakes" have provided a man-made substitute, several with
walking areas such as Prairie Creek Reservoir, Summit Lake State Park,
Westwood Park, Wildcat Creek Reservoir and Raccoon State Recreation
Area at Cecil M. Harden Lake Reservoir. The nature preserves that have
been set aside are special and include Louis A. Bibler Nature Preserve,
McVey Memorial Forest, Oscar and Ruth Hall Woods Nature Preserve,
Pine Hills Nature Preserve and Rocky Hollow-Falls Canyon Nature
Preserve at Turkey Run State Park.

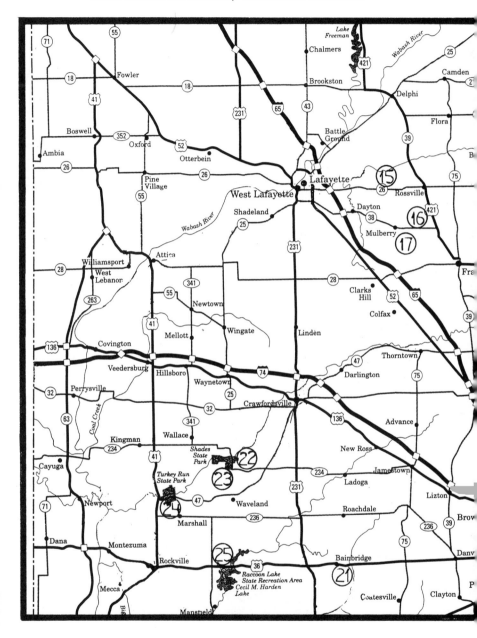

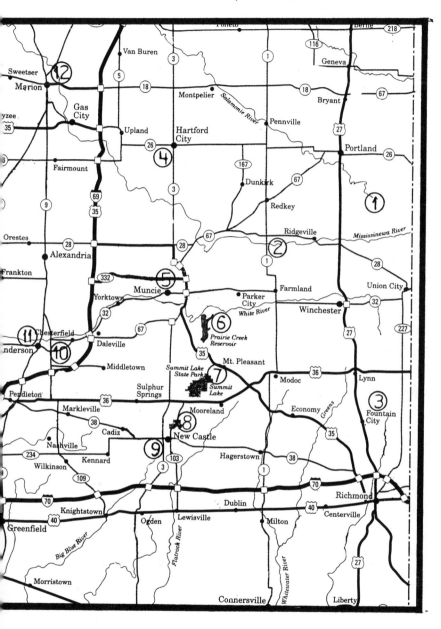

1. JESSE KANTNER MEMORIAL FOREST & LOUIS A. BIBLER NATURE PRESERVE

Boundary City, IN/Jay County
USGS MAP(s): Deerfield 1:24,000
TRAIL(s): DISTANCE: jkmf 2 miles/bnp 2 miles
ACREAGE: bnp 105 acres/jkmf 85 acres
ACTIVITIES: nature walks, nature study

Situated at the headwaters of the Little Salamonie River in southeastern Jay County are two nature preserves that are open to hiking; the Jesse Kantner Memorial Forest and the Louis Bibler Nature Preserve. Both properties share a common boundary that may be freely crossed on foot although each natural area has separate parking areas, trailheads and trail systems.

The Jesse Kantner Memorial Forest was established as a memorial forest for nature study by Jesse Kantner in 1948 and is now overseen by seven trustees that reside in Jay County. The maturing mixed woods is bisected by the meandering Little Salamonie River. The approximate two miles of foot trails begin and end at the meeting house and parking area. There are two trail loops; one looping about in the south property woods along the stream and the other in the reforested deciduous and pine plantations west of the parking area.

To reach the parking area for the memorial forest from the CR 173 and CR 201 crossroads at Boundary City, drive east on CR 201 about 0.5 mile (past the east boundary memorial granite stone) to a gravel lane on the left/north side of CR 201. Follow the lane about 0.2 mile north, curving west to the parking area, meeting house and pit toilets. The trails begin just west of the parking area.

Adjacent north and east of the Kantner Memorial Forest is the Bibler Nature Preserve which was acquired by ACRES, Inc. in 1989. The nature preserve was part of the Bibler homestead known as Spring Brook Farm. The land is mostly regenerating forest and grasslands bisected by Spring Brook, which flows to the Little Salamonie River. Bibler has recently authored an autobiography of life growing up at Spring Brook Farm during the 1920s entitled, Back Home Again.

The trailhead begins at the parking lot on CR 179. From the Boundary City junction of CR 173 and CR 201, go east on CR 201, 1.2 miles to CR 179 and turn left/north. Proceed on CR 179, 0.4 miles to the parking area on the left/west side of the road. The marked trail loops about the preserve.

342

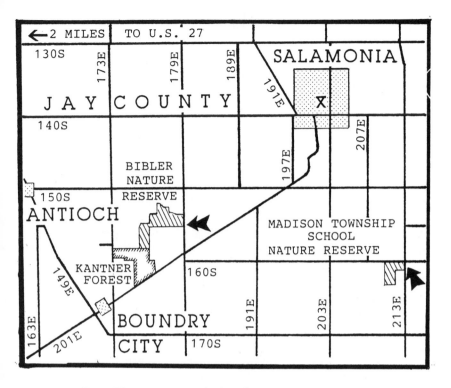

Jesse Kantner & Louis A. Bibler Nature Preserves

To reach Boundary City from Main Street in Portland, the county seat of Jay County, drive south on US 27 about 6.75 miles to CR 164 at Bluff Point, Indiana and turn left/east at the road sign. Follow CR 164 east just over two miles to the "T" junction with CR 1491 Boundary Pike and turn right/south. Follow CR 149/Boundary Pike 0.25 mile to the junction with CR 201 and turn left/east. Drive east on CR 201 (the Greenville Treaty Line) through the village of Boundary City to the access points of the two properties.

2. McVEY MEMORIAL FOREST

Brinckley, IN/Randolph County
USGS MAP(s): Redkey 1:24,000
TRAIL(s) DISTANCE: 4 trails total appx. 2 miles
ACREAGE: 406 acres
ACTIVITIES: nature walks, nature study, historic sites

Four color coded interconnecting foot trails lead through the wood, grass and crop lands of the McVey trust property that is maintained by the Randolph County Soil and Water Conservation District. The 0.5 mile Yellow Fitness Trail is considered the best overall walk along a terrace bluff of Bush Creek, a short tributary of Elkhorn Creek that joins the Mississinewa River. There is considerable shagbark hickory along the linear upland forest path which concludes at CR 750N. Retrace the route back to the trailhead at parking lot #2 on CR 700N. Connecting to the Yellow Fitness Trail are two adjoining loop trails; the 0.5 mile Orange Wildlife Trail and the 0.33 mile Blue Trail. The 0.5 mile Red Trail is a linear walk from the McVey Memorial Site parking lot #1 along Indiana 1, east along grassy-wooded edge, crossing a large suspension bridge and Bush Creek, to a second foot bridge to join the Yellow Fitness Trail.

There is a nature trail guide booklet/map available at the trailhead sheltered information booth that focuses on tree identification and forest ecology. There are rest benches enroute. A canoe exit site has been developed on the property at CR 750N near the Mississinewa River. In addition, 65 acres have been planted with trees along Indiana 1 and 20 acres seeded in wildlife grasses.

Half a mile north of parking lot #1 on the east/right side of Indiana 1 is the historic ghost village site of Steubenville, at the confluence of the Elkhorn River with the Mississinewa River. Follow the farm lane east 0.25 mile from the small parking lot to the old cemetery and down to the river to the old ford site and foundation of an old covered bridge. North 0.25 mile of the old historic Steubenville site on Indiana 1, beyond the river bridge crossing on the west side of the highway, is another historic site; this one concerning the Battle of Mississinewa.

South on Indiana 1 from the McVey Memorial parking lot 1 less than a mile, is the 385 acre Herbert Davis Forest Farm that is owned and managed by Purdue University. The farm contains one of the world's largest marked forests with each tree identified. The 50 acre natural undisturbed old growth forest is a living example of the pre-agricultural central Till Plain of Indiana. The forest is open by tour appointment at (317) 468-7022.

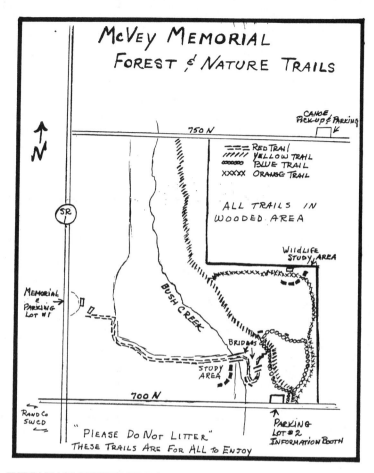

McVey Memorial Forest & Nature Trails

750 N

CANOE Pick-up & Parking

=== RED TRAIL
////// YELLOW TRAIL
∞∞∞∞∞ BLUE TRAIL
XXXXX ORANGE TRAIL

ALL TRAILS IN WOODED AREA

WILdLIFE STUDY AREA

MEMORIAL & PARKING LOT #1

BUSH CREEK

BRIDGES

STUDY AREA

700 N

RAND Co SWCD

PARKING LOT #2 INFORMATION BOOTH

"PLEASE DO NOT LITTER" THESE TRAILS ARE FOR ALL TO ENJOY

3. INDIANA'S HIGHEST POINT (El. 1,275 ft.)
Arba, IN/Wayne County
USGS MAP(s): Fountain City, Whitewater 1:24,000
TRAIL(s) DISTANCE: 60 yards
ACTIVITIES: natural landmark

The rolling morainal plateau of northeast Wayne County is the site of Indiana's highest elevation point above sea level, the headwaters of three rivers. The present site is an unsuspecting formerly grazed woodlot on a privately owned farm, whose owners permit visitation to one of the fifty highest points in the United States.

From US 36, 4.4 miles east of Lynn, Indiana, near the Randolph-Wayne county line, turn right and drive south on Arba Pike, 3.2 miles to the community of Arba. Continue through the village to the south edge and CR 1200E/County Line Road and turn left/east. Drive one mile east on

County Line Road to CR 800S/ Elliott Road. Proceed south 0.3 mile on Elliott Road to the southeast corner of a woodlot and farm lane, just past the farmhouse, on the right/west side of Elliott Road

Turn right/west into the farm lane and park. Walk towards the fence stile and cross over to the signed stone cairn, "Indiana's Highest Point, El. 1,275' ". A register is here for climbing enthusiasts who would like to sign in their "was here" or leave their calling card. No doubt, some climbers have been to all fifty states.

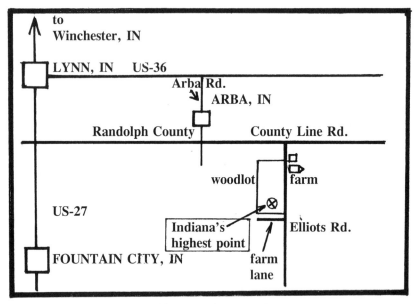

Indiana's Highest Point

4. WILDERNESS PARK
Hartford City, IN/Blackford County
USGS MAP(s): Hartford City East 1:24,000
TRAIL(s) DISTANCE: 2 loop trails total 0.5 mile
ACREAGE: 55 acres
ACTIVITIES: nature walk, fitness trail, picnicking, playfields, ball park

The Hartford City park may seem like a wilderness in a well farmed area of the Till Plain. However, Wilderness Park, unlike the name suggests, is actually a ball park fringed by a natural area with a nature and exercise trail system. The wood chipped paths are two people wide. The traveller should note this nature-oriented community park as a place to stop, picnic, walk the trails, and rest. Wilderness Park is one of the largest Hartford City parks.

To reach Wilderness Park in Hartford City from I-69 exit 55 east on Indiana 26 and drive about twelve miles to west Hartford City, turning right/south on Ford Street. Follow Ford Street south a few blocks to Fulton Street and turn right/west. Continue to the intersection of Fulton and West and turn left/south on West Street, proceeding to park area on the south end of West Street. Hartford City is the county seat of Blackford County, one of Indiana's smallest counties.

Wilderness Park, Hartford City

5. BALL STATE UNIVERSITY CAMPUS WALK

Muncie, IN/Delaware County
USGS MAP(s): Muncie West 1:24,000
WALKING DISTANCE: appx. 5 miles
ACREAGE: 995 acre campus
ACTIVITIES: nature walks, tree walks, greenhouses, planetarium observatory, picnicking, shelter

The Ball State University campus grounds are beautifully landscaped and the old campus area features many old growth tree specimens and the Christy Woods nature area. There are three color coded loop trails, each a mile long, that identify over 100 different species and hybrids. The Campus Tree Trail Guide identifies each plant individually via the Green Trail (old campus), Blue Trail (central campus) and the Red Trail (sport facilities area). Each walk requires about an hour. For information, call the Supervisor of Grounds, at (317) 285-5092.

On the campus west end is Christy Woods, a 17 acre natural area and arboretum, with gardens, greenhouses, and outdoor education center. Wide limestone based trails encircle and bisect the woodland areas of Christy Woods, where there are prolific spring wildflowers, open grassy areas with flower beds, many with native perennial species, two wetland areas, and other horticultural plantings and displays. One greenhouse displays the Wheeler Orchid collection and Species Bank, while the second greenhouse protects a subtropical and tropical plant collection. Since 1919, Christy Woods has been a outdoor education center for the University, Muncie, and surrounding communities. There are bulletin boards at the three entrance areas, natural history exhibits, and a picnic shelter. Illustrated tree and wildlife identification brochures are available for sale.

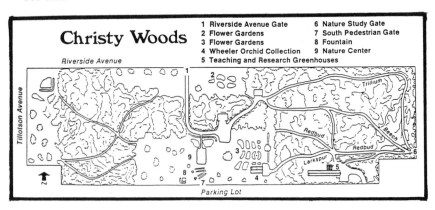

Christy Woods, Ball State University

Parking is available along Riverside Avenue to the north of Christy Woods, and in the Faculty, Student, and Visitor parking lot south of Christy Woods, off University Avenue. Weekends and summer are less hectic regarding parking. Gates are open Monday through Friday from 7:30 am to 4:30 pm, Saturday 8 am to 4:30 pm throughout the year, and Sunday 1 to 5 pm from April to October. Call (317) 285-8820 for information.

Another enjoyable Ball State nature experience involves astronomy. The observatory and planetarium (building No. 24) are open to the general public during selected times in November and March, closed during the summer. Each semester a number of weekend presentations are given for the community. After a 45-60 minute presentation during the evening at the planetarium, weather permitting, the observatory is open afterwards.

Scheduled program information may be obtained by calling the Department of Physics and Astronomy (317) 285-8871. The planetarium has 77 seats and is located at the southeast ground floor of the Cooper Science Complex on old campus commons. The observatory seats 30 and is upstairs five flights.

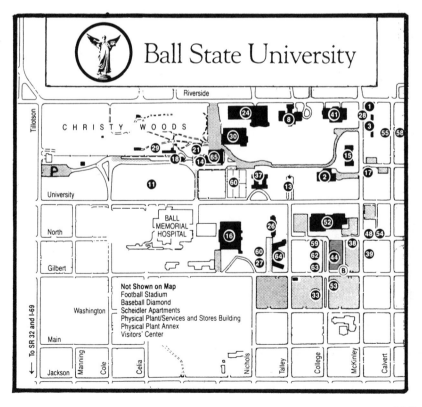

6. PRAIRIE CREEK RESERVOIR PARK
Muncie, IN/Delaware County
USGS MAP(s): Muncie East, Mt. Pleasant 1:24,000
TRAIL(s) DISTANCE: appx. 0.5 mile shoreline walk
ACREAGE: 2,300 a., 1,252 a. lake
ACTIVITIES: nature walk, picnicking, shelters, fishing, boating, launch
ramp, docks, playgrounds, playfields, beach, bathhouse, swimming,
lifeguards, wind surfing, sailing, model boat & airplane ports, camping
FEE(s): beach, shelter, boat & lodge rentals, launch permit, dock rental,
wind surfing launch, camping

Prairie Creek Reservoir, a state park sized, regional-like, city maintained
park, is the result of a cooperative agreement between the Muncie Parks
and Recreation Department and the owners, Indiana American Water
Company. Winter hours are limited. The reservoir park is fully
operational from April 15 to October 15. However, the park grounds are
open year around for walking. The west shore is about a mile long, north
to south strand with few finger coves, allowing for easier walking. The
area has an open prairie-like appearance and feel.

Prairie Creek Reservoir, the largest of the Muncie area parks, is located
five miles southeast of Muncie near Mt. Pleasant. From U.S. 35 east,
access the county roads on the west by CR 475E, south by CR 550S, east
by CR 540E, CR 544E, CR 560E and north by CR 300S.

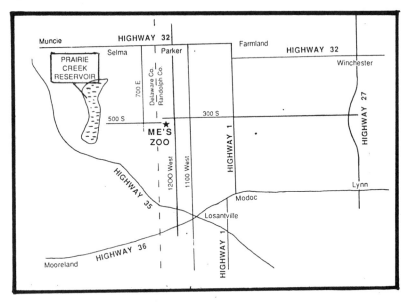

Prairie Creek Reservoir Park & ME's Zoo

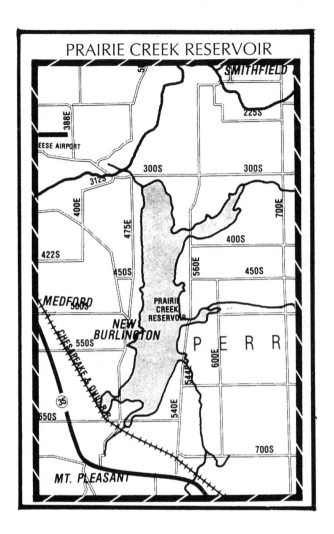

At the south edge of the reservoir, an access trail will link-up with the 50 mile long Cardinal Trail, a bike-hike path that will be open in the near future. The Cardinal, CSX rail-to-trail, connects Gaston, Muncie and Richmond.

Just east of the Prairie Creek Reservoir near the Delaware and and Randolph county line, is a small commercial zoo (ME'S) of 100 exotic animals that would be of interest to families with small children. The hours from May 1 to October are Tuesday, Wednesday and Thursday 10 am to 6 pm, Saturday 10 am to 7 pm and Sunday noon to 7 pm. The address is RR #1, Box 387, Parker City, IN 47368 (317) 468-8559 near CR 300S in Randolph County.

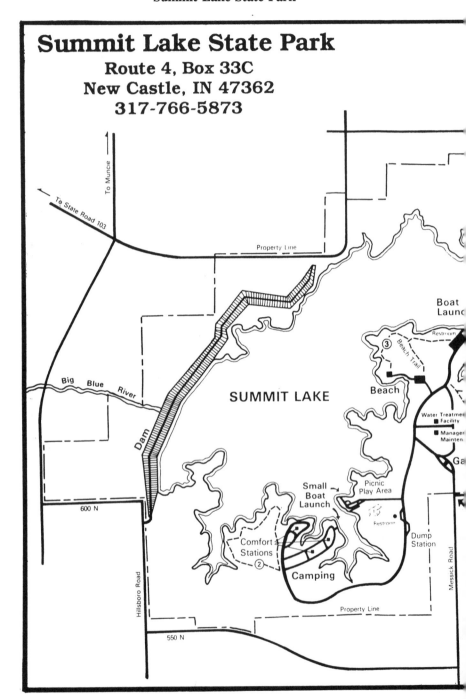

Summit Lake State Park
Route 4, Box 33C
New Castle, IN 47362
317-766-5873

Summit Lake State Park

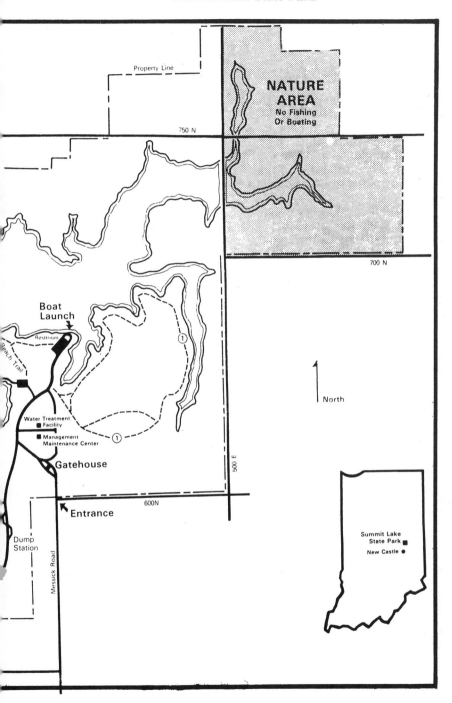

Property Line

NATURE
AREA
No Fishing
Or Boating

750 N

700 N

Boat
Launch

Restroom

Beach Trail

North

Water Treatment
■ Facility

■ Management
Maintenance Center

500 E

Gatehouse

600N

Entrance

Dump
Station

Messick Road

Summit Lake
State Park ■

New Castle ●

7. SUMMIT LAKE STATE PARK

New Castle, IN/Henry County
USGS MAP(s): Mt. Pleasant, New Castle East 1:24,000
TRAIL(s): DISTANCE: 3 trails total 3.75 miles
ACREAGE: 2,680 acres, 800 acre lake
ACTIVITIES: nature walks, nature study, seasonal naturalist, nature preserve, birding, picnicking, shelters, beach, swimming, bathhouse, lifeguards, fishing, boating, launch ramps, winter sports, cultural arts program, Class A camping, concessions
FEE(s): seasonal entrance, camping, rentals of shelters, boat launching, canoe, paddleboats, rowboats

In east central Indiana, lakes are rare and Summit Lake, like Prairie Creek Reservoir a few miles to the north, is one of the larger water bodies in the area. The man-made lake is an important stopover for migratory birdlife. The recently acquired state park was developed by the Big Blue River Conservancy District and the Indiana DNR. Much of the acreage is retired revegetating fields. However the 127 acre Zeigler Woods Nature Preserve is an old growth beech-maple woodlot and abandoned field overlooking Summit Lake at the southwest corner of the dam.

A trail system is just being established and currently there are three trails: the Beach Trail, Trail 1 and Trail 2:

Beach Trail: The 0.5 mile Beach/Trail 3 is easy going and is a connecting path to the boat launch and beach from the parking area. Some of the best views of Summit Lake are at this jutting point.

Trail 1: Trail 1 is the longest and most remote trail. A loop path moves through a young mix woodland and old herbaceous fields, as well as recently established prairie, between two finger coves, east of the beach and boat launch area.

Trail 2: Trail 2 is west to the Class A campground. The loop trail is a mix of oak-hickory forest and open field centering on the lake. A connecting trail is planned to trace a loop west to Zeigler Woods Nature Preserve. Future trails are being planned that will loop and interconnect throughout the property, improving with time.

Summit Lake State Park is located northeast of New Castle, east of Mt. Summit and west of Mooreland in Henry County. Access to the main park entrance is reached by turning north on Messick Road from Indiana 36. The address is 5993 North Messick Road.

8. WILBUR WRIGHT FISH & WILDLIFE AREA
New Castle, IN/Henry County
USGS MAP(s): New Castle East 1:24,000
TRAIL(s) DISTANCE: service roads total appx. 5 miles
ACREAGE: 970 acres
ACTIVITIES: nature walks, nature study, river canoe access, fishing, hunting, shooting ranges

Just south and west of Summit Lake State Park a few miles, is the smallest state fish and wildlife area, Wilbur Wright. The Fish and Wildlife Area was established in 1975 from retired farm land donated from the former dairy farm operation of the New Castle State Hospital.

The day-use area is open to hiking and the best nature walk is along the east bank of the Big Blue River. The linear walk is along two separate segments of about a mile each, bisected by CR 200N from Indiana 103, going west to the east side of the bridge on CR 200N. The service road parallels the Big Blue River for about 1.5 miles along the property's west boundary. The Unit 2 upland area east of Indiana 103 is accessible via service roads from parking areas near the property headquarters. The mile long service road crosses the Little Blue River, which runs through the fish and wildlife area for about two miles. Best place to begin a visit is to the property headquarters on the west side of Indiana 103. There are parking areas on all four units.

East of New Castle between US 36 and Indiana 38, between Mooreland and Millville, at CR 200N and CR 750E, is the five acre Wilbur Wright Memorial, the birthplace of Wilbur Wright (1867-1912), aviation pioneer.

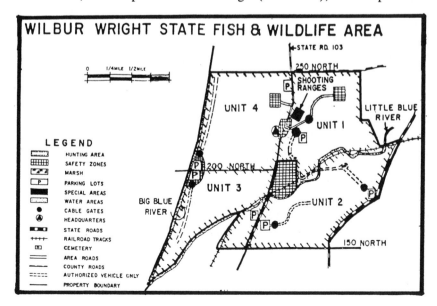

WILBUR WRIGHT STATE FISH & WILDLIFE AREA

0   1/4MILE 1/2MILE

STATE RD. 103

250 NORTH

SHOOTING RANGES

UNIT 4

LITTLE BLUE RIVER

UNIT 1

LEGEND

- HUNTING AREA
- SAFETY ZONES
- MARSH
- PARKING LOTS
- SPECIAL AREAS
- WATER AREAS
- CABLE GATES
- HEADQUARTERS
- STATE ROADS
- RAILROAD TRACKS
- CEMETERY
- AREA ROADS
- COUNTY ROADS
- AUTHORIZED VEHICLE ONLY
- PROPERTY BOUNDARY

200 NORTH

UNIT 3

BIG BLUE RIVER

UNIT 2

150 NORTH

9 WESTWOOD PARK
New Castle, IN/Henry County
USGS MAP(s): New Castle West 1:24,000
TRAIL(s) DISTANCE: 0.5 mile foot loop, appx. 6.5 mile bridle/hiking
trail
ACREAGE: 450 a. land, 180 a. lake
ACTIVITIES: nature walk, bridle/hiking trail, picnicking, shelters, play-
ground, playfields, fishing, boating, launch ramp, fishing, docks,
primitive & modern camping
FEE(s): entrance, shelter rental, camping

The size and setting of Westwood Park makes it an attractive day hike
or overnight camp site. Owned and managed by the Big Blue River
Conservancy District, Westwood Park is located on the western edge of
the Big Blue River valley with hundreds of acres of rolling "Raintree
County" scenic land, southwest of New Castle, Indiana. The lake waters
are derived from damming Westwood Run, a tributary to the Big Blue
River, which flows through the Wilbur Wright State Fish and Wildlife
Area, northeast of New Castle.

Westwood Park is comprised of abandoned fields, woodlands, meadows,
and the 180 acre reservoir. The regional park features a 0.5 mile foot trail

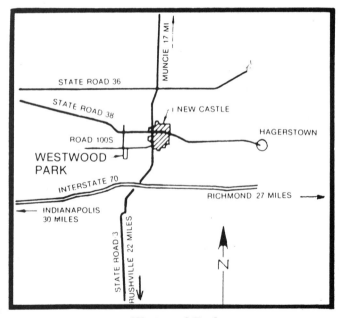

Westwood Park

only that runs between the park facilities such as the campground, playground, picnic area, boat ramp and day-use horse area on the southwest shore. A six and one half mile bridle/hiking trail follows the perimeter of the property around the reservoir. The trail is open to adventuresome hikers.

Westwood Park is open all year. To reach Westwood from Indiana 38 at the west edge of New Castle, drive west on IN 38 to CR 275W and go south 2 miles to the entrance at 1900 South CR 275W.

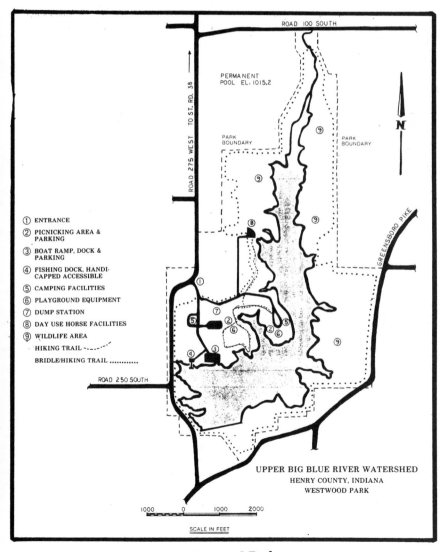

① ENTRANCE
② PICNICKING AREA & PARKING
③ BOAT RAMP, DOCK & PARKING
④ FISHING DOCK, HANDI-CAPPED ACCESSIBLE
⑤ CAMPING FACILITIES
⑥ PLAYGROUND EQUIPMENT
⑦ DUMP STATION
⑧ DAY USE HORSE FACILITIES
⑨ WILDLIFE AREA
　HIKING TRAIL
　BRIDLE/HIKING TRAIL

UPPER BIG BLUE RIVER WATERSHED
HENRY COUNTY, INDIANA
WESTWOOD PARK

1000　0　1000　2000
SCALE IN FEET

Westwood Park

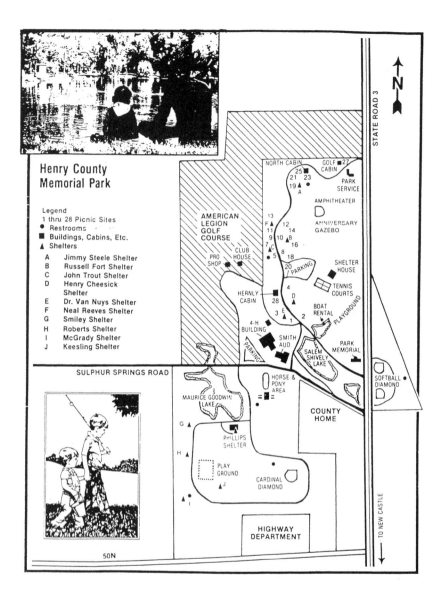

Henry County
Memorial Park

Legend
1 thru 28 Picnic Sites
● Restrooms
■ Buildings, Cabins, Etc.
▲ Shelters

A   Jimmy Steele Shelter
B   Russell Fort Shelter
C   John Trout Shelter
D   Henry Cheesick
     Shelter
E   Dr. Van Nuys Shelter
F   Neal Reeves Shelter
G   Smiley Shelter
H   Roberts Shelter
I   McGrady Shelter
J   Keesling Shelter

The nearby <u>Henry County Memorial Park</u>, owned and managed by the
Henry County Parks and Recreation Department, is a more active urban
counterpart of rural Westwood Park. The Memorial Park was created after
World War 1, one of the largest war memorial parks in Indiana, and the
large shady trees are showing their age by their large size.

Memorial Park is located one mile north of New Castle on Indiana 3, six
miles north of I-70 exit 123, at 2221 North Memorial Drive.

10. MOUNDS STATE PARK

Anderson, IN/Madison County
USGS MAP(s): Anderson South, Middletown 1:24,000
TRAIL(s) DISTANCE: 4 foot trails total 4 mile, 2.5 mile bridle trail
ACREAGE: 288 acres
ACTIVITIES: nature walks, nature study, naturalist, nature center, picnicking, shelters, bridle trail, playground, playfields, swimming pool, bathhouse, lifeguards, fishing, river launch, cultural arts program, Class A campground, camp store, special events
FEE(s): seasonal entrance, shelter rental, canoe rental, building rental

Mounds State Park is a major prehistoric site where Indian tribes of Adena and Hopewell cultures thrived two to three thousand years ago. This golden age of Eastern Woodland tribes is evident by the burial mounds they created, and a dozen of these mounds are found along the riverbluff park. The ceremonial Great Mound (360' diameter) is the largest earthwork in the park and trails 1 and 4 explore the mound area. Information about the ancient prehistoric woodland cultures may be obtained from the nature center and naturalist stationed at the Bronnenberg House near the park entrance.

The four nature walking trails interconnect and are accessed from the Main Pavilion parking area, just northwest of the gatehouse. The four trails and bridle trail are summarized briefly:

Trail 1: This could easily be known as the "Great Mound Trail". Trailhead begins at main pavilion parking area. The one mile easy loop merges with and becomes Trail 2 , 4 and the bridle trail. Dips down into a river ravine, follows the river bluff and loops back through the mounds. Walk Trail 4 for full mound appreciation.

Trail 2: The trailhead is the same for Trail 1 and so is the first segment to the bridle trail "T". Go right/east upstream on the bridle trail, past the Trail 3 junction to Trail 2. Walk right on Trail 2 looping back along Trail 2 & 3 to the pavilion. Dense floodplain and upland forest.

Trail 3: The longest foot trail of 1.75 miles. Follows a section of bridle trail at northeast end of park. Starts at pavilion and traces a loop in the floodplain and ravines of the White River's south bank and Little Bronnenberg Creek. Combines with Trail 2 and the bridle trail.

Trail 4: Trail 1 and Trail 4 are mound hikes. Begins between Great Mound and Fiddleback Mound. Great 0.5 mile foot trail loop around the mounds complex.

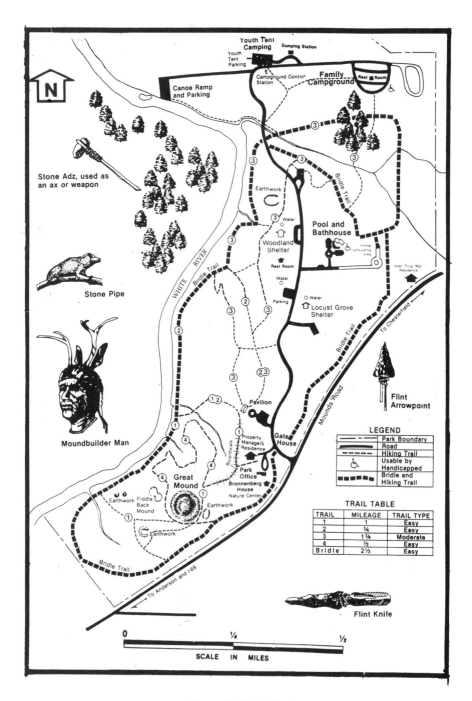

N

Youth Tent Camping

Youth Tent Parking

Canoe Ramp and Parking

Dumping Station

Campground Control Station

Family Campground

Rest Room

Stone Adz, used as an ax or weapon

Earthwork

Bridle Trail

Water

Woodland Shelter

Pool and Bathhouse

Horse Unloading Area

Asst. Prog. Mgr. Residence

Stone Pipe

WHITE RIVER

Bridle Trail

Rest Room

Water

Parking

Water

Locust Grove Shelter

To Chesterfield

Bridle Trail

Mounds Road

Flint Arrowpoint

Moundbuilder Man

Pavilion

Property Manager's Residence

Gate House

Boardwalk

Park Office

Bronnenberg House

Nature Center

Great Mound

Earthwork

Fiddle Back Mound

Earthwork

Earthwork

Bridle Trail

To Anderson and I-69

LEGEND

Park Boundary
Road
Hiking Trail
♿ Usable by Handicapped
Bridle and Hiking Trail

TRAIL TABLE

TRAIL	MILEAGE	TRAIL TYPE
1		Easy
2	¾	Easy
3	1¾	Moderate
4	½	Easy
Bridle	2½	Easy

Flint Knife

0	¼	½

SCALE IN MILES

Mounds State Park

Bridle Trail: Trails 1, 2 and 3 merge with the 2.5 mile bridle trail that encircles the perimeter of the park. Heavy use and heavy rain or flooding can make the equestrian path impossible for hikers at times.

An extension of the city of Anderson's Indian Trails Riverwalk along the White River is being planned and implemented that will extend the recreational trail to Mounds State Park. If Mounds were recently "discovered" and developed today, it would probably be designed as an interpretive historic site, similar to Angel Mounds at Evansville, Indiana.

Mounds State Park, one of Indiana's smallest state parks, is located two miles east of Anderson on the north side of Indiana 232. From I-69 exit 34, go west on Indiana 32 to Chesterfield, Indiana and turn on Anderson Road left, which becomes Mounds Road. The address is 4306 Mounds Road.

Mounds State Park

11. INDIAN TRAILS RIVERWALK
Anderson, IN/Madison County
USGS MAP(s): Anderson South 1:24,000
TRAIL(s) DISTANCE: 3 segments total 5.7 miles, (to be expanded)
ACTIVITIES: nature walk, historic walk, bicycling, picnicking, shelters,
   fitness trail, fishing, canoeing, launch ramp, special events

This city's rivergreenway along the White River West Fork and a
tributary, Killbuck Creek is inviting to wildlife as well as humans. The
most natural areas include 15 acre Killbuck Wetlands at the confluence of
Killbuck Creek and the White River and the Shadyside Recreation Area
and Lake. Three miles of trails meander along Killbuck Creek and
encircle Shadyside Lake, once a dump site and gravel pits.

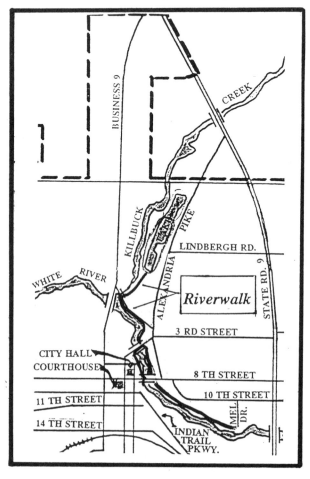

Indian Trails Riverwalk, Anderson

At the confluence of Killbuck Creek with the White River, the Indian Trails Riverwalk begins and heads upstream, east through Athletic Park, and Edgewater Park to conclude at Imel Drive on the north bank of White River. Plans and trail implementation are being made to extend the Riverwalk east to Mounds State Park, a total of seven miles. Future plans call for the merging of the Riverwalk with other trail networks from Muncie to Indianapolis. The Indian Trails Riverwalk is mostly paved asphalt interspersed with boardwalks, overlooks and gazebo. Historic sites enroute include former village and home site of Delaware Chief Anderson or Kikthawenund and the "Old Vesuvius" gas well near Eisenhower Bridge. The Riverwalk has added recreation, protects wildlife and has made eyebrights from eyesores. The Indian Trails Riverwalk and other city parks are managed by the Anderson Parks and Recreation Department at 101 East Oak Street near Shadyside Park, Indiana 9 entrance.

To access the three interconnecting trails of Shadyside Recreation Area, Killbuck Wetlands and Indian Trails Riverwalk, park at Shadyside Park adjacent to Indiana 9, the Killbuck Wetlands parking area along Grand Avenue, limited streetside parking along Main and Central Avenue, Athletic Park, at Wilcon Street and Edge Water Park at 10th Street.

The city of Anderson is easily accessed from I-69 exits 22, 26, and 34, Indiana State Roads 32 and 9. Consider visiting Mounds State Park while in the Anderson-area.

12. MISSISSINEWA RIVERWAY TRAIL
Marion, IN/Grant County
USGS MAP(s): Marion 1:24,000
TRAIL(s): DISTANCE: 2.75 miles
ACTIVITIES: urban river walk, bicycling, picnicking, shelters, city parks
enroute

The Mississinewa Riverway Trail is a thread of green forest edge and bluegray river parkway through the community of Marion, Indiana. The 2.75 mile natural corridor extends from Washington Street downtown, west and north to Matter Park, Plans are to extend the walk 4 miles.

The riverine park parallels River Drive most of its linear paved route. Two other community parklands that connect the riverway trail include Riverside Park near Wabash Avenue and River Drive and Charles Mill Park at the river-end of Charles Street. Both are small pocket park overlooks of the river. Matter Park, at the north terminus of River Drive, north of Huntington Road, offers picnicking, and ball fields. An additional

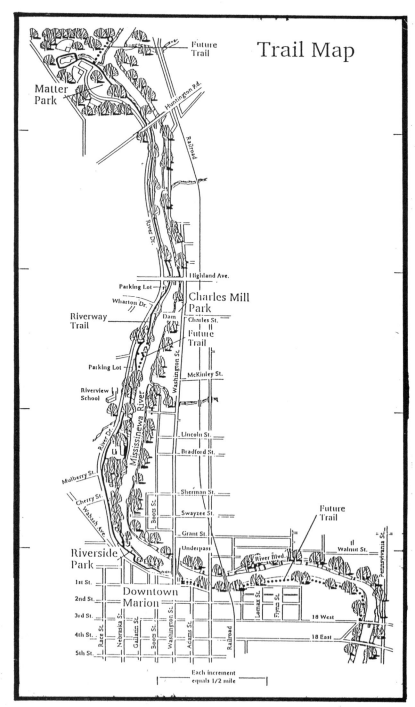

Mississinewa Riverway Trail, Marion

park, Mississinewa, is also connected by the walkway and lays on the west edge of the Mississinewa River across from Charles Mill park. The Mississinewa Riverway Trail is a model for other communities and areas.

Additional attractions include the international walkway of 250,000 Christmas lights which illuminate the walkway from Thanksgiving to the New Year. Also the annual Riverfest, held for 3-4 days before July 4th, includes river raft races, concerts, fireworks, and other festivities.

To reach Marion from I-69 exit 64 onto Indiana 18 and drive west a few miles to the limits. State highways 15 and 9 also access the county seat of Grant County.

13. KOKOMO NATURE PLACES
Kokomo, IN/Howard County
USGS MAP(s): Kokomo East, Kokomo West 1:24,000
TRAIL(s) DISTANCE: appx. 3 miles
ACREAGE: 4 parks total 140 acres
ACTIVITIES: nature walks, picnicking, shelters, historic sites, museum, arboretum, bandstand, swimming pool, bathhouse, lifeguards, senior citizen center, ballfields & courts, winter sports, concessions, special events

One of the major cities of the central Till Plain, Kokomo's Parks and Recreation Department maintains nearly 30 parks of which four are sizeable nature oriented green spaces, in-town and at the suburban fringe. All four parks (and soon a fifth one), vary in experience, each uniquely urban and suburban.

Highland Park (A) at 900 West Deffenbaugh is the premier park of the Kokomo Parks and Recreation Department. The 83 acre green space is positioned on both sides of Kokomo Creek. A user trail system, known as Indian Trails extends from Deffenbaugh to Webster Street. Highland Park features "Old Ben, the Steer", a stuffed glass-enclosed Hereford of record size, "The Stump", a sycamore tree stump 51 feet in circumference, and the Vermont Covered Bridge. At the intersection of South Webster and Boulevard is the Elwood Haynes Museum, the inventor's home. Across the avenue is the Bicentennial Park arboretum. Highland Park is also the headquarters of the Kokomo Parks and Recreation Department.

Foster Park (B), at 721 West Superior is a 30 acre city park situated near the heart of downtown Kokomo along both banks of Wildcat Creek. The busy park includes the Seashore swimming pool, a senior center,

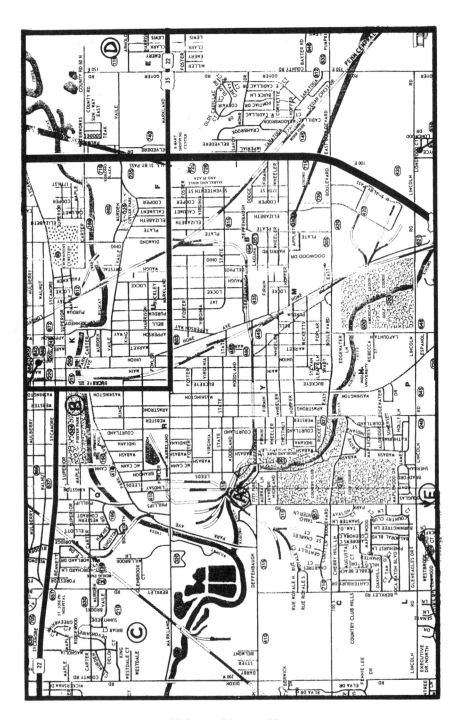

Kokomo Nature Places

playfields, tennis courts, as well as natural areas for picnicking, fishing and walking. A pleasant green space enveloped by busy city streets.

Westdale Park (C), is a small 3.8 acre neighborhood park enclosed by suburban housing, mostly wooded and trails lead through the young woodland. There is picnicking and a playground. To reach Westdale Park at 2000 Westdale Court go west on Markland Avenue/Indiana 22 to Dixon Road and turn right/north. Follow Dixon Road to the first street east or Wesdale Court. Drive to the cul de sac and park near the park entrance.

The Darrough Chapel Park (D), a 25 acre suburban park on the city's eastside offers ballfields, basketball, tennis courts, plus a playground, picnicking shelters, hiking trails and a natural area. To reach Darrough Chapel Park go east on Indiana 22/US 35 one mile from the intersection of Reed Road/US 31 and Indiana 22/US 35/ Markland Avenue, east to Goyer Road and turn left/north. Follow Goyer Road to the intersection of Goyer and Arnold Drive and the park.

The future construction of Jackson Morrow Park (E) at CR 100W/Park Avenue and Center/CR 300S will add interpretive trails and a nature center along Little Wildcat Creek, as well as activity play areas. In an area where land values are at the top in the state, acquiring parkland by payment is difficult.

Vermont Covered Bridge, Highland Park, Kokomo

14. WILDCAT CREEK RESERVOIR PARK

Kokomo, IN/Howard County
USGS MAP(s): Kokomo East, Greentown 1:24,000
TRAIL(s) DISTANCE: 2 trails total appx. 5 miles
ACREAGE: 1,025 acres
ACTIVITIES: nature walks, nature study, picnicking, shelters, playgrounds, playfields, fishing, pier, sailing, canoeing, launch ramps

The Wildcat Creek Reservoir Park is comprised of 1,025 land and water acres, which is also known as the Kokomo Reservoir. The reservoir and surrounding land are currently under lease from the Indiana American Water Company and is maintained by the Kokomo Parks and Recreation Department. There are two separate trailhead locations a few miles apart.

The Main Trail begins/ends at the parking area on CR 500E. The path follows the south shore of the Reservoir to the dam site which is popular with fishermen at CR 400E. Most of the 0.8 mile trail (one-way) is open grasslands and young forest with vistas north to the reservoir lake. There is an upland trail portion through regenerating woods and where the park boundary meets active farm fields. This will extend the hike 0.3 miles.

To reach the Wildcat Reservoir and Main Trail parking and trailhead from Kokomo, go east on US 35/Indiana 22 about four miles from the intersection with US 31, to CR 500E and turn left/north. Drive one mile north on CR 500E to the main reservoir parking area on the left/west side of CR 500E. The trailhead begins at the south end of the circle drive.

Upstream on Wildcat Creek is the second trailhead, seemingly far removed from the reservoir but vitally connected. Continue east on U.S. 35/Indiana 22 and instead of turning north to the main reservoir, go to Greentown, Indiana and Indiana 213. Turn right/south on Indiana 213 and drive about 1.2 miles to Wildcat Creek and a parking area located on both side of the stream on the west side of the highway.

The Pe-che-wah Trail begins/ends on the north side of Wildcat Creek. The linear path follows a portion of a historic corduroy road and stays high and dry, following the field-bordered bluffs. Pe-che-wah is the Miami personal name of Chief Jean John Baptiste Richardville or "the wild cat" for whom the stream is named. Actually there are three interconnecting trails that follow the north streambank which are:

1. Pe-che-wah Trail: 0.5 mile horseshoe loop
2. Fisherman's Trail: 1.5 miles
3. Woodland Trail: 1.4 miles, ends at CR 100S

Since the Fisherman's Trail and Woodland Trail are non-looping, it will be necessary to retrace your steps back to the Indiana 213 parking lots. There are several spur trails leading down to the stream from the bluffs. Also a fine place to launch a canoe and float nine miles downstream to the reservoir.

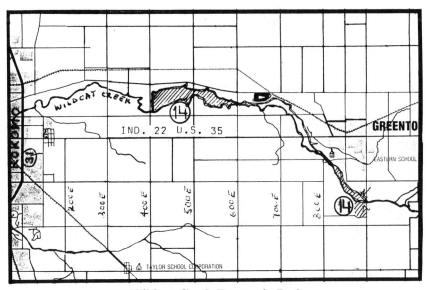

Wildcat Creek Reservoir Park

15. KNOP LAKE PUBLIC FISHING AREA

Owasco, IN/Carroll County
USGS MAP(s): Pyrmont 1:24,000
TRAIL(s) DISTANCE: appx. 1.5 mile lake & river fisherman's paths
ACREAGE: 49 acres, 10 acre lake
ACTIVITIES: nature walk, nature study, picnicking, shelters, fishing, canoeing, launch ramp, primitive camping, hunting
FEE(s): camping

Knop Lake is a green and watery oasis in the till plain. Nature walks can be made along the fisherman's user paths that encircle 10 acre Knop Lake and along the south bank of Wildcat Creek North Fork. The meandering North Fork joins the South Fork to form Wildcat Creek at Wildcat Park in northeast Lafayette. Jerry Clegg Botanic Garden and the Wabash River are just downstream. The fish and wildlife property provides a canoe camp and travellers may enjoy Knop Lake as a place to picnic, explore and rest.

Knop Lake Public Fishing Area is located in the extreme southwest corner of Carroll County. From Indiana 39/US 421, just south of Wildcat Creek at Owasco, Indiana, go west on CR 700W to CR 650S, 2.3 miles to the gravel road entrance. Follow the road signs.

While on the Wildcat Creek North Fork, head upstream via county roads to the 1872 Adams Mill and Lancaster Covered Bridge, located one mile northeast of Cutler (Indiana 75), and seven miles west of Burlington, (Indiana 29), at the east side of Carroll County. There is a Wildcat Creek North Fork canoe access at the mill and bridge site, CR 440S on CR 50E.

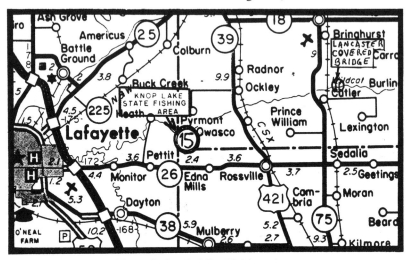

Knop Lake Public Fishing Area

16. EUNICE HAMILTON BRYAN NATURE PRESERVE
Hamilton, IN/Clinton County
USGS MAP(s): Frankfort 1:24,000
TRAIL(s) DISTANCE: appx. 1.25 miles
ACREAGE: 29 acres
ACTIVITIES: nature walk, nature study

Cut off from a greater expanse of forest, this tree "island" refuge is found in northwest Clinton County, where agricultural lands utilized over 80% of Clinton County. The woodland was willed by Henry R. Smith in honor of his mother-in-law and the sanctuary is by far the best old growth forest within miles.

The trailhead begins next to the parking area alongside CR 450W and heads east about 0.2 mile along a farm lane to the forest edge. A detailed trail brochure is available at the self-registration box at the parking lot trailhead. At the forest, there is a self-guiding long and short nature loop trail that moves through the block-shaped, dense canopied woodlot.

The forest has several wet depressions and high points that support a great variety of hardwoods and wildflowers over the 29 acres. White, red, bur and pin oaks, beech, basswood, black haw, and buttonbush, sugar maple, paw paw, spicebush, red maple, and winterberry thrive in the nature preserve, which is slowly evolving to beech-maple forest. The two trails are shaped in a figure 8 double loop, laying on its side, and both trails have numbered stations that correspond to the trail brochure. Mosquitoes can be pesky during rainy periods.

To reach Eunice Hamilton Bryan Nature Preserve from Frankfort, Indiana, drive north on Indiana 39 about five miles and turn left/ on Indiana 38 at Mattix Corner. Follow Indiana 38, 1.2 miles west to CR 450W and go north one mile to the small parking lot on the east side of CR 450W. The trail goes east from the parking area.

The preserve's hours are dawn to dusk.

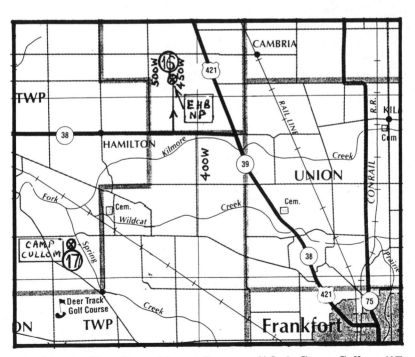

Eunice Hamilton Bryan Nature Preserve (16) & Camp Cullom (17)

17. CAMP CULLOM
Mulberry, IN/Clinton County
USGS MAP(s): Mulberry 1:24,000
TRAIL(s) DISTANCE: 3 trails total appx. 3 miles
ACREAGE: 50 acres
ACTIVITIES: nature walks and study, seasonal nature center, naturalist, picnicking, shelters, boating, winter sports, youth group camping, lodge

Camp Cullom is one of the most scenic nature places in Clinton County. The educational youth camp is comprised of 50 acres of stream bottoms, marsh, pond and forested rolling uplands. Spanning both banks of Spring Creek, a tributary of the nearby Wildcat Creek South Fork, Camp Cullom was donated to the Clinton County Youth Foundation in 1941 by the Cullom family who wanted to provide a natural area for youth to enjoy and learn nature's ways. The camp is now primarily funded by the United Way and staffed by volunteers. A naturalist/park manager resides near the park entrance, who also presents programs and leads hikes.

The three short interpretive trails traverse spring fed Spring Creek and its riparian forest, encircles a marsh, and through upland forest perched above the compact valley. All three trails interconnect and have self guiding trail brochures that correspond to marked posts along the trails.

The Wetland Trail loops about a marsh and follows Spring Creek upstream along a narrow path. The Tree Trail begins near the nature center and follows the ridge top. The Upland Trail traces a loop around the eastern high ground portion of the property. Visitors entering the private property must register at the gate. The hours are dawn to dusk.

To reach Camp Cullom from Frankfort, Indiana, drive north on Indiana 39/US 421 a few miles to the signed CR 200N/Farmers Road and turn left/west. There is a highway directional sign for Camp Cullom at this intersection. The camp entrance is five miles west on CR 200N/Farmers Road on the left/south side of the county road, after crossing Spring Creek

The nearby city and county seat of Frankfort has six city parks, the largest is the TPA Park, which is located near Kyger Street and Burlington Avenue in northeast Frankfort. The Traveller's Protective Association, a fraternal beneficiary society of professional men, purchased the 85 rolling scenic acres and established a public park in 1911.

The TPA Park is unique with its expansive field stone work, historic log cabins, nature center, zoo and petting zoo. The handsome park is also a fine place to picnic and enjoy the playfields and playgrounds.

18. LEBANON CITY PARKS
Lebanon, IN/Boone County
USGS MAP(s): Lebanon 1:24,000
TRAIL(s) DISTANCE: appx. 1 mile
ACREAGE: 3 parks total 95 acres
ACTIVITIES:nature walks, nature study, arboretum, picnicking, shelters, playgrounds, playfields, swimming pool, lifeguards, ball diamonds, football, soccer, volleyball, tennis, basketball, fitness course, concerts, hayrides, mini-camp, special events

Rural Boone County is big on corn and soybean production but short on public parklands. However if passing through or visiting Lebanon, the county seat, there are six roadside-handy city parks adjacent to or close by Indiana 39/Lebanon Street. Three of these are ideal for nature walks.

Located about two miles south of Lebanon on the east side of Indiana 39 is the Brookshire Arboretum [1]. The 14 acre woody plant collection of Indiana's native trees was donated to the Lebanon parks department in 1987 by Ruth Brookshire Sedgewick. The arboretum is currently undergoing development, and is an ideal site for nature activities. Park and walk about the rolling landscape.

Going north under the I-65 overpass, turn at the first street right, or Birchwood Drive. Follow Birchwood Drive to the next street left/north and turn onto S. East Street. Continue on S. East Street north to Thompson Street and turn right/east. Proceed on Thompson Street to Abner Longley Park [2] and parking area. Named for the community's first pioneer citizen, there is a 0.25 mile interpretive nature trail south of the Stokes Elementary School. This open green space is a fine place to picnic

Memorial Park [3] is the main activity park of the city and the headquarters of the parks and recreation department at 130 E. Ulen Drive. Memorial Park is located on the east side of Indiana 39/North Lebanon Street at the north edge of Lebanon.

Also in Lebanon is Hot Pond Park, a 3 acre picnic and fishing area just off Indianapolis Avenue on Noble Street. There is also James Hill Park and Rolling Meadows Play Area, both small neighborhood play area parks.

Lebanon City Parks

19. STARKEY NATURE PARK/NANCY BURTON MEMORIAL PATH

Zionsville, IN/Boone County
USGS MAP(s): Zionsville 1:24,000
TRAIL(s) DISTANCE: 6 trails total appx. 5 miles
ACREAGE: 77 a. snp/32 a. nbmp
ACTIVITIES: nature walks, nature study, picnicking

Starkey Nature Park is Zionsville's largest park and most nature oriented. The 77 acre sanctuary is named for Lucille Starkey, who bequeathed a large portion of land to the community. The recently acquired rail-to-trail segment that accesses Starkey Park is named in honor of donor benefactor, Nancy Burton.

The five interconnecting trails of Starkey Park begins at the trailhead parking area at the dead end of Sugarbush Drive in southwest Zionsville. Trail 1 and 1A lead into the old growth mixed forest of the uplands and ravines to access Trails 2 and 3. Trail 2 follows the upland ridge down to the floodplain of Eagle Creek and loops back, accessing Trail 5 for a complete loop back to the parking area. Trail 2 also connects Trail 3 at the junction with Trail 5. Trails 3 and 3A are floodplain meadow and creek frontage paths that access Trail 4, a square-shaped trail through the herbaceous old field in the bottoms. The total distance of all five trails and their side loops is about four miles.

From Trail 2 at the park's northeast end is a series of boardwalk that switches back up the railroad embankment to the 32 acre linear Nancy Burton Memorial Park Path. The former Penn Central/Conrail segment from Indiana 334/Oak Street southeast to the railroad trestle bridge is now a mile long rail-to-trail, open to walkers and bicyclists. The views of Eagle Creek from the trestle bridge overlooks the natural area.

To reach Starkey Park [19] and Nancy Burton Memorial Path in Zionsville, drive west from the downtown village on Oak Street/ Indiana 334 and turn left/south on 6th Street. Follow 6th Street south about five blocks to Starkey Avenue and turn right/west. Proceed on Starkey Avenue west, crossing Nancy Burton Memorial Path, curving southwest to Sugarbush Drive, turning left/south. Continue on Sugarbush Drive to the dead end parking area and the trailheads. Additional parks in Zionsville to visit include the downtown Lincoln Park and Jennings Field on the northwest side.

Zionsville, in southeast Boone County, is easily accessed from the west via I-65 to Indiana 334/Oak Street or from I-465 to US 421, west at Indiana 334.

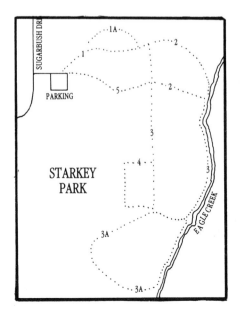

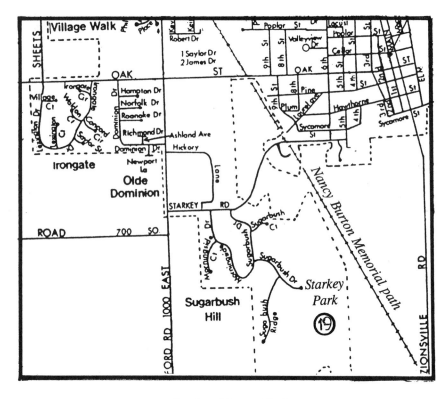

Starkey Nature Park

20. COOL CREEK PARK

Carmel, IN/Hamilton County
USGS MAP(S): Noblesville, Fishers 1:24,000
TRAIL(S) DISTANCE: appx. 3 miles total
ACREAGE: 90 acres
ACTIVITIES: nature walks, nature study, naturalist hikes, programs, picnicking, shelters, playground, playfields
FEE(S): shelter rental

Cool Creek County Park is owned and administered by the Hamilton County Parks and Recreation Department. Cool Creek is one of several Hamilton County parks that have recently been developed or under development, in the face of growing population of a greater Indianapolis.

As the name implies, Cool Creek is the main natural feature of the county park where three miles of nature trails parallel the streambanks and

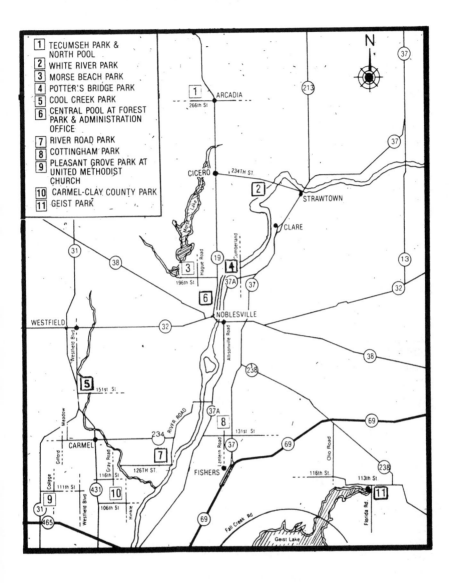

Hamilton County Parks & City Parks

the adjacent rolling uplands, all within a couple of hundred yards from US 31 and McDonalds restaurant. Naturalist-led hikes are a common warm weather occurrence. The property also includes picnicking areas, five shelters, a playground and a softball/soccer field, and amphitheatre. A nature center and volleyball courts are planned.

377

Cool Creek County Park (**5** on map) is located at 2,000 East 151st St., south of Westfield. A south entrance is on 151st St. and a west entrance is just east of the intersection of Westfield Boulevard and US 31. Both entrances can be accessed from US 31, between Westfield and Carmel.

Two additional Hamilton County nature-oriented parks are currently being developed at 17 acre Geist Park (**11** on map) along Fall Creek and upper Geist Reservoir at 113th Street and Florida Road, and the 63.7 acre River Road Park (**7** on map) at 126th Street and River Road near the White River. A Hamilton County campground is at White River Park (**2** on map). The 25 acre county park has 100 Class A campsites, boat launch, camp store, picnic shelter and playground. The campground park is located at the west bank of the White River at 11299 East 234th Street, between Cicero and Strawtown, Indiana.

Bitternut Woods Nature Preserve, a Nature Conservancy owned property, is a 22 acre tract of floodplain along Williams Creek near Carmel. However accessing the preserve is difficult since there is no parking area and no trails. A half mile west of US 31 on West 106th Street.

Ritchey Woods is a 42 acre rolling woodland and floodplain plus cultivated acreage that is owned and managed by The Children's Museum. Permission must be obtained before visiting the preserve by calling (317) 924-5431. Both Bitternut Woods and Ritchey Woods are located in fast growing suburban areas of south Hamilton County.

Nearby community parks to visit include Forest Park (**6** on map) at Noblesville and Flowing Well at Carmel. Forest Park, a 68 acre active city park also includes a 40 acre golf course. A three mile trail loops around the park's perimeter. At one point, the trail follows the river banks of the White River. There are several road crossings. Forest Park is located at 701 Cicero Road in northwest Noblesville. There is also picnicking, shelters, pool swimming, ball diamonds, playgrounds, a Transportation Museum, a nature preserve and wildflower grove.

Flowing Well (**10** on map) at the northeast corner of Gray Road and 116th Street is a 17 acre riparian woodland park with a natural flowing well that has been spouting water at a rate of 15 gallons a minute since 1902. People come and go to fill their water containers. There is a small parking area adjacent to the well along 116th Street on the north side of the street, east of the intersection of Gray Road and 116th Street.

21. OSCAR & RUTH HALL WOODS NATURE PRESERVE
Bainbridge, IN/Putnam County
USGS MAP(s): Roachdale 1:24,000
TRAIL(s) DISTANCE: 1 mile loop
ACREAGE: 128 acres
ACTIVITIES: nature walk, nature study

This old growth nature preserve occupies the west bank of Big Walnut Creek, about a mile east of Bainbridge, Indiana. Forested ridgetops, deep lush ravines and valley floodplain are the essence of this sanctuary. The number of different tree species is considerable. From the parking area, a loop trail ventures through the level upland of white oak-dominated woods and descends gradually about 80 feet into the sharp ravines to the riparian plain. The property was acquired by gift and purchase by The Nature Conservancy but is now owned by the DNR Division of Nature Preserves and managed as a dedicated state nature preserve.

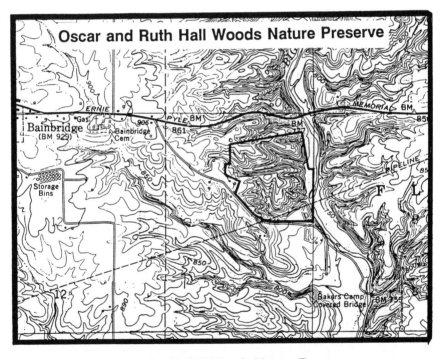

Oscar & Ruth Hall Woods Nature Preserve

To reach Oscar and Ruth Hall Woods from Bainbridge in north central Putnam County, drive east on US 36 one half mile and turn right/southeast on a gravel road. Continue one half mile on the gravel county road to the preserve on the left/north side of the road where there is a parking area and trailhead. Of further interest, the gravel road continues east to cross Big Walnut Creek via Bakers Camp Covered Bridge.

22. PINE HILLS NATURE PRESERVE
Waveland, IN/Montgomery County
USGS MAP(s):
TRAIL(s) DISTANCE: 1.3 mile loop
ACREAGE: 599 acres
ACTIVITIES: nature walk, nature study, historic sites

Dedicated in 1971, Pine Hills was Indiana's first official nature preserve. The special area includes a myriad of outstanding natural features: forested hills, 100 feet deep gorges, sandstone cliffs, box canyons, "backbone" ridges and five miles of streams from Clifty and Indian creeks. Not only are the geological features unique but so are the botanical resources of eastern hemlock, Canada yew, white pine, wintergreen, snow trillium as well as old growth oak-hickory and beech-

Mill Cut Notch, Pine Hills Nature Preserve

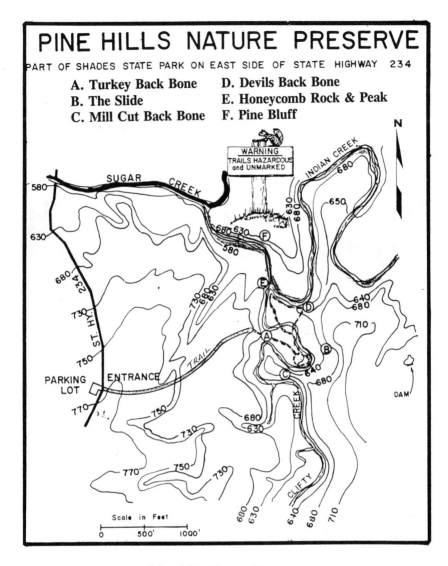

PINE HILLS NATURE PRESERVE

PART OF SHADES STATE PARK ON EAST SIDE OF STATE HIGHWAY 234

A. Turkey Back Bone   **D. Devils Back Bone**
B. The Slide   **E. Honeycomb Rock & Peak**
C. Mill Cut Back Bone   **F. Pine Bluff**

Pine Hills Nature Preserve

maple forest cover. Pine Hills was originally acquired by The Nature Conservancy and is now owned and managed by the DNR Division of State Parks; considered an addition to Shades State Park. Pine Hills is also included in the National Registry of National Landmarks.

The parking area and trailhead are located along and bisected by Indiana 234, about two miles north of Shades State Park and 0.5 mile south of Deer's Mill Covered Bridge over Sugar Creek. (The preserve is accessible

Overlook, Turkey Backbone, Pine Hills Nature Preserve

from Trail 10 of Shades State Park). From the parking area on the west side of the highway, cross over Indiana 234 to the east side and climb over the fence stile, register and obtain a trail brochure from the registration box. The trail through Pine Hills has two segments: the entrance and double loop trail.

The linear <u>entrance trail</u> to <u>Turkey Backbone</u> must be walked out and back. From Turkey Backbone, one of four ridges formed by meandering stream erosion, there are excellent views of the gorge and the hillside ridges. Cross the narrow backbone and descend through the eastern hemlock grove to the valley below via stairs. The streamside trail leads to the former 1870 site of the Pine Hills Woolen Mill Company and the U-shaped flume cut in <u>Mill Cut Backbone</u>.

From the <u>Mill Cut Backbone</u>, the shady trail leads along Clifty Creek past the geological <u>Slide</u> appearing on the east canyon wall. Continue to follow the trail signs and cross Clifty Creek to the <u>Devil's Backbone</u>. The trail climbs and crosses over the backbone (nearly a natural bridge) and descends to <u>Honeycomb Rock</u>, recrosses the creek and proceeds back to the original trail out. The preserve is open dawn to dusk daily.

23. SHADES STATE PARK

Waveland, IN/Montgomery, Parke & Fountain Counties
USGS MAP(s): Alamo 1:24,000
TRAIL(s) DISTANCE: 10 trails total 10 miles
ACREAGE: 3,082 acres
ACTIVITIES: nature walks, nature study, seasonal naturalist, nature preserves, picnicking, shelters, playgrounds, playfields, stream fishing, canoeing, canoe launch (Deer's Mill Covered Bridge), canoe camp, Class B campground, youth camp, back pack camp (April-October), airport flight strip, cultural arts program
FEE(s): seasonal entrance, camping, shelter rental, bicycle rental, airplane landing fee

Established in 1947, Shades State Park is one of the most natural and less developed of Indiana's state parks. Sugar Creek, canyons, waterfalls, ravines, overlooks, evergreen hemlock groves, and old growth deciduous forest are the main natural attractions. North of Sugar Creek is the 730 acre Pedestal Rock Nature Preserve which is open by appointment with the seasonal naturalist. The Pine Hills Nature Preserve, northeast of the park, is connected by Trail 10. Trail-wise, there is plenty to explore at Shades and the paths lead visitors to the most varied natural beauties and scenic points of interest. The trails can prove a challenge with climbing, slippery streambeds, staircases and ladders.

The ten foot trails are briefly summarized as follows:

Trail 1: The 0.75 mile loop trail is one of the most popular walks in Shades State Park. The lower trail begins at the Devil's Punch Bowl, a pool-like basin, and follows the smooth and also at times slippery streambed to Silver Cascade Waterfalls. The upper trail leads to Inspiration and Prospect points; 210 feet majestic overlooks of Sugar Creek. Trail 1 connects Trail 6.

Trail 2: The 1.25 mile rugged loop trail begins at Dell Shelter parking area and leads to Lover's Leap overlooking Sugar Creek. The trail continues and descends to Steamboat Rock along Sugar Creek and then follows Pearl Ravine streambed to Maidenhair Falls and back to Dell Shelter. High water and heavy rains may close the trail.

Trail 4: The 0.6 mile loop begins at the west end of the main parking area and follows narrow Frisz Ravine down to Sugar Creek and back along an adjacent ravine. There are steps and ladders and high water and heavy rains may close the trail. Connects Trails 7 and 5.

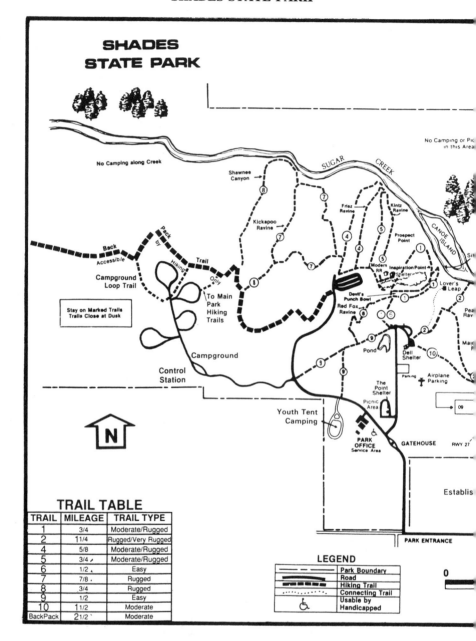

TRAIL TABLE

TRAIL	MILEAGE	TRAIL TYPE
1	3/4	Moderate/Rugged
2	1 1/4	Rugged/Very Rugged
4	5/8	Moderate/Rugged
5	3/4	Moderate/Rugged
6	1/2	Easy
7	7/8	Rugged
8	3/4	Rugged
9	1/2	Easy
10	1 1/2	Moderate
BackPack	2 1/2	Moderate

LEGEND

――――	Park Boundary
	Road
▬ ▬ ▬	Hiking Trail
· · · · · ·	Connecting Trail
♿	Usable by Handicapped

SHADES STATE PARK

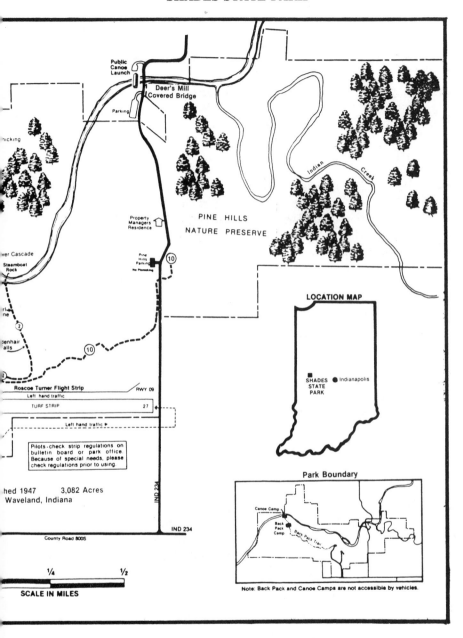

Public Canoe Launch

Deer's Mill Covered Bridge

Parking

Picking

Property Managers Residence

PINE HILLS NATURE PRESERVE

Indian Creek

ver Cascade

Steamboat Rock

Pine Hills Parking
No Picnicking

10

le

denhair alls

10

Roscoe Turner Flight Strip   RWY 09

Left hand traffic

TURF STRIP   27

Left hand traffic ►

Pilots-check strip regulations on bulletin board or park office. Because of special needs, please check regulations prior to using.

hed 1947   3,082 Acres
Waveland, Indiana

IND 234

IND 234

County Road 800S

LOCATION MAP

■ SHADES STATE PARK   ● Indianapolis

Park Boundary

Canoe Camp

Back Pack Camp

Back Pack Trail

Note: Back Pack and Canoe Camps are not accessible by vehicles.

¼   ½

SCALE IN MILES

Trail 5: Similar to Trail 4. The 0.75 mile loop path begins at the west end of the main parking area. The upper section follows the ridge separating Frisz Ravine from Kintz Ravine to Sugar Creek. The trail returns along Kintz Ravine streambed which may be closed during periods of excessive rain and high stream waters. There are steps and ladder.

Trail 6: The 0.5 mile loop trail is considered one of the easiest walks in the park. The trail begins west of Dell Shelter parking area and follows a portion of Trail 1 north to Red Fox Ravine and heads left/west, following the ravine to Trail 9. Turn left/ east at the Trail 9 junction and go past the pond back to the parking area.

Trail 7: The 0.88 mile rugged loop ravine trail begins at the west end of the main parking area and follows a short segment of Trail 4 to connect with Trail 7 trail-head. The trail leads to Sugar Creek and returns along Kickapoo Ravine. Connects Trail 8. Trail 7 can be difficult to negotiate at times of high water.

Trail 8: The 0.75 mile rugged trail begins at the intersection with Trail 7. Trail 8 follows Sugar Creek and turns inland to continue up Shawnee Canyon streambed. Trail 8 connects and travels a segment of Back Pack Trail, reconnects to Trail 8 and Trail 7.

Trail 9: The easy 0.5 mile trail is primarily a connector trail from the youth and main campground areas to the central trail system. For day visitors, the level trail begins at Dell Shelter parking area and goes southwest past the pond to the campgrounds.

Trail 10: A linear 1.5 mile (one-way) trek from the east end of Dell Shelter to Indiana 234 and Pine Hills Nature Preserve, where a 1.3 mile path loops about the 599 acre preserve. Trail 10 returns along the original route.

Back Pack Trail: The 2.5 mile linear route begins at the main parking area and heads west, skirting the main campground (several spur access trails), moving through a variety of successional areas to conclude at the Back Pack campground and Canoe Camp areas. Return along the same route you arrived.

To reach Shades State Park from I-74 exit 34 at Crawfordsville, Indiana and drive south through the city on US 231 to the junction with Indiana 47. Go south on Indiana 47 to Indiana 234 and turn right/west. Follow Indiana 234 west to the park entrance.

24. TURKEY RUN STATE PARK

Marshall, IN/Parke County
USGS MAP(s): Wallace 1:24,000
TRAIL(s) DISTANCE: 10 trails total 13.5 miles
ACREAGE: 2,382 acres
ACTIVITIES: nature walks, nature study, naturalist, nature center, planetarium, nature preserve, historic sites, picnicking, shelters, canoeing, canoe launch ramp, stream fishing, playgrounds, playfields, tennis courts, saddle barn, bridle trail for rental horses, hayrides, bicycling, swimming pool, bathhouse, lifeguards, inn, restaurant, Class A campground, walk-in tent sites, youth camp, camp store, cultural arts programs
FEE(s): seasonal entrance, shelter rental, camping, inn, conference facilities, bicycle rental

Established in 1916, Turkey Run is Indiana's second oldest state park, following McCormick Creek's founding earlier the same year. Richard Lieber, the "Father of Indiana's State Parks", made a considerable effort to secure Turkey Run as a state park and a memorial to Lieber is located at Sunset Point.

Over two-thirds of the picturesque park is dedicated nature preserve, located in Rocky Hollow and Falls Canyon on the undeveloped north side of Sugar Creek, accessible from the suspension bridge. Like Shades State Park upstream on Sugar Creek a few miles, Turkey Run is noted for its narrow sandstone canyons, gorges, ravines, overlooks, eastern hemlock groves and virgin old growth deciduous forest. Additional points of interest include the various historic sites such as the Salmon Lusk home, the Narrows and Cox Ford covered bridges, the 1829 old mill site, the 1848 Lieber Cabin, the 1871 log church, and the Juliet Strauss Memorial, a tribute to an Indiana writer. The nature center and planetarium have many scheduled programs throughout the year.

The ten interconnecting foot trails are summarized as follows:

Trail 1: The three mile trail is the longest of the ten park trails. The foot path begins at the suspension bridge and parallels Sugar Creek heading east, upstream to the Narrows Covered Bridge. Enroute there are several virgin black walnut and sycamore trees and Goose Rock is the death site of the last Miami in the area. Trail 1 continues south to Trail 2, merges and interconnects with Trail 2 and concludes at Canyon picnic area.

For a near loop, continue on the park road west to the circle cul de sac turn-around and trailhead for Trail 2. Follow Trail 2 downslope to the

TURKEY RUN STATE PARK

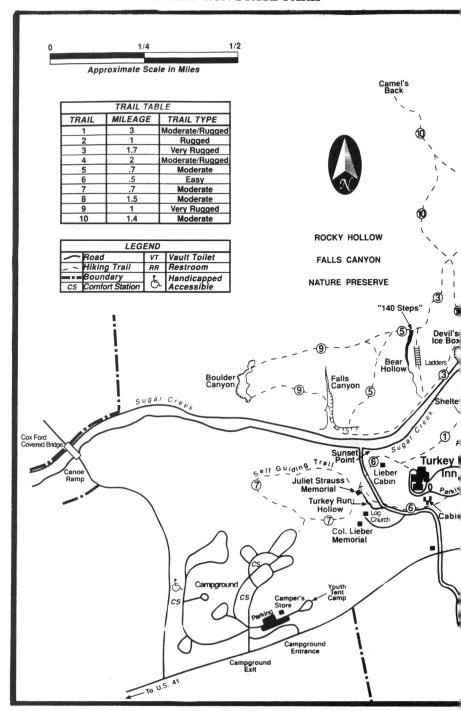

Approximate Scale in Miles

0   1/4   1/2

TRAIL TABLE		
TRAIL	**MILEAGE**	**TRAIL TYPE**
1	3	Moderate/Rugged
2	1	Rugged
3	1.7	Very Rugged
4	2	Moderate/Rugged
5	.7	Moderate
6	.5	Easy
7	.7	Moderate
8	1.5	Moderate
9	1	Very Rugged
10	1.4	Moderate

LEGEND			
Road		VT	Vault Toilet
Hiking Trail		RR	Restroom
Boundary		♿	Handicapped
CS	Comfort Station		Accessible

ROCKY HOLLOW

FALLS CANYON

NATURE PRESERVE

Camel's Back

"140 Steps"

Devil's Ice Box

Bear Hollow

Ladders

Boulder Canyon

Falls Canyon

Shelter

Sugar Creek

Cox Ford Covered Bridge

Canoe Ramp

Self Guiding Trail

Sunset Point

Lieber Cabin

Turkey Inn

Juliet Strauss Memorial

Turkey Run Hollow

Log Church

Col. Lieber Memorial

Campground

Camper's Store

Youth Tent Camp

Parking

Campground Entrance

Campground Exit

To U.S. 41

TURKEY RUN STATE PARK

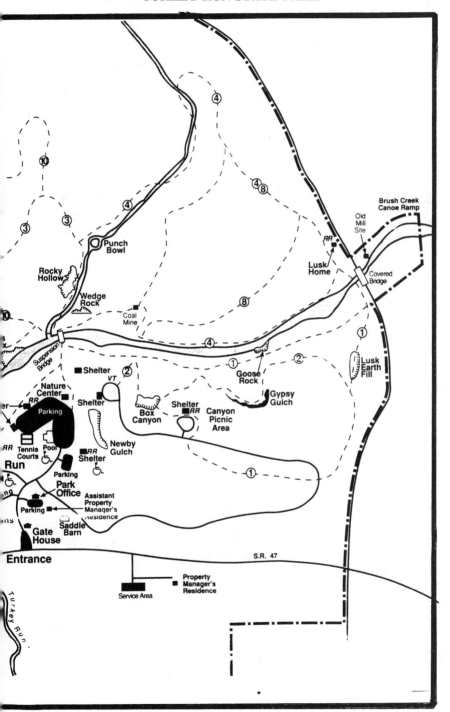

Rocky Hollow Trail, Turkey Run State Park

creek bank and <u>Trail 1</u>. Go left/west back to the suspension bridge. A segment of <u>Trail 1</u> leads from Turkey Run Inn east to the suspension bridge along Sugar Creek's south bank.

<u>Trail 2</u>: The one mile near-loop begins at the cul de sac circle turn around west of Canyon picnic area. Follow the trail downslope to near Sugar Creek where the cliffside trail skirts past Box Canyon and Gypsy Gulch. The east bound trail merges with <u>Trail 1</u> and loops back to Canyon picnic area.

<u>Trail 3</u>: The 1.7 mile rugged trail traces a loop in the Rocky Hollow Falls Canyon Nature Preserve. Cross the suspension bridge and go left/west along the stream past the Ice Box to Bear Hollow and turn right/north. Climb the series of ladders up to the top and go right/east and loop back through Rocky Hollow and Wedge Rock to the suspension bridge crossing. Connects <u>Trails 5</u>, <u>10</u> and <u>4</u>.

<u>Trail 4</u>: The two mile loop is also located in Rocky Hollow-Falls Canyon Nature Preserve. From the suspension bridge walk right/east past the old hand dug coal quarry to the <u>Trail 8</u> junction. Turn right/south back to the stream. Follow the north bank of Sugar Creek upstream to the Narrows Covered Bridge and head north past the Lusk Home and merges with <u>Trail 8</u> for a distance before looping back along a intermittent stream

to the Punch Bowl and Trail 3. Continue left/south on Trail 3 through Rocky Hollow and Wedge Rock back to the suspension bridge.

Trail 5: The 0.7 mile loop begins at the suspension bridge and follows Trail 3 downstream west to the Trail 5 junction at Falls Canyon. Walk right/north and climb the ladders to the top and go left/west. Follow Trail 5 west a short distance and turn south at the trail junction with Trail 9. Continue south down the ravine towards Sugar Creek and turn left/east, following the streambank back to Trail 3 and the suspension bridge.

Trail 6: A 0.5 mile loop trail that begins west of Turkey Run Inn. The short trail connects Sunset Point, Lieber Cabin, and crosses Turkey Run to Juliet Strauss Memorial, and ends near the cabin area adjacent to the inn. Accesses Trails 1 and 7.

Trail 7: The 0.7 mile loop trail is self-guiding with 15 numbered stations that correspond to a trail brochure. The trailhead begins/ends near Sunset Point and crosses Turkey Run over a footbridge to trace a loop in the forest uplands and ravines. Trail 7 connects the campground and Trail 6.

Trail 8: The 1.5 mile loop trail begins at the suspension bridge in Rocky Hollow-Falls Canyon Nature Preserve. From the bridge go right/east on Trail 8/4 past the coal mine and turn right/ south to Sugar Creek. Trail 8 separates from Trail 4 and goes northeast through the woodland to merge once again with Trail 4 north of the Lusk Home. Follow Trail 8/4 north to Trail 8 junction and turn south and west back to the coal mine and on to the suspension bridge.

Trail 9: The one mile rugged loop trail begins at the suspension bridge and follows Trail 3 downstream to the Trail 3, 5 and 9 junction. Continue west into Falls Canyon and on west to Boulder Canyon, looping back to Trail 5 junction. Follow Trail 5 south down the ravine to Trail 3 junction and go left/upstream back to the suspension bridge.

Trail 10: The 1.4 mile loop begins at the suspension bridge and follows Trail 3 west a short distance to access Trail 10, which heads north, crosses Trail 3 and continues north to an overlook known as Camel's Back. Trail 10 loops back to the suspension bridge via Trail 3 through Rocky Hollow and Wedge Rock.

To reach Turkey Run State Park from US 41 in north central Parke County, turn east on Indiana 47 and drive about two miles to the park entrance on the left/north side of the highway. Turkey Run is located eight miles north of Rockville, Indiana, the county seat of Parke County.

Along Trail 3, Turkey Run State Park

25. RACCOON STATE RECREATION AREA
Hollandsburg, IN/Parke County
USGS MAP(s): Bellmore, Mansfield 1:24,000
TRAIL(s) DISTANCE: 12 trails total appx. 3 miles
ACREAGE: 4,065 acres total, 2,060 lake reservoir
ACTIVITIES: nature walks, nature study, picnicking, shelters, playfields, playfields, swimming, beachhouse, lifeguards, pier, marina, fishing, boating, launch ramps, waterskiing, athletic courts, camp store, Class A, B & C campgrounds, cultural arts program, interpretive programs, limited hunting
FEE(s): seasonal entrance, shelter & boat rentals, camping

Raccoon State Recreation Area forms a peninsular land extension from the north shore into <u>Cecil M. Harden Lake</u> reservoir, a flood control project in the Raccoon Creek and Wabash River watersheds. Although there are other recreational sites surrounding the U. S. Army Corps dam and lake reservoir, Raccoon SRA is the only area where established and maintained nature trails are found. Twelve short interconnecting trails are located along the east side of the recreation area. The trails may be divided into two areas: the campground-marina area and the campground north to the beach area.

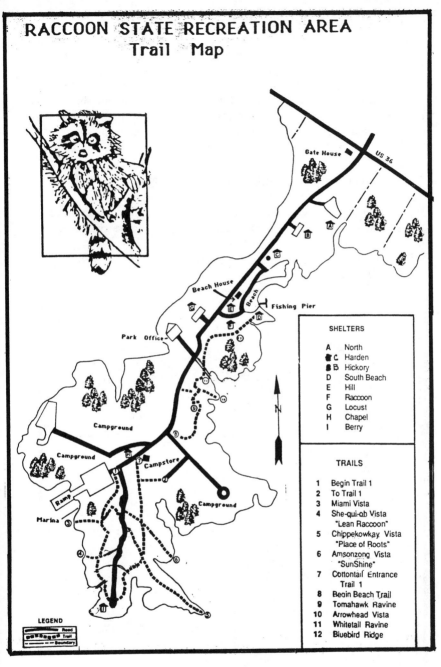

RACCOON STATE RECREATION AREA
Trail Map

Gate House

US 36

Beach House

Beach

Fishing Pier

Park Office

Campground

Campground

Campstore

Ramp

Marina

N

SHELTERS

A	North
C	Harden
B	Hickory
D	South Beach
E	Hill
F	Raccoon
G	Locust
H	Chapel
I	Berry

TRAILS

1	Begin Trail 1
2	To Trail 1
3	Miami Vista
4	She-qui-ob Vista "Lean Raccoon"
5	Chippekowkay Vista "Place of Roots"
6	Amsonzong Vista "SunShine"
7	Cottontail Entrance Trail 1
8	Begin Beach Trail
9	Tomahawk Ravine
10	Arrowhead Vista
11	Whitetail Ravine
12	Bluebird Ridge

LEGEND
Road
Trail
Boundary

Raccoon State Recreation Area

The trails are summarized as follows:

Trail 1: The main trail in the campground-marina area which basically forms a loop along the ridgetop with several spur trails radiating off to the lake. Trail 1 begins at the northeast corner of the boat ramp parking area and heads south, paralleling the park road to the Berry picnic shelter. The trail loops north crossing the park road and following the ridgeline west to conclude at the rear of the camp store. A U-shaped trail.

Trails 2, 3, 4, 5, 6, and 7 all lead from Trail 1 to the lake's edge except Trail 2, which is a connector trail from the campground to Trail 1.

Trail 8: Travels north along a linear route from the intersection of the main park road and the primitive camping area to the beach.

Trails 9, 10, and 11 are spur trails that lead from Trail 8 to the park road to the lake's edge.

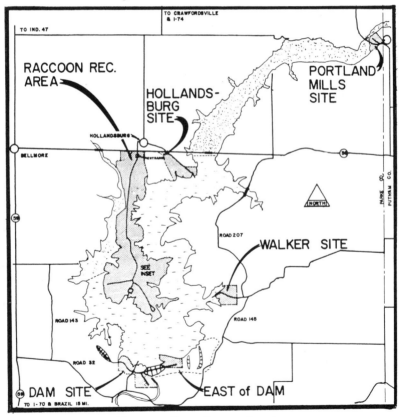

Raccoon State Recreation Area

Additional recreational sites surrounding Cecil M. Harden Lake reservoir include the dam area where picnicking and boat ramp are found; east of the dam area where there is picnicking; the <u>Hollandsburg</u> <u>site</u> where there is picnicking and a boat ramp; the <u>Portland Mills</u> site which has a boat ramp, shelter house, and picnicking area; and the <u>Walker</u> site, which also has a boat ramp and picnicking.

Raccoon State Recreation Area is located nine miles east of Rockville, Indiana on US 36 at Hollandsburg, Indiana.

The water that flows downstream a few miles from Harden Lake powers the restored 1819 <u>Mansfield Roller Grist Mill</u> near Mansfield, Indiana, six miles south of US 36 and Indiana 59. The mill is open February to December, Wednesday through Sunday, from 10 am to 5 pm.

Lily Pads

OHIO BORDERLANDS - NORTH

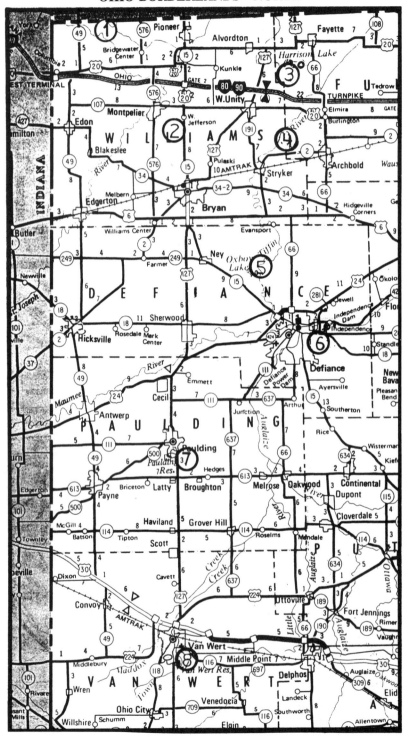

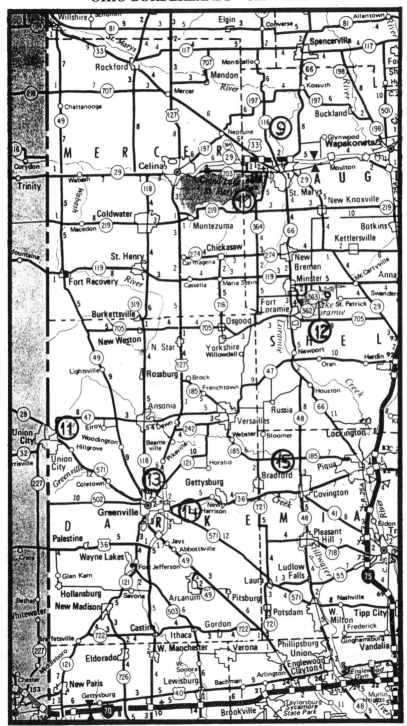

1. LAKE LA SU AN WILDLIFE AREA

c/o Area Manager
Route 1, Box 88
Montpelier, Ohio 43543
(419) 459-4676

Nearly bordering Michigan, the 1,161 acre wildlife area has several walking paths around the shorelines of most of the fourteen lakes and ponds that dot the property of which 82 acre Lake La Su An is the largest. Virtually two-thirds of the area is in beech-maple forest and brushlands while the remainder is divided between cropland, grassy meadow, marshland and wooded swamp. The West Branch of the St. Joseph River cuts through the middle of the area. The property is easily accessible from the nine parking lots. Best time to visit is during the off hunting season.

Lake La Su An Wildlife Area is situated in Bridgewater and Northwest Townships in the northwest corner of Williams County, seven miles west of Pioneer, Ohio. Williams County Road R provides access to the area from Ohio SR 576. The area can also be reached from Williams CR 7, three miles north of US 20. Parking areas are also along CR S and CR 8.

Open Daily, Dawn to Dusk

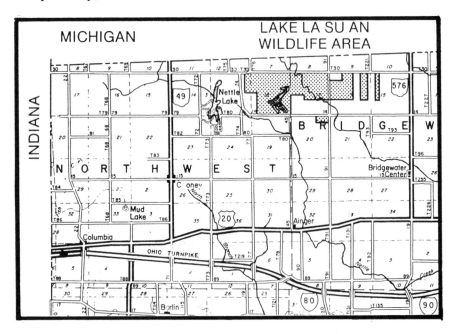

Lake La Su An Wildlife Area

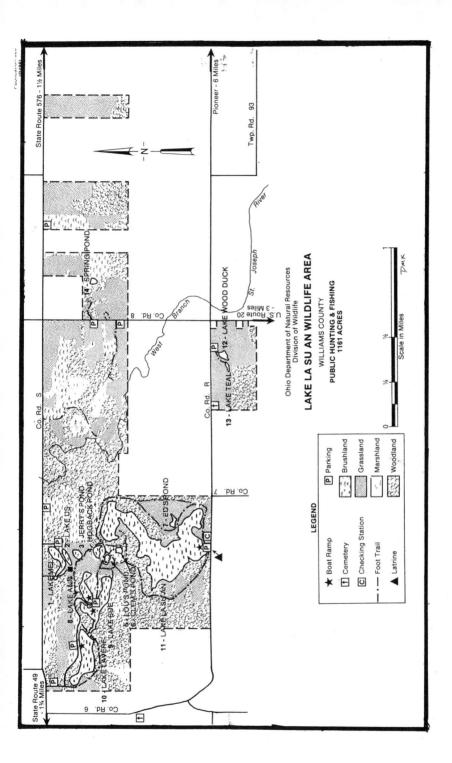

Ohio Department of Natural Resources
Division of Wildlife

LAKE LA SU AN WILDLIFE AREA

WILLIAMS COUNTY

PUBLIC HUNTING & FISHING
1161 ACRES

LEGEND

★ Boat Ramp   P Parking
T Cemetery   Brushland
C Checking Station   Grassland
-·- Foot Trail   Marshland
▲ Latrine   Woodland

Scale in Miles

0   ¼   ½   1

1 - LAKE SMELT
2 - LAKE US
3 - LAKE ALUS
5 - LOUS POND / SLEM'S POND
8 - LAKE RYE
9 - LAKE LATERRE
10 - LAKE LA TERRE
11 - LAKE LA SU AN
12 - LAKE TEAL
13 - LAKE WOOD DUCK
14 - SPRING POND

JERRY'S POND
HOGBACK POND
ED'S POND

State Route 49 - 1¼ Miles
Co. Rd. 6
Co. Rd. 7
Co. Rd. R
Co. Rd. 8
Co. Rd. S
State Route 576 - 1½ Miles

West Branch
St. Joseph River

Pioneer - 6 Miles
Twp. Rd. 93
U.S. Route 20 - 3 Miles

2. GEORGE BIBLE PARK
Junction of CR 13 & CR J
c/o Williams County Commissioners
County Courthouse
Bryan, Ohio 43506
(419) 636-2509
(419) 636-2825

The 60 acre day-use rural park is situated at the near center of Williams County, southeast of Montpelier, Ohio. Hiking paths have been established through the beech-maple woods, the revegetating natural area and around a seven acre pond. Picnicking tables and a shelter are also at hand.

George Bible Park (location #2 on map) may be reached by driving north five miles from Bryan, Ohio on Ohio SR 15 to CR J. Turn west/left on CR J and proceed one mile to the junction with CR 13 and the park entrance.

Open Year Around, Dawn to Dusk

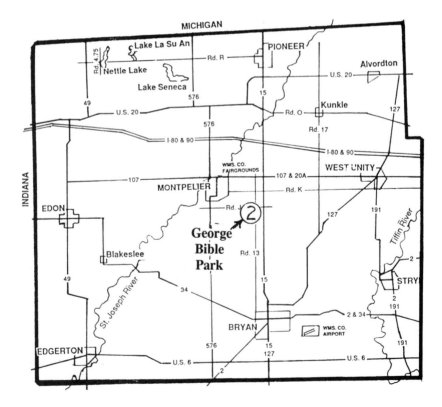

3. HARRISON LAKE STATE PARK
Route 1, CR 27
Fayette, Ohio 43521
(419) 237-2593

In the midst of Ohio's most productive agricultural region, Harrison Lake State Park stands out as one of the few recreational areas in what was once the "Black Swamp Forest".

A three and half mile nature trail encircles 105 acre Harrison Lake, a man made water body created from the dam waters of Harrison Creek. The state park also offers picnicking, shelters, a beach, swimming, boat launch ramp, non-motorized boating, fishing, winter sports and Class A, B, group and rent-a-tent camping.

Harrison Lake State Park is located five miles southwest of Fayette, Ohio off of US 20 between US 127 and Ohio 66, near the Fulton and Williams county line. Follow the roadside signs.

Open Year Around

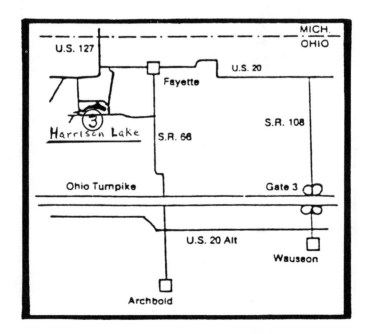

Harrison Lake State Park

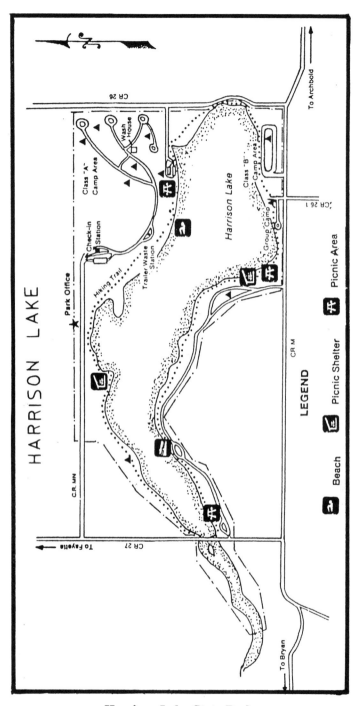

Harrison Lake State Park

4. GOLL WOODS NATURE PRESERVE
Ranger in Residence
Route 3, Box 67
Archbold, Ohio 43502
(419) 445-3276

Goll Woods is a prime remnant of the "Black Swamp Forest" that covered northwest Ohio before settlement. The 80 acre state nature preserve remains one of the most outstanding near virgin swamp woodlands in Ohio. Some oaks are nearly 500 years old.

The 3.75 miles of gravel and earth nature trails with such names as Cottonwood, Burr Oak, Tuliptree and Toadshade, loop and shortcut, and begin and end at the parking lot on Township Road 26. The preserve is divided into east and west woods separated by TR 26. A portion of trail follows the Tiffin River and leads past the Goll Cemetery and a thick pine plantation in the west woods. An exceptional well illustrated trail booklet is available to enhance your walk.

To reach Goll Woods from Bryan, Ohio drive east on Ohio 34 to Ohio 66 and turn north/left. Proceed on Ohio 66 to Archbold, Ohio and continue 1.6 miles to Township Road F and turn left/west. Drive 2.8 miles on TR F to TR 26 and turn left/south. The parking lot will be 0.2 mile south of the junction of TR F and TR 26.

Open Daily, Dawn to Dusk

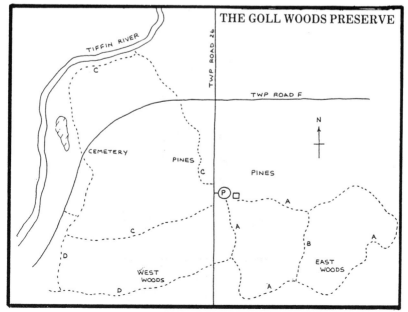

THE GOLL WOODS PRESERVE

5. OXBOW LAKE WILDLIFE AREA
c/o Ohio Division of Wildlife
District 2 Office
952 Lima Avenue
Findlay, Ohio 45840
(419) 422-6757

Foot-wise, the 415 acre wildlife area has no maintained hiking trails but the adventuresome will discover fisherman's paths around Oxbow Lake, Little Oxbow Lake and along Mud Creek which divides the property. In places along Mud Creek the slopes are steep. The Tiffin River confluence is not far to the east. Birders will find 38 acre Oxbow Lake and marsh prairie surroundings suitable for waterfowl and songbirds. Woodcock and Hungarian partridge may be seen. The area is also used for picnicking, fishing, non-motorized boating, a launch ramp, hunting and trapping.

The wildlife area was established in 1948. The property headquarters is at the junction of Schick Road/CR 67 and the entry road/Trinity Road. Two parking areas are at Oxbow Lake and one at 4.5 acre Little Oxbow Lake.

To reach Oxbow Lake Wildlife Area drive 12 miles northwest of Defiance, Ohio on Ohio SR 15 and turn right/east on Schick Road just northwest of the Olive Branch Church. Follow Schick Road two miles to the property. There are directional signs. Use caution during hunting season.

Open Daily, Dawn to Dusk

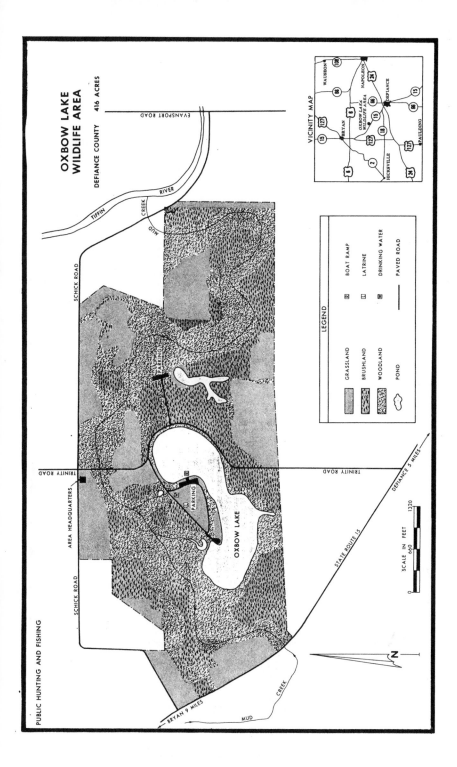

OXBOW LAKE
WILDLIFE AREA

DEFIANCE COUNTY   416 ACRES

PUBLIC HUNTING AND FISHING

VICINITY MAP

LEGEND

GRASSLAND

BRUSHLAND

WOODLAND

POND

BOAT RAMP

LATRINE

DRINKING WATER

PAVED ROAD

AREA HEADQUARTERS

OXBOW LAKE

PARKING

PARKING

TRINITY ROAD

SCHICK ROAD

SCHICK ROAD

EVANSPORT ROAD

TIFFIN   RIVER

MUD   CREEK

MUD   CREEK

STATE ROUTE 15

DEFIANCE 5 MILES

BRYAN 9 MILES

SCALE IN FEET

0   660   1320

N

6. INDEPENDANCE DAM STATE PARK
Route 4, Ohio SP 424
Box 27722
Defiance, Ohio 43512
(419) 784-3263

The 604 acre state park occupies a narrow strip of land six miles long and about 50 yards wide, lying between Ohio 424 and the Maumee River, three miles east of Defiance. The original dam supplied water for the Miami-Erie and Wabash canals of the early to mid-19th century. The three mile linear Miami & Erie Canal Towpath Trail provides level easy walking. Picnicking with shelters, fishing, boating, launch ramp, and camping are other outdoor enjoyments.

While in the Defiance area consider visiting the historic Au Glaize Village Farm Museum at Kramer Road, 0.5 mile south of US 24 and the Defiance city parks of Pontiac, Ft. Defiance, and Kingsbury; all three are located at the confluence of the Au Glaize and Maumee rivers.

Open Year Around

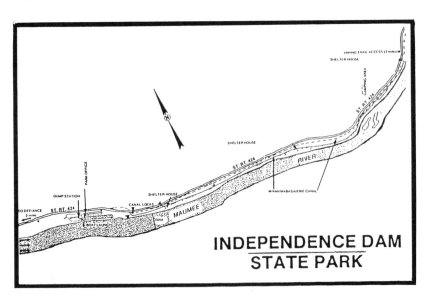

**INDEPENDENCE DAM
STATE PARK**

7. PAULDING PONDS WILDLIFE AREA
c/o Paulding County Commissioners Court House
Paulding, Ohio 45879

The three small man made ponds that were former settling ponds of a sugar beet factory on the outskirts of Paulding give rise to the wildlife area's place name. The 56 acre county owned nature area has a wide variety of wildlife attracted to the wetlands that includes Flatrock Creek, an Au Glaize River tributary. The Paulding County Wildlife Association has developed the preserve as a conservation education area and there are foot trails.

Paulding Ponds is located near the fairgrounds off of CR 107 in Paulding, Ohio, the county seat of Paulding County.

Open Daily, Dawn to Dusk

8. HIESTAND WOODS PARK
Hospital Drive
c/o Van Wert Jaycees
P. O. Box 21
Van Wert, Ohio 45891

An oak-hickory woodland remnant in southeast suburban Van Wert. The Jaycee community park of 20 acres has a developed nature trail in the south end of the maturing woodland alongside a stream. A nice oasis to picnic and there is a playground.

The park entrance is located east of Ohio SR 127 in south Van Wert, Ohio along Hospital Drive across from the golf course and east of the Van Wert County Hospital and the city reservoir where walking is also permitted around the shore.

Open Daily, Dawn to Dusk

9. MIAMI & ERIE CANAL TRAIL
Delphos, Ohio, south to Lake Loramie State Park
c/o Grand Lake St. Marys State Park
Division of Watercraft
834 Edgewater Drive
St. Marys, Ohio 45885
(419) 394-3611

The historic trail follows the former towpath of the canal from Delphos, Ohio, south to Lake Loramie State Park, a distance of 40 miles. Several county and state roads are crossed enroute. Makes a good early spring hike. Portions of the trail vary from urban to wild. Historically the canal was dug by hand, forging a 248 mile waterway between Cincinnati and Toledo, Ohio. Some locks and aqueducts have been restored and historical markers abound. The Belle of St. Mary, a replica canal boat, may be viewed at the municipal park in St. Marys, Ohio. Numerous access points in the communities along the point-to-point trail. The Miami & Erie Canal Trail makes up a segment of the state wide Buckeye Trail.

Open Daily, Dawn to Dusk

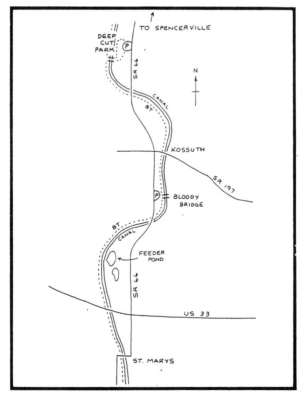

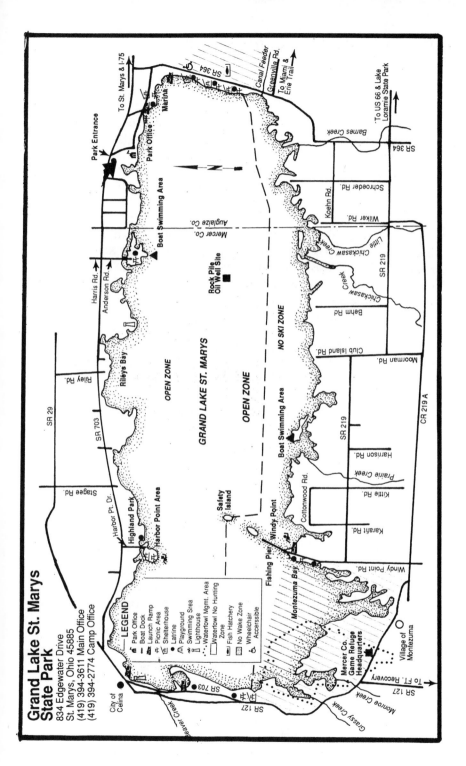

Grand Lake St. Marys
State Park

834 Edgewater Drive
St. Marys, Ohio 45885
(419) 394-3611 Main Office
(419) 394-2774 Camp Office

LEGEND

🏢 Park Office
⚓ Boat Dock
Launch Ramp
🚻 Picnic Area
Shelterhouse
Latrine
△ Playground
Swimming Area
Lighthouse
Waterfowl Mgmt. Area
Waterfowl No Hunting Zone
Fish Hatchery
No Wake Zone
♿ Wheelchair Accessible

GRAND LAKE ST. MARYS

OPEN ZONE

OPEN ZONE

NO SKI ZONE

Rock Pile Oil Well Site

Boat Swimming Area

Boat Swimming Area

Safety Island

Fishing Pier

Windy Point

Montezuma Bay

Mercer Co. Game Refuge Headquarters

Village of Montezuma

Rileys Bay

Highland Park

Harbor Point Area

Marina

Park Office

Park Entrance

To St. Marys

Harris Rd.
Anderson Rd.
Riley Rd.
SR 29
SR 703
Stagee Rd.
Harbor Pt. Dr.
SR 703
SR 127
Beaver Creek
City of Celina

To St. Marys & I-75
SR 364
Canal Feeder
Greenville Rd.
To Miami & Erie Trail
Barnes Creek
To US 66 & Lake Loramie State Park
SR 364
Schroeder Rd.
Koehn Rd.
Wilker Rd.
Little Chickasaw Creek
SR 219
Chickasaw Creek
Behm Rd.
Club Island Rd.
Moorman Rd.
CR 219 A
SR 219
Harrison Rd.
Prairie Creek
Kittle Rd.
Cottonwood Rd.
Karafit Rd.
Windy Point Rd.
Monroe Creek
Grassy Creek
SR 127
To Ft. Recovery

Mercer Co.
Auglaize Co.

10. GRAND LAKE ST. MARYS STATE PARK
834 Edgewater Drive Box 308
St. Marys, Ohio 45885
(419) 394-3611

In addition to the 420 acre state park which is scattered around the lakeshore in separate tracts, there are several local parklands located on the 52 mile shore of Grand Lake St. Marys. The lake was built during the late 1830's as a feeder lake for the Miami-Erie Canal. Actually there are no designated trails, but the open spaces on the vast 13,500 acre lake are worth seeing.

The city of Celina has several beach parks in Pullman Bay and the birding is superb. The 1,408 acre Mercer County Game Refuge on the southwest shore allows bird viewing from the parking lots. The state park entrance, headquarters and campground lies south of Ohio 703 at the northeast shore and a tourable state fish hatchery is on the east shore. There are even lighthouses.

West of the lake, bicyclists will enjoy the 4.5 mile paved path between Celina at Schunck Road and Coldwater, Ohio created from an abandoned rail line.

Ohio State Road access highways include 703, 364, 219, and 127 .

Open Year Around

11. COPPESS NATURE SANCTUARY
Ohio 47 & Young Road South
Darke County Park District
Greenville, Ohio 45331
(513) 548-0165

The Nature Conservancy originally purchased the land which is now owned and managed by the Darke County Park District. The nature walk through the 32 acre beech-maple forest is a 0.5 mile loop on flat terrain.

From Greenville, Ohio, the county seat, go northwest on Ohio 49 to the junction with Ohio 47. Go west two miles on Ohio 47 to Young Road and turn left/south. Continue about 0.33 mile to the preserve parking lot on the east side of Young Road. The preserve is located midway between Ansonia, Ohio and Union City, Ohio.

Open Daily, Dawn to Dusk

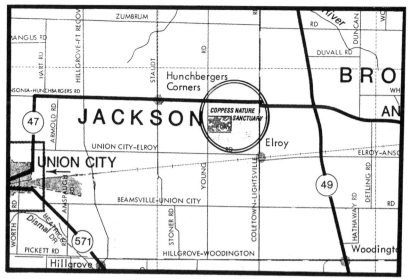

Coppess Nature Sanctuary

12. LAKE LORAMIE STATE PARK
11221 Ohio SR 362
Minster, Ohio 45865-9311
(513) 295-2011

Like Grand Lake St. Marys, Lake Loramie was constructed as a feeder dam lake for the Miami-Erie Canal of the early to mid-1800s. The 1,655 acre reservoir is surrounded by 400 acres of public lands. There are eight miles of trails and the best long distance hike is the 4.5 Blackberry Island Trail. A footbridge leads to the island and the trail loops about the east end.

Lake Loramie State Park is also the south terminus of the 40 mile long Miami-Erie Canal Trail and also part of the statewide Buckeye Trail and the North Country National Scenic Trail There is also picnicking, shelters, swimming, fishing, boating, launch ramp, winter recreation and camping.

From I-75 exit at Anna, Ohio and drive west on Ohio 119, crossing Ohio 29. Continue west on Ohio 363 to Minister, Ohio and Ohio 66. Turn south on Ohio 66 and drive south to the edge of Minister and turn left/east on Canal Street and proceed to Ohio 362. Turn south/right and drive to the park entrance (map on page 414-15).

Open Daily

Lake Loramie State Park

☐ Public Hunting Area

Lake Loramie State Park

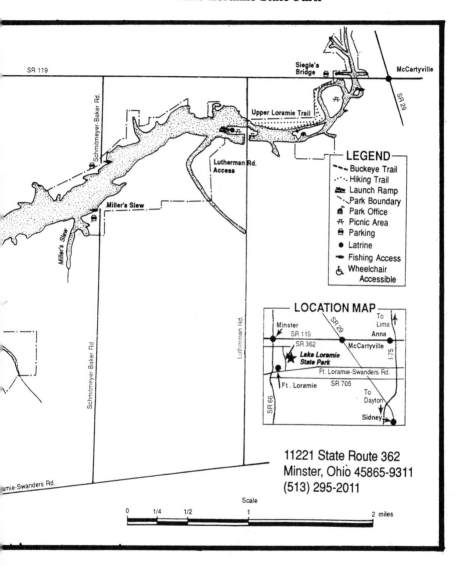

SR 119

Siegle's
Bridge

McCartyville

SR 29

Upper Loramie Trail

Lutherman Rd.
Access

Miller's Slew

Miller's Slew

Schmitmeyer-Baker Rd.

Schmitmeyer-Baker Rd.

Lutherman Rd.

amie-Swanders Rd.

LEGEND

- ➤➤ Buckeye Trail
- ⋯ Hiking Trail
- ⚓ Launch Ramp
- Park Boundary
- ⌂ Park Office
- ⅌ Picnic Area
- ⛟ Parking
- ● Latrine
- ➤ Fishing Access
- ♿ Wheelchair
  Accessible

LOCATION MAP

Minster
SR 119

SR 362

Fo Loramie-Swanders Rd.

Ft. Loramie   SR 705

SR 66

To
Lima

Anna

McCartyville

I-75

SR 29

**Lake Loramie
State Park**

To
Dayton

Sidney

**11221 State Route 362
Minster, Ohio 45865-9311
(513) 295-2011**

Scale

0   1/4   1/2   1   2 miles

413

13. GREENVILLE, OHIO PARKS & PRESERVE
c/o Greenville Park & Recreation Department
Greenville, Ohio 45331
(513) 548-1314

The site of present day Greenville is important in the history of early
Ohio and this pioneer history is reflected in the city's parks. Bordering
Greenville Creek along Wilson Drive is the Treaty of Greenville State
Park and the 90 acre city Memorial Park along Park and Harmon Drives.
The vast open green space with lagoons and ponds commemorates the
1795 U.S. and Indian Treaty that was signed at the old fort with General
Wayne. The main park entrance is from Ohio 118/Broadway.

Tecumseh Point Walkway, a triangular shaped park at the confluence of
Greenville and Mud creeks, is also rich in historical significance. The site
was Chief Tecumseh's Prophetstown encampment during the summer of
1795. There are trails along and over Greenville Creek. Entrance to
Tecumseh Point Walkway from Walnut Street foot bridge, north of Main
Street, east of the circle. Future plans are to develop a continuation of the
walkway southeast along Mud Creek to the Darke County Park District
owned Prairie Preserve, south of Winchester Avenue/Ohio 502.

Another historic site five miles southwest of Greenville, Ohio at Ft.
Jefferson, Ohio is one of a series of frontier forts along the west edge of
pioneer Ohio. The park is on a knoll at the corners of Ohio 121 and
Weavers-Ft. Jefferson Road.

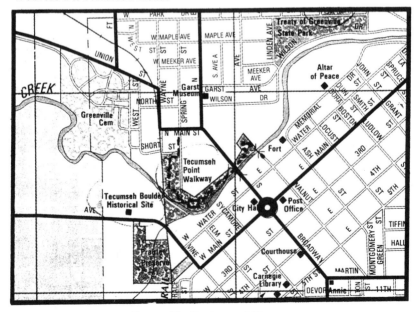

14. ROUTZONG PRESERVE
Routzong Road N from Ohio 571
Darke County Park District
Greenville, Ohio 45331
(513) 548-0165

This 55 acre old growth forest preserve is located on Routzong Road just over five miles southeast of Greenville, Ohio off Ohio SR 571. Visitors may walk on paths which wind through the level to gently rolling land.

The parking lot is located on the west side of Routzong Road, about 0.2 mile from Ohio 571, before McCool Road east of Greenville, Ohio. Park and enter a small pasture and walk 0.2 mile to the trail through seasonally wet mixed woods.

Open Daily, Dawn to Dusk

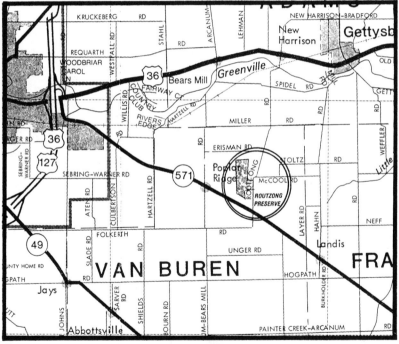

Routzong Preserve

15. STILLWATER PRAIRIE RESERVE
Ohio SR 185 & Ohio SR 48
Miami County Park District
Troy, Ohio

The 217 acre Miami County reserve is a western Ohio tallgrass prairie of bluestem grasses and wildflowers along the banks of the Stillwater River, a state designated scenic river. There are two and more miles of trail and boardwalk loops that begin and end at the two parking lots. The trail crosses the river at one point along the mile long river reserve floodplain. There are also old fields, mature forest, marsh and pond. Picnicking with shelters.

To reach Stillwater Prairie Reserve from I-75 exit onto US 36 west and drive to Piqua, Ohio. Continue west on Ohio 185, 8.5 miles, crossing Ohio 48. The reserve lies 1.5 miles west of the junction of the state roads 185 and 48.

Open Daily, Dawn to Dusk

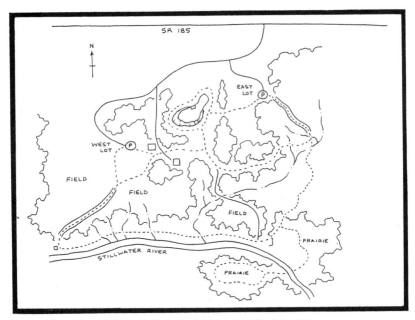

STILLWATER PRAIRIE PRESERVE

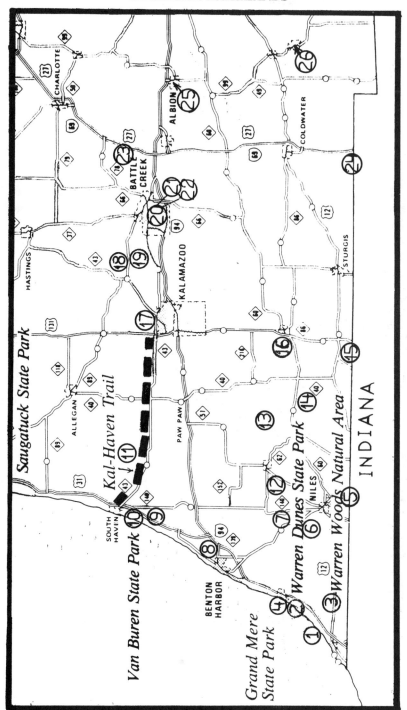

1. ROBINSON PRESERVE

c/o The Nature Conservancy
Michigan Chapter
2840 East Grand River Avenue. Suite 5
East Lansing, Michigan 48823
(517) 332-1741

Fifty acres of level oak savanna uplands grade north to thirty acres of climax beech-maple forest along deep ravines cut by woodland streams. A service road trail leads north from the parking area on East Road to the lush woodland trails.

To reach Robinson Preserve from I-94 exit 6 north and proceed about two miles to Lakeside, Michigan. From Lakeside turn right/ east onto East Road and drive just over one mile to the entrance which is on the left/north side of East Road. The entrance is marked by a routed sign.

Open Daily, Dawn to Dusk

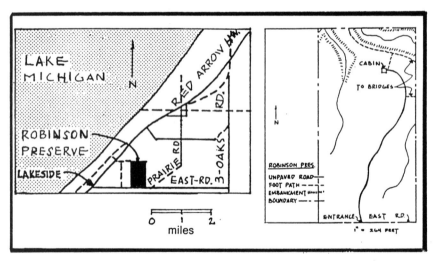

Robinson Preserve

2. WARREN DUNES STATE PARK
Route 1, Red Arrow Highway
Sawyer, Michigan 49125
(616) 426-4013

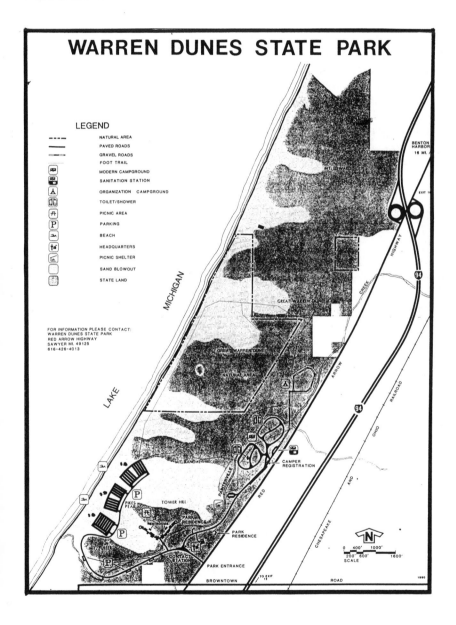

419

The massive dunes of this Michigan state park are well known by many dune-loving Hoosiers. Besides the two miles of beach strand there are nature trails that explore the Great Warren Dune Natural Area, Mt. Randall, Mt. Fuller, Mt. Edward, Tower Hill, Pikes Peak and Painterville Creek.

In addition to hiking, the park offers x-country skiing, tobaggoning, wind surfing, hang gliding, swimming, beach house, picnicking, playgrounds, concessions and camping.

Warren Dunes is located three miles southeast of Bridgman, Michigan. From I-94 exit 16 west and south on Red Arrow Highway to the park entrance.

Open Daily, Admission Fee

3. WARREN WOODS NATURAL AREA

Warren Woods & Elm Valley Roads
Three Oaks, Michigan
c/o Warren Dunes State Park
Route 1, Red Arrow Highway
Sawyer, Michigan 49125
(616) 426-4013

A few miles south of Warren Dunes State Park is the 480 acre Warren Woods Natural Area that contains a virgin beech-maple climax forest which is accessible along walking paths. The primeval woods was bought by E. K. Warren in 1879 to preserve what has come to be southwest Michigan's last stand of untouched forest. The National Natural Landmark is administered by Warren Dunes State Park, as is Grand Mere State Park.

From I-94 exit 12 onto Sawyer Road and drive west 0.5 mile to Three Oaks Road and turn south/left. Follow Three Oaks Road about five miles to Warren Woods Road, just about one mile north of the community of Three Oaks and US 12. Turn west/right on Warren Woods Road and drive one mile to the preserve on the south side of the county road where there are pullouts. A second entry and parking area is located on Elm Valley Road, one mile south, where there is a picnicking area.

Open Daily, Dawn to Dusk

4. GRAND MERE STATE PARK & NATURE AREA
Willow Road
Stevensville, Michigan 49127
c/o Warren Dunes State Park
Route 1, Red Arrow Highway
Sawyer, Michigan 49125
(616) 426-4013

North of Warren Dunes State Park, about six road miles are 985 acres more of sand dunes and beach that are publicly accessible state lands. Several trails interwind along the wooded dunes, lakeshore and wetlands of this National Natural Landmark. The interdunal ponds are an interesting feature and include a cranberry bog. Natural groves of eastern hemlock conifers thrive and the birding is especially good in spring and fall when migrating.

Grand Mere may be reached from I-94 exit 22 at Stevensville, Michigan by driving south on Thornton Road (adjacent west of I-94) about two miles to Willow Road and the park entrance. Day-users are required to have a daily permit displayed on their windshield. There is no camping. Trails begin and end at the parking lot.

Open Daily, Day-Use Only, Admission Fee, Entry Permit Required

GRAND MERE STATE PARK

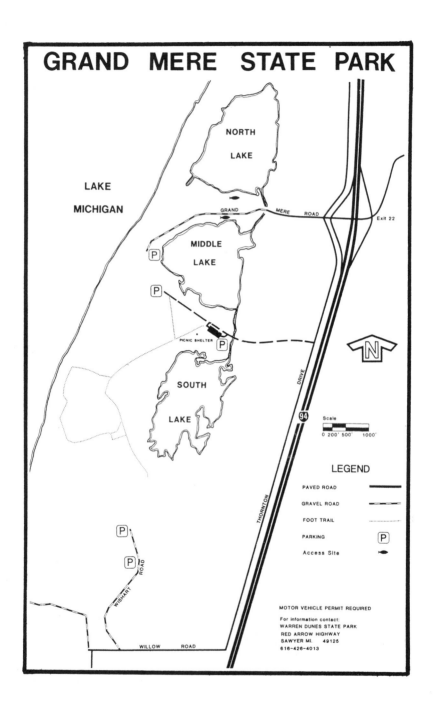

NORTH LAKE

LAKE MICHIGAN

GRAND MERE ROAD

Exit 22

MIDDLE LAKE

PICNIC SHELTER

SOUTH LAKE

N

94

Scale
0 200' 500' 1000'

THORNTON DRIVE

WISHART ROAD

WILLOW ROAD

LEGEND

PAVED ROAD	━━━━
GRAVEL ROAD	┄┄┄
FOOT TRAIL	··········
PARKING	P
Access Site	➤

MOTOR VEHICLE PERMIT REQUIRED

For information contact:
WARREN DUNES STATE PARK
RED ARROW HIGHWAY
SAWYER MI.   49125
616-426-4013

422

5. MADELINE BERTRAND COUNTY PARK

3038 Adams Road
Niles, Michigan 49120
(616) 683-8280
(616) 983-7111, ext. 435

Named in honor of a Potawatomi woman, this Berrien County park borders St. Patricks (St. Joseph County, Indiana) County Park, north of South Bend, Indiana. Besides park boundaries, hiking trails are also shared by the bi-state county parks. Bertrand Park also offers x-country skiing, a visitor center, naturalist, picnicking with shelters, playground, swimming, canoeing and a popular 18 hole frisbee disc golf course.

The park entrance is west of US 33, south of Niles, Michigan. Follow State Line Road west to Adams Road and turn north.

Open Year Around
Admission Fee, Closed gate Mondays

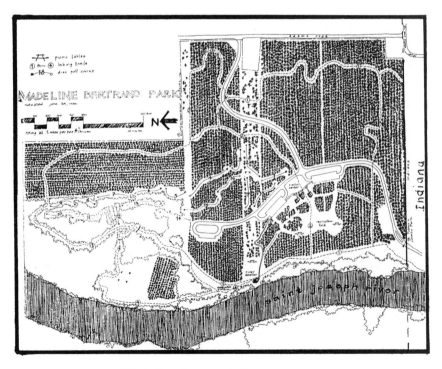

Madeline Bertrand County Park

6. FERNWOOD

13988 Range Line Road
Niles, Michigan 49120
(616) 695-6491
(616) 683-8653

Fernwood is a privately run nature center, botanic garden, and arts and crafts center between Niles and Buchanan, Michigan, along the east bank of the St. Joseph River. The 105 acre sanctuary features numerous beautiful theme gardens, a visitors center, tea room, library, classrooms and a gift shop, art and pottery studios and a fern house. Twelve nature trails cover three miles and Arboretum Trail is the longest. Woodlands, prairie, ravines and floodplain surround the formal garden area. Fern Trail has 100 varieties of ferns alongside the path. Classes, lectures and workshops are open to the public

Fernwood is easy to reach from Indiana via the US 31 bypass around South Bend. Fernwood is located northeast of Buchanan, Michigan via River Road or Geyer Road to Range line Road. Follow the directional signs from the US 31 bypass along the east bank of the St. Joseph River.

Open Year Around
Monday - Friday 9 am - 5 pm
Saturday 9 am - 6 pm; Sunday Noon - 6 pm
Winter Hours Vary, November - March
Admission Fee, Membership Available

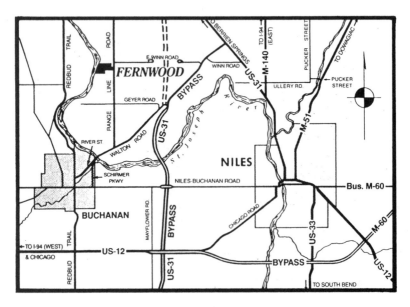

7. LOVE CREEK COUNTY PARK & NATURE CENTER
9228 Huckleberry Road
Berrien Center, Michigan 49102
(616) 471-2617

Nearly six miles of hiking/skiing trails cut thru the 100 acres of creeks, marshes, meadows and forests of this Berrien County park. The year round naturalist can usually be found at the nature center adjacent west of the parking area, where there are also exhibits, a classroom, bird observation window and a nature book shop. The thirteen hiking trails fan out from the nature center to explore the Love Creek valley and adjoining uplands.

Love Creek County Park is located east of Berrien Springs, Michigan between Pokagon and Deans Hill Roads. From Berrien Springs, drive east and south on US 31 across the St. Joseph River about 0.5 mile to Pokagon Road and turn left/north and east. Continue on Pokagon Road two miles to Huckleberry Road and turn north/left. The entrance is located one mile north and on the west/left side of Huckleberry Road.

Trails Open Daily, Dawn to Dusk
Nature Center Hours:
Tuesday & Thursday 11 am - 5 pm; Wednesday & Friday 9 am - 5 pm
Saturday 11 am - 5 pm; Sunday 11 am - 6 pm
Closed Mondays, Admission Fee

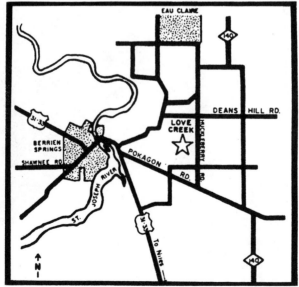

Love Creek County Park & Nature Center

LOVE CREEK COUNTY PARK TRAIL MAP

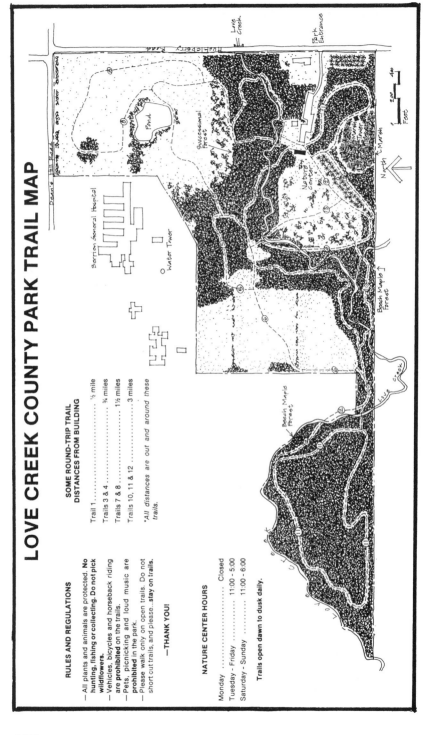

RULES AND REGULATIONS

— All plants and animals are protected. **No hunting, fishing or collecting. Do not pick wildflowers.**
— Vehicles, bicycles and horseback riding are **prohibited** on the trails.
— Pets, picnicking and loud music are **prohibited** in the park.
— Please walk only on open trails. Do not short cut trails, and please...**stay on trails.**

—THANK YOU!

NATURE CENTER HOURS

Monday	Closed
Tuesday - Friday	11:00 - 5:00
Saturday - Sunday	11:00 - 6:00

Trails open dawn to dusk daily.

SOME ROUND-TRIP TRAIL DISTANCES FROM BUILDING

Trail 1	½ mile
Trails 3 & 4	¾ miles
Trails 7 & 8	1½ miles
Trails 10, 11 & 12	3 miles

*All distances are out and around these trails.

Huckleberry Road

Berrien General Hospital

Water Tower

Pond

Successional Forest

Nature Center

North Marsh

Love Creek

Park Entrance

Beech Maple Forest

Beech Maple Forest

200   400
Feet

8. SARETT NATURE CENTER
2300 Benton Harbor Road
Benton Harbor, Michigan 49022
(616) 927-4832

The 362 acre wildlife sanctuary is an educational center of the Michigan Audubon Society. Five trails total nearly six miles along the Paw Paw River, Alder Creek and surrounding uplands. Elevated boardwalks and foot bridges traverse floodplains, marshes, bogs, and streams where observation towers provide bird's eye views of the sanctuary and there are several resting benches at scenic spots. Michigan's champion red oak tree resides at Sarett. The nature center adjacent to the parking area contains meeting rooms, exhibits and a gift shop. A trail guide is available.

Sarett Nature Center is situated northeast of Benton Harbor, Michigan. From the intersection of I-94 and I-196/US 31 drive north on I-196 about one mile to the first exit, Red Arrow Highway. Turn southwest on Red Arrow Highway and drive approximately 0.5 mile to Benton Harbor Road. Turn north/right and drive one mile to the entrance on the west side of the paved road.

Trails Open, Dawn to Dusk
Nature Center Hours: Tuesday-Friday 9 am - 5 pm
Saturday 10 am - 5 pm; Sunday 1 pm - 5 pm; Closed Monday
Membership Available, Donations Accepted

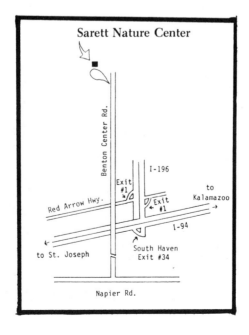

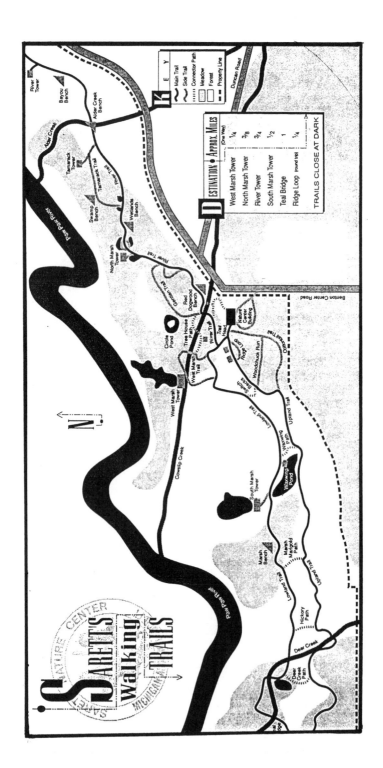

Sarett's
Walking
TRAILS

SARETT NATURE CENTER
MICHIGAN

N →

KEY
- Main Trail
- Side Trail
- Connector Path
- Meadow
- Forest
- Property Line

DESTINATION	APPROX. MILES (One Way)
West Marsh Tower	1/4
North Marsh Tower	3/8
River Tower	3/4
South Marsh Tower	1/2
Teal Bridge	1
Ridge Loop (round trip)	1/4

TRAILS CLOSE AT DARK

Duncan Road

Benton Center Road

River Tower
Bayou Bench
Alder Creek Bench
Alder Creek
Tamarack Bench
Tamarack Trail
Paw Paw River
Swamp Bench
Wetlands Bench
North Marsh Tower
River Trail
Gentian Trail
Red Dogwood Bench
Circle Pond
Tree House Path
Trail Head
Nature Center Building
River Trail
Roost
Woodchuck Run
Sassafras Trail
West Marsh Trail
West Marsh Tower
Cowslip Creek
Lowland Trail
Waxwing Path
Waxwing Pond
South Marsh Tower
Upland Trail
Marsh Bench
Marsh Marigold Path
Paw Paw River
Lowland Trail
Upland Trail
Hickory Path
Deer Creek
Deer Creek Path

9. ROSS PRESERVE

c/o The Nature Conservancy
Michigan Chapter
2840 East Grand Avenue, Suite 5
East Lansing, Michigan 48823
(517) 332-1741

Three coastal plain marshes feature plants that are normally found growing in marshes along the Atlantic Coastal seaboard. Oak forest, hemlock forest, swamp forest, and old field also comprise the 1,214 acre preserve that was once the shoreline of preglacial Lake Nipissing. A linear foot trail crosses a foot bridge over Brandywine Creek into the preserve, heading southwest, skirting the marshes.

From I-196 exit 13 at Covert, Michigan go east on 32nd Avenue two miles to 76th Street and turn right/south. Proceed south on 76th Street 1.5 miles to 38th Street and turn right/west. Continue 2.25 miles on 38th Street to the road's end and park along the roadside.

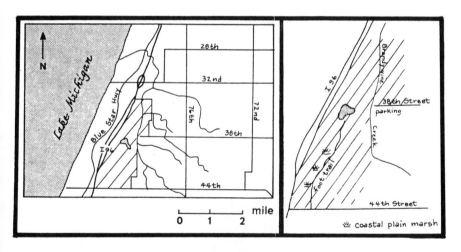

Ross Preserve

10. VAN BUREN STATE PARK
23960 Ruggles Road
P. O. Box 122-B
South Haven, Michigan 49090
(616) 637-2788

Compared to the lakeside state parks located further south at Warren Dunes and Grand Mere, Van Buren is smaller and seemingly more developed. The 326 acre dune and woods park has several nature trails and a 0.75 mile long beach. The state beach park is the westernmost terminus of the 34 mile Kal-Haven bike/hike trail currently under development. The proposed Blossomland River Trail will connect the Kal-Haven Trail with a hiking/biking trail to South Bend, Indiana. Van Buren also offers swimming, lifeguards, a beachhouse, picnicking, shelters, camping and concessions.

To reach Van Buren State Park from I-196 exit 18 west, five miles south of South Haven. The park entrance is located off of US 31/Blue Star Highway at Ruggles Road. Follow directional signs.

Open Year Around
Day Use Hours: 8 am - 10 pm
Admission Fee, Kal-Haven Trail Fee

Dunes along Lake Michigan

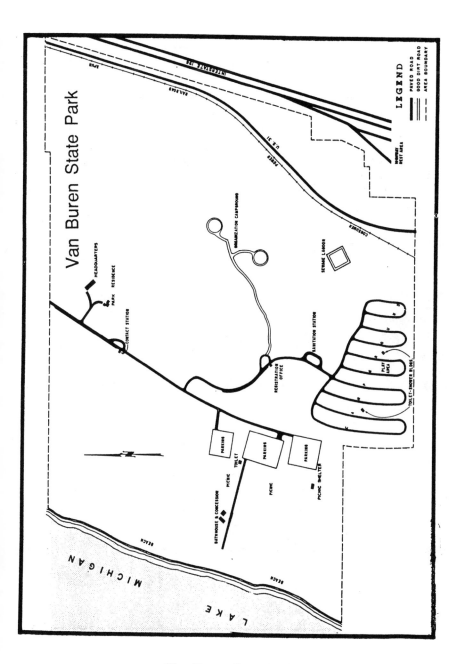

Van Buren State Park

11. KAL-HAVEN TRAIL SESQUICENTENNIAL STATE PARK
c/o Van Buren State Park
23960 Ruggles Road
South Haven, Michigan 49090
(616) 637-4984
(616) 637-2788

The Kal-Haven Trail is a scenic 34 mile long linear biking & hiking trail (also horses, skiing and snowmobiles) that connects Kalamazoo with South Haven on Lake Michigan via a converted abandoned railroad track. The trail, a multi-use recreational trail, provides a corridor of forests, open fields, wetlands, and stream crossings including the Black River near South Haven.

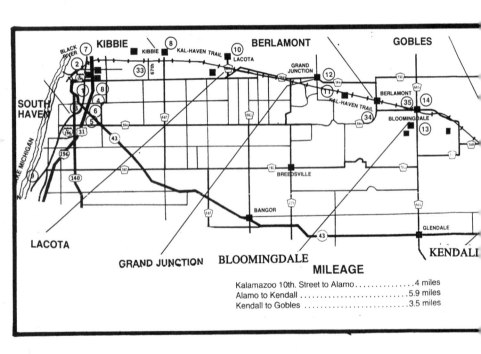

MILEAGE

Kalamazoo 10th. Street to Alamo . . . . 4 miles
Alamo to Kendall . . . . 5.9 miles
Kendall to Gobles . . . . 3.5 miles

KAL-HAVEN TRAIL

The east terminus is located on 10th Street in Oshtemo Township near the city of Kalamazoo's west side. The community of Bloomingdale is the mid-point of the trail. The west terminus is near the lake in South Haven. Individual and family passes are available at the east and west trailheads, Bloomingdale, and any business displaying the trail logo. Since no tax dollars are spent for trail operations, all funding comes from user fees and private donations.

Trail Open
Sunrise to 10 pm Year Around
Admission Fee

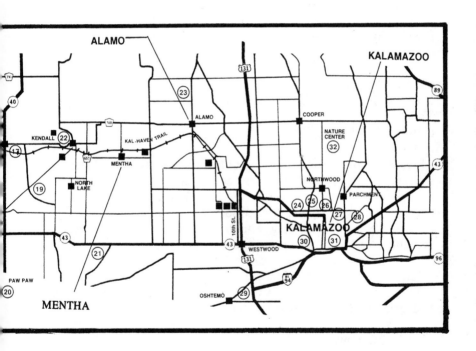

KAL-HAVEN TRAIL

12. DOWAGIAC WOODS
c/o Michigan Nature Association
P. O. Box 102
Avoca, Michigan 48006

The 220 acre sanctuary is owned and managed by the Michigan Nature Association and represents one of the largest undisturbed deciduous woodland tracts left in the Wolverine state. Four hundred known plants including 45 different tree species and 20 kinds of ferns thrive. Three trails explore the woodlands. Spring wildflowers and fall foliage are exceptional. Fine birding forest.

From the community of Dowagiac, go west on M-62 for about four miles to Sink Road and turn south/left. Continue on Sink Road and drive one mile to Frost Road and turn east/left. Proceed on Frost Road one mile to the parking area on the north side of the road.

Open Daily, Dawn to Dusk

13. RUSS FOREST
Marcellus Highway & Decatur Road
Volinia, Michigan
(616) 445-8611

Fred Russ donated over 700 acres of hardwood forest to Michigan State University, which uses the forest as a research station for forestry management. Visitors are welcome to hike/ski the forest trails and visit the historic Newton House. A small portion of the forest is a Cass County Park where trails, picnicking with shelters and a playground are also available. A Class A trout stream flows through this national landmark.

Russ Forest is located midway between Dowagiac and Marcellus, Michigan in north central Cass County. The entrance is west of Volinia, Michigan on Marcellus Highway, 0.4 mile east of Decatur Road.

Open Daily, Dawn to Dusk

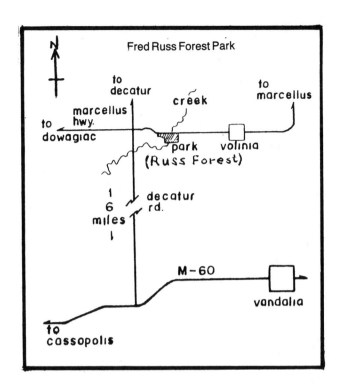

14. DR. T. K. LAWLESS COUNTY PARK
15122 Monkey Run Street
Vandalia, Michigan 49095
(616) 476-2730
(616) 445-8611

Seven trails total over five miles of hiking/skiing in this east central Cass County park of 640 acres. The color coded trails penetrate and explore the upland forest and shorelines of Hogback and Doane lakes. Picnicking with shelters, playfields and playground facilities have been developed

The county park is located nine miles east of Cassopolis on M-60. Turn south on Lewis Lake Road, go one mile and turn on Monkey Run Road east to the park entrance. Follow the park signs (location 14 on map).

Crane Pond State Game Area lies north of M-60 in separate tracts and Forked Lake is the closest best accessible parcel. From M-60 drive north on Born Street to Savage Road north (located in plat 20 on map).

Open Daily, Dawn to Dusk, Admission Fee

435

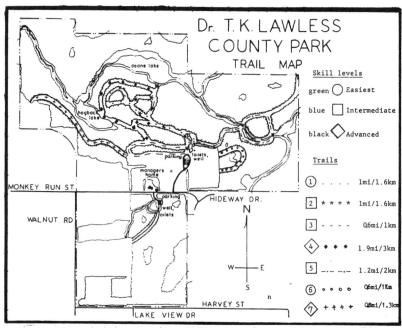

Dr. T.K. LAWLESS COUNTY PARK
TRAIL MAP

<u>Skill levels</u>

green ◯ Easiest

blue ▢ Intermediate

black ◇ Advanced

<u>Trails</u>

① 1mi/1.6km

② * * * * 1mi/1.6km

③ - - - - 0.6mi/1km

④ ◆ ◆ ◆ 1.9mi/3km

⑤ —..—..— 1.2mi/2km

⑥ ◦ ◦ ◦ ◦ 0.6mi/1Km

⑦ + + + + 0.8mi/1.3km

doane lake

hogback lake

parking toilets, well

managers home

MONKEY RUN ST.

WALNUT RD

parking well toilets

HIDEAWAY DR.

N

W — E

S

HARVEY ST

LAKE VIEW DR.

Dr. T.K. Lawless County Park & Crane Pond State Game Area

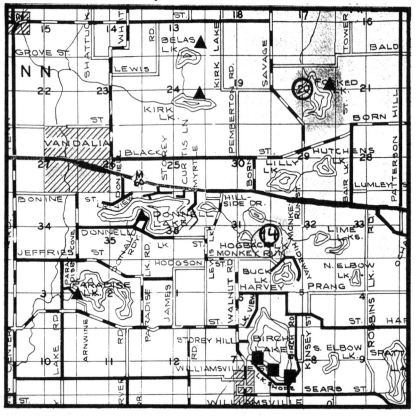

15. WHITE PIGEON RIVER NATURE SANCTUARY

Burke & Silver Creek Roads
White Pigeon, Michigan 49099
c/o Michigan Nature Association
P. O. Box 102, Avoca, Michigan 48006

Situated one mile north of the Indiana-Michigan state line, the White Pigeon Nature Sanctuary is 58 acres of floodplain, old river channels, lagoons, steep slopes and bluffs. A nature trail accesses the sanctuary which is the summer home of 55 bird species including the rare prothonotary warbler or golden swamp warbler which prefers to nest in dead tree cavities.

To reach the sanctuary drive two miles west from the junction of US 12 and US 131 on US 12 to Burke Road. Turn south/left on Burke Road and continue one mile to the junction with Silver Creek Road and the property's west boundary (plat location 16 on map). Park alongside the road. The trail begins beyond the gate.

Nearly a mile west on Silver Creek Road is <u>Vistula Park</u>, a riverside county facility that offers picnicking, fishing and a canoe launch on the White Pigeon River.

Open Daily, Dawn to Dusk

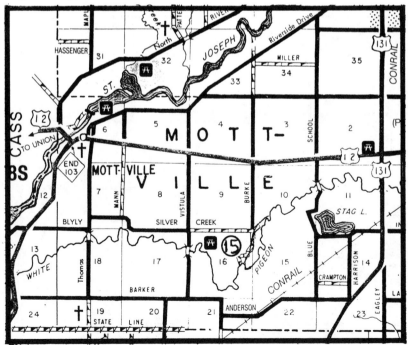

White Pigeon River Nature Sanctuary

16. MEYER BROADWAY & COON HOLLOW PARKS

Roberts & West Broadway Roads
Three River, Michigan 49093
(616) 467-6361
(616) 273-4444

The 149 acre St. Joseph County park features a three mile hiking/skiing trail that follows the perimeter of this nature oriented facility that also serves as a county nursery. Winter sports such as snow tubing, ice skating and hockey and x-country skiing are popular pursuits. Ecology tours are given and a bluebird trail has been established. Picnicking, playfields and courts are also available.

The county park is located west of US 131 bypass from Three Rivers on Broadway or Coon Hollow roads.

The St. Joseph County Parks and Recreation Department has several small natural parks scattered throughout the county. For more information, contact the department at P. O. Box 427, Centreville, Michigan 49032 (61.6) 467-6361 or the River Country Tourism Council, Box 70, 150 W. Main, Centreville, Michigan (616) 467-4505 or (616) 447-2821.

Open Daily 10 am - 6 pm

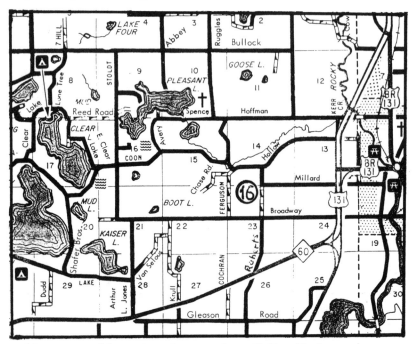

Meyer Broadway & Coon Hollow Parks

17. KALAMAZOO NATURE CENTER
7000 North Westnedge Avenue
Kalamazoo, Michigan 49007
(616) 381-1574

In size, the Kalamazoo Nature Center is the largest nature center in Michigan and its facilities and programs are second to none. Several miles of nature trails lead to a rich variety of demonstration areas as well as the center's natural areas. Separated by North Westnedge Avenue, the property is divided into two unique areas.

Bordering the Kalamazoo River, the west property includes an arboretum, a butterfly hummingbird garden, prairie restoration area, crop land, a barnyard and the interpretive center that includes a library, natural history exhibits, classrooms and a book shop. The east property along West E Avenue features a pioneer 19th century farm, an Indian village and a trout stream. Alternative energy sources are also demonstrated especially solar. The nature center is also the state headquarters for the Michigan Audubon Society.

To reach the nature center from US 131 exit east on Avenue D and continue three miles to Westnedge Avenue. Turn right/south on Westnedge and drive one mile to the entrance on the east side of the road.

Nearly 1.5 miles south of the nature center on Westnedge Avenue is the 160 acre Maple Glen Park. The Kalamazoo County regional park has walking trails that cover the natural areas of this green space.

Additional nature-oriented parklands in Kalamazoo County include River Oaks, Coldbrook, Scotts Mill, Prairie View, West Lake Nature Preserve, Fort Custer State Recreation Area and Gourdneck State Game Area.

Open Year Around
Nature Center Hours:
Monday-Saturday 9 am - 5 pm
Sunday 1 pm - 5 pm
Main Gates Close at 6 pm
Closed Thanksgiving, Christmas, New Year's Day
and Two Weeks in September After Labor Day
Admission Fee, Members Free

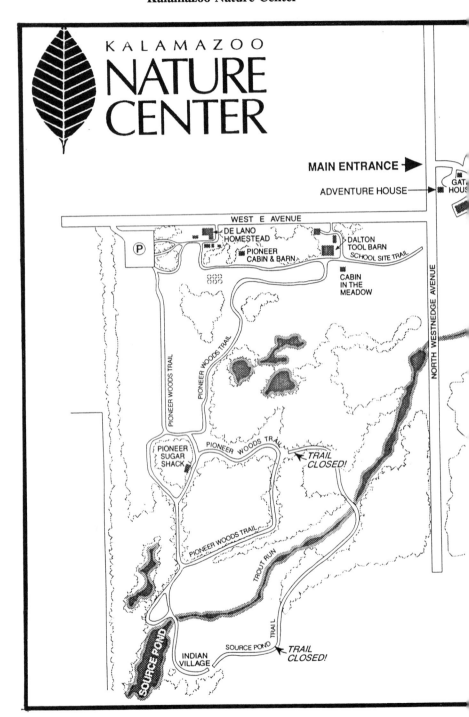

Kalamazoo Nature Center

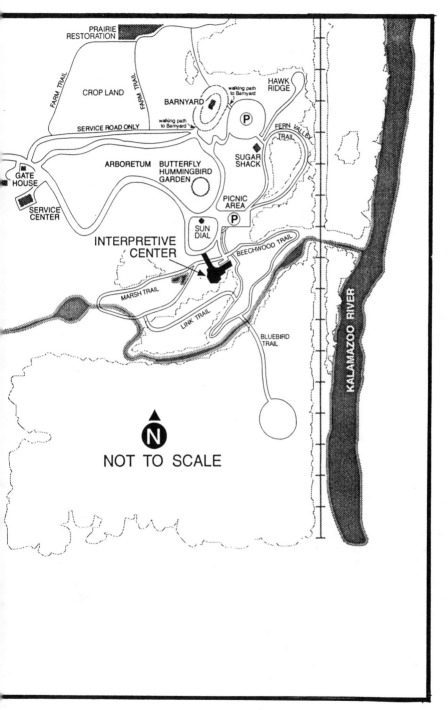

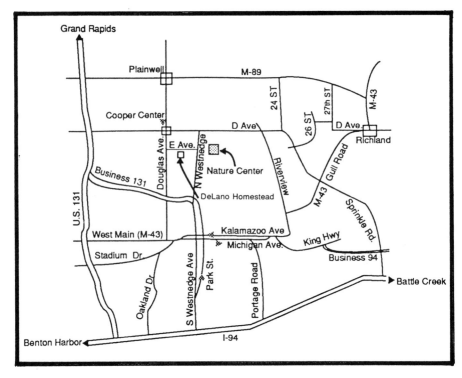

Kalamazoo Nature Center

18. KELLOG BIRD SANCTUARY
Michigan State University
12685 East C Avenue
Augusta, Michigan 49012
(616) 671-2510

Located near Gull Lake in northeastern Kalamazoo County, the bird sanctuary had its beginnings in the 1920's when cereal magnate, W. K. Kellogg donated his private refuge to Michigan State University. Paved walkways with barrier free trails allow visitors to observe up close numerous birds of prey in outdoor flight cages. A large number of waterfowl including swans, swim, dive and feed at Wintergreen Lake where the Overlook Museum features displays and exhibits. A bookstore for environmental education has resource materials and gifts.

To reach the bird sanctuary from M-89 north of Augusta, Michigan turn north on 40th Street and drive one mile to C Avenue. Turn left/west on C Avenue and drive 0.25 mile to the entrance and parking.

Open Daily
Summer Hours: May - October 9 am - Dusk
Winter Hours: November - April 9 am - 5 pm
Admission Fee

19. KELLOG FOREST
Michigan State University
7060 North 42nd Street
Augusta, Michigan 49012
(616) 731-4597

Southwest of the Kellogg Bird Sanctuary a few miles is the Kellogg Forest which is owned by Michigan State University and managed by the Department of Forestry. The 716 acre experimental forest has more than 200 species of trees. The 2.5 miles of auto road provides access to 35 miles of self-guiding hiking trails, many service roads. Plenty of picnicking areas.

Kellogg Forest lies northwest of Augusta, Michigan on the corner of M-89 and 42nd Street. The entrance is on 42nd Street.

Open Daily
Summer Hours: 8 am - 8 pm
Winter Hours: 8 am - 5 pm

20. BATTLE CREEK LINEAR PARK
c/o Battle Creek Parks & Recreation
124 East Michigan Avenue
Battle Creek, Michigan 49017
(616) 966-3431

The Battle Creek Linear Park is a paved vehicle-wide path that meanders for miles through the city along the Kalamazoo and Battle Creek rivers, connecting parks, open spaces, wooded areas, and neighborhoods. Residents and visitors alike enjoy walking, jogging, roller skating, bicycling, picnicking, exercise fitness, playgrounds, fishing and canoeing along the linear parkway.

BATTLE CREEK LINEAR PARK

N

Map Symbols

P	PARKING
K	PICNICKING
L	GAZEBO
I	FITNESS COURT
	SCHOOL
	BRIDGE
	LINEAR PATH
L	PLAYGROUND
	FISHING DECK

Points of Interest

(A) Kellogg World Headquarters
(B) Willard Library
(C) Y-Center
(D) City Hall
(E) Horseshoe Bend/Boardwalk
(F) Riverview Park
(G) Verona Dam
(H) Bailey Park
(I) Kellogg Community College (KCC)

(J) Stouffer/McCamly Arena
(K) Irving Park
(L) Valentine Center
(M) Takasaki Gardens
(N) Federal Center
(O) Leila Arboretum / Kingman Museum
(P) Union Pump
(Q) W.K. Kellogg Foundation Headquarters

There are four color coded loops of which the longest is over ten miles. The linear park also connects cultural centers such as the Takasaki Gardens and the Leila Arboretum and Kingman Museum of Natural History. Additional connecting sites include the Willard Library, Horseshoe Bend/Boardwalk, Riverview Park, Verona Dam, Bailey Park, Kellogg Community College, Irving Park, Valentine Center and Union Pump.

Open Daily, Dawn to Dusk

21. LEILA ARBORETUM & KINGMAN MUSEUM OF NATURAL HISTORY
West Michigan Avenue/M-89 at 20th Street
Battle Creek, Michigan 49017
(616) 969-0270 arboretum society
(616) 965-5117 museum

The Leila Arboretum is a 72 acre Battle Creek city park which was given to the city in 1922 by Mrs. Leila Post Montgomery. The majority of the plantings occurred around 1928 in the design of a historic English landscape garden. There are exceptional collections of mature conifers, demonstration sun and shade perennials with several new garden displays planned in the future for this rolling acreage. There is a 0.75 mile self-guiding Deciduous Tree Trail.

Located on the arboretum grounds is the Kingman Museum of Natural History which was built in 1933. The three floors of the museum features hands-on exhibits focusing on natural history, a planetarium, library, and "Fun to Discover" displays, plus a gift shop. (See Battle Creek Linear Park map for location).

Arboretum Grounds
Open Dawn to Dusk
Museum Hours:
Tuesday - Saturday 9 am - 5 pm
Sunday 1 pm - 5 pm
Closed Monday Except July & August
Admission Fee for Museum

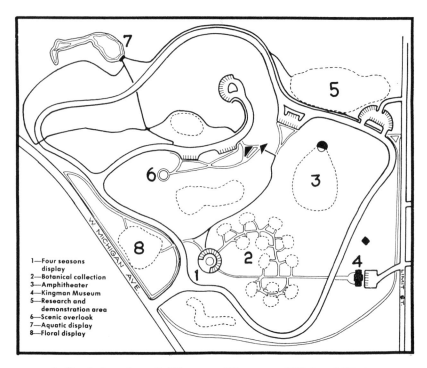

1—Four seasons
    display
2—Botanical collection
3—Amphitheater
4—Kingman Museum
5—Research and
    demonstration area
6—Scenic overlook
7—Aquatic display
8—Floral display

Leila Arboretum & Kingman Museum of Natural History

22. BINDER PARK ZOO
7400 Division Drive
Battle Creek, Michigan 49017-9500
(616) 979-1351

Binder Park Zoo features eighteen exotic and fourteen domestic animal exhibits that are designed with natural settings. Habitat Trail takes visitors down shaded boardwalks and brick paths that wind through the zoo and along Harper Pond. Miller Children's Zoo, a "zoo within a zoo", includes one of the largest dinosaur replicas, domestic animal exhibits and interactive hands-on displays for children. The zoo is involved in a variety of conservation programs to help preserve species like cheetahs, white-handed gibbons, ruffed lemurs, red pandas and other animals. The zoo includes picnicking areas, a restaurant, gift shop and a mini-Z.0.& 0. railroad.

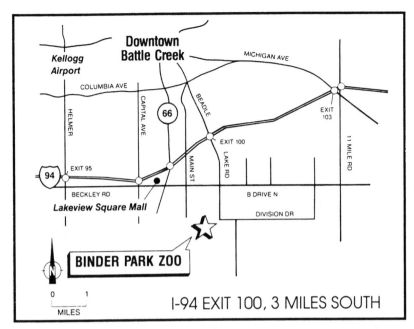

Binder Park Zoo

To reach Binder Park Zoo in Battle Creek from I-94 exit 100 south onto Beadle Lake Road and drive three miles to the intersection with Division Drive.

Open Daily Mid-April-Mid-October
Zoo Hours:
Monday - Friday 9 am - 5 pm
Saturdays & Holidays 9 am - 6 pm
Sundays 11 am - 6 pm
Admission Fee

23. BERNARD W. BAKER SANCTUARY

16 Mile Road
Convis Township, Calhoun County
c/o Michigan Audubon Society
409 West E. Avenue
Kalamazoo, Michigan 49007

In 1941, Bernard W. Baker, a Muskegon businessman and conservationist, purchased nearly 500 acres of wetlands northeast of Battle Creek known as the Big Marsh and gave the property to the Michigan Audubon Society as a refuge for nesting sandhill cranes. Today the sanctuary has grown to 871 acres and is the largest holding for the state-wide environmental organization. The Iva E. Doty Native Flower Trail begins near the nature center near the parking area. The 1.5 mile trail enters several habitats.

To reach the sanctuary from I-69 exit 42, take the first exit north of I-94 and I-69, and turn left/west on N Drive North a short distance to 16 Mile Road. Turn right/north on 16 Mile Road and proceed 3.3 miles to the property, just north of Garfield Road and east of Big Marsh Lake (plat location 11 on map).

Open Daily, Dawn to Dusk

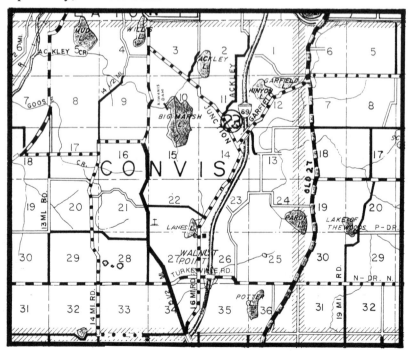

Bernard W. Baker Sanctuary

24. KOPE KON NATURE SANCTUARY & KERSHAW WOODS
Kope Kon Road
Lake George, Michigan
c/o Michigan Nature Association
P. O. Box 102
Avoca, Michigan 48006

Kope Kon and Kershaw Woods are situated on the north shore of Lake George, a body of water straddling the Steuben County, Indiana and Branch County, Michigan state line. Both preserves join to form 56 acres and both are owned and managed by the Michigan Nature Association. Two loop trails are found in the sanctuary and two trails have been established in the adjoining Kershaw Woods. From aquatic shore inland to upland forest, these two preserves represent ecological diversity.

To reach the area from I-69 exit 2, the first Michigan exit beyond the state line, and drive west on Copeland Road a short distance to Old US 27. Turn south on Old US 27 and proceed about two miles to Kope Kon Road and turn right/west. Follow the road about a mile to the dead end.

A few miles north and east, the Coldwater Lake State Park is currently undergoing development and will be open in the next few years.

Open Daily, Dawn to Dusk

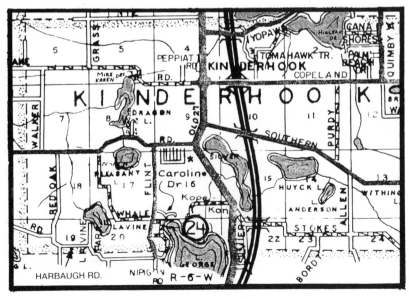

Kope Kon Nature Sanctuary & Kershaw Woods

25. WHITEHOUSE NATURE CENTER
of Albion College
Farley Drive East
Albion, Michigan 49224
(517) 629-2030

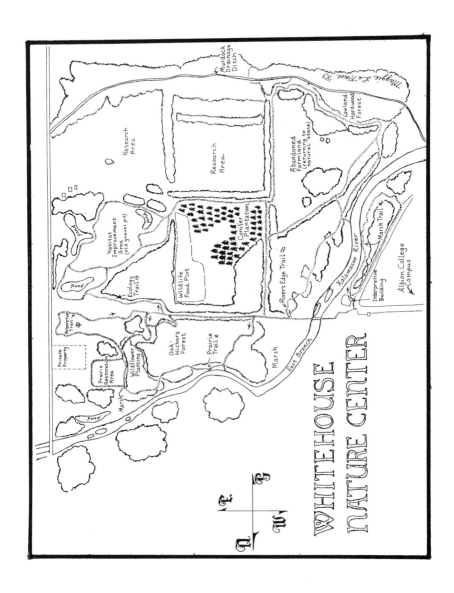

Whitehouse Nature Center

Situated along the banks of the Kalamazoo River, the 135 acre nature center is owned and operated by Albion College. Three self guiding upland nature trails and one marsh trail total over five miles in distance. The paths lead through a variety of natural and man altered habitats. The one mile Arboretum Trail enters an area set aside for Michigan trees and shrubs. The nature center on the west bank adjacent to the parking area is where to begin your visit. A foot bridge over the river leads to the trails and gardens in the east property.

The Whitehouse Nature Center is located 0.25 miles southeast of Albion College main campus on the east branch of the Kalamazoo River at the end of the athletic field. Park at the nature center entrance at the east end of Farley Drive. Farley Drive is located just south of the Erie-South Hannah Street intersection.

Trails Open Daily, Dawn to Dusk
Nature Center's Hours:
Monday - Friday 9 am - 4:30 pm
Weekends Noon to 5 pm

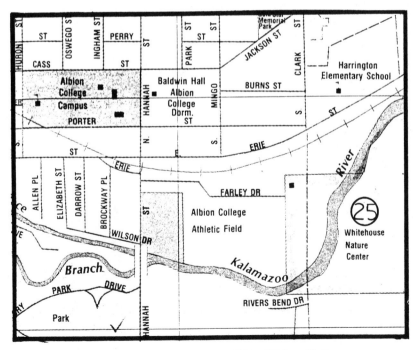

Whitehouse Nature Center (25), Albion College

26. SLAYTON ARBORETUM
of Hillsdale College
Barber Drive
Hillsdale, Michigan 49242

The scenic arboretum had its beginnings from land donated by Mr. and Mrs. George Slayton. Over 1,100 plant species cover the 40 acres today including fine collections of lilac, magnolia, and crabapple. Additional features include fieldstone gazebos, a lagoon, rock gardens, an amphitheatre and a waterfall. The arboretum is open to the public at no charge, dawn to dusk.

Additional parks to visit in the Hillsdale area include the nearby 90 acre Lewis Emery Park on East State Street. Easy hiking around five ponds plus fishing, picnicking and playgrounds.

Outside of Hillsdale southeast is the Lost Nation State Game Management Area located south of M-34 and Pittsford, Michigan on the Pittsford Road. The area contains 3,000 acres to hike and tent camp (April-October).

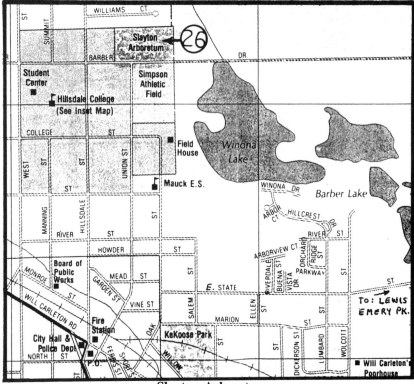

Slayton Arboretum

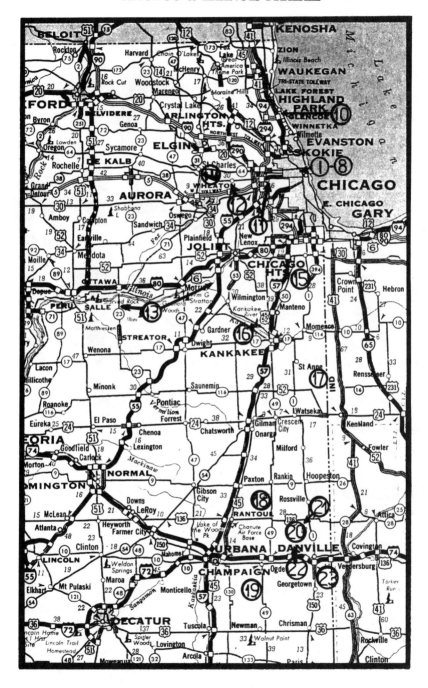

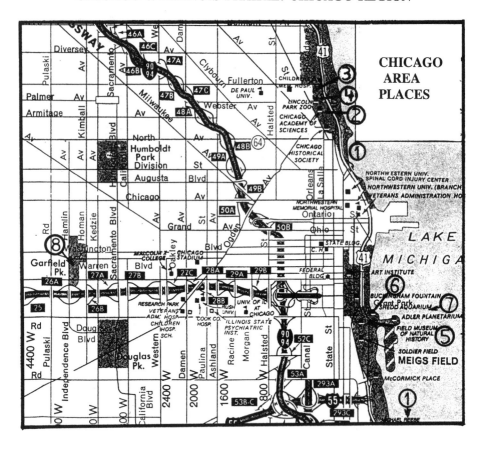

1. CHICAGO'S LAKE MICHIGAN BEACHES

c/o Chicago Park District 425
East McFetridge Drive
Chicago, Illinois 60605
(312) 294-2492, (312) 294-2274, (312) 294-2200

Thirty-one public beaches and several city parks line Chicago's 29 miles of lakefront. From Foster Avenue Beach at Winnemack Park south to Rainbow Park near 79th Street, the lakefront beaches are part of what makes Chicago great.

Some of the more popular beach parks include Montrose Wilson near Winnemack Park, North Avenue at Lincoln Park, Oak Street at Lake

Shore Park, 12th Street near Grant Park, 31st Street at Burnham Park and the 49th, 57th and 67th Streets at Jackson and Rainbow parks. The 3,000 foot long Navy Pier landmark at 600 East Grand Avenue is a place to stroll, fish and/or picnic from 6 a.m. to 8 p.m. daily.

There are fishing piers at Farwell, Montrose, McCormick Place, and North Avenue and launch ramps at Diversity Harbor, Burnham Harbor, Calumet Harbor, Jackson Park, Inner Harbor and Montrose Harbor . Whatever outdoor activity you are engaged in be sure to dress for the cooler weather at the lakefront.

Chicago beaches are accessible from Lake Shore Drive/ US 41/14.

2. CHICAGO ACADEMY OF SCIENCES MUSEUM
2001 North Clark Street & Armitage Avenue
Lincoln Park
Chicago, Illinois 60614
(312) 549-0607
(312) 871-2668

For nearly a century and a half, Chicago's first science museum has always specialized in the natural history of Chicago and the Midwest. The museum experience is billed as "going on an indoor wilderness expedition. Permanent exhibitions include an Illinois ice cave, prehistoric Chicago, a 1900 Chicago wilderness, and a Children's Gallery. A museum gift and book shop has a fine selection for aspiring naturalists. Educational programs, workshops, field trips, scientific research and membership are open to the public.

The Chicago Academy of Sciences Museum is located in Lincoln Park near the Lincoln Park Conservatory and Zoo. South on North Clark at North Avenue is the Chicago Historical Society Museum.

Open Daily, 10 am - 5 pm
Closed Christmas Day
Admission Fee, Mondays Free

3. LINCOLN PARK CONSERVATORY

2400 North Stockton Drive & Fullerton Avenue
Lincoln Park
Chicago, Illinois
(312) 294-4770

Lincoln Park, like Grant Park a few block south of the Chicago River, is a several hundred acre city park located between the lakeshore and the skyscrapers. The 3.5 acre conservatory, designed by J. L. Silsbee, features four floral shows annually. There are permanent displays all year in the exotic palm, fern and cacti display rooms. For birders, Lincoln Park is a "migrant trap" for migratory birds when they funnel through the Great Lakes flyway. The 1,200 acre park is the largest in Chicago.

Lincoln Park lies along Lake Shore Drive from North Avenue north to Hollywood Avenue. There are several beaches and outdoor recreational facilities.

Open Daily, 9 am - 5 pm
Extended Hours for Floral Shows

4. LINCOLN PARK ZOO

2200 North Cannon Drive
Lake Shore Drive & Fullerton Avenue
Lincoln Park
Chicago, Illinois 60614
(312) 294-4660

Like neighboring Brookfield Zoo, the 35 acre Lincoln Park Zoo is one of the world's best and most popular. Twenty-five hundred animals that comprise over 600 species live at the beautifully landscaped zoo. Major exhibits include the large mammal area, the antelope and zebra area, a zoo nursery, the sea lion pool and the great ape house. The Children's Zoo includes a living five acre Illinois farm-at-the-zoo. Zoo tours, classes, educational programs and membership are available to the public.

Lincoln Park Zoo is located in Lincoln Park, north of downtown Chicago near the lake.

Open Daily, 9 am - 5 pm

5. FIELD MUSEUM OF NATURAL HISTORY
Roosevelt Road at Lakeshore Drive
Grant Park south
Chicago, Illinois 60605
(312) 922-9410

Nearly ten acres of natural history artifacts are on display at this first class world museum located near the south end of Grant Park. The Field Museum was established to house the 1893 Columbian Exposition's natural history collections.

Nature "paths" explore the animal, plant and mineral kingdoms that all begin in Stanley Field Hall where the African elephants appear real. Walk on a South Pacific beach and learn about the Oceanic cultures. Discover a Pawnee plains earth lodge. There is a museum gift shop and restaurant. The Field Museum scientists study natural and social diversity the world over.

Park free in the north lot or pay fee parking in Soldier Field. Parking areas can fill rapidly on weekends and free day. The Shedd Aquarium and the Adler Planetarium are nearby along the lakefront.

Open Daily, 9 am - 5 pm
Closed Thanksgiving, Christmas & New Year's Day.
Admission Fee, Thursday Free

6. JOHN G. SHEDD AQUARIUM
1200 South Lake Shore Drive
Grant Park south
Chicago, Illinois 60605
(312) 939-2426

Facing Lake Michigan, one of the world's largest freshwater lakes, the Shedd Aquarium, "the ocean by the lake", is the world's largest indoor aquarium. There are six galleries of aquatic life including 6,000 aquatic animals representing 700 species in 200 naturalistic habitats. A 90,000 gallon tank harbors a tropical coral reef where angelfish, barracuda, tarpon, eels and sharks swim. Nature "trails" lead along a Pacific northwest coastline in the four level Oceanarium. Five seawater pools hold whales, dolphins, seals and sea otters. The Shedd produces its own seawater. In addition the aquarium has an auditorium, amphitheater, gift shop, a library, programs and membership.

The Shedd Aquarium is located east of the Field Museum and west of the Adler Planetarium. The aquarium, museum and planetarium are at the south end of 300 acre Grant Park.

Open Daily, 9 am - 6 pm
Closed Christmas & New Year's Day
Admission Fee, Thursday Free

7. ADLER PLANETARIUM
1300 Lake Shore Drive south
Chicago, Illinois 60605
(312) 322-0300

The lakeside planetarium has been bringing the universe closer to the public at Northerly Island Park since the summer of 1930. Multi-media Sky Shows for all ages are varied in topic as the stars in the seasonal heavens. The Doane Observatory provides views via closed circuit television of the celestial bodies and a solar telescope allows visitors to see solar storms. Three museum floors of exhibits and displays about "the Final Frontier". The planetarium store offers a variety of astronomical books and gifts. Programs, lectures, workshops, research and membership available.

The Adler Planetarium is east of the Field Museum and Shedd Aquarium, north of Meigs Airfield. All three "earth, sea and sky museums" are within walking distance of each other. Bus routes stop at all three.

Open Daily 9:30 am - 4:30 pm
Friday 9:30 am - 9 pm
Closed Thanksgiving Day and Christmas Day
Admission Fee, Tuesday Free

8. GARFIELD PARK & CONSERVATORY
300 North Central Park Boulevard
Garfield Park north at Lake Street
Chicago, Illinois
(312) 533-1281
c/o Chicago Park District
425 East McFetridge Drive
Chicago, Illinois 60605
(312) 294-2492

The main attraction at 185 acre Garfield Park is the 4.5 acre conservatory, designed by Jens Jensen, prairie landscape designer and former employee of the Chicago Park District. Thousands of exotic plant species are displayed in the Cactus, Aroid, Palm and Economic houses and exhibit halls at the westside landmark. There are four annual flower shows in Horticultural Mall and Show House. Both Lincoln Park Conservatory and the Garfield Conservatory are without a doubt the greenest places in Chicago during winter. Garfield Park also has its share of ballfields and courts. Cross country skiing in winter.

To reach Garfield Park and Conservatory from bordering I-290/Eisenhower Expressway exit 26A onto Hamlin Avenue and drive north alongside the park's west boundary. Parking is near the conservatory. Hours are 9 am to 5 pm daily.

For further information about Chicago's other city parks such as Douglas Park (fine gardens), Marquette (rose gardens), Lincoln Park's Conservatory & Zoo, Jackson Park's Museum of Science & Industry and the downtown Grant Park Museum complex, contact the Department of Public Information, Chicago Park District.

459

9. FOREST PRESERVE DISTRICT OF COOK COUNTY, ILLINOIS
Cummings Square
536 North Harlem Avenue
River Forest, Illinois 60305
(708) 366-9420

Scattered around the perimeter of Chicago in suburban Cook County are nearly 67,000 acres of forest preserves. Wild forest, prairie and wetland sanctuaries have outdoor recreation areas such as picnicking, playfields, launch ramps and winter sports developed along their edges. The preserves are made accessible to hikers by 150 miles of trails.

The following ten forest preserve divisions are open for visitation usually from 8 am to 5 pm or longer:

A. Skokie: north Cook County, home of the Chicago Botanic Garden in Glencoe, Illinois.

B. North Branch: north Cook County, has several nature reserves and winter tobbaggoning.

C. Des Plaines: northwest Cook County, borders the Des Plaines River, River Trail Nature Center.

D. Indian Boundary Preserve: west Cook County, entire preserve borders Des Plaines River, historic site.

E. Salt Creek: west Cook County, home of the Brookfield Zoo, a National Historic Site, the Chicago Portage is here.

F. Palos & Sag Valley: southwest Cook County, borders Des Plaines River, Calumet Sag Channel and the Illinois & Michigan Canal Trail, Little Red Schoolhouse Nature Center.

G. Finley Creek: southwest Cook County, ravines and woods along Tinley Creek, north portion of park.

H. Thorn Creek: south Cook County, three nature preserves and Sand Ridge Nature Center, west of the Indiana-Illinois state line, adjacent to the Calumet Expressway, 159th and Paxton Avenue.

I. Calumet: south edge of Chicago, south of Powers Conservation Area at Wolf Lake, borders Grand and Little Calumet Rivers.

CHICAGO NATURE WALK LOCATIONS 1 - 13

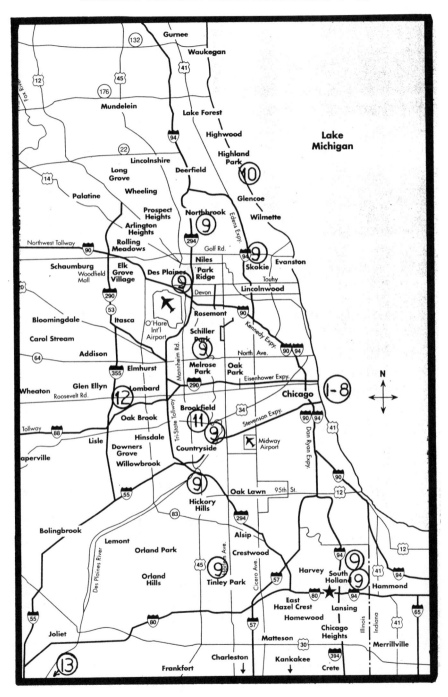

10. CHICAGO BOTANIC GARDEN
1000 Lake Cook Road
Glencoe, Illinois 60022
(708) 835-5440

Walking trails wind through and loop around the 300 lovely rolling acres of theme gardens, the Skokie Lagoons, and a Japanese Garden with three islands. The demonstration gardens are especially of interest to home gardeners looking for ideas. The Education Center has a library, exhibition hall and ten greenhouses. Tram tours also. The Chicago Botanic Garden is owned by the Cook County Forest Preserve District and operated by the Chicago Horticultural Society.

The garden is located 25 miles north of Chicago, just west of Lake Michigan in Glencoe, Illinois. More specifically, 0.5 mile east of the I-94/Edens Expressway exits 30A-B or 29 to Lake Cook Road.

Open Daily 8 am - Dusk, Closed Christmas Day
Parking Fee

11. BROOKFIELD ZOO
First Avenue and 31st Street
Brookfield, Illinois
(708) 485-0263

One of the first American zoos to exhibit animals in natural settings was the Brookfield Zoo. Opened since 1934, the 200 acre zoo is owned by the Forest Preserve District of Cook County and operated by the Chicago Zoological Society. Chicago's largest zoo contains 2,300 animals and 425 species within 24 exhibit areas.

Within the zoo is Tropic World, a five acre African, Asian, and South American rainforest and indigenous fauna, Fragile Kingdom, Seven Seas Panorama with bottle-nosed dolphins, Australian House, Aquatic Bird House, Reptile House, Perching Bird House, Wolf Woods, Pachyderm House and Children's Zoo and more.

Brookfield Zoo is located 14 miles west of the downtown Chicago loop in Brookfield, Illinois. The zoo is easily accessed from the I-290/Eisenhower Expressway, I-55/Stevenson Expressway and I-294/ Tri-State Tollway.

Open Daily 9:30 am - 6 pm Memorial Day - Labor Day
Rest of Year 10 am - 5 pm

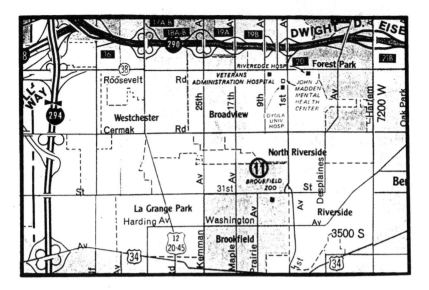

Brookfield Zoo

12. THE MORTON ARBORETUM
Illinois SR 53, north of I-88
Lisle, Illinois 60532
(708) 968-0074

The scientific and educational Morton Arboretum uses its collections and natural areas for people to study and enjoy. The 1,500 acre arboretum was founded in 1922 by Joy Morton, founder of Morton's salt company, on the grounds of his estate. His influential father, J. Sterling Morton, was founder of Arbor Day. There are 4,800 species and varieties of woody plants growing on the grounds of the arboretum.

There are several miles of self-guiding trails with guide booklets available and many unmarked trails. The Illinois Tree Trail covers most of the east property collections while the Evergreen and Joy Morton trails traverse the west portion across Illinois 53. There are outstanding tree groupings of similar species. Additional points of interest include the visitor's center complex, Frost Hill, a prairie restoration, and the estate of Joy Morton. Motorized one-way drives access the property collections.

The Morton Arboretum is 0.25 mile north at the Illinois 53 exit of the east-west tollway I-88, north of Lisle, Illinois.

Grounds Open Daily Weather Permitting
9 am - 4, 5, & 6 pm, Seasonal hours

The Morton Arboretum

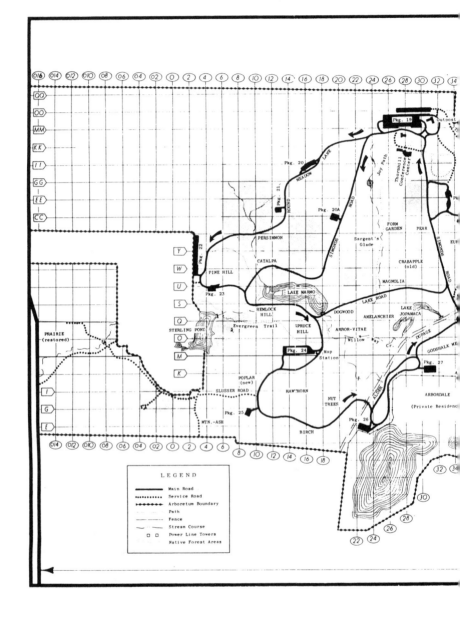

LEGEND

▬▬▬	Main Road
••••••••	Service Road
▸━▸━▸	Arboretum Boundary
········	Path
———	Fence
—··—	Stream Course
▫ ▫	Power Line Towers
	Native Forest Areas

THE MORTON ARBORETUM

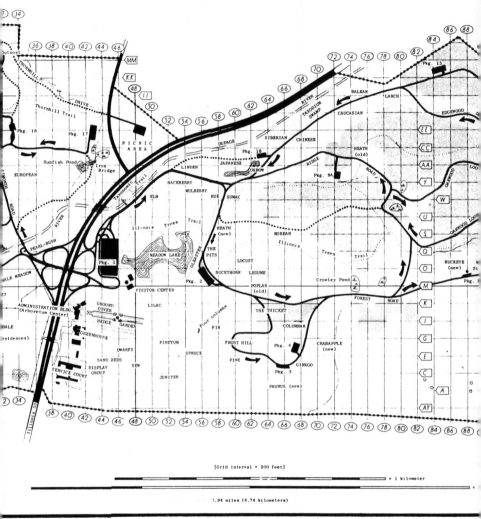

[Grid interval = 200 feet]

= 1 kilometer

1.94 miles (4.74 kilometers)

The Morton Arboretum

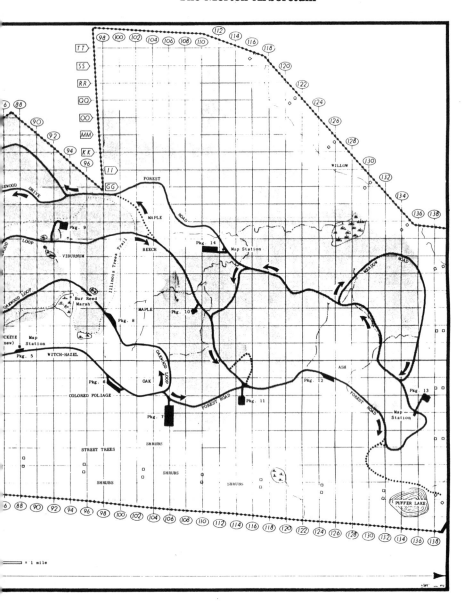

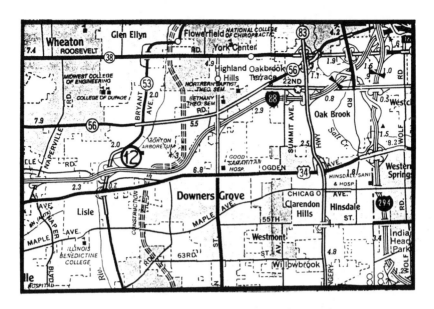

The Morton Arboretum

13. ILLINOIS & MICHIGAN CANAL NATIONAL HISTORIC CORRIDOR

Illinois & Michigan Canal State Trail

c/o I & M Canal NHC
15701 South Independence Blvd.
Lockport, Illinois 60441
(815) 740-2047

c/o I & M Canal State Trail
P. O. Box 272
Morris, Illinois 60450
(815) 942-0796

The I & M Canal was the first navigable route to the Mississippi River from Lake Michigan, opening in 1848. The canal made another first a few years ago when it became the first National Heritage Corridor.

The corridor begins at the south branch of the Chicago River and continues southwest nearly 100 miles before joining the Illinois River at Peru, Illinois. Perhaps the best place to begin is the Chicago Portage Site at the Salt Creek Division of the Cook County Forest Preserve. The route is mostly motorized until reaching Channahon, Illinois where the I & M Canal State Trail begins, ending at Lazily, Illinois. The limestone trail follows the old former towpath adjacent to the canal and the Des Plaines and Illinois rivers. Natural and social history sites enroute include Goose Lake Prairie in Morris, Illini State Park in Marseilles, the Effigy Tumuli. and Buffalo Rock State Park at Utica, Illinois.

Open Daily, Dawn to Dusk

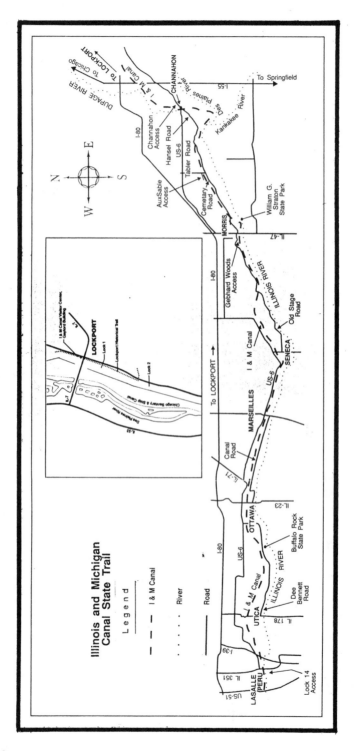

Illinois and Michigan Canal State Trail

Legend

— — — I & M Canal

········· River

——— Road

14. ILLINOIS PRAIRIE PATH

220 South Villa
Villa Park, Illinois 60181
(708) 941-9223
(708) 752-0120

The Illinois Prairie Path is a 43 mile recreational trail that follows a former rail road bed and was one of the first rails-to-trails projects in the nation. Proposed by naturalist and author, May Theilgaard Watts in 1963 and taken up by dedicated volunteers who gave their time and money, the trail was taken over to be administered by DuPage County in 1987.

The multi-use prairie path stretches from Maywood west to Wheaton, Illinois then splits into four spur trails that extend west to the Fox River communities of Elgin, Geneva, Batavia and Aurora. Prairie remnants, wetlands, historic sites, and parks are enroute. The trailhead in the east is south of St. Charles Road in Maywood, Illinois, running west to and from Elmhurst, Illinois.

Open Year Around

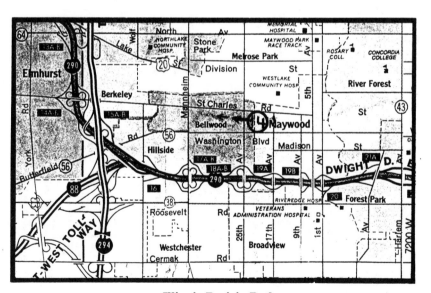

Illinois Prairie Path

15. FOREST PRESERVE DISTRICT OF WILL COUNTY, ILLINOIS
U.S. 52 & Cherry Hill Road, R.R. 4
Joliet, Illinois 60433
(815) 727-8700

A short distance west of the Indiana state line and Lake County, IN is the eastern portion of Will County, Illinois. Thanks to the Forest Preserve District of Will County, there are three forest preserves, easily accessible and not in areas highly congested as Cook County to the north. The preserves are located east of I-57 and are open daily from 8 a.m. to 8 p.m. in summer and 8 a.m. to 5 p.m. in winter, excepting major holidays.

A. Thorn Creek Nature Preserve is an 808 acre area on the Will-Cook County line in Park Forest, Illinois. From US 30 drive south on Orchard Drive to Monee Road and go right/west to the entrance.

B. Raccoon Grove Forest Preserve is noted for spring wildflowers and Rock Creek in its 150 woodland acres. From I-57 exit 335 east and continue a mile or so to Monee, Illinois and Illinois SR 50/Governors Highway. Turn south/right and continue to Paulding Road and turn east/left. Go 1/8 mile to the preserve entrance.

C. Goodenow Grove Forest Preserve is 400 acres of diverse landscape along Plum Creek. There is an excellent nature center with year around programs. The preserve is located between Crete, Illinois and Beecher, Illinois on Goodenow Road south to South Park Avenue, then north to preserve. Limited camping in summer. Access from Illinois SR 1 at Goodenow, Illinois.

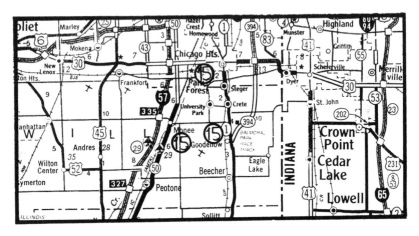

Forest Preserve District of Will County

16. KANKAKEE RIVER STATE PARK
P. 0. Box 37, Route 102
Bourbonnais, Illinois 60914
(815) 933-1383

The Kankakee River and its tributary Rock Creek are the essence of this sizeable 3,512 acre state park. Located six miles northwest of Kankakee, Illinois, the park occupies both banks of the river for 11 miles. There are several miles of foot trails on the north bank (south bank horses and snowmobiles trails). Rock Creek has formed a limestone canyon and waterfalls. There is a loop trail in the west portion of the park near a dedicated nature preserve. Besides trails, the park also offers picnicking, shelters, x-country skiing, biking, canoeing, hunting, rentals, concessions and A-B-C-D and horse camping is popular.

From I-57 exit onto Illinois 50 in north Kankakee and drive south to Armour Road and turn right/west. Continue west on Armour Road to the "T" with Main Street/Illinois 102 and turn right/west. Proceed to the park entrance in about six miles. Illinois 102 on the north and Illinois 113 on the south border access the park.

Additional Kankakee area parks that have established walking paths include <u>Bird Park</u>, <u>River Road Park</u>, <u>Hieland Road Park</u>, <u>Legion Park</u> and <u>Small Memorial Park</u>.

Open Year Around

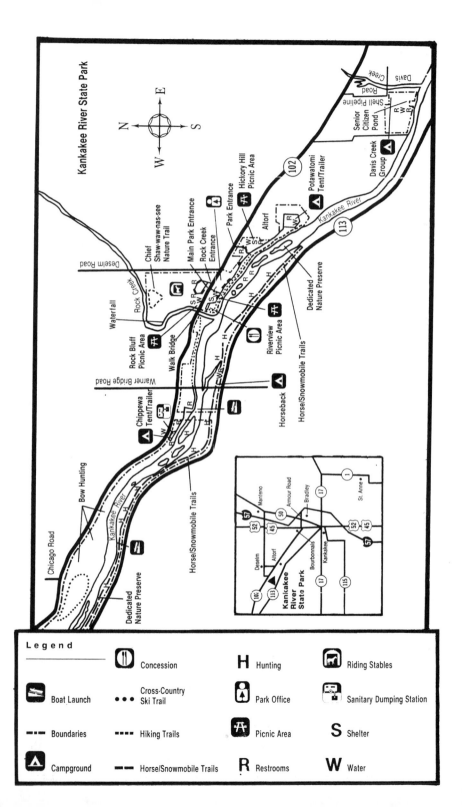

Kankakee River State Park

Davis Creek

Shell Pipeline Road

Senior Citizen Pond

Davis Creek Group

Potawatomi Tent/Trailer

Hickory Hill Picnic Area

Park Entrance

Altorf

102

113

Kankakee River

Dedicated Nature Preserve

Main Park Entrance

Rock Creek Entrance

Chief Shaw-waw-nas-see Nature Trail

Deselm Road

Waterfall

Rock Creek

Rock Bluff Picnic Area

Walk Bridge

Riverview Picnic Area

Horse/Snowmobile Trails

Warner Bridge Road

Horseback

Chippewa Tent/Trailer

Bow Hunting

Chicago Road

Kankakee River

Horse/Snowmobile Trails

Dedicated Nature Preserve

Inset map

Manteno

Armour Road

Bradley

St. Anne

1

17

57

50

52

45

52

45

57

Deselm

Altorf

Bourbonnais

Kankakee

Kankakee River State Park

102

113

17

115

Legend

🍴 Concession	**H** Hunting	🏠 Riding Stables
🚤 Boat Launch	••• Cross-Country Ski Trail	🚮 Sanitary Dumping Station
--- Boundaries	---- Hiking Trails	**S** Shelter
▲ Campground	— Horse/Snowmobile Trails	**W** Water
	🅿 Park Office	
	🎪 Picnic Area	
	R Restrooms	

17. IROQUOIS COUNTY STATE WILDLIFE AREA SITE
Superintendent
Beaverville, Illinois 60912
(815) 435-2218

Five miles west of Willow Slough Fish & Wildlife Area and the Indiana-Illinois state line is the Iroquois County Wildlife Area. First purchased as a prairie chicken refuge, the 2,480 acre wildlife area has one of the largest oak-savanna nature preserves in Illinois. The 480 acre Hooper Brand Savanna is situated in the northeast area of the property. There are two loop trails east of headquarters and there are about 12 miles of firelanes. Picnicking but no camping.

The area is located nine miles southeast of St. Anne, Illinois and about six miles northeast of Beavervile, Illinois. Best access is from Illinois 1 and US 41, exiting west at Morocco, Indiana.
Open Year Around

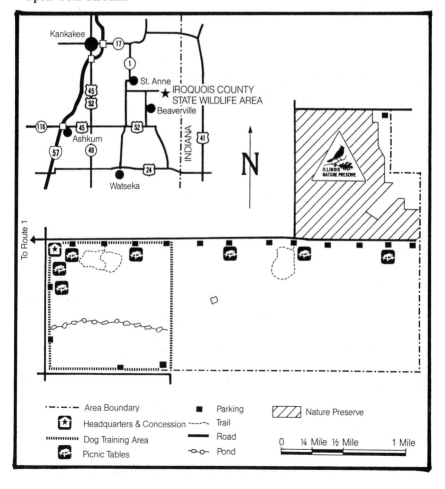

18. MIDDLE FORK RIVER FOREST PRESERVE
Champaign County Road 22
Penfield, Illinois
c/o Forest Preserve District of Champaign County
(217) 586-3360

Retired farmlands of over 1,500 acres are now preserved and returning to their natural state thanks to the Champaign County Forest District. There are outdoor activities available such as picnicking, playgrounds, building rentals, fishing lakes and river, swimming beach, modern campgrounds and several miles of trails.

The preserve is located in northeast Champaign County near the Ford, Vermillion and Champaign county lines. From I-57 at Rantoul, Illinois exit east onto US 136 and drive about 14 miles to CR 22 north of Penfield and turn left/north. Drive about five miles and turn west and go 0.75 miles to the property. Follow the roadside directional signs (Location M on Champaign County location map).

The Nature Conservancy's Grandma Jane Patton's Timber Preserve is nearby. The 14 acre oak-hickory forest has an interpretive trail. From Clarence, Illinois, north of the forest preserve, drive south 4.5 miles on the blacktop to the road "T". Turn right/west and go one mile to the next road and turn left/south. The preserve is located on the west side of the road after a quarter mile.

Open Year Around

19. SALT FORK RIVER FOREST PRESERVE
Homer, Illinois
c/o Forest Preserve District of Champaign County
(217) 586-3360

The 789 acre preserve surrounds Homer Lake, north of Homer, Illinois in east central Champaign County. The education center features programs and interpretive displays of the natural and social history of the area. In addition to the river, two fishing lakes may be fished and sailed. There are picnicking areas, playgrounds and building rental. The hiking trails serve also as x-country ski trails in winter.

The forest preserve is located 1.5 miles northwest of Homer, Illinois, and 1.5 miles west of Illinois 49. To reach the day-use forest preserve exit I-74 at Ogden, Illinois south onto Illinois 49 and drive about five miles to a signed country road and turn right/west. Proceed 1/3 mile to the next county road and turn south/left and go 1/3 mile to the preserve (location **S** on Champaign County map).

Open Year Around, 7:00 am - Dusk

A further excursion west of Champaign at I-74 and IL-47 is <u>Lake of the Woods County Park</u> which occupies almost 900 acres along the corridor of the Sangamon River with hiking trails, swimming beach, and an early American Museum and Garden (location **L** on map).

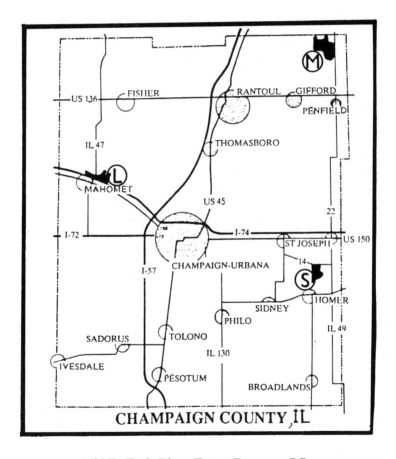

Middle Fork River Forest Preserve (M)
Salt Fork River Forest Preserve (S)
Lake of the Woods County Park (L)

20. MIDDLE FORK STATE FISH & WILDLIFE AREA
c/o Kickapoo State Park
R. R. 1, Box 374
Oakwood, Illinois 61858
(217) 442-4915

The morainal hills and valley of this wildlife area lie upstream from Kickapoo State Park along the Middle Fork of the Vermillion River. There are 35 miles of service roads that are primarily used by equestrians. The property's two nature preserves, Horseshoe Bottoms and Windfall Prairie are to the east across the river and best accessible from Kennekuk County Park. All marked trails are accessible from the parking lot near the office at 2400N, just off Newtown Road where day use parking is available. The 3,015 acre wildlife area is also open to fishing, canoeing, picnicking, and walk-in and equestrian camping.

The Middle Fork State Fish & Wildlife Area is five road miles north of Kickapoo State Park, west of Danville, Illinois and eight miles north of I-74 exit at Oakwood, Illinois.

Open Year Around

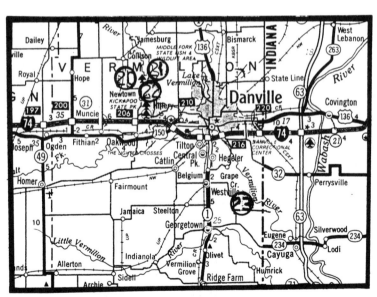

Middle Fork State Fish & Wildlife Area (20)
Kennekuck Cove County Park (21)
Kickapoo State Park (22)
Forest Glen Preserve (23)

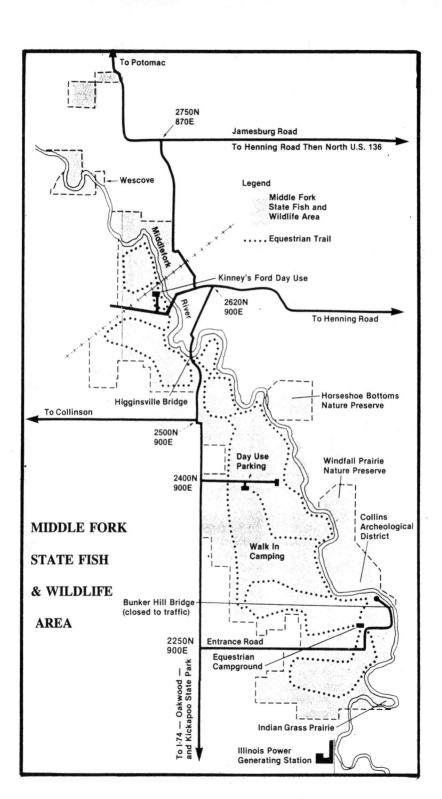

To Potomac

2750N
870E

Jamesburg Road

To Henning Road Then North U.S. 136

→ Wescove

Legend

Middle Fork
State Fish and
Wildlife Area

····· Equestrian Trail

Middlefork

Kinney's Ford Day Use

2620N
900E

To Henning Road

River

Higginsville Bridge

Horseshoe Bottoms
Nature Preserve

To Collinson

2500N
900E

Day Use
Parking

Windfall Prairie
Nature Preserve

2400N
900E

Collins
Archeological
District

MIDDLE FORK

STATE FISH

& WILDLIFE

AREA

Walk In
Camping

Bunker Hill Bridge
(closed to traffic)

2250N
900E

Entrance Road

To I-74 — Oakwood —
and Kickapoo State Park

Equestrian
Campground

Indian Grass Prairie

Illinois Power
Generating Station

KENNEKUK COVE COUNTY PARK

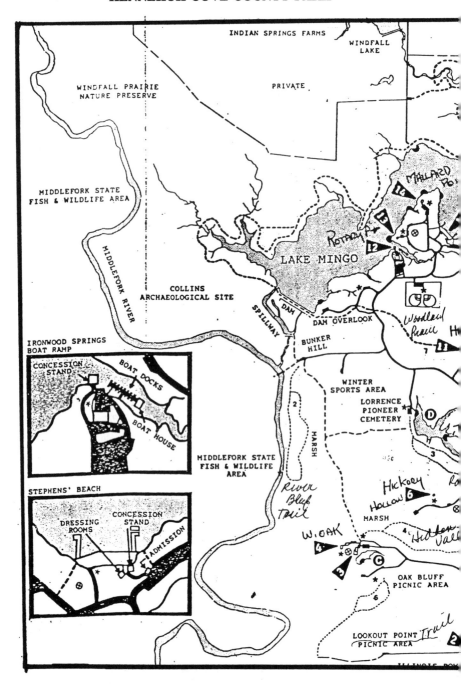

KENNEKUK COVE COUNTY PARK

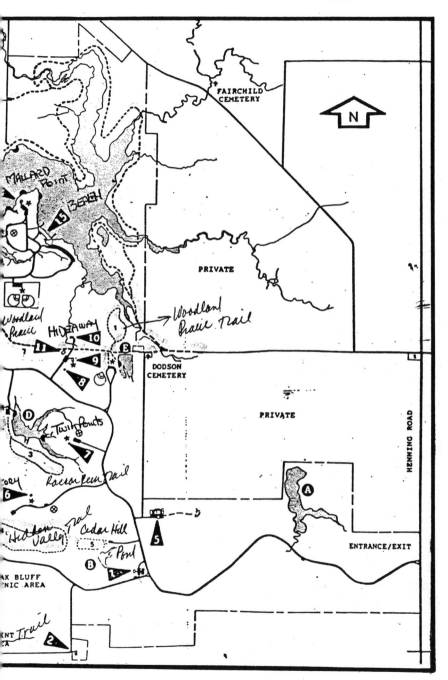

21. KENNEKUK COVE COUNTY PARK
North Henning Road
Danville, Illinois 61832
(217) 442-1691
Vermillion County Conservation District

This 3,000 acre Vermillion County park is located eight miles northwest of Danville, Illinois at Henning Road, north of Kickapoo State Park and east of Middle Fork State Fish & Wildlife Area. The outstanding county park has an exceptional trail system. All seven trails, of varying lengths and difficulties, radiate and loop from the picnic shelter area south of Lake Mingo, and some are self-guiding such as Took Out Point and Raccoon Run trails. The longest trail is the 7.5 mile Lake Mingo Trail that skirts the finger peninsulas of the north shoreline.

The visitors and nature center features natural and social history displays of the local area. Swimming is at Stephen's Beach, a protected cove on 160 acre Lake Mingo. Historical buildings such as a chapel, school and store are occasionally open. Winter sports, fishing and hunting are other park activities.

Open Year Around

22. KICKAPOO STATE PARK
R. R. 1, Box 374
Oakwood, Illinois 61858
(217) 442-4915

Strip mine ponds, hills and the outstanding Middle Fork of the Vermillion River valley comprise the 2,842 acre state park. Despite the history of strip coal mining, the area is one of the most scenic areas in east central Illinois. The difficult 7.6 mile Out & Back Trail is highly scenic. Easier and shorter hikes are the 0.75 mile High Pond Trail, 0.75 Walnut-White Tail Nature Trail, and the Clear Pond Trail. Fisherman paths around the ponds can be explored. The 83 acre Middle Fork Woods Nature Preserve protects a special area. Besides hiking, fishing, boating, canoeing, canoe rental, pond SCUBA diving, picnicking with shelters, winter sports, hunting and camping are activities and facilities within the park.

Kickapoo State Park is located two miles west of Danville, Illinois. From I-74 exits 206 and 210 onto CR 850E and Illinois 150 north access the park.
Open Year Around

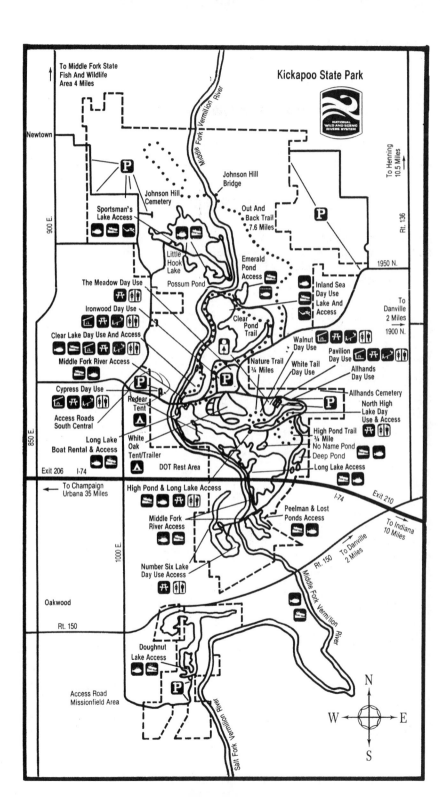

23. FOREST GLEN PRESERVE
Rural Route 1, Box 495A
Westville, Illinois 61883
(217) 662-2142
Vermillion County Conservation District

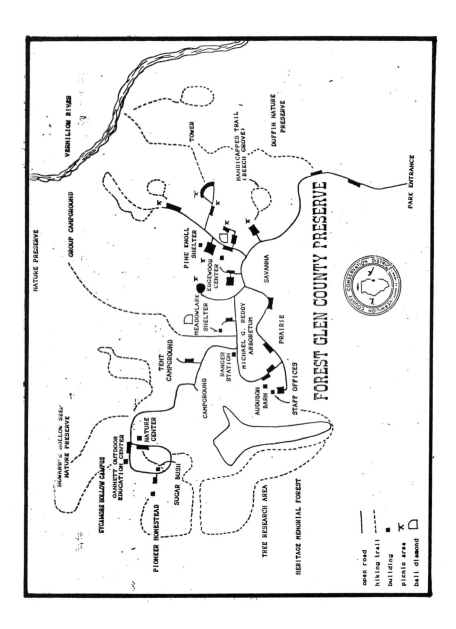

The first established Vermillion County park has wooded ravines, grassy meadows, ponds, prairie and river forest along the Vermillion River. The 1,800 acre county park has eleven trails of varying length and three miles of river frontage. The eleven mile long River Ridge Trail has overnight camping. Six trails have interpretive self-guiding brochures, available at the trailheads. Additional park features include a pioneer homestead, an observation tower, a sugar maple "bush", three nature preserves, a 20 acre arboretum, a 40 acre restored prairie, an environmental education campus, and also fishing, boating, picnicking, bicycling and camping.

Forest Glen Preserve is 4.5 miles southeast of Westville, 6.0 miles northeast of Georgetown, Illinois, and 4.5 miles east of Illinois 1 on the southwest side of the river.

Open Year Around

American Beech, Along the Trail

HELPFUL BOOKS

ACRES, Inc. The Nature Preserves of ACRES, Inc. Ft. Wayne, IN: Updated annually.

American Medical Association. Handbook of First Aid and Emergency Care. New York: Random House, 1980.

Angel, Heather, and Wolseley, Pat. The Water Naturalist. New York: Facts on File, 1982.

Baker, Ronald L., and Carmony, Marvin. Indiana Place Names. Bloomington, IN: Indiana University Press, 1975.

Borror, D.J., and White, R.E. A Field Guide to the Insects of America: North of Mexico. Boston, MA. Houghton Mifflin, Peterson Field Guide Series, 1970.

Brock, Kenneth J. Birds of the Indiana Dunes. Bloomington, IN: Indiana University Press, 1986.

Brown, Vinson. Knowing the Outdoors in the Dark. New York: Macmillan Publishing, 1969.

Brown, Vinson. Reading the Woods. New York: Macmillan Publishing, 1969.

Brown, Vinson. The Amateur Naturalist's Handbook. New York: Prentice-Hall, 1980.

Brown, Tom. Tom Brown's Field Guide to Nature Observation and Tracking. Berkley Books, 1977.

Buchholtz, K. P., Grisgby, B. H., Lee, O. C., et al. Weeds of the North Central States. Champaign, IL: Agricultural Experimental Station, 1954.

Bull, John, and Farrand, John. The Audubon Society Field Guide to North American Birds: Eastern Region. New York: Alfred Knopf, 1977.

Bull, Alvin T., and Runkel, Sylvan T. Wildflowers of Indiana Woodlands. Iowa City, IA: University of Iowa Press (2nd ed.), 1993.

Carra, Andrew J. ed. The Complete Guide to Hiking and Backpacking. New York: Winchester Press, 1977.

Conant, Roger. Peterson Field Guide to Reptiles and Amphibians of the United States and Canada. Boston, MA: Houghton Mifflin Company (2nd ed.), 1975.

Daniel, Glenda. Dune Country: A Hiker's Guide to the Indiana Dunes. Athens, OH: Swallow Press, 1984

Danielsen, John A. Winter Hiking and Camping. Glen Falls, NY: Adirondack Mountain Club, 1977.

Deam, Charles C. Flora of Indiana. Indianapolis, IN: Indiana Department of Conservation, Division of Forestry, 1940.

Deam, Charles C. Grasses of Indiana. Indianapolis, IN: W. B. Burford, 1929.

Deam, Charles C. Shrubs of Indiana. Indianapolis, IN: Indiana Department of Conservation, 1932.

Doan, Marlyn. Hiking Light. Seattle, WA: Mountaineers Books, 1982.

Downing, Elliott R. A Naturalist in the Great Lakes Region. Chicago, IL: University of Chicago Press, 1922.

Durand, Herbert. Field Book of Common Ferns. New York: G. P. Putnam and Sons, 1928.

Ellsworth, Henry William. Valley of the Upper Wabash River. New York: Arno Press, 1975.

Fletcher, Colin. The Complete Walker III. New York: Alfred Knopf, 1984.

Foster, Lynne. Take A Hike!: The Sierra Club Kid's Guide to Hiking and Backpacking. Boston, MA: Little, Brown and Company, 1991.

Franklin, Kay. The Indiana Dunes: A Selected Bibliography. Hammond, IN: Regional Studies Institute, Purdue University Calumet Campus, 1980.

Frey, Robert W., and Lane, Michael A. editors. A Survey of Indiana Geology. Bloomington, IN: Indiana University Department of Geology, 1966.

Gerking, Shelby D., and Nelson, Joseph S. Annotated Key to the Fishes of Indiana. Bloomington, IN: Indiana University Department of Zoology, 1968.

Golden Guide Series. Racine, WI: Golden Press.

Harper, Samuel A. A Hoosier Tramp. Chicago, IL: The Prairie Club, 1928.

Hedge, Christine. Indiana: A Guide to State Forests, Parks and Reservoirs. Indianapolis, IN: Department of Natural Resources, 1987.

Henbest, Nigel. A Spotter's Guide to the Night Sky. Mayflower Books, 1979.

Homoya, Michael A. Orchids of Indiana. Bloomington, IN: Indiana University Press, 1992.

Indiana Department of Natural Resources. Directory of Indiana's Dedicated Nature Preserves. Indianapolis, IN: 402 W. Washington Street, Room 267, 46204, 1991.

    In addition the Indiana DNR publications include maps, canoeing, lakes, wetland conservation areas, & wildlife viewing guides, Outdoor Indiana magazine, and statewide flora and fauna information.

Jensen, Jens. Siftings. Baltimore, MD: John Hopkins University Press, 1990.

Kals, W. S. The Stargazer's Bible. New York: Doubleday, 1980.

Kellar, Charles E., Shirley A., and Timothy C. Indiana Birds and their Haunts. Bloomington, IN: Indiana University Press, 1979.

Kellar, James H. An Introduction to the Prehistory of Indiana. Indianapolis, IN: Indiana Historical Society, 1983.

Klots, Elsie B. The New Field Book of Freshwater Life. New York: G. P. Putnam & Sons, 1966.

Komaiko, Jean, and Schaeffer, Norma. Doing the Dunes. Beverly Shores, IN: Dunes Enterprises, 1990.

Kuntzleman, Charles T. The Complete Book of Walking. New York: New York: Simon and Schuster, 1978.

Lawrence, Gale. A Field Guide to the Familiar. New York: Prentice-Hall, 1984.

Lindsey, Alton A., ed. Natural Features of Indiana. Indianapolis, IN: Indiana Academy of Science, Indiana State Library, 1966.

Lindsey, Alton A., Schmelz, D. V., and Nichols, S. A. Natural Areas in Indiana and their Preservation. Lafayette, IN: Purdue University, Department of Biological Sciences, 1969.

Long, Judith Reick. Gene Stratton Porter: Novelist and Naturalist. Bloomington, IN: Indiana University Press, 1990.

MacFarlan, Alan. Exploring the Outdoors with Indian Secrets. Harrisburg, PA: Stackpole Books, 1982.

Madison, James. History of Indiana. Bloomington, IN: Indiana University Press, 1986.

Madson, John. Where the Sky Begins. New York: Houghton Mifflin, 1982.

Martin, Laura C. Wildflower Folklore. Charlotte, NC: East Woods Press, 1984.

McClane, A. J. Field Guide to Freshwater Fishes of North America. New York: Holt, Rinehart and Winston, 1978.

McPherson, Alan J. Indian Names in Indiana. Monticello, IN: The Blasted Works. 1993.

McPherson, Alan, and Clark, Sue A. Wild Food Plants of Indiana. Monticello, IN: The Blasted Works (2nd edition), 1994.

Milne, L., and Milne, M. Audubon Society Field Guide to North American Insects and Spiders. New York: Alfred Knopf, 1980.

Mitchell, Christie, and Mitchell, Frank. Practical Weather Forecasting. New York: Barron's, 1978.

Mitchell, Edwin V. The Pleasures of Walking. New York: Vanguard Press, 1948.

Mumford, Russell E., and Keller, Charles E. The Birds of Indiana. Bloomington, IN: Indiana University Press, 1984.

Mumford, Russell E. and Whitaker, John 0. Mammals of Indiana.
Bloomington, IN: Indiana University Press, 1982.

Niering, William A. The Life of a Marsh. New York: McGraw-Hill,
1966.

Niering, William A. Wetlands: An Audubon Society Nature Guide. New
York: Random House, 1985.

Peattie, Donald Culross. Flora of the Indiana Dunes. Chicago, IL: Field
Museum of Natural History, 1930.

Pennak, Robert W. Freshwater Invertebrates of the United States. New
York: John Wiley & Sons, 1978.

Perry, T. G. Fossils: Prehistoric Animals in Hoosier Rocks. Bloomington,
IN: Indiana Geological Survey, Circular #7, 1959.

Peterson Field Guide Series. New York: Houghton Mifflin Company.

Petrides, George A. Field Guide to Trees and Shrubs. New York:
Houghton Mifflin, 1972.

Pitcher, Emma Bickham. Up and Down the Dunes. Beverly Shores, IN;
Shirley Heinze Environmental Fund, 1987.

Pough, Frederick. A Field Guide to the Rocks and Minerals. Boston, MA:
Houghton Mifflin, 1976.

Schaeffer, Norma, and Franklin, Kay. Round and About the Dunes.
Beverly Shores, IN: Dunes Enterprises, 1984.

Scifres, Bill. Indiana Outdoors: A Guide to Wild Crops, Fishing, and
Hunting. Bloomington, IN: Indiana University Press, 1976.

Seng, Phil T., and Case, David J. Indiana Wildlife Viewing Guide.
Helena, MT: Falcon Press, 1992.

Shaver, Robert H. Adventures With Fossils. Bloomington, IN: Indiana
Geological Survey, Circular # 6, 1959.

Shedd, Randall. Indiana Landscapes. Bloomington, IN: Indiana University
Press, 1992.

Shull, Ernest M. The Butterflies of Indiana. Indianapolis, IN: Indiana
Academy of Science, 1987.

Simons, Richard S. The Rivers of Indiana. Bloomington, IN: Indiana
University Press, 1985.

Smith, Alexander H., and Weber, Nancy Smith. The Mushroom Hunter's
Field Guide. Ann Arbor, MI: University of Michigan Press, 1963.

Starling, Bud. Enjoying Indiana Birds. Bloomington, IN: Indiana
University Press, 1978.

Stephens, H. A. Poisonous Plants of Central United States. Lawrence,
KS: University Press of Kansas, 1984.

Stokes, Donald W. A Guide to Observing Insect Lives. Boston, MA:
Little, Brown and Company, 1983.

Swink, Floyd and Gerould, Wilhelm. Plants of the Chicago Region. Lisle, IL: Morton Arboretum, 1979.

Sussman, Aaron. The Magic of Walking. New York: Simon and Schuster, 1980.

Taylor, Robert M., et al. Indiana: A New Historical Guide. Indianapolis, IN: Indiana Historical Society, 1989.

The Nature Conservancy. A Guide to Indiana Preserves and Projects. Indianapolis, IN: Update annually.

Thomas, Bill. Talking With the Animals. New York: William Morrow & Company, 1985.

Thomas, Bill, and Thomas, Phyllis. Indiana Off the Beaten Path. A Guide to Unique Places. Chester, CT: Globe Pequot Press, 1985.

Thomas, Lowell J., and Sanderson, Jay L. First Aid for Backpackers and Campers. New York: Holt, Rinehart, and Winston, 1978.

Invitation to Adventure, Merry Lea Environmental Learning Center and Nature Preserve. Lake Plains (22)

INDEX

ABBREVIATION USAGE

Am.	American	nat.	native
appx.	appproximately	NF	National Forest
arb.	arboretum	NM	National Memorial
ave.	avenue	NP	Nature Preserve
BSA	Boy Scouts of Am.	NWR	National Wildlife Ref.
CCC	Civilian Conser. Corps	OH	Ohio
conser.	conservation	Pk.	park
co.	county	Pl.	place
CP	County park	Pt.	point
div.	division	PFA	Public Fishing Area
elev.	elevation	Planet.	Planetarium
est.	established	Pres.	Preserve
ft.	foot	Pub.	Public
FWA	Fish & Wildlife Area	Recr.	Recreation
hist.	historic, history	Res.	Reservoir
Hq.	headquarters	SF	State Forest
HT	horse trail	SFA	State Fish & Wildlife Area
I	Interstate	SP	State park
IN, Ind	Indiana	sp.	species
IL	Illinois	SR	State Road
KY	Kentucky	SRA	State Recreation Area
Lk.	lake	Tr.	Trail
Land.	landing	USGS	United States Geol. Survey
Mem.	memorial	wild.	wilderness
Mus.	museum	WR	Wildlife Refuge
N	north		

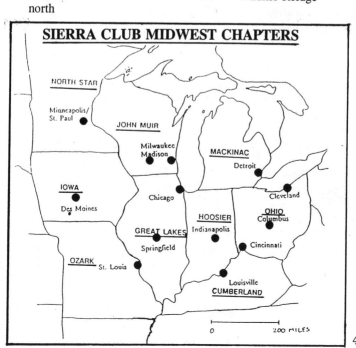

SIERRA CLUB MIDWEST CHAPTERS

S ince 1892, the Sierra Club has been working to preserve our magnificent wild places and protect our natural environment. The Sierra Club has played a major role in the formation of America's National Park and Wilderness Preservation Systems, safeguarding over 132 million acres of irreplaceable public land.

With your help, we can continue working to preserve wilderness areas that remain at risk from encroaching development. As a Sierra Club member you will have the satisfaction of knowing that you are helping to preserve and protect our natural heritage.

☐ **Yes**, I want to join! I want to help safeguard our nation's precious natural heritage. My payment is enclosed.

My Name _____

Address_____

City/State_____ZIP _____

Phone (Optional) (   ) _____

Please charge my ☐ Mastercard ☐ Visa

Cardholder Name:_____

Card Number:_____ Expiration Date:_____ /_____

Contributions or gifts to the Sierra Club are not tax deductible as charitable contributions. Annual dues include subscription to *Sierra* ($7.50) and chapter publications ($1), and other member only benefits.

MEMBERSHIP CATEGORIES
for 1996

	INDIVIDUAL	JOINT
REGULAR	☐ **$35**	☐ **$43**
SUPPORTING	☐ $50	☐ $58
CONTRIBUTING	☐ $100	☐ $108
LIFE	☐ $750	☐ $1000
SENIOR	☐ $15	☐ $23
STUDENT	☐ $15	☐ $23
LIMITED INCOME	☐ $15	☐ $23

Sierra Club
P.O. Box 52968
Boulder, Colorado
80322-2968

W 652 -1 Entity

F94Q W99901

One Earth, One Chance®